THE
COMPLETE small-
BUSINESS
SOURCEBOOK

THE
COMPLETE small-
BUSINESS
SOURCEBOOK

Information, Services, and Experts
Every Small and Home-Based
Business Needs

CARL HAUSMAN
and
WILBUR CROSS

A Stonesong Press Book

TIMES BUSINESS

RANDOM HOUSE

Copyright © 1998 by The Stonesong Press, Inc.
A Stonesong Press Book

All rights reserved under International and Pan-American Copyright Conventions. Published in the United States by Times Books, a division of Random House, Inc., New York, and simultaneously in Canada by Random House of Canada Limited, Toronto.

Library of Congress Cataloging-in-Publication Data

Hausman, Carl
    The complete small-business sourcebook : information, services,
and experts every small and home-based business needs / Carl
Hausman.
        p.   cm.
    Includes bibliographical references and index.
    ISBN 0-8129-2824-5
    1. Small business—Information services.   2. Small business—
Management.   3. New business enterprises—Management.   4. Home-
based businesses—Management.   5. Success in business.   I. Title.
HD2341.H356   1998
658.02′2—dc21   98-18633

Random House website address: www.randomhouse.com
Printed in the United States of America on acid-free paper
9 8 7 6 5 4 3 2
First Edition

PREFACE

Learning from your experience can be expensive, inconvenient, and sometimes disastrous when it comes to starting a small business. But learning from the experience of others is painless and profitable.

That's why we have put together this directory of information resources for the entrepreneur. Somewhere, someone has been through it before and has the answer to your question. The answers may come from a trade association, Web site, book, or even from the U.S. Government—but the information is out there, waiting to be harvested.

What's your question? Do you want to know . . .

- How to find start-up money for your small business?
- What to do about employee drug testing?
- How to start importing and exporting?
- What sort of computer you need?
- How to set up your books?

The answers are here. In some areas, we've provided a "Tip Sheet" that leads you through the more common small-business scenarios. In other instances, we recommend books, Web sites, or trade associations that can bring considerable knowledge and experience to bear on your particular issue. Because we devote so much space to sources of information, this book will remain a dynamic reference throughout the life of your business.

Using this book is simple: Look through the contents and index to find entries that relate to your situation or browse through it for ideas, inspiration, and sources of help. The entries contain factual data, how-to advice, and listings of resources. The complete contact information for all organizations listed, including address, phone and fax numbers, and Web site, can be found in Part Three.

The authors wish to acknowledge research associates Jeannie Rujikarn, Susan Posternock, Angela Starita, and Alice Richey. Their diligence and creativity helped make this book comprehensive and cohesive.

CARL HAUSMAN
WILBUR CROSS

CONTENTS

PART ONE

A Crash Course in Starting and Growing a New Business

CHAPTER 1

The Idea

It may come to you all at once. Or maybe you have been turning the idea over in your mind for years. But now you've made the decision: you'll start your own business. You're convinced that the idea is viable. You're sure there is a hungry market for your products or services.

 ## TESTING THE CONCEPT

A great idea is an excellent beginning, but it's only a beginning. You have a lot of important homework to do. Now is the time to investigate:

- Is enough capital available, or can it be acquired, to launch the enterprise and maintain its momentum?
- Is a suitable location available?
- Can the population in the area surrounding the location support your kind of business?
- Is the local economy, or the market in which you will compete, in a healthy condition?
- Can suitable employees or contractors be recruited?
- Will the business be resistant to economic fluctuations, fickle consumer tastes, or changing legislation?
- Could any legal entanglements or extraordinary legal risks cause unexpected financial liability?

Above and beyond these basic requirements, you need patience. It will take time for the business to become known, gather paying customers, and reach a break-even point. This precarious introductory period is when most failures occur. Your total personal commitment is a must. Even though you may be steadily adding employees in the initial stage, you must hold a tight rein on the business, controlling all the major management and operational functions. During this period, you may be working days, nights, and weekends, and consistent profitability may be a mirage on a distant horizon.

 ## Do You Have What It Takes? A Self-Test

The start-up period can be expected to continue for a year or two—or longer, for a more complicated enterprise. Financially, personally, and psychologically, these can be punishing years. Are you up to the challenge? Ask yourself these questions before you make the decision to become an entrepreneur:

- Do I have the *self-confidence* needed to undertake the venture? Can I get on the phone and make calls to prospective customers, or make cold sales calls on the street?

- For the business I have in mind, is the *timing* right, both seasonally and from the viewpoint of consumers' buying trends?

- Are my *personal attributes* right for the task? Am I self-motivated, a hard worker, comfortable managing other people whom I will need for assistance, and willing to sacrifice my private interests and leisure time to devote a full effort to the job?

- Do I have the *competitive spirit* required to run a business in the face of stiff and persistent rivals—other owners and managers who will be aiming at the same clients and/or customers? Do I have the drive and the imagination to compete in the marketplace?

- Am I willing to make the necessary *financial sacrifices*—to focus my monetary efforts on this new business, even if it means investing my own nest egg? Or do I have enough fortitude and poise to approach banks or other prospective lenders and obtain the necessary financing?

- Can I survive a situation in which I have *no regular, dependable paycheck* and sometimes may have to hold off some creditors until my business reaches a point where I can pay myself a salary or expenses? Can I cut back on my personal financial obligations in order to avoid unmanageable debt?

- Have I prepared a *professional "road map"* to guide me in the direction I want the business to take? Have I clearly marked the route for long-term growth and development of the firm?
- Do I know how to *take advantage of the resources,* public and private, that are available to help me chart the best course to my goals?

This sourcebook has been prepared to help you answer the last question affirmatively and, in the process, to help you meet all the other requirements for being a successful entrepreneur.

 ## PUTTING THE BUSINESS PLAN ON PAPER

An essential job, early in the venture's creation, is development of a *business plan,* a meticulous definition of the business you are starting. The business plan is useful both as an initial road map and, later, as a vehicle for obtaining loans and funding. Your plan should cover the following subject areas:

- *Management:* The names and qualifications of the owner(s) and manager(s) of the new business, their addresses and other vital statistics.
- *Financial needs:* How much funding you will require now and later on, for what purpose, and from what classification of lender; your expected income and expenses, sources of additional capital, and projected time periods for reducing debt.
- *The market:* The potential outlets today and in the future, and the methods you expect to use to attract customers, make sales, and provide related services.
- *Competition:* How strong your rivals are, and how you expect to survive and prosper in spite of them.
- *Duties and responsibilities:* Who will do what, and how pertinent functions and operations will be handled on a day-to-day basis.
- *Future prospects:* What they are and why they are realistic; an evaluation of the market area and where your new company will fit in.

- *Regulations and restrictions:* The external controls that will affect your business: the licenses, entitlements, permits, and authorizations, from the federal, state, county, or municipal governments, that are needed to conduct business in your area.

- *Taxes and fees:* The charges imposed by each government level. Plan to open a Taxes account, to keep tax collections related to sales, Social Security, income, and so on, separate from business revenues and receivables.

- *Record-keeping methods:* Of the types that are available, the ones best used in your particular business. You must keep all business transactions separate from your personal expenses.

- *Profit-and-loss statements/Balance sheets:* How often you must prepare them, and what form they should take. If you are not sure, find out what the industry practices are for your kind of business.

- *Personnel administration:* A wide range of duties and responsibilities, including recruitment, screening, hiring, compensation, orientation, training, assigning, and discharging. Personnel activities are affected, at least in part, by government regulations, union demands, and the laws of supply and demand. Most small businesses have problems locating qualified and efficient employees whose compensation demands are within the fledgling company's budget.

Several chapters in Part Two, "Resources by Category," provide detailed guidance on getting your business off the drawing board and into action. Chapter 6 explains the structure of the business plan, and Chapter 7 tells you how to use the plan to garner funding. Chapter 8 provides a quick briefing in accounting, and Chapters 9 through 11 clarify various aspects of compensation, management, and law.

CHAPTER 2

Surveying the Business Landscape— Locating Resources

No single directory can contain everything you need to know as a new business owner. Nothing can substitute for on-the-spot personal intelligence gathering—the localized contacts and sources that will bring your business's picture into sharp focus. Even as you are mining the information presented in this sourcebook, begin searching for your own personal and territorial data. This chapter points you toward places to start.

CHAMBERS OF COMMERCE

Your local Chamber of Commerce (or the one in the area in which you intend to do business) can give you a concise summary of the local business climate, the number and size of firms that might be your competitors, and the failure rate of small and home-based businesses in the district. Associated with the Chambers of Commerce in many areas are Small Business Resource Centers (SBRCs), that can be of invaluable help to owners and managers of small and home-based businesses. Besides locating local sources and resources, SBRCs provide marketing workshops, business-to-business expositions, conferences, speakers, and liaisons between business and government.

SERVICE CORPS OF RETIRED EXECUTIVES

Complete contact information for the Service Corps of Retired Executives (SCORE) appears in Part Three, "A to Z Listings." SCORE has local offices in all fifty states, the District of Columbia, and Puerto Rico. SCORE is a valuable resource because its members live in the communities where the SCORE offices are located, and they have an intimate knowledge of the local economy. The organization is composed of retired executives, many of whom ran their own businesses. SCORE volunteers will sit down with you and honestly evaluate your chances of success. They will guide you to alternative resources, help you write a business plan, and perform other invaluable services—all without charging any fee.

SCORE also offers counseling by e-mail. You can locate experts via the SCORE Web page. The address is:

www.score.org

The SCORE Databank lists over 750 skills that can be discussed with a counselor, who is just another click away. Here is a slightly condensed version of the Databank topics:

Accounting
Accounting and budgeting
Accounting systems
Acquisitions and mergers
Acquisitions and long-range
   planning
Activity-based costing
Administration
Adult day care
Adult education programs
Advanced technology
Advertising
Advertising and promotion
Advertising copy and layout
Aerospace
Aerospace engineering
Aerospace software
Agri-business
Agricultural loans
Agriculture
Air conditioning
Aircraft overhaul

Aircraft/aerospace
   engineering
Airline management
Airline operations
Aluminum forging
Amateur radio operations
Americans with Disabilities Act
   (ADA)
Animal health and nutrition
Antitrust
Apparel manufacturing
Appliances
Appraisal
Arbitration
Architectural engineering
Architectural metals
Architecture
Arts and crafts
Audio control facilities
Auditing
Author
Automotive dealer

Automotive industry
Automotive service

Banking
Bankruptcies
Bar code technology
Bed and breakfast management
Beverage distribution and
    management
Beverages
Bio-remediation
Boarding kennels
Boating: power/sail/instruction/
    charter/piloting
Body shop operations
Book publishing
Bookkeeping
Brochure concepts
Budget and management systems
Budgeting
Budgets and controls
Building construction and
    maintenance
Business and industrial
    management
Business acquisitions
Business administration
Business analysis
Business appraisals and valuations
Business automation
Business continuity and recovery
    planning
Business credit
Business development
Business entities
Business evaluation
Business forms
Business management
Business operations

Business organization
Business planning
Business plans
Business plans for loan
    presentations
Business plans management
Business problem solving
Business records storage
Business startup
Business systems
Business valuations
Buy and sell agreements
Buyouts
Buying and selling a business

Capital requirements
Cash control
Cash flow
Cash flow analysis
Cash flow consulting
Cash flow management
Cash management
Catalogs
Cellular phone retail operations
Certified public accountant
Chain store operations
Change management
Charter aircraft operations
Charter boat operations
Chemical engineering
Chemical research and
    development
Chemicals
Chemistry
Child day care
Children's summer camps
Civil engineering
Clothing retail
Collateral evaluation

Commercial banking
Commercial leasing
Commercial printing
Commercial real estate
Commodity trade
Communications
Compliance with state requirements
Computer accounting
Computer accounting applications
Computer applications
Computer consulting
Computer counseling
Computer credit database systems
Computer hardware and software
Computer integration
Computer operations systems
Computer programming
Computer science
Computer skills
Computer systems
Computer systems analysis
Computer systems and applications
Computer technology
Computer training
Computer usage
Computer utilization
Computerized accounting and
   bookkeeping systems
Computing
Consolidations
Construction
Construction and operations
Construction loans
Consulting (engineering-medical)
Consulting (technical)
Consumer credit
Consumer electronics industry
Consumer finance
Consumer loans

Consumer products: financial
Consumer products: sales
Continuous process improvement
Contract administration
Contract proposals
Contract writing
Contracting
Contracting with particular
   emphasis on DOD
Contracts management
Copyrights
Corporate strategic planning
Cost accounting
Cost control
Cost controls
Costs
Court mediator
Credit
Credit collections
Credit policy and procedures
Crisis management
Customer service

Data processing
Day care centers
Debt
Decorative bath product
   manufacturing
Dental practice management
Department store sales
Department store retailing
Design
Design and manufacturing of
   sterling silver jewelry
Direct mail
Disaster preparedness
Disaster recovery (hi-tech)
Display
Distribution

Distribution systems
Durable medical equipment: sales
  and rentals

Economic growth bonds
Electrical contracting
Electrical engineering
Electronic engineering
Electronic engineering operations
Electronic packaging/designing/
  manufacturing
Electronic product design;
  business plans
Electronics
Electronics industry
Employee benefits
Employee compensation
Employee training
Employment agency
Engineering
Engineering—aircraft
Engineering—electrical
Engineering—mechanical
Engineering—physics
Entrepreneurship
Envelope production and
  marketing
Environmental corrosion
Environmental products
Equipment
Equipment rentals
Equity
Evaluation
Event planning
Expense forecasting
Export assistance programs
Export trade
Export trade shows
Export/import

Factory experience
Fashion merchandising
Fast foods
Federal and state income tax
  preparation training
Federal government
  proposals/contracts/contracting
Fiber optics
Fiberglass products
Finance
Finance analyst
Finance and banking
Financial and plant management
Financial analysis
Financial controls
Financial controls and analysis
Financial management
Financial management analysis
Financial planning
Financial services
Financial statements
Financial statements analysis
Financial systems
Financial targets
Financing
Financing commercial real estate
  and small businesses
Fixed price contracting
Fleet transportation
Floor covering sales
Floor covering specifications
Flying
Food administration
Food and beverage management
Food broker
Food distribution
Food manufacturing
Food marketing
Food processing

Food research
Food sales
Food service
Forms of business
Forms of ownership
Foundry operations (iron and lost wax)
Franchises
Franchising
Funding sources
Furniture manufacturing

General accounting and auditing practices
General business
General contracting
General furniture retail
General management
General manufacturing
General office administration
Gift and card shops
Giftware
Government
Government contracting
Government contracting/sales and marketing
Government contracts
Government operations
Government procurement
Government uniform fabrics
Grant writing
Graphic arts
Growth issues

Hardware
Hardware and industrial equipment
Health care
Health care services
Heating installation and service
Heavy-duty construction

Heavy machinery
Heavy manufacturing
High-tech manufacturing
High-tech program management
High-tech: operations of research and development
High technology
Hiring and training
Home-based business
Home building
Home furnishings
Home health services
Home repair
Hospitality industry
Hotels
Household products
Human relations
Human resources
Human resources management
Human resources/personnel management

Image development
Imaging equipment sales
Importing
Imports
Income properties and rental
Income taxes
Industrial and commercial light fixtures and signs
Industrial and electric engineering
Industrial engineering
Industrial park management
Industrial relations
Information management
Information systems
Information technology
Inspection systems
Insurance

Insurance business
Insurance needs
Intellectual property management
Intellectual property patents and
 trademarks
Intellectual property protection and
 inventrepreneurship
Intellectual property transfer
International marketing
International operations
International sales: Europe/Asia
International trade
International trade—financing
International trade—import/export
International trade—management
Internet
Internet development and use
Internet marketing
Interpreting
Inventions
Inventory
Inventory control and management
ISO 9000

Jams and jellies processing
Jewelry stores
Job descriptions
Just-in-time manufacturing

Labor relations
Ladies' ready-to-wear stores
Land development
Latin American importing
Laundromat operations
Laundry and dry cleaning
Law
Law office administration
Licensing
Licensing of intellectual property
Life insurance

Light manufacturing (food/apparel)
Lighting equipment marketing for
 retail and wholesale
Limited partnerships
Linen rentals
Livestock production/processing/
 marketing
Loan packages
Location selection
Logistics
Logistics/distribution
Long-range planning
Low-interest bonds

Machine shops
Machine tools
Machinery and fabrication
Magazine advertising
Mail order
Mail order marketing
Mainframe computers
Major appliance distribution
Management
Management consulting/strategic
 planning
Management control systems
Management development
Management of financial
 institutions
Management and leadership
 coaching
Management and office
 administration
Management and planning
Management services
Manufacturers' representative
Manufacturing
Manufacturing of boys', young
 men's, and men's apparel

Manufacturing children's wear
Manufacturing consumer goods
Manufacturing costs
Manufacturing: domestic and off
   shore
Manufacturing food products
Manufacturing management
Manufacturing medical devices
Manufacturing of modular homes
Manufacturing plastics/composites
Manufacturing representative
Marina operations
Marine transportation
Market planning
Market research
Market testing
Marketing
Marketing: consumer goods
Marketing avionics
Marketing generalist
Marketing management
Marketing strategy
Marketing: word-of-mouth
   specialty
Marketing and sales: industrial
   products
Marketing and sales: management
Material control
Materials management
Meat processing
Mechanical
Mechanical engineering
Media
Medical hospital supplies
Medical insurance
Medical personnel registry
Men's sportswear
Menswear sales
Merchandising

Mergers
Mergers and acquisitions
Metal forming
Metal stamping of auto parts
Metalworking
Micro chip technology
Microfilm systems
Microsoft office 95
Military marketing
Military vehicle development
Milk marketing
Mini-malls
Minority women's programs
Mission statements
Mortgages
Motels
Motivation
Motor transportation

New business development
Newsletters
Nonferrous metals processing
Nonprofit organizations 501(c)(3)
Nonprofit startups
Nursing

Objective setting
Office administration
Office administration and
   management
Oil production
Operational and strategic planning
Operations
Operations modeling
Order picking systems
Organic farming
Organization
Organization planning/structuring
   business
Organizational alignment

Organizational behavioral
Overhead analysis
Owner's manuals

Paints and coatings
Partnerships
Party rentals
Patents
Payroll
Payroll taxes
Peachtree accounting for DOS
Personnel
Personnel/labor relations
Personnel management and training
Personnel operations
Pet services
Pharmacist
Photographic equipment and
    supplies
Photography
Physics
Planning
Plant layout
Plant management
Plant production management
Plastics
Plastics and metals
Plumbing
Pool service
Power boating
Pricing
Print purchasing and production
Printing
Private investigation
Private lenders
Problem solving
Process design
Process improvement
Producing

Product development
Product safety
Product and sales management
Production control
Production controls
Production planning and control
Profit improvement
Profit and loss control
Project engineering
Project management
Project management operations
Project planning
Promotions
Property appraisal
Property management
Proposal writing
Protection
Public accounting
Public relations
Public service bodies
Publishing
Publishing/graphic arts
Purchases
Purchasing
Purchasing systems

Quality assurance/control
Quality control
Quality giftwares
Quality improvement
Quality sciences
Quality systems

Radio stations
Real estate
Real estate loans
Record keeping
Recruiting and training
Registered engineer
Rehabilitation equipment

Remodeling

Research

Research and development

Research and development: consultation

Research and development: funding

Research and development: marketing (federal)

Research and development: plastics/composites/fabrics

Restaurants

Restaurants: planning

Restaurants: startup and established operations

Restructuring

Retail

Retail (discount; chain and jewelry stores; advertising; promotions)

Retail (ladies' ready-to-wear: sales and management)

Retail clothing business

Retail electronics

Retail grocery

Retail hardware store

Retail leasing

Retail lumber and hardware

Retail management

Retail marketing

Retail operations

Retail sales

Retail shoe stores

Retail sporting goods

Retail store management

Retail store operations

Retail tire and service stores

Retail trade

Retail wines and spirits

Retailing

Retailing (advertising; accounting; display; internal control; purchasing; sales training)

Risk management

S corporations

Safety

Sailing equipment/rigging/sails

Salary administration

Sales

Sales: airline

Sales: working with agents and distributors

Sales campaigns

Sales of chemicals

Sales to federal and state governments

Sales forecasting

Sales incentives

Sales management

Sales and product manuals

Sales and service literature

Sales training

SBA export loan program

SBA loans

SBIR program

School/office installation and sales

Self-storage

Service

Service companies

Services

Shopping center

Small boats

Small business operations

Soft drink bottling plant operations and sales

Software

Software management

Software systems

Software testing
Spice trade
Sports
Spreadsheet applications
Staff meetings
Staff training programs
Start-up financing
Startups
Stocks and bonds
Strategic alliances
Strategic market analysis
Strategic planning
Strategy and policy
Styled apparel
Subcontracting
Supermarkets
Supplier partnerships
System engineering
Systems
Systems analysis
Systems management

Tax-exempt bonds
Tax planning
Tax problems
Taxes
Taxicab operations
Technical knowhow
Technical management
Technical products
Technical writing
Technology transfers
Telecommunications
Telecommunications management
and consulting
Telemarketing
Telephone and communication
equipment
Textile importing

Textiles
Total Quality Management (TQM)
Total quality planning
Town engineer
Trade secrets
Trade show—USA plans
Trade shows
Trademarks
Training
Transportation
Trucking
Truss manufacturing
Turnaround management

Unemployment compensation
Uniform rental service

Warehousing
Web page construction
Website critique and review
Website design
Wheelchair distributor
Wholesale distribution
Wholesale and retail building
supplies
Wholesale sales
Wholesale shoes
Wholesale tire distribution
Wholesale trade
Wholesaling
Windows 95
Women's networking groups
Work flow analysis
Workers' compensation
Workplace safety and health
Workshops and seminars
Writing and editing

Zero-based budgeting

LOCAL BUSINESS LIBRARIES

Your local library is likely to contain two essential sources:

- *Back copies of area newspapers:* The business sections can give you specific, home-front accounts of the local business economy.
- *Clipping folders:* These should contain news items about specific businesses and regional market conditions.

See whether the libraries in your area will answer phone queries. Some large public libraries, such as the Brooklyn Public Library and the New York Public Library, have staffers assigned to answering questions over the phone. Larger public libraries and university libraries often feature extensive business sections. Some newspapers will, for a fee, have a professional news librarian search their holdings for you.

The Web is another avenue for searching library holdings. This is mostly a do-it-yourself proposition, but, with a little experience, you can pose the right question and get a useful answer. For starters, visit the mammoth directory of library resources at:

www.danbury.lib.ct.us/org/dpl/lib.htm

 ## FRATERNAL ORGANIZATIONS

Organizations such as Kiwanis, Elks, and Knights of Columbus have many members who own small businesses and are often more than willing to share their experiences with you. A little probing and informal discussion can be more rewarding than hiring a professional consultant.

 ## GOVERNMENT PRINTING OFFICE

Many publications on starting and managing a small business, and related topics, are available from the Government Printing Office. GPO bookstores are located in twenty-four major cities; for a list of addresses, see Part Three, "A to Z Listing." You can obtain a subject bibliography by writing to Government Printing Office, Superintendent of Documents, Washington, DC 20402-9328, or visit the GPO Web site:

www.access.gpo.gov

Location of U.S. Government Bookstores by State

Through the Superintendent of Documents, the U.S. Government Printing Office (GPO) operates twenty-four U.S. government bookstores across the country. Each bookstore carries a selection of at least 1,500 of the most popular Federal government publications, subscriptions, and electronic products. Each bookstore can order any of over 12,000 titles for sale by GPO. Visit or contact any bookstore for more information. MasterCard and VISA are welcome. Maps to GPO stores are available at:

www.access.gpo.gov/su_docs/sale/abkst001.html

U.S. Government Printing Office
710 N. Capitol Street, NW
Washington, DC 20401
(202) 512-0132 FAX: (202) 512-1355
Hours: 8:00 A.M.–4:00 P.M.,
Monday–Friday, except federal holidays
Branch:
1510 H Street, NW
Washington, DC 20005
(202) 653-5075 FAX: (202) 376-5055
Hours: 9:00 A.M.–4:30 P.M.,
Monday–Friday, except federal holidays

The following is a state-by-state list of GPO bookstores:

ALABAMA
Birmingham (35203)
O'Neill Building
2021 Third Avenue, North
(205) 731-1056/731-3444 (Fax)
Hours: 8:30 A.M.–4:30 P.M.,
Monday–Friday, except federal holidays

CALIFORNIA
Los Angeles (90071)
ARCO Plaza, C-Level
505 South Flower Street
(213) 239-9844/239-9848 (Fax)
Hours: 8:00 A.M.–4:00 P.M., Monday–
Friday, except federal holidays

San Francisco (94107)
Marathon Plaza, Room 141-S
303 2nd Street
(415) 512-2770/512-2776 (Fax)
Hours: 8:00 A.M.–4:00 P.M., Monday–
Friday, except federal holidays

COLORADO
Denver (80202)
1660 Wynkoop Street, Suite 130
(303) 844-3964/844-4000 (Fax)
Hours: 8:00 A.M.–4:00 P.M., Monday–
Friday, except federal holidays

Pueblo (81003)
Norwest Banks Building
201 West 8th Street
(719) 544-3142/544-6719 (Fax)
Hours: 8:30 A.M.–4:30 P.M., Monday–
  Friday, except federal holidays

FLORIDA
Jacksonville (32202)
100 West Bay Street, Suite 100
(904) 353-0569/353-1280 (Fax)
Hours: 8:30 A.M.–4:30 P.M., Monday–
  Friday, except federal holidays

GEORGIA
Atlanta (30309-3964)
First Union Plaza
999 Peachtree Street, NE, Suite 120
(404) 347-1900/347-1897 (Fax)
Hours: 8:30 A.M.–4:00 P.M., Monday–
  Friday, except federal holidays

ILLINOIS
Chicago (60605)
One Congress Center
401 South State Street, Suite 124
(312) 353-5133/353-1590 (Fax)
Hours: 8:30 A.M.–4:30 P.M., Monday–
  Friday, except federal holidays

MARYLAND
Laurel (20707)
Warehouse Sales Outlet
8660 Cherry Lane
(301) 953-7974, 792-0262/498-8995 (Fax)
Hours: 8:30 A.M.–3:45 P.M., Monday–
  Friday, except federal holidays

MASSACHUSETTS
Boston (02222)
Thomas P. O'Neill Building
10 Causeway Street, Room 169
(617) 720-4180/720-5753 (Fax)
Hours: 8:00 A.M.–4:00 P.M., Monday–
  Friday, except federal holidays

MICHIGAN
Detroit (48226)
Federal Building
477 Michigan Avenue, Suite 160
(313) 226-7816/226-4698 (Fax)
Hours: 8:00 A.M.–4:00 P.M., Monday–
  Friday, except federal holidays

MISSOURI
Kansas City (64137)
120 Bannister Mall
5600 E. Bannister Road
(816) 765-2256/767-8233 (Fax)
Hours: 10:00 A.M.–9:00 P.M., Monday–
  Saturday and 12:00 A.M.–6:00 P.M.,
  Sunday, except Easter, Thanksgiving,
  and Christmas

NEW YORK
New York (10278)
Federal Building
26 Federal Plaza, Room 2-120
(212) 264-3825/264-9318 (Fax)
Hours: 8:15 A.M.–4:15 P.M., Monday–
  Friday, except federal holidays

OHIO
Cleveland (44199)
Federal Building
1240 E. 9th Street, Room 1653
(216) 522-4922/522-4714 (Fax)
Hours: 8:00 A.M.–4:00 P.M., Monday–
  Friday, except federal holidays
Columbus (43215)
Federal Building
200 N. High Street, Room 207
(614) 469-6956/469-5374 (Fax)
Hours: 8:00 A.M.–4:00 P.M., Monday–
  Friday, except federal holidays

OREGON
Portland (97201-5801)
1305 SW First Avenue
(503) 221-6217/225-0563 (Fax)
Hours: 8:30 A.M.–4:30 P.M., Monday–
  Friday, except federal holidays

PENNSYLVANIA
Philadelphia (19103)
Robert Morris Building
100 North 17th Street
(215) 636-1900/636-1903 (Fax)
Hours: 8:00 A.M.–4:00 P.M., Monday–
Friday, except federal holidays
Pittsburgh (15222)
Federal Building
1000 Liberty Avenue, Room 118
(412) 395-5021/395-4547 (Fax)
Hours: 8:00 A.M.–4:00 P.M., Monday–
Friday, except federal holidays

TEXAS
Dallas (75242)
Federal Building
1100 Commerce Street, Room IC50
(214) 767-0076/767-3239 (Fax)
Hours: 8:00 A.M.–4:00 P.M., Monday–
Friday, except federal holidays

Houston (77002)
Texas Crude Building
801 Travis Street, Suite 120
(713) 228-1187/228-1186 (Fax)
Hours: 8:30 A.M.–4:30 P.M., Monday–
Friday, except federal holidays

WASHINGTON
Seattle (98174)
Federal Building
915 Second Avenue, Room 194
(206) 553-4270/553-6717 (Fax)
Hours: 8:00 A.M.–4:00 P.M., Monday–
Friday, except federal holidays

WISCONSIN
Milwaukee (53203)
Reuss Federal Plaza
310 W. Wisconsin Avenue, Suite 150
(414) 297-1304/297-1300 (Fax)
Hours: 8:15 A.M.–4:15 P.M., Monday–
Friday, except federal holidays

 ## CONTINUING EDUCATION CENTERS

Continuing education courses in nearby colleges that have business curricula can be valuable. A single course may not offer advice specifically tailored for your purposes, but brushing elbows with business faculty members and other professionals could help you to evaluate the regional business environment. As an alternative to taking the courses, you might make your own arrangements to consult with members of the business faculty and gain their evaluations of the market and consumer needs. Chapter 21, "Training and Continuing Education," provides descriptions of many resources. Part Three, "A to Z Listing," contains a list of the major American business schools.

 ## COMPETITORS

Extracting information from established rivals-to-be is difficult, but no one in the area will have a better understanding of the potential for your business. Much of what you seek may be available publicly; for example, a competitor may post a list of prices and services on a Website. Sometimes, undercover research is effective. Think about asking a friend or relative who is a customer of a future competitor to scope out your competitor's products, services, and reputation for satisfying customers.

Each chapter in Part Two, "Resources by Category," lists useful national and state resources. Chapters 16 and 20 specifically address aspects of market research.

 ## *ENTREPRENEUR* **Magazine Group (EMG)**

This Group publishes numerous periodicals of interest to small businesses and entrepreneurs. Its primary publication, *Entrepreneur,* covers many subjects of direct concern to the owners and managers of small businesses, such as starting, promoting, and building a business. Each month, *Entrepreneur* offers case histories of entrepreneurs who have been successful in fields ranging from auto repairing and bookselling to innkeeping, printing, showmanship, and yogurt making. During the course of a year, the Group reviews a wide range of franchises. Its annual directory of some one thousand franchises gives statistics about the type of ownership, start-up costs, royalties, financing, advertising, and profitability.

In addition to its monthly magazine and special issues, the Group publishes *Business Startups, Guide to Franchise and Business Opportunities, Business Start-Up Guides,* and fact sheets and literature on various kinds of franchises and entrepreneurial ventures. Its three-volume *Small Business Encyclopedia* is a major reference work for business executives of all kinds, whether involved with franchises or not.

Entrepreneur publishes dozens of start-up guides, in areas such as business services, computers, personal services, maintenance services, auto services, retail business, and food services. Individual titles have included how to start: a child care service, personal shopping service, travel agency, hair salon, sandwich shop, temporary help service, utility and telephone bill auditing service, vitamin and health food store, wholesale distribution business, herb farm, freight brokerage, consignment clothing store, and many others. Call 800-421-2300 for further information.

STATE INFORMATION CENTERS

State information centers can connect you with the appropriate government agency for questions you have or information you may need about state law, regulations, and resources. A state-by-state list can be found in Part Three, "A to Z Listing."

3

Start-up Options

When you decide to start a business, you must select the legal format of your organization-to-be. These are your choices.

 ## CORPORATION

A corporation is a specific legal entity that is distinct from the individuals who own or manage it. Generally, it is the option associated with large or middle-range companies rather than small businesses. However, some small businesses with quick growth possibilities elect to start life as a corporation.

 ## S CORPORATION

An S corporation is a specific type of corporation with advantages for a one- or two-person company. The paperwork is simpler, but the S corporation still offers the advantage of relieving company principals of some of their personal liability in the event of a lawsuit or bankruptcy.

 ## PROPRIETORSHIP

A proprietorship is the simplest of all legal formats. The owner is customarily the manager and does not share control of the business with others.

The sole proprietor, however, bears unlimited personal responsibility for the debts of the business.

 ## PARTNERSHIP

A partnership is an arrangement under which two or more people own the business jointly, under a mutual agreement. The partnership agreement usually specifies duties, responsibilities, accountability, guidelines for administration and management, and long-range contingencies for the eventual dissolution of the business. The problem with a partnership is that each partner assumes unlimited liability for the business actions of the other partner or partners.

See Chapter 12 for detailed guidance on choosing a business form.

Managing the New Business

Management has been defined as: the art and science of getting things done through other people. For small-business owners, the definition must include self-management—knowing how to plan your own time properly, and developing the discipline to follow and expedite the business plan.

 ## MANAGEMENT FUNCTIONS

Management is a complex activity that requires individuals to take charge in five crucial spheres of action:

1. *Planning:* The ability to: visualize what is necessary to keep the venture on an even keel today and in the future; set goals that are realistic; and outline steps and procedures for meeting those goals.

2. *Organization:* The allocation of assignments to individuals and groups in a way that (a) matches tasks with skills, facilities, and tools, and (b) establishes timetables to accomplish the stated goals of the organization. In a small company, good organization also involves skills in dealing with outside personnel on whom the owner depends, such as suppliers, servicers, and agencies.

3. *Staffing:* The evaluation of the demographics of the geographical area(s) in which a business is conducted, to determine the company's personnel needs and estimate whether the existing workforce pool can meet those needs.

4. *Leadership:* The ability to motivate other people, both inside and out-side the company, to become involved in and take actions that will be beneficial to the organization. The ability to lead and motivate may be inborn or acquired. It is best achieved by owners and managers who are themselves strongly motivated, or even inspired, and are thus able to influence others to be productive.

5. *Exercising control:* An essential long-term attribute. Many small-business owners and managers are effective in pursuing the first four principles of good management, but they fall short when they must retain control. Failure to maintain standards of performance, to measure performance against these standards, and to take prompt corrective action when standards are not met, leads to loss of control.

 ## MANAGEMENT TOOLS

Among the proven tools for small-business management are:

1. A clear-cut, written, *long-range plan* that includes the company's original business plan, the financial projections, a description of the operational system, production capabilities (if applicable), and a sales or marketing plan.

2. A comprehensive *budget,* in writing, that allows for anticipated expenses; salaries and other compensation; payables and receivables; and all other financial obligations. Budgeting on a monthly basis is standard practice. No budget period should be longer than a fiscal quarter.

3. *Job descriptions* that clearly establish duties and areas of responsibility. If the company has no employees, work descriptions should be prepared for part-time help, professional services, commercial services, and consultants.

4. A detailed *calendar* that displays timetables for reaching specific goals and fulfilling production or distribution schedules, and highlights dates relating to various activities or obligations that have to be met.

5. A list of *priorities,* indicating their role in operations and their timing. They should be arranged in descending order of importance and urgency. One of the hallmarks of good administration is the ability of management to envision and specify priorities.

6. A formal statement of *company policies* that relate to such matters as employee conduct, product quality, caliber of service, the environment, community relations, productivity, and advertising/promotion standards.

 ## MANAGEMENT PITFALLS

When the business-rating firm of Dun & Bradstreet conducted a nation-wide study to compile a list of pitfalls that proved to be the undoing of small-business managers, these were among the most dangerous characteristics or activities:

- Lack of experience.
- Inadequate financing for the business, both at the start and during the early stages of growth.
- Selecting the wrong location for the business site or the wrong geographical areas for operation and marketing.
- Mismanaging inventory—having too much or too little.
- Investing too heavily in capital equipment.
- Extending too much credit to customers.
- Attempting to expand the business too soon, or to an unreasonable extent.
- Placing the blame for failures and negligence on others when management itself was at fault.

Chapter 10 provides information and resources related to management; also see related topics in Chapters 8 and 9, and 11 through 14.

Coping with Problems
Down the Road

When the growth stage of a small enterprise starts to level off, the business reaches *maturity,* the point at which it is realizing its top potential and achieving its peak earnings. At maturity, one of two things will happen:

1. The business will show signs of going downhill, leaving the owner skeptical about the future and inclined to consider selling out.
2. It will continue on a fairly level course for an indefinite period.

 ## THE PSYCHOLOGICAL SIDE EFFECTS OF LIMITED GROWTH

According to the Center for Entrepreneurial Management, many owners are not content to see their brainchild—on which they have lavished so much time and care—simply coast along. When growth does not occur, even those managers who were once very competitive become downhearted and passive. Or, if they still have the old entrepreneurial spark, they start looking around for other ventures to which they can devote their energy and imagination anew.

A limited-growth condition can dominate the workplace for years, persuading some owners that they have been fortunate because their business is now stabilized and they can transfer its management to an associate or an outsider while they enjoy holidays and vacations.

But signs of imminent decline can arise as quickly as a summer squall. Among those signs are: profits becoming harder to achieve, recruiting

becoming difficult, employees drifting away, advertising failing to stimu-
late sales, and maintenance expenses and upkeep getting out of hand.
Faced with these signs, some owners panic, realizing that they might have
sold the business for a tidy sum some months earlier, when it was still in
maturity, and they now may have to sell at a sacrifice price or risk greater
losses if the business declines still further.

 ## AVOIDING THE TYPICAL CAUSES OF FAILURE

Failure is nothing new to the small-business world. One often-cited statistic points to four out of five businesses failing during their first five
years of operation. Some economists dispute this high percentage rate;
but in fact, the short life expectancy of these modest enterprises has dis-
couraged many would-be entrepreneurs from getting involved. Data from
the Administrative Office of the U.S. Courts documents the fact that
more than 95 percent of the business filings for bankruptcy in the 1980s
and 1990s were for businesses that were classified as small. The basic
reasons for failure include the following (not necessarily in order of impact or degree):

- The inability of owners to make clear decisions.
- Failure to anticipate market trends.
- Insufficient capital.
- Overextension of credit to customers.
- Poor communications and relations with suppliers.
- Sloppy inventory control.
- Lack of basic business training.
- Reluctance to seek professional counsel and help.
- Insufficient knowledge of merchandise or equipment.
- Inadequate record keeping.
- Disregard of competition.

The essential point of this chapter is that many of the landmines have
been clearly marked, and experience has demonstrated that the dangers
lurk during the entire development of a small business.

That is one reason why this reference directory has been compiled—as a beacon to guide you in the right direction. Each of the book's chapters deals with a particular aspect of small business, and leads you to resources that allow you to learn from the advice and experience of others. Useful information is presented in the Tip Sheets—concise guides to various aspects of starting and running your own small business.

Resources by Category

Crafting the Funding Blueprint: Your Business Plan

INTRODUCTION

By definition, a *business plan* is a formal statement that describes in great detail an enterprise that is about to be launched, substantially reorganized, or expanded. The business plan is usually prepared and presented to request financing and to secure necessary permits and approvals for legalizing the venture. But the document also is an essential road map for the entrepreneur, and is useful for recruiting managers, partners, employees, suppliers, and others who might be essential to the successful operation of the business.

Most business beginners seriously underestimate both the importance of planning and the time it takes to research and prepare a competent plan and a well-documented presentation. A sound business plan should contain the following basic components: description of the venture, nature of products and/or services, the market (its geography and consumer profile), competition, location, management, personnel, current financial condition, and short-term and long-term financing needed.

The importance of planning must not be underestimated. The plan should be prepared in an objective manner—with attention to the weaknesses, as well as the strengths, of the new enterprise. In some cases, a realistic and detailed business plan can help avoid the birth of an enterprise that is doomed to failure. If the proposed venture is not sound, it probably won't make sense on paper, and the principals will lose only their time and a few marginal research expenses.

SOURCES OF INFORMATION

American Business Association (ABA)

The American Business Association is for businesspeople from firms employing fewer than fifty persons. The ABA also encourages membership by individuals who are professionals, consultants, or specialists, but are not affiliated directly with a business firm. The ABA provides a number of benefits to small-business members, including assistance with business planning, financial services, loans, group travel packages, group insurance, and discounts.

American Small Businesses Association (ASBA)

The American Small Businesses Association was established to allow small-business owners access to many of the same advantages and assistance programs that larger companies enjoy. Members of the ASBA enjoy many opportunities and benefits, such as medical insurance savings and consumer/business discounts. Among the variety of support services available are: business planning and organization, a bimonthly business magazine, seminars and workshops, and access to private forums online. The ASBA also provides an open door to Congress, where the organization wields enough power to help shape political policies. The ASBA staff monitors state and federal issues that impact small businesses.

Membership is low-cost and recommended. However, nonmembers can contact the association for reports about small-business issues or obtain references to other sources of information. ASBA publications include *ASBA Today* and *What's New With ASBA Online*.

Associated Business Writers of America (ABWA)

The Associated Business Writers of America is an excellent source for small-business owners/managers who need accomplished writers to help with their company's communications efforts or with the preparation of formal business plans. No fee is charged by the association when it matches its member writers with businesses that need assistance. In addition to writing articles for business papers and trade journals, many ABWA members work with business clients in the development of articles, books, and other publications aimed at enhancing businesses and/or building customer relationships.

ABWA members who work with businesses are particularly valuable in that they are well qualified and have been "editor-approved" for giving assistance to clients in achieving their communications aims.

The ABWA publishes the *Professional Freelance Writers Directory,* which contains information on members' background and the subject areas in which they write. This directory has proven useful to small-business owners and managers seeking help in writing and publishing documents such as business and marketing plans.

Business Information Centers (BICs)

Business information Centers are joint ventures between the U.S. Small Business Administration and private partners. BICs offer state-of-the-art personal computers, graphics workstations, and CD-ROM technology for use in creating a business plan. The tools available at the BICs can also help to improve marketing and sales techniques, price products, and investigate the possibilities of exporting. A complete list of Business Information Centers can be found in Part Three.

The Entrepreneurship Institute (TEI)

The Entrepreneurship Institute serves people who are "planning, creating, developing, or growing a small business." The institute gives assistance in a host of small-business-related matters: planning, proposals, financial advice, legal assistance, and computer programming. Consultation is available on accounting, management, marketing, advertising, public relations, and selling. Membership is not required of users of these services.

TEI also promotes sharing information among entrepreneurs; develops one-on-one discussions between small-business owners and the managers of community resources; conducts research; and sponsors workshops.

Minority Business Development Agency (MBDA)

The Minority Business Development Agency offers an array of services to minority-owned businesses in a number of operational areas, including business planning, administration, marketing, finance, and technology. Its Minority Enterprise Growth Assistance Centers are strategically located across the United States.

National Association for Business Organizations (NAFBO)

The National Association for Business Organizations offers support for small-business owners who feel they have the capabilities to expand their reach from local to regional or national markets. When a business is growing or is changing in scope and is considering a joint venture, merger, or other affiliation, the NAFBO can be a source of information or referral to appropriate sources and resources that can help with effective business expansion plans.

National Business Association (NBA)

The National Business Association developed *The First Step Software Series* in conjunction with the U.S. Small Business Administration. It was revised and updated in 1995, and Windows and Macintosh versions have been released. The series is designed to assist a small-business owner or prospective entrepreneur in writing a comprehensive business plan and compiling all information necessary for a small-business loan package. *The First Step Software Series* is free to NBA members and available to nonmembers at a cost of $15. The NBA also publishes a resource library on topics such as sales, advertising, and funding resources. It's available to both members and nonmembers.

Service Corps of Retired Executives (SCORE)

The Service Corps of Retired Executives, a national organization sponsored by the U.S. Small Business Administration, is an excellent source of information on business planning, diversification, research and development, and similar functions and operations. It provides help at little or no cost. SCORE experts, often retired executives who have prepared many successful business plans for their own enterprises, will advise on how to lay out a presentation, what to include, and how to phrase appropriate language. For additional information on this organization, see the listing in Part Three.

Small Business Development Centers (SBDCs)

Small Business Development Centers, which are sponsored by the U.S. Small Business Administration in partnership with state and local governments, the educational community, and the private sector, can assist with business planning and the preparation of a business plan.

Tip Sheet

Complete Guide to Developing a Business Plan

The following outline is excerpted from the SBA's "Road Map to Success" Workshop on preparing a business plan. You can use this model as a guide when developing a business plan for your own business.

ELEMENTS OF A BUSINESS PLAN

I.   Cover sheet
II. Statement of purpose
III. Table of contents
   1. The Business
      A. Description of business
      B. Marketing
      C. Competition
      D. Operating procedures
      E. Personnel
      F. Business insurance
      G. Financing
   2. Financial Data
      A. Loan applications
      B. Capital equipment and supply list
      C. Balance sheet
      D. Break-even analysis
      E. Pro forma income projections (profit and loss statements)
         • Three-year summary
         • Detail each month (first year)
         • Detail each quarter (second and third years)
         • Assumptions on which projections are based

    F. Pro forma cash flow
- Follow guidelines for section E (above)

  3. Supporting Documents
    A. Tax returns of principals for past three years
    B. Personal financial statement (all banks have these forms)
    C. For a franchised business, a copy of the franchise contract and all supporting documents provided by the franchisor
    D. Copy of proposed lease or purchase agreement for building space
    E. Copies of licenses and other legal documents
    F. Copies of resumes of all principals
    G. Copies of letters of intent from suppliers, etc.

BUSINESS PLANS: THE BASIC CONTENT

What information *must* be given in business plans? This is an excellent question, but too many new and potential small-business owners don't ask it. The body of a business plan should, at a minimum, cover: (1) description of the business; (2) marketing plan; (3) management plan; and (4) financial management plan. Addenda to the business plan should include the executive summary, supporting documents, and financial projections.

☐ Description of the Business

You should provide a detailed description of your business. Ask yourself: "What business am I in?" To answer this question, consider your products, market, and services, as well as the characteristics that make your business unique. Remember, however, that as you develop your business plan, you may have to modify or revise your initial questions.

    This section includes a business description that has three primary divisions: (1) business description, (2) product or service offered, and (3) location—and why this location is desirable (if you have a franchise, some franchisors assist with site selection).

1. Business Description

When describing your business, generally you should explain:

- *Origin:* Is it a new independent business, a takeover, an expansion, a franchise?
- *Legalities:* Business form; such as proprietorship, partnership, corporation, and the licenses or permits you will need.
- *Business type:* Merchandizing, manufacturing, or service.

- *Product:* What your product or service is.
- *Value:* Why the business will be profitable. What are the growth opportunities, and will franchising impact growth?
- *Operation:* When your business will be open (days, hours)?
- *Management:* What you have learned about your kind of business from outside sources (e.g., trade suppliers, bankers, other franchise owners, franchisors, publications).

A cover sheet should fall before the description. On it, include the name, address, and telephone number of the business and the names of those who are principal participants involved in the business. In the description of your business, describe its unique aspects and how or why they will appeal to consumers. Emphasize —explaining how and why—any special features you believe will encourage that appeal. The description of your business should clearly identify your business goals and objectives, and it should clarify why you are, or why you want to be, in business.

2. Product or Service

Describe the benefits of your goods and services from your customers' perspective. Successful business owners know, or at least have an idea of, what their customers want and expect from them. This type of anticipation can be helpful in building customer satisfaction and loyalty, and it certainly is a good strategy for beating the competition or retaining your competitiveness. Describe your product or service by answering the following questions:

- What am I selling?
- How will the product or service benefit the customer?
- Which products or services are in demand? Will there be a steady cash flow?
- What is different about the product or service my business is offering?

3. Location

The location of your business can play a decisive role in its success or failure. Build around your customers; the location should be accessible and provide a sense of security. Consider these questions when addressing this section of your business plan:

- What are my location needs?
- What kind of space will I need?
- Why is the area and/or the building desirable?
- Is the location easily accessible? Is public transportation available? Is street lighting adequate?
- Are market shifts or demographic shifts occurring in the area?

It is a good idea to create your own checklist of questions you identify when developing your business plan. Categorize the questions, and as you answer each question, remove it from your list.

THE MARKETING PLAN

Because marketing plays a vital role in making business ventures successful, how well you market your business can ultimately determine the business's degree of success or failure. The key element of a successful marketing plan involves knowing your customers—their likes, dislikes, expectations. By identifying these factors, you can develop a marketing strategy that will allow you to arouse and fulfill their needs.

Identify your customers by their age, sex, income and education level, and residence. At first, target only those customers who are likely to purchase your product or service. As your customer base expands, modify the marketing plan to include other customers.

To initiate development of your business's marketing plan, answer the questions that follow (potential franchise owners will have to use the marketing strategy developed by their respective franchisor):

- Who are my customers? Define your target market(s).
- Are the markets steady? Are they growing or declining?
- Is the market share steady, growing, or declining?
- How will you attract, hold, increase your market share? If a franchise, will the franchisor provide assistance in this area? Based on the franchisor's strategy, how will you promote your sales?
- If a franchise, how is the market segmented?
- Are the markets large enough to expand?
- What pricing strategy have you devised?

Appendix 1, "Marketing," contains a sample marketing plan and Marketing Tips, Tricks, and Traps, a condensed guide on how to market your product or service. Study these documents carefully when developing the marketing portion of your business plan.

☐ Competition

Competition is part of life. We compete for jobs, promotions, scholarships, sporting awards, and so on; there is competition in almost every aspect of our lives. Nations compete for consumers in the global marketplace as do individual business owners. Advances in technology can send profit margins of a successful business into a tailspin, causing them to plummet within just a few hours. When considering these factors, we can conclude that business is a highly competitive, volatile arena, an arena where it is important to know about your opponents. Answers to the following questions can help:

- Who are my five nearest direct competitors?
- Who are my indirect competitors?
- How are the competitors' businesses: steady? increasing? decreasing?
- What can be learned from their operations and advertising?
- What are their strengths and weaknesses?
- How does their product or service differ from mine?

To better understand your competitors and how they operate their businesses, maintain a file on each of your competitors. Fill manila envelopes with their advertising and promotional materials and pricing-strategy techniques. Review these files periodically, determining when and how often your competitors advertise, sponsor promotions, and offer sales. Study the copy used; for example, is it short, descriptive, or catchy? How much are prices reduced for sales?

☐ Pricing and Sales

Pricing strategy is another marketing technique used to improve a business's overall competitiveness. Investigate the pricing strategies of your competitors to determine if your prices are in line with your market area and with industry averages. Some of the pricing strategies are as follows:

Retail cost and pricing.
Competitive position.
Pricing below competition.
Pricing above competition.
Price lining.
Multiple pricing.
Service costs and pricing (for service businesses only):
—Service components.
—Material costs.
—Labor costs.
—Overhead costs.

The key to success is to develop a well-planned strategy, establish your policies, and constantly monitor prices and operating costs to ensure profits. Even in a franchise where the franchisor provides operational procedures and materials, keep abreast of the changes in the marketplace because these changes can affect your competitiveness and profit margins.

Appendix 1, "Marketing," contains a sample price/quality matrix. Review it for ideas on pricing strategies of your competitors, determining which of the strategies they use and if and why it is effective.

☐ Advertising and Public Relations

How you advertise and promote your goods and services also can make or break your business. Having a good product or service and not advertising and promoting it is like not having a business at all. Many business owners operate under the mistaken concept that the business will promote itself; thus, they channel money that should be used for advertisements and promotions to other areas of the business. Yet, public relations is the lifeline of a business and should be treated as such.

Devise a plan that uses advertising and networking as a means to promote your business. With short, descriptive copy (text material), clearly identify your goods or services, their prices, and your business's location. Construct catchy phrases to arouse the interests of your readers, listeners, and/or viewers. In the case of a franchise, the franchisor will provide advertising and promotional materials as part of the franchise package; you may need approval to use any materials that you and/or your staff develop. Whether this is the case, as a courtesy, allow the franchisor opportunity to review, provide feedback, approve these materials before using them. Make sure the advertisements you create are consistent with the image the franchisor is trying to project. Remember that the more care and attention you devote to your marketing program, the more successful your business will be.

THE MANAGEMENT PLAN

Managing a business requires more than the desire to be your own boss. It demands dedication, persistence, and the ability to make decisions and to manage employees and finances. Your management plan, along with your marketing and financial plans, sets the foundation for and facilitates the success of your business.

Like plants and equipment, people, too, are resources; they are the most valuable asset of a business. Employees and staff play important roles in the total operation of your business; consequently, it is imperative to know which skills you possess and which you lack since you will be hiring personnel to complement your abilities. Additionally, you should know how to manage and communicate with your employees. Make them a part of the team: keep them informed of, and get their feedback regarding, changes. Employees oftentimes have excellent ideas that can lead to new market areas, innovations to existing products or services or new product lines, or services that can improve the business's competitiveness. Your management plan should answer the following questions:

- How do past experiences help me with this business?
- What are my weaknesses, and how can I compensate for them?
- Who will be on the management team? What are their strengths and weaknesses?
- What are their duties? Are these duties clearly defined?
- If a franchise, what type of assistance can I expect from the franchisor? Will this assistance be ongoing?
- What are my current personnel needs?
- What are my plans for hiring and training personnel?
- What salaries, benefits, vacations, and holidays will I offer? If a franchise, are these issues covered in the management package the franchisor will provide?
- What benefits, if any, can I afford to provide at this point?

If a franchise, the operating procedures, manuals, and other materials provided by the franchisor should be included in this section of the business plan. Study these documents carefully when writing your business plan, and be sure to incorporate this material. The franchisor should assist you with managing your franchise. Take advantage of his or her expertise and develop a management plan that will ensure success for your franchise and satisfy the needs and expectations of your employees, as well as of your franchisor.

THE FINANCIAL MANAGEMENT PLAN

Sound financial management is necessary for your business to remain profitable and solvent. How well you manage the finances of your business is the cornerstone of every successful business venture; each year thousands of potentially successful businesses fail because of poor financial management. As a business owner, you will need to identify and implement policies that will lead to and ensure your meeting all financial obligations.

To effectively manage your finances, create a sound, realistic budget by determining the actual amount of money needed to open your business (start-up costs) and that needed to keep it open (operating costs). The first step to building a sound financial plan is to devise a start-up budget. Your start-up budget will usually include such one-time-only costs as major equipment, utility deposits, down payments, and so forth. The start-up budget should allow for the following expenses:

- Personnel (costs prior to opening).
- Legal, professional, and/or fees.
- Occupancy.
- Licenses and/or permits.
- Equipment and supplies.
- Insurance.
- Advertisements and/or promotions.
- Income.
- Utilities.
- Payroll expenses.

An operating budget is to be prepared when you are actually ready to open for business. This budget should reflect your priorities in terms of how you will spend the business's money, the expenses that will be incurred and how you will meet those expenses (income). The operating budget also should include money to finance the business's first three to six months of operation. It should allow for the following expenses:

- Personnel.
- Insurance.
- Rent.
- Depreciation.
- Loan payments.
- Advertisements and/or promotions.
- Legal and/or accounting fees.
- Miscellaneous expenses.
- Supplies.
- Payroll expenses.
- Utilities.
- Dues and/or subscriptions.
- Taxes.
- Equipment/maintenance.

This section of your financial management plan should include any loan applications you have filed, a capital equipment and supply list, balance sheet, break-even analysis, pro forma income projections (profit and loss statement), and pro forma cash flow. The income statement and cash flow projections should include a three-year summary, detailed by month for the first year, then by quarter for the second and third years.

The accounting and inventory control systems you will be using are also generally addressed in this section of the business plan. If a franchise, the franchisor may stipulate, in the franchise contract, the type of accounting and inventory systems to be used. If this is the case, he or she will have a system intact and you will be required to adopt this system. Whether you develop the accounting and inventory systems yourself, contract an outside financial adviser to develop them, or find them provided by the franchisor, you need to acquire a thorough understanding of each segment and how it operates. (A financial adviser can assist you in developing this section of your business plan.) Answers to the following questions should help you to determine the amount of start-up capital needed to purchase and open a franchise:

- How much money do I have?
- How much money will I need to purchase the franchise?
- How much money will I need for startup?
- How much money will I need to stay in business?

Other questions to consider are:

- What type of accounting system will I use? Is it a single-entry or dual-entry system?
- What will be my sales and profit goals for the coming year? If a franchise, will the franchisor set these goals, or will he or she expect me to reach and retain a certain sales level and profit margin?
- What financial projections will I need to include in the business plan?
- What kind of inventory control system will I use?

Your plan should include an explanation of all projections. Unless you are thoroughly familiar with financial statements, get help in preparing your balance sheet and cash flow and income statements. Your aim is not to become a financial wizard, but to understand available financial tools well enough to gain their benefits. Your accountant or financial adviser can help you accomplish this goal.

Sample balance sheets, income projections (profit and loss statements), and cash flow statements are included in Appendix 2, "Financial Management." For a detailed explanation of these and more complex financial concepts, contact your local SBA office. You can find its telephone number listed under the U.S. Government section of your local telephone directory.

☐ **Self-Paced Activity**

Review the development of a business plan by performing the following activities:

1. Briefly describe what is included in a business plan.
2. Identify advantages of developing marketing, management, and financial management plans.

3. List financial projections included in the financial management plan.

4. Jot down an outline for your own business plan.

APPENDIX 1: MARKETING

☐ **The Marketing Plan**

I. Market Analysis

    A. Target Market: Who Are the Customers?

        1. We will be selling primarily to (check all that apply):

		Total Percent of Business
a.	Private sector	_____	_____
b.	Wholesalers	_____	_____
c.	Retailers	_____	_____
d.	Government	_____	_____
e.	Other	_____	_____

        2. We will be targeting customers by:

           a. Specific product lines and/or services. We will target lines _____

           b. Geographic area(s) _____

           c. Sales _____

           d. Industry _____

           e. Other _____

3. How much will our selected market spend on our type of product or service this coming year? $_____

    B. Competition

        1. Who are our competitors?

           Name: _____

           Address: _____

           _____

           Years in business _____

           Market share _____

           Price/strategy _____

           Product/service features _____

Name: _____

Address: _____

Years in business   _____

Market share   _____

Price/strategy   _____

Product/service features   _____

2. How competitive is the market?

High   _____

Medium   _____

Low   _____

3. List your strengths and weaknesses compared with those of your competition (consider such areas as location, resources, reputation, service, personnel, etc.):

Strengths	Weaknesses
_____	_____
_____	_____
_____	_____
_____	_____

C. Environment

1. The following are some important economic factors that will affect our product or service (such as trade area growth, industry health, economic trends, taxes, rising energy prices, etc.):

_____

_____

_____

2. The following are some important legal factors that will affect the market:

_____

_____

_____

3. The following are some important government factors:

_____

_____

_____

4. The following are environmental factors that will affect the market, but over which we have no control:

_____

_____

_____

II. Product or Service Analysis
   A. Description
      1. Describe the product or service is and what it does:

          _____

          _____

          _____

   B. Comparison
      1. What advantages does your product or service have over that of the competition (consider such things as unique features, patents, expertise, special training, etc.)?

          _____

          _____

          _____

      2. What are the disadvantages?

          _____

          _____

          _____

   C. Additional Considerations
      1. Where will you get your materials and supplies?

          _____

          _____

          _____

      2. List Other:

          _____

          _____

          _____

III. Marketing Strategies: Market Mix
   A. Image
      1. What kind of image do I want the business to project (such as cheap but good, or exclusiveness, or customer-oriented or highest quality, or convenience, or speed, or . . .)?

          _____

          _____

          _____

   B. Features
      1. List the features to be emphasized:
          a. _____
          b. _____
          c. _____

C. Pricing
    1. We will be using the following pricing strategy:
        a. Markup on cost   ____   What percent markup? ____
        b. Suggested price   ____
        c. Competitive   ____
        d. Below competition   ____
        e. Premium price   ____
        f. Other   ____
    2. Are our prices in line with our image?
        Yes____   No____
    3. Do our prices cover costs and leave a margin of profit?
        Yes____   No____

D. Customer Services
    1. List the customer services we provide:
        a. _____
        b. _____
        c. _____
    2. These are our sales/credit terms:
        a. _____
        b. _____
        c. _____
    3. The competition offers the following services:
        a. _____
        b. _____
        c. _____

E. Advertisement/Promotion
    1. These are the things we wish to say about the business:
        _____
        _____
        _____
    2. We will use the following advertising/promotion sources:
        1. Television   _____
        2. Radio   _____
        3. Direct mailings   _____
        4. Personal contacts   _____
        5. Trade associations   _____
        6. Newspapers   _____
        7. Magazines   _____

8. Yellow Pages   _____
9. Billboards   _____
10. Other: _____

3. The following are reasons why we consider the media we have chosen to be the most effective:

_____

_____

_____

☐ **Marketing Tips, Tricks and Traps**

Marketing Steps

- Classifying your customers' needs
- Targeting your customer(s)
- Examining your niche
- Identifying your competitors
- Assessing and managing your available resources
  —Financial
  —Human
  —Material
  —Production

Notes and Strategies for Your Business: _____

_____

_____

_____

Marketing Positioning

- Follower versus leader
- Quality versus price
- Innovator versus adaptor
- Customer versus product
- International versus domestic
- Private sector versus government

Notes and Strategies for Your Business: _____

_____

_____

_____

Sales Strategy

- Use customer-oriented selling approach by constructing agreement
  —Phase One: Establish rapport with customer by agreeing to discuss what the customer wants to achieve.
  —Phase Two: Determine customer objective and situational factors by agreeing on what the customer wants to achieve and those factors in the environment that will influence these results.
  —Phase Three: Recommend a customer action plan by agreeing that using your product or service will indeed achieve what customer wants.
  —Phase Four: Obtaining customer commitment by agreeing that the customer will acquire your product or service.
- Emphasize Customer Advantage
  —Must be read: When a competitive advantage cannot be demonstrated, it will not translate into a benefit.
  —Must be important to the customer: When the perception of competitive advantage differs between supplier and customer, the customer wins.
  —Must be specific: When a competitive advantage lacks specificity, it translates into mere puffery and is ignored.
  —Must be promotable: When a competitive advantage is proven, it is essential that your customer know it, lest it not exist at all.

Notes and Strategies for Your Business: _____
_____
_____
_____

Benefits versus Features

- The six *O's* of organizing customer buying behavior:
  Origins: Who buys it?
  Objectives: What do they buy?
  Occasions: When do they buy it?
  Outlets: Where do they buy it?
  Objectives: Why do they buy it?
  Operations: How do they buy it?
- Convert features to benefits using the "which means" transition:

Features	"Which Means"	Benefits
Performance		Time saved
Reputation		Reduced cost

Features	*"Which Means"*	*Benefits*
Components		Prestige
Colors		Bigger savings
Sizes		Greater profits
Exclusive		Greater convenience
Uses		Uniform production
Applications		Uniform accuracy
Ruggedness		Continuous output
Delivery		Leadership
Service		Increased sales
Price		Economy of use
Design		Ease of use
Availability		Reduced inventory
Installation		Low operating cost
Promotion		Simplicity
Lab Tests		Reduced upkeep
Terms		Reduced waste
Workmanship		Long life

Buying Motives

Rational	*Emotional*
Accurate performance	Convenience
Availability	Curiosity
Complete servicing	Desire to be unique
Curiosity	Desire to create
Desire to be unique	Desire to imitate
Durability	Desire for prestige
Ease of installation	Desire for recognition
Ease of repair	Desire for security
Economy of purchase	Desire for variety
Economy of use	Fear
Efficient profits	Pride of appearance
Good workmanship	Pride of ownership
Increased production	Safety
Increased profits	
Labor-saving	
Low maintenance	
Simple construction	
Simple operation	
Space-saving	
Thorough research	
Time-saving	

- Sales maxim: Unless the proposition appeals to their *interest*, unless it satisfies their *desires*, and unless it shows them a *gain*—then they will not buy!
- Quality customer leads:
  Ability to pay.
  Accessibility.
  Authority to pay.
  Business history.
  Level of need.
  One-source buyer.
  Reputation (price or quality buyer).
  Sympathetic attitude.

Notes and Strategies for Your Business: _____
_____
_____
_____

☐ **Price/Quality Matrix Sales Appeals**

PRICE

		High	Medium	Low
QUALITY	**High**	Rolls-Royce	We Try Harder	Best Buy
	Medium	Out Performs	Piece of the Rock	Smart Shopper
	Low	Feature Packed	Keeps on Ticking	Bargain Hunter

APPENDIX 2: FINANCIAL MANAGEMENT

☐   The Income Projections Statement

To control business operations the income projections (projections include profits and losses) statement is valuable as a planning tool and a key management
tool. It enables the owner and/or manager to develop a preview of the amount of
income generated monthly and/or yearly, based on reasonable predictions levels
of sales, costs, and expenses.

As monthly projections are developed and entered into the income projections statement, they serve as definite goals to be considered when controlling
business operations. As actual operating results become known each month,
they should be recorded for comparison with the monthly projections. A completed income statement allows the owner and/or manager to compare actual
figures with monthly projections and to take the necessary steps to correct any
problems. See the sample income projection statement on page 57.

Industry Percentage

In the industry percentage column, enter the percentages of total sales (revenues) that are standard for your industry, which are derived by dividing:

$$\frac{\text{Costs} / \text{Expenses} \times 100\%}{\text{Total net sales}}$$

These percentages can be obtained from various sources, such as trade associations, independent accountants, and banks. The reference librarian in your
nearest public library also can refer you to documents that contain the required
percentage figures.

Industry figures serve as a useful benchmark with which to compare cost
and expense estimates that you develop for your firm. Compare the figures in the
industry percentage column with those in the annual percentage column.

Total Net Sales (Revenues)

Determine the total number of units of products or services you realistically expect to sell each month in each department at the prices you expect to get. Use
this step to create the projections to review your pricing practices: What returns,
allowances and markdowns can be expected? Exclude any revenue not strictly
related to the business.

Cost of Sales

The key to calculating your cost of sales is that you do not overlook any costs
you have incurred. Calculate cost of sales of all products and services used to

INCOME PROJECTION STATEMENT

Industry Percentage	Use a Column for Each Month			Annual Total	Annual Percentage
	Jan.	Feb.	... Dec.		
Total net sales (revenues)					
Cost of sales					
Gross profit					
Gross profit margin					
Controllable expenses					
Salaries/wages					
Payroll expenses					
Legal/accounting					
Advertising					
Automobile and travel					
Office supplies					
Dues/subscriptions					
Utilities					
Miscellaneous					
Total controllable expenses					
Fixed expenses					
Rent					
Repair/maintenance					
Depreciation					
Utilities					
Insurance					
Licenses/permits					
Loan payments					
Miscellaneous					
Total fixed expenses					
Total expenses					
Net profit (loss) before taxes					
Taxes					
Net profit (loss) after taxes					

determine total net sales. Where inventory is involved, do not overlook transportation costs. Also include any direct labor.

Gross Profit

Subtract the total cost of sales from the total net sales to obtain gross profit.

Gross Profit Margin

The gross profit is expressed as a percentage of total sales (revenues). It is calculated by dividing:

$$\frac{\text{Gross profits}}{\text{Total net sales}}$$

Controllable (Variable) Expenses

The following is a list of common business expenses necessary for the business to maintain routine operations. These expenses are variable in that they can be modified to more readily reflect the interests of the business:

- Salaries/wages—Base pay plus overtime.
- Payroll expenses—Include paid vacations, sick leave, health and unemployment insurance, and social security taxes.
- Legal/accounting—Outside professional services.
- Advertising—Include desired sales volume and classified directory advertising expenses.
- Automobile and travel—Include charges if personal car is used for business, including parking, tools, travel expenses, and so on.
- Office supplies—Services and items purchased for use in the business.
- Repair/maintenance—Regular maintenance and repair, including periodic large expenditures such as painting.
- Miscellaneous—Include costs of subcontracts, overflow work, and special or one-time services.

Fixed Expenses

The following includes those regular payments for which nearly every small business must account:

- Rent—List only real estate used in business.
- Repair/maintenance.
- Depreciation—Amortization of capital assets.
- Utilities—Water, heat, light, and so on.

- Insurance—Fire or liability on property or products. Include workers' compensation.
- Licenses/permits.
- Loan payments—Interest on outstanding loans.
- Miscellaneous—Unspecified, small expenditures without separate accounts.

Net Profit (Loss)

To find your business's net profit (before taxes), subtract the total expenses from gross profit.

Taxes

Where taxes are to be noted on the statement, include all taxes incurred by the business: inventory, sales, excise, real estate tax, and so on.

Net Profit (Loss)

To calculate your business's net profit (after taxes), subtract total taxes from the net profit (before taxes).

Annual Total

For each of the sales and expense items in your income projections statement, add all the monthly figures across the table and put the result in the annual total column.

Annual Percentage

Calculate the annual percentage by dividing:

$$\frac{\text{Annual total} \times 100\%}{\text{Total net sales}}$$

Now compare this figure with the industry percentage in the table's first column.

☐ The Balance Sheet

Figures used to compile the balance sheet are taken from the business's previous and current balance sheets as well as the current income statement. (The income statement is usually attached to the balance sheet.) At the top of the balance sheet, fill in the legal name of the business: the type of statement, balance sheet, and the day, month, and year the statement was completed. Essential elements of the balance sheet are discussed in the following text. (A sample balance sheet can be found on pages 60–61.)

BALANCE SHEET

Company Name

As of _____ , 20 _____

Assets

Current Assets

    Cash $_____

    Petty cash _____

    Accounts receivable _____

    Inventory _____

    Short-term investments _____

    Prepaid expenses _____

Long-Term Investments _____

Fixed Assets

    Land _____

    Buildings _____

    Improvements _____

    Equipment _____

    Furniture _____

    Automobile/vehicles _____

Other Assets

    1. _____

    2. _____

    3. _____

    4. _____

Total Assets _____

Liabilities

Current Liabilities

    Accounts payable _____

    Notes payable _____

    Interest payable _____

Taxes Payable

    Federal income tax _____

    State income tax _____

    Self-employment tax _____

    Sales tax (SBE) _____

    Property tax _____

    Payroll accrual _____

Long-Term Liabilities

    Notes payable _____

Total Liabilities _____

Net Worth (owner equity)   _____

Proprietorship or Partnership
    Equity [name]   _____
    Equity [name]   _____
Corporation
    Capital stock   _____
    Surplus paid in   _____
    Retained earnings   _____

Total Net Worth   _____

Total Liabilities and Total Net Worth   _____

Assets

List anything of value that is owned or legally due the business as an asset. Total assets include all net values. These are the amounts derived when you subtract depreciation and amortization from the original costs of acquiring the assets.

Current Assets

Your total of all cash and other items of value includes the following:

- Cash—Cash and resources that can be converted into cash within 12 months of the date of the balance sheet (or during one established cycle of operations). Include any money on hand and demand deposits in the bank: for example, checking accounts and regular savings accounts.
- Petty cash—A fund for small miscellaneous expenditures. If your business has such a fund, include its total here.
- Accounts receivable—Amounts due from customers in payment for a product or service.
- Inventory—Includes raw materials on hand, work in progress, and all finished goods; either manufactured or purchased for resale.
- Short-term investments—Also called *temporary investments* or *marketable securities,* these include interest- or dividend-yielding holdings expected to be converted into cash within one year. List stocks and bonds, certificates of deposit, and time-deposit savings accounts at either cost or market value, whichever is less.
- Prepaid expenses—Goods, benefits, or services a business buys or rents in advance. Examples include office supplies, insurance protection, and floor space.

Long-Term Investments

Also called *long-term assets,* these are holdings the business intends to keep for at least one year and that typically yield interest or dividends. Included are stocks, bonds, and savings accounts earmarked for special purposes.

Fixed Assets

Also called *plant and equipment,* fixed assets include all resources a business owns or acquires for use in operations and does not intend to resell. Fixed assets may be leased, and depending on the leasing arrangements, the value and liability of the leased property may need to be listed on the balance sheet. The following is a list of commonly held fixed assets:

- Land—List original purchase price without allowances for market value.
- Buildings.
- Improvements.
- Equipment.
- Furniture.
- Automobile/vehicles.

Liabilities

Your tally of what you owe includes the following:

Current Liabilities

List all debts, monetary obligations and claims payable within 12 months or one cycle of operations. Typically, such liabilities include the following:

- Accounts payable—Amounts owed to suppliers for goods and services purchased in connection with business operations.
- Notes payable—The balance of principal due to clear short-term debt for borrowed funds. Also includes the current amount due of total balance on notes whose terms exceed 12 months.
- Interest payable—Any accrued fees due for use of short- and long-term borrowed capital as well as credit extended to the business.
- Taxes payable—Amounts estimated by an accountant to have been incurred during the accounting period.
- Payroll accrual—Salaries and wages currently owed.

Long-term Liabilities

List notes and any contract or mortgage payments due over a period exceeding 12 months or one cycle of operations. They are listed by the outstanding balance less the current position due.

Net Worth

Also called *owner's equity,* net worth is the claim of the owner(s) on the assets of the business. In a proprietorship or partnership, equity is each owner's original investment plus any earnings that remain after withdrawals.

Total Liabilities and Net Worth

The sum of these two amounts always must match that for total assets.

MONTHLY CASH FLOW PROJECTION

Name of Business: _____	**Date:** _____

Year: _____	**Use a Column for Each Month** **Jan. Feb. . . . Dec.**

1. Cash on hand (beginning month)
2. Cash receipts
   - (a) Cash sales
   - (b) Collections from credit accounts
   - (c) Loan or other cash injections (specify)
3. Total cash receipts (2a + 2b + 2c = 3)
4. Total cash available (before cash out) (1 + 3)
5. Cash paid out:
   - (a) Purchases (merchandise)
   - (b) Gross wages (excludes withdrawals)
   - (c) Payroll expenses (taxes, etc.)
   - (d) Outside services
   - (e) Supplies (office and operating)
   - (f) Repairs and maintenance
   - (g) Advertising
   - (h) Car, delivery, and travel
   - (i) Accounting and legal
   - (j) Rent
   - (k) Telephone
   - (l) Utilities
   - (m) Insurance
   - (n) Taxes (real estate, etc.)
   - (o) Interest
   - (p) Other expenses (specify each)
   - (q) Miscellaneous (unspecified)
   - (r) Subtotal
   - (s) Loan principal payment
   - (t) Capital purchases (specify)
   - (u) Other start-up costs
   - (v) Reserve and/or escrow (specify)
   - (w) Owner's withdrawal

(Continued)

MONTHLY CASH FLOW PROJECTION

Name of Business: _____ **Date:** _____

	Use a Column for Each Month
Year: _____	**Jan. Feb. . . . Dec.**

6. Total cash paid out (5a–5w)
7. Cash position (end of month) (4 – 6)

Essential operating data (non-cash flow
information)
   (a)   Sales volume (dollars)
   (b)   Accounts receivable (end of month)
   (c)   Bad debt (end of month)
   (d)   Inventory on hand (end of month)
   (e)   Accounts payable (end of month)

Instructions
1. Cash on hand (beginning of month)—Cash on hand same as (7), cash position, previous month.
2. Cash receipts:
   (a)   Cash sales—All cash sales. Omit credit sales unless cash is actually received.
   (b)   Gross wages (including withdrawals)—Amount to be expected from all accounts.
   (c)   Loan or other cash injection—Indicate here all cash injections not shown in 2(a) or 2(b) above.
3. Total cash receipts (2a + 2b + 2c = 3)
4. Total cash available (before cash out) (1 + 3).
5. Cash paid out:
   (a)   Purchases (merchandise)—Merchandise for resale or for use in product (paid for in current month).
   (b)   Gross wages (including withdrawals)—Base pay plus overtime (if any).
   (c)   Payroll expenses (taxes, etc.)—Include paid vacations, paid sick leave, health insurance, unemployment insurance (this might be 10 percent to 45 percent of 5[b]).
   (d)   Outside services—This could include outside labor and/or material for specialized or overflow work, including subcontracting.
   (e)   Supplies (office and operating)—Items purchased for use in the business (not for resale).
   (f)   Repairs and maintenance—Include periodic large expenditures, such as painting or decorating.
   (g)   Advertising—This amount should be adequate to maintain sales volume.
   (h)   Car, delivery, and travel—If personal care is used, charge in this column; include parking.
   (i)   Accounting and legal—Outside services, including, for example, bookkeeping.
   (j)   Rent—Real estate only (see 5[p] for other rentals).
   (k)   Telephone.
   (l)   Utilities—Water, heat, light, and/or power.
   (m)   Insurance—Coverage on business property and products (fire, liability); also worker's compensation, fidelity, and so on. Exclude executive life (include in 5[w]).
   (n)   Taxes (real estate, etc.)—Plus inventory tax, sales tax, excise tax, if applicable.
   (o)   Interest—Remember to add interest on loan as it is injected (see 2[c] above).

MONTHLY CASH FLOW PROJECTION

Name of Business: _____ **Date:** _____

Use a Column for Each Month

Year: _____ Jan. Feb. ... Dec.

  (p) Other expenses (specify each).

_____

_____

Unexpected expenditures may be included here as a safety factor

_____

Equipment expenses during the month should be included here (non-capital equipment)

_____

When equipment is rented or leased, record payments here.

_____

  (q) Miscellaneous (unspecified)—Small expenditures for which separate accounts would be practical.

  (r) Subtotal—This subtotal indicates cash out for operating costs.

  (s) Loan principal payment—Include payment on all loans, including vehicle and equipment purchases on time payment.

  (t) Capital purchases (specify)—Nonexpensed (depreciable) expenditures such as equipment, building purchases on time payment.

  (u) Other start-up costs—Expenses incurred prior to first-month projection and paid for after startup.

  (v) Reserve and/or escrow (specify)—Example: insurance, tax or equipment escrow to reduce impact of large periodic payments.

  (w) Owner's withdrawals—Should include payment for such things as owner's income tax, social security, health insurance, executive life insurance premiums, and so on.

6. Total cash paid out (5a–5w).

7. Cash position (end of month) (4 – 6)—Enter this amount in (1) Cash on hand following month—

Essential operating data (non-cash flow information)—This is basic information necessary for proper planning and for proper cash flow projection. Also with this data, the cash flow can be evolved and shown in the above form.

  A. Sales volume (dollars)—This is an important figure and should be estimated carefully, taking into account size of the facility and employee output as well as realistic anticipated sales (actual sales, not orders received).

  B. Accounts receivable (end of month)—Previous unpaid credit sales plus current month's credit sales, less amounts received current month (deduct "C").

  C. Bad debt (end of month)—Bad debts should be subtracted from "B" in the month anticipated.

  D. Inventory on hand (end of month)—Last month's inventory plus merchandise received and/or manufactured current month minus amount sold current month.

  E. Accounts payable (end of month)—Previous month's payable plus current month's payable minus amount paid during month.

  F. Depreciation—Established by your accountant, or value of all your equipment divided by useful life (in months) as allowed by IRS.

Tip Sheet

Diversification, Growth, and Financial Viability

You diversity your business when you extend your operations to fields outside of your expertise, whether related or unrelated, to *augment product lines, exploit more promising opportunities,* or otherwise *increase profitability* and long-term potential. Diversification into new businesses, however, has been rated as one of the highest types of business risks, according to the National Business Information Center, which notes that fewer than 20 percent of the businesses in America have been successful when they tried to diversity. The chief reasons for failed diversification include the following:

- Poor selection of enterprises into which to diversify.
- Lack of experience in, or knowledge about, the "new" field of business.
- Overallocation of investment capital to an untried field of operations.
- Increased management responsibilities by way of additional commitments and time-consuming problems.
- Neglect of existing business to attend to the demands of the new business.

Proper business planning, well in advance of any attempt at diversification, can measurably improve your chances of success.

 ## RECOMMENDED READING

Dethomas, Art, *Financing Your Small Business: Techniques for Planning, Acquiring and Managing Debt.* Edited by Vickie Reierson (Grants Pass, Oregon: Oasis, 1992). Variety of methods for all financial circumstances.

Graybill, John O., *Entrepreneur's Road to Business Success and Personal Freedom: 101 Proven Tips for Your Small Business* (New York: Amacom, 1995). Tips for small business owners interested in accurate planning, expanding their business, and locating a solid client base.

Hughes, Charles L., *Goal Setting* (New York: Amacom, 1979). Practical guidance on setting short- and long-term goals, with emphasis on breaking large goals into small steps.

Inc. Business Resources, a division of *Inc.* magazine, publishes several good resources about business plans, including the "Guide to Creating a Successful Business Plan," Inc. PLAN Software, and the video "How to Really Create a Successful Business Plan." Call 617-248-8000, or you can find a variety of Inc. publications at: www.inc.com/incmagazine/

J.K. Lasser Institute, *How to Run a Small Business* (New York: McGraw-Hill, 1993). Revision of popular handbook covering issues pertinent to small business—insurance, taxes, personnel, location, and so forth—along with advice on how to incorporate those issues into your business plan.

Lasher, William, *The Perfect Business Plan Made Simple* (New York: Doubleday, 1994). Comprehensive yet compact guide, long on practical information. Many examples of successful business plans, along with important information on working with lawyers and accountants.

McDeever, Mike, *How to Write a Business Plan* (Seattle: Nolo Press, 1992). Writing a business plan that will impress banks and potential investors. Includes model plans for different types of businesses.

The Portable MBA in Entrepreneurship. Edited by William Bygrave (New York: Wiley, 1997). Informative chapter on creating a successful business plan.

Sherman, Andrew J., *The Complete Guide to Running and Growing Your Business* (New York: Times Books, Random House, 1997). Insightful chapters include "Business Planning and Strategies for Raising Equity Capital" and "Debt Financing for Growing Companies."

"Small Business Advisor." *Entrepreneur* magazine. Has both an excellent overview on developing a business plan as well as an extensive sample business plan.

Raising and Using Capital

 ## INTRODUCTION

The word *capital* carries different meanings and implications to various players in the business world. To most business executives, capital means any type of material wealth, such as money, real estate, or precious metals, accumulated by individuals or organizations. In economic theory, however, capital is one of the major factors of production—the others being labor and property. Within this theory, distinctions are made between circulating capital (e.g., raw materials, finished goods, and wages) and fixed capital (e.g., railroads, and other transportation facilities, and major installations, such as factories and machinery). In financial markets, capital is associated with investments in productive assets that yield income. In accounting, capital relates to those parts of the net worth of an organization that represent claims on assets. In this sense, for tax records, the gain on capital—*capital gain*—is the value of assets computed over an extensive period of time.

With regard to small business, capital initially invested is generally cash from the owner's pockets, money lent against collateral, or money lent for a stake in the business. The business, then, accumulates its own capital, some of which is used for operations and some for investments.

 ## SOURCES OF CAPITAL

The National Business Association (NBA) lists the following six basic sources for start-up funds or expansion capital:

1. *Personal savings,* from your own savings and those of friends and relatives. The NBA advises drawing up a formal agreement when pledging collateral, viewing the participants as business associates.

2. *Private investors,* such as accountants, attorneys, and other professionals, looking for higher investment returns than they might obtain in traditional markets.

3. *Venture capital firms* that generally want equity or part ownership of a business in exchange for money. They are interested in sharing the venture and having input with regard to the business's management.

4. *Bank financing and credit unions,* the former being the primary source of loans guaranteed by the ASBA (see pages 78–79 for more information). In the case of the latter, you must be a member of the credit union to apply for a loan.

5. *Commercial lenders,* of which there are hundreds that lend money to small businesses. Customarily, lenders seek higher interest rates and shorter payback terms than banks.

6. Federal, state, and local *government agencies,* which rarely (with the exception of the ASBA) lend money to small or home-based businesses.

Other sources of capital include: Certified Development Companies (CDCs), Small Business Investment Companies (SBICs), State Government Small Business Centers, and the sale of stock in your company.

 ## UNDERSTANDING VENTURE CAPITAL

Venture capital refers to funds invested in new, sometimes speculative, enterprises without a proven track record, with the hope of clearing a profit. Venture capitalists and venture capital firms lend money to new businesses, but they differ from banks and other lending institutions in that they have a longer-range vision and look to the more distant future to recoup their investments.

To be sure, venture capitalists are concerned with many of the same factors that influence bankers in their evaluations of business loan applications. They want to know the past financial records of the people who will be managing the venture, amount and intended use of the funds requested, and objectives and projected earnings of the new business. But venture capitalists also meticulously study the features of the products, nature of the services, and market potential.

Venture capital firms become part owners of the business in which they invest. They generally hold stock in the company, augmenting its equity base with their invested capital.

Venture capitalists aim to multiply their investments at least three times in five years or five times in seven years. They may achieve capital gains of 300 to 500 percent on only a limited portion of their total investments, but their intent is to offset—by a wide margin—any ventures that produce losses.

Most venture capital firms are interested only in potential projects that require $500,000 or more because investigation, evaluation, and administration are costly and do not justify a venture capital firm's involvement at a lower financial level. While a firm may receive as many as 1,000 business proposals a year, it typically will investigate less than 10 percent and may actually invest in only 3 or 4 percent.

There are several types of venture capital firms. The following are the most common:

- *Insurance companies:* Insurance companies often hold a portion of equity as a condition of their loans to smaller companies; this works as a hedge against inflation.

- *Investment banking firms:* Although investment bankers usually trade in established securities, they occasionally form investor syndicates for venture proposals.

- *Manufacturing companies:* A few Fortune 500 manufacturers become involved with venture capital projects as a way to keep abreast of technological innovations related to the companies' being funded. Others look upon investment in smaller companies as a means of supplementing their research and development programs.

- *Professionally managed pools:* Operating much like those who participate in traditional partnerships, some venture capitalists solicit and pool institutional money for venture investments.

- *Small Business Investment Corporations (SBICs):* Licensed by the Small Business Administration, which may provide management assistance as well as venture capital, these corporations often are interested in venture capital opportunities, as well as long-term lending.

- *Traditional partnerships:* Often established by wealthy families or groups of well-to-do individuals, these partnerships manage portions of their funds by aggressively investing in small companies.

Some venture capitalists are individual private investors and finders. *Finders,* either individuals or firms, often are knowledgeable about the capital industry and can help entrepreneurs locate investment money, though themselves they generally are not sources of capital.

 ## SOURCES OF INFORMATION

American Bankers Association (ABA)

The American Bankers Association offers information about banks and banking, and can sometimes provide information not easily available locally. The ABA is the national trade and professional association for America's full-service banks, representing about 95 percent of the banking industry. The association not only promotes legislation beneficial to the banking public, but also sponsors seminars and workshops, and produces literature for business owners, managers, and professionals. Many such programs are scheduled in liaison with local banks.

The ABA distributes booklets, press releases, and fact sheets on topics of interest to business owners and managers, including business loans, commercial checking accounts, personnel records, auto financing, credit cards, credit ratings, and retirement budgets.

American Financial Services Association (AFSA)

The American Financial Services Association refers business owners to the association's members who can provide reliable answers about capital management, direct credit lending, use of credit, and other monetary matters. The AFSA is composed of financial services providers of small businesses and their customers and associates. The group studies issues relating to the capitalization of small businesses.

National Association of Development Companies (NADC)

The National Association of Development Companies is a useful resource for anyone looking for capital to expand a small business. The NADC is the trade association for Certified Development Companies, which are community-based nonprofit organizations that promote small-business expansion and job creation through the Small Business Administration's "504 Loan Program." This program offers fixed, market-rate competitive loans to qualified businesses for the purchase of fixed assets, such as real estate, machinery, or equipment. During the past 15 years, this program has benefitted some 20,000 small businesses, which, in turn, have created more than 400,000 jobs. All 504 funding, which is usually about 40 percent of total project costs, is guaranteed by the SBA. Through NADC, small business owners can obtain contact information from their local Certified Development Company. In addition to the SBA 504 loan program, CDCs often administer other federal, state, and regional loan programs.

National Association of Small Business Investment Companies

This is a trade association for more than 200 firms that make equity capital and credit available to small, independent businesses. SBICs are licensed by the Small Business Association, but set their own policies and investment decisions. In effect, they function like private venture capital firms but have authority to receive financial support from the SBA, thus increasing their capacity to underwrite small businesses.

National Venture Capital Association (NVCA)

The National Venture Capital Association may not be of much assistance to entrepreneurs in terms of providing loans, but it can provide business owners with a better understanding of what venture capital is and is not. It also can refer you to venture capitalists who might be interested in a company of your size and location, as well as the nature of the business.

Small Business Investment Company (SBIC) Program

One practical way to locate venture capital is through the Small Business Investment Company Program. Congress created the SBIC Program in 1958 to fill the gap between the availability of venture capital and the needs of small businesses in start-up and growth situations. SBICs, licensed and regulated by the Small Business Administration, are privately owned and managed investment firms that use their own capital, plus funds borrowed at favorable rates with an SBA guarantee, to make venture capital investments in small businesses.

Virtually all SBICs are profit-motivated businesses. They provide equity capital, long-term loans, debt-equity investments, and management assistance to qualifying small businesses. Their incentive is the chance to share in the success of the small business as it grows and prospers. There are two types of SBICs: regular and specialized, also known as 301(d) SBICs. Specialized SBICs invest in small businesses owned by entrepreneurs who are socially or economically disadvantaged. The Program makes funding available to all types of manufacturing and service industries. Many investment companies seek out small businesses with new products or services because of the strong growth potential of such firms. Some SBICs specialize in the field in which their management has special knowledge or competency. Most, however, consider a wide variety of investment opportunities.

You can find out more by calling the SBA or visiting the SBIC Web site at:

www.sbaonline.sba.gov/INV/sbinfo.html

Tip Sheet
Finding Venture Capital on the Web

The World Wide Web offers unparalleled access to venture capital intelligence and sources. One of the best places to start is at the Price Waterhouse Venture Capital Survey, which tracks the investments of more than 1,000 venture capital firms. You can search by keyword for a particular type of business funding. Visit this massive site at:

www.pw.com/vc

Biz Planit-Entrepreneur Links features well-organized links to many venture capital and business planning sources. Its Web address is:

www.bizplanit.com/links.htm

There are several venture capital Web publications. One with a particularly useful section matches capital providers with capital seekers. Visit Venture Capital On-Line at:

www.vcapital.com

NOWA Capital Consultants maintains an excellent Web page at the following site:

www.nowa.com/ventcap.htm

This site offers informative sections about legalities and procedures in finding venture capital and provides direct links to the following firms:

Accel Partners	Equity Ventures Limited
Adams Capital Management	Eurolink Services Limited
Agio Capital Partners	Fairfax Partners II
Alliance Technology Ventures	Focus Capital Group
Alpine Technology Ventures	Gemini Israel Fund
Asset Management Associates	Geocapital Partners
Atlas Ventures	Global Asset Management
Austin Ventures	Howard Industries, Inc.
AVI Capital, L.P.	Hummer Winblad Venture Partners
Avix Ventures	Idanta Partners
Bachow and Associates	InnoCal
BancBoston Capital	Institutional Venture Partners (IVP)
Benchmark Capital	Intersouth Partners
Bessemer Venture Partners	Interwest Partners
BG Affiliates, LLC	ITP Ventures
Boston Capital Ventures	J.L. Albright Venture Partners, Inc.
Bridge Ventures	Kansas City Equity Partners
Canaan Partners	Kestrel Venture Management
CCG Venture Partners	Kirk Ventures
CMG@Ventures	Kirkland Capital
Commonweath Development	Kleiner Perkins Caufield & Byers
Crosspoint Venture Partners	Korea Technology Finance
Danish Development Finance	Levine Leichtman Capital Partners
DICO A/S–Copenhagen, Denmark	Levy Trajman Management Investment
Digital Technology Partners	Matrix Partners
Draper Fisher Associates	New Enterprise Associates
Dreyfus Capital Management	Northland Business Capital
Edison Venture Fund	Norwest Venture Capital
Embryon Capital	Olympic Venture Partners
EnerTech	Onset Ventures
Environmental R&D Capital	Opus Capital

Pacific Venture Group	Summit Partners
Partech International, Inc.	TA Associates
Pioneer Capital	Technologieholding
Platinum Venture Partners	Technology Management & Funding
Ponte Vedra Ventures	Tribune Ventures
Quaestus Management	Trident Capital, L.P.
Redleaf Venture Management	Trinity Ventures
Richards Investment Capital	VenCom
Rossein Ventures	Venrock Associates
RRE Investors, LLC	Venture Resources
Sierra Ventures	VækstFonden
St. Paul Venture Capital	

Tip Sheet

Investments for Start-up Businesses

Investments are vital to a start-up business, a fact that runs counter to the intuition of many businesspeople, who may feel that there is so little money sitting idle during the start-up stage that company investments are far down on the priority list. However, even the smallest businesses must exercise some form of leverage to increase their purchasing and operational powers by maintaining investments that will not only keep pace with inflation, but also bring additional funds. This section discusses a few common investment types that can accomplish small-business financial objectives.

MONEY MARKET FUNDS (MMFS)

Money market funds are practical because they enable business owners—and others—to start an investment program with very little cash. They offer security (you can invest in insured MMFs), a reasonable return on your money, and a good degree of liquidity. MMFs are basically mutual funds that invest in short-term, interest-earing securities, such as Treasury bills (T-bills), government bonds, and certificates of deposit (CDs).

REAL ESTATE

Many small firms have grown by buying or renting slightly more office or warehouse space than they require, then renting the surplus space at a profit. The resultant income helps to underwrite the cost of certain company operations from month to month.

LONG-TERM SECURITIES

Long-term securities are not for every entrepreneur because they demand strong and experienced financial management if they are to achieve the typical goals of small businesses. Many factors have to be considered, such as the size of your portfolio, degree of risk, and nature of the markets in which you do business.

COMMODITIES

Purchasing futures contracts in commodities (livestock, cotton, sugar, and wheat, for example) is a tricky and volatile form of investment, not for the timid or the inexperienced. Nevertheless, this can be a reasonable type of investment for companies whose fields of activity relate to commodities, or whose management has a close and continuing acquaintance with the products traded on the commodities market.

SPECIALIZED INVESTMENTS

Some small firms have made profits—usually over the long-term—by purchasing precious metals, rare coins, gemstones, or antiques. Such investing makes sense only if the buyers are knowledgeable in the specialized field of their choice and if they can afford to sit on their purchases for the long-term.

Tip Sheet

Getting a Small-Business Grant

A *grant* is money awarded to an individual or organization that does not have to be repaid in cash. There are more than 1,000 federal assistance programs; hundreds of others are administered by state and regional agencies and private philanthropies. A business cannot qualify for a grant without documenting a need that will benefit the *public,* as well as the recipient. Examples of businesses meeting such a requirement follow:

- A forest products company learned the bark of certain trees in its woodlands contained valuable elements for medicinal applications. The company was awarded $200,000 to determine how to process the bark, that was then being dumped as waste, to make it marketable to pharmaceutical manufacturers.

- The owner of two printing firms, one in New Mexico and the other on the coast of South Carolina, had made numerous complaints that the paper company supplying both plants was shipping an inferior product. But on further investigation, he found that at the factory the quality of the paper was exactly the same. When the owner then suspected that salt air and humidity were the culprits affecting paper temporarily held in stock, he applied for, and received, a research grant to reduce in-plant humidity and test other types of mold-resistant paper available at no increase in cost. The grant was given on the hypothesis that other printing firms and the paper industry would benefit from the research findings.

- Plagued by complaints from customers that their vehicles were sloppily serviced and often had dangerous defects, a truck-leasing dealer in the Midwest traced the problem to a frustrating regional economic climate that made it virtually impossible to find and hire properly trained mechanics. He solved the problem by convincing the state department of motor vehicles that a grant to add a mechanic's curriculum be allocated to his county's technical trade school. His mechanics were able to attend the program at little cost. Although the grant did not go directly to the dealer, it greatly improved his customer relations.

A study cited by the SBA reported that more than 15 percent of those businesses who applied for business research grants were approved, not a high figure when compared with a success rate of about 70 percent for business loans. Bear in mind, however, that almost half of all grant applications are initially rejected because of sloppy or inadequate proposals. In addition, many are motivated by an individual's highly inflated conception of what he or she can do to improve and upgrade business or society.

The key is to prepare a grant proposal that is realistic, presents your case in a positive manner, and itemizes the benefits to be derived from the grant. Suggestions for the preparation of proposals are detailed in several of the books cited in this chapter's "Recommended Reading," as well as in literature you can obtain through the SBA. Here are some additional tips:

- Aim your request for a grant at the right agency or committee.
- Ask for assistance in a positive way, not looking at such funding as charity or a handout.
- Use an enthusiastic sales approach to be assertive (not aggressive) in presenting your cause.
- Enumerate the benefits to the business world and/or community that would follow the work made possible by the grant.

- Be specific, bearing in mind that this need not be totally altruistic. You might, for example, emphasize that by helping your company to improve a business situation, the grant would provide new jobs to the community.
- Picture the recipients of your grant proposal and how you would react to your reasoning if you were in their shoes.
- Before even attempting to draft anything on paper, request from the grant committee (or similar body) a written description of its criteria for proposals.
- Fine-tune the technical details of your proposal, following instructions from the grant committee, and making sure your facts are accurate and to the point.
- Employ a respectful tone and dignified style in your presentation. If you are uneasy about your writing skills, seek professional help. (Here again, SCORE can provide excellent advice, and at no fee.)
- If at first you don't succeed, try again.

Tip Sheet

How to Qualify for Small-Business Loans

For the small-business owner seeking a loan, the SBA is the most comprehensive resource, if not for the loan itself, for information and counsel. The criteria for SBA loans can be an excellent yardstick for outlining the steps to be taken and the requirements to be met to obtain financial aid.

The procedure for an SBA loan is that the small business submits a loan application to a lender for initial review. If the lender finds the application acceptable, it forwards the application and its credit analysis to the nearest SBA office. After SBA approval, the lending institution closes the loan and disburses the funds. The borrower then makes loan payments to the lender under the latter's terms; the length of time for repayment depends on the use of the proceeds and the ability of the business to repay. SBA standards call for an interest rate that cannot exceed 2.75 percent over the prime rate. As a loan applicant, you must:

- Be of good character and reputation in your community.
- Demonstrate sufficient management experience and responsibility to be successful in your business.
- Maintain enough funds in the company, plus personal moneys, to operate the business on a sound financial basis. If you are a new business, the financial requirement includes sufficient resources to withstand

start-up expenses and the initial operating phase when losses are likely to occur.

- Prove that the past earnings record and estimated future earnings will be sufficient to repay the loan in a timely fashion.
- Pledge specific, identifiable assets to adequately secure the loan.
- Be willing and able to provide personal guarantees, personally and from any associates who are principals in your business.
- Submit a current personal financial statement of all principals and stockholders.
- Prepare a current balance sheet listing all assets, liabilities, and net worth.

To be eligible under SBA standards, a company must be operated for profit, meet small-business size and earnings standards, and not engaged in speculation or investment in rental real estate. Eligibility of a company varies according to the industry within which it functions. Examples include:

- *Manufacturing:* The maximum number of employees may range from 500 to 1,500, depending on the type of product manufactured.
- *Retailing:* Average annual receipts may not exceed $5 million to $21 million, depending on the industry.
- *Wholesaling:* The maximum number of employees may not exceed 100.
- *Service firms:* Average annual receipts may not exceed $2.5 million to $14.5 million, depending on the industry.
- *Construction:* Average annual receipts may not exceed $17 million.
- *Agriculture:* Average annual receipts can range from $500,000 to $7 million, depending on the products and services.

Tip Sheet
Your Chances of Obtaining a Loan

According to the business loan unit of the SBA, the success ratio for obtaining a loan is about seven out of every ten applicants. Remember, though, this figure considers that group of applicants who (a) prepared solid, presentable proposals to accompany their applications; (b) turned to SCORE or an SBA Small Business Development Center beforehand for assistance in preparing and presenting the loan application; and (c) ensured the application was presented to an officer at the bank who was familiar with the SBA loan programs.

Tip Sheet

Forecasting Profits and Losses

For many small-business owners, forecasting profits and losses may seem a little like fortune telling. While it is admittedly difficult to predict the future, a business seldom gets in trouble overnight, and there are numerous signs that indicate the possibilities of success and chances of failure. Reading those signs is the main reason why a business owner uses forecasting devices.

A key forecasting devise is the *profit-and-loss ratio.* To apply it to your business, use two figures for computation: current assets and current liabilities. Divide the total of the first by the total of the second to obtain the ratio. The resultant figure might look like this: 1.7:1 (or 1.7 to 1). That is your current ratio, which by itself is meaningless until it is compared with past ratios from month to month, or quarter to quarter, and then projected into the future as you proceed. If, on the one hand, the ratio of assets to liabilities is decreasing, such as a change from 1.7:1 to 1.3:1, your business is becoming less liquid and you can expect to have greater difficulty meeting financial obligations. If, on the other hand, you see that the asset figure is increasing in relation to the liability figure, your financial balance is improving.

A change in the ratio in either direction, from one period to the next, is not necessarily cause for concern (or euphoria), since cash and liquidity patterns fluctuate in most small businesses. Thus, measure the *long-term* patterns and trends attending to periods you thought were good but that turned out to be downtrends, or vice versa. Determine the points at which changes up or down are no longer insignificant variations but indicate major financial trends in your business.

Tip Sheet

Preparing Profit and Loss Statements

Perhaps the information an owner and/or manager wants most about the performance of the business is its profitability. For a particular period of time, did the company make a profit or experience a loss? The Profit and Loss Statement (sometimes called the Income Statement) describes the net result, over a period of time, of revenue less expenses. A familiar term, *the bottom line* refers to the last line on the Profit and Loss Statement, the one indicating the company's net profit (or loss). Stated simply, the Profit and Loss Statement is represented by the equation:

Revenue – Expenses = Income

What follows is an example of the format and types of categories commonly found on a Profit and Loss Statement. The first thing to notice on the statement is the dates. A Profit and Loss Statement always covers a particular period of time—a month, quarter, year, and so forth. This means that revenue and expense items appearing on the statement were actually incurred during the time indicated. The element of time should be kept in mind when examining the various accounts listed on the statement.

Profit and Loss Statement
October 1–December 31, 20XX

	Dollars	Percent
Net Sales	$68,116	100.0
Cost of Goods Sold	47,696	70.0
Gross Profit on Sales	$20,420	30.0
Expenses		
Wages	$ 6,948	10.0
Delivery Expense	954	1.4
Bad Debts Allowance	409	0.6
Communications	204	0.3
Depreciation Allowance	409	0.6
Insurance	613	0.9
Taxes and Licenses	1,021	1.5
Advertising	1,566	2.3
Interest	409	0.6
Other Charges	749	1.1
Total Expenses	$13,282	19.5
Net Profit	$ 7,138	10.5
Other Income	886	1.3
Total Net Income	$ 8,024	11.8

NET SALES

Net sales refers to the total sales for a period, less necessary adjustments. To arrive at a net sales figure, use the following process:

Gross Sales	$XX,XXX
Less Sales Returns and Allowances	–X,XXX
Net Sales	$XX,XXX

Many small businesses treat sales returns and allowances as direct reductions of the sales figure. However, it is advisable to establish a separate account to record sales returns and allowances. This will aid the owner and/or manager in determining if too much merchandise is being returned.

Another, less frequent, reduction to the total sales figure involves the sale of merchandise to be delivered at a later time. The concern on a Profit and Loss Statement is to match revenues and expenses. To record a sale that will be completed later may be misleading. In such a case, it is advisable to check with an accountant for suggestions on the best way to record the sale.

COST OF GOODS SOLD

The primary expense incurred in selling merchandise is the cost of the goods sold. The process for arriving at this cost is controlled by the merchandise inventory valuation methods discussed in the previous chapter and is calculated as follows:

Beginning Inventory	$XX,XXX	
Add Merchandise Purchased	+XX,XXX	
Merchandise Available for Sale		$XX,XXX
Less Ending Inventory		–XX,XXX
Cost of Goods Sold		$XX,XXX

Start with the beginning inventory, the inventory on hand on the first day of the period covered by the Profit and Loss Statement. Add the total of merchandise purchased during that period, less any items returned to the supplier. The resultant figure represents merchandise that was available for sale. From this figure, subtract the ending inventory as of the last day of the period covered. The difference is the cost of goods sold. This cost can then be entered on the Profit and Loss Statement.

Notice the column on the far right of the statement titled "Percent." The various costs of doing business are expressed as a percentage of sales in this column. The cost of goods sold in this example is 70 percent of sales. This means that 70 percent of sales dollars were eaten up by the cost of the merchandise.

GROSS PROFIT ON SALES

The gross profit on sales (or gross margin) in the example provided is 30 percent. This figure is found by subtracting the cost of goods sold from net sales. The percentage is computed by dividing the amount of gross profit on sales by the net sales figures.

EXPENSES

All business expenses are recorded on the Profit and Loss Statement and totaled; the total is then subtracted from the gross profit on sales. Expenses are often split into two categories to aid in identifying problem areas. One type may be categorized as operating expenses. These expenses generally vary with the level of sales. Sales commission expense, for example, varies relative to the volume of sales. The second expense category is often referred to as fixed (or overhead) expenses. Rental expense, for instance, stays the same from month to month, regardless of the level of sales. The sample Profit and Loss Statement contains common expense accounts. Wages expense includes all employee reimbursement and comes from the gross salaries account recorded in the Cash Disbursements Journal. Delivery expenses represents costs associated with delivering merchandise to customers. Freight costs associated with receiving merchandise are treated as part of the cost of the merchandise and not included in this category.

Bad debt allowance is an estimate of the amount of Accounts Receivable that will not be paid. While the exact amount that will turn out to be uncollectible cannot be determined in advance, reasonable estimates can be made based on past experience. Communication expense refers to the various activities involved in conducting business communications—telephone, mail, and related expenses.

DEPRECIATION

Depreciation allowance refers to an account established to recognize the cost of property in generating income. A delivery truck, for example, may be purchased at a cost of $15,000. Because the truck will be used over a number of years, its cost should be spread over its useful life. This matches expenses with revenues. Because depreciation systems may change through Congressional legislation, always refer to the latest Publication 534 from the Internal Revenue Service.

☐ What Can Be Depreciated

Depreciable property is property for which a depreciation deduction is allowed. Many different kinds of property can be depreciated, such as machinery, buildings, and equipment. Property is depreciable if it meets the following requirements:

1. It must be used in business or held for the production of income.
2. It must have a determinable life of longer than one year.

3. It must be something that wears out, decays, is used up, becomes ob-
    solete, or loses value from natural causes.

In general, if property does not meet all three of these conditions it is not depreciable.

ACRS Method

Accelerated cost recovery system (ACRS) is mandatory for most tangible depreciable assets placed in service after 1980. Other methods require you to make
determinations on matters such as useful life and salvage value. Under ACRS,
salvage value and useful life are not relevant. ACRS allows you to recover the unadjusted basis of recovery property over a recovery period. Your property's
recovery period is determined by its class life. Generally, the class life of property
places it in a 3-year, 5-year, 10-year, 15-year, or 18-year class. A recovery percentage for each year of the recovery period is prescribed for figuring your ACRS
deduction. The deduction is figured by multiplying your unadjusted basis in the
property by the applicable recovery percentage. (For detailed information on
ACRS, see Internal Revenue Service Publication 534.)

☐   Recovery Property

Recovery property is tangible, depreciable property that was placed in service
after 1980 and is not excluded property. It usually includes new or used property
acquired after 1980 for use in trade or business or to be held for the production
of income. Property acquired and used for any purpose before 1981 is not recovery property.

Classes of Recovery Property

The class to which an item of recovery property is assigned is determined in part
by whether it is section 1245 or section 1250 class property. Section 1245 class
property is any depreciable property that is (a) tangible personal property; (b) a
special purpose structure or storage facility that is also depreciable tangible
property. A building or its structural components may not be included. The facility must be an integral part of a certain business activity, such as a research
facility used in connection with this activity, or a bulk storage facility for replace-
able commodities set in connection with this activity. Such an activity includes
manufacturing, production, extraction, or the furnishing of transportation, communications, electrical, energy, gas, water, or sewage disposal services; (c) a
single purpose agricultural (livestock) or horticultural structure; or (d) a storage
facility (other than a building or its structural components) used in connection
with the distribution of petroleum or any primary product of petroleum.

Section 1250 class property is all depreciable real property not classified as section 1245 property. An elevator and escalator are included in this category.

☐ Unadjusted Basis

The ACRS deduction is figured by multiplying the unadjusted basis in recovery property by its applicable percentage for the year. Salvage value is disregarded under ACRS. The unadjusted basis may not be reduced by any salvage value when figuring deductions under ACRS.

☐ Recovery Periods

Note: There have been IRS revisions to this section. Each item of recovery property is assigned to a class of property. These classes of recovery property establish the recovery periods over which the unadjusted basis of items in a class are recovered. The six classes with examples of inclusive property are:

1. Three-year property (automobile and light-duty trucks).
2. Five-year property (office furniture and fixtures).
3. Ten-year property (manufactured homes).
4. Fifteen-year real property (real property placed in service before March 16, 1984).
5. Low-income housing.
6. Eighteen-year real property (real property placed in service after March 15, 1984).

☐ Excluded Property

VACRS may not be used for certain property placed in service before 1981 but transferred after 1980. Property that does not come under ACRS must be depreciated under other methods of depreciation, such as straight line or declining balance. In addition, owners may elect to exclude certain property from the application of ACRS.

Election to Exclude Certain Property

If you depreciate property under a method of depreciation not based on a term of years, such as the unit-of-production method, you may elect to exclude that property from ACRS. A depreciation deduction under the unit-of-production method is figured by dividing the cost or other basis (less salvage) by the estimated number of units to be produced during the life of the asset. The resultant amount is then applied to the units produced in a year to arrive at the depreciation for that year.

☐ Dispositions

Gain or loss from an asset is usually recognized on its disposition or retirement. Nonrecognition rules may, however, allow the postponement of some gain. (See Internal Revenue Service Publication 544, "Sales and Other Dispositions of Assets.")

☐ Other Depreciation Methods

Before ACRS was enacted, other methods were used to figure depreciation. If property was placed in service before 1981, or if the property does not qualify for ACRS, these methods must be used. However, these methods may not be used for property that qualifies for ACRS. Because some states do not accept the ACRS method for state taxes, check with your state tax office to determine how to reconcile state requirements with the ACRS method now required by the federal government.

There are many different methods of figuring depreciation. Any method that is responsible may be used if it is applied consistently. These methods, such as the straight-line method, sum-of-the-years-digits methods, and declining-balance method are not discussed here. They are described in numerous references, including SBA's Business Development Booklet SBMS No. 32, "Financial Recordkeeping for Small Stores."

REMAINING EXPENSES

Insurance expense includes the cost of various insurance policies. If an insurance policy premium is paid for a period exceeding the period covered by the Profit and Loss Statement, include only the portion paid for the statement period. The remaining portion of the paid premium becomes a temporary asset called Prepaid Insurance (or Prepaid Expenses) and is recorded on the Balance Sheet.

Taxes and licenses expense includes governmental fees, license fees, sales taxes, and so forth. It does not include tax on business income. Income tax is computed on the Net Income.

Advertising expense includes all costs associated with advertising the business. Again, prepaid advertising is not included as an expense, but treated as an asset and recorded on the Balance Sheet. Interest expense is the interest paid on any loans during the period covered by the statement. Other charges is a category used to record miscellaneous expenses that are incurred. Total expenses is derived by adding all the expenses listed on the statement.

Net profit can then be determined by subtracting total expenses from Gross Profit on Sales. Net profit can be thought of as operating income or profit earned on operations. Total Net Income is the sum of Net Profit and Other Income.

RECOMMENDED READING

Blechman, Bruce Jan, and Jay Conrad Levinson, *Guerrilla Financing: Alternative Techniques to Finance Any Small Business* (Boston: Houghton Mifflin, 1992). Getting results even if you're not a corporate giant. Related titles of interest also by Levinson: *Guerrilla Advertising: Cost-Effective Techniques for Small-Business Success* and *The Way of the Guerrilla: Achieving Success and Balance As an Entrepreneur in the 21st Century.*

Blum, Laurie, *Free Money for Small Business and Entrepreneurs* (New York: Wiley, 1995). One in a series of books by Blum on mining sources of funding. An excellent sourcebook for information on grants. Also, detailed sections on research funds, and other non-traditional sources.

Corporate Finance Sourcebook (national Register Publishing, published annually). The Sourcebook lists about 3,500 entries on capital investment resources and financial services available to the business community. There are 18 classifications of resources; all listings include address, personnel, and financial information. Chapters include U.S. venture capital lenders, major private lenders, and a list of contact personnel at commercial banks. Call 800-323-4958 for information.

Dawson, George M., *Borrowing for Your Business: Winning the Battle for the Banker's "Yes"* (Denver: Upstart Publishing, 1991). No-holds-barred survey. Special attention given to hard-to-borrow enterprises.

Flanagan, Lawrence, *Money Connection: Where and How to Solve the Problems of Growing Companies* (Grants Pass, Oregon: Oasis Press, 1995). Explains where to find funding sources and how to write various types of proposals to obtain that funding. Includes a generous listing of federal, state, and private resources.

Merrill, Ronald E., and Henry Sedgwick, *New Venture Handbook: Everything You Need to Start and Run Your Own Business* (New York: Amacom, 1995). A guide to starting a small business deemed by *Inc.* magazine as "a small-business bible."

Pratt's Guide to Venture Capital Sources-1998 (Venture Economics). Annual guide to major venture capital firms. Expensive ($355) but comprehensive.

Seglin, Jeffrey, *Financing Your Small Business* (New York: McGraw-Hill, 1992). Comprehensive with thorough explanations of banks and their inner workings.

Accounting

 INTRODUCTION

The most basic function of accounting is simple, day-to-day bookkeeping. Bookkeeping records include:

- Income from the sale of products or services.
- Expenses of business operations.
- Costs of merchandise produced.
- Overhead expenses, such as employee compensation, rent, and transportation.

Accounting involves using these bookkeeping records for business planning. Accounting principles determine which financial events and transactions should be recorded in the bookkeeper's ledgers, journals, and computer disks. The review and evaluation of these records is the primary function of accounting.

Financial statements produced by accountants furnish businesses with the basis for financial planning and control; they also provide outside investors and government agencies with data that can be used to make decisions regarding these organizations. Accounting systems provide statistical access to a firm's financial condition for three broad categories:

1. *Management,* which needs such information to evaluate financial performance over given periods of time and to make decisions regarding the future.

2. The *general public,* especially stockholders or dealers in securities, who cannot make investment decisions without knowing the financial status of a company over the previous quarter or year.

3. *Regulatory departments* of the various levels of government which are concerned with taxes and regulations. Accountants also perform similar functions for government agencies and nonprofit organizations.

Today's system of accounting has developed to meet the rising needs for accurate financial reports, as well as to provide reports to meet government regulations. In the field of law, the development of the corporation has had the greatest impact because it allowed public scrutiny of internal financial affairs, something unheard of in earlier forms of business ownership. Equally significant have been increases in the available quantity and kind of financial instruments used in the past generation, escalating professional demands placed on accountants, even within small businesses.

 ## SOURCES OF INFORMATION

American Institute of Certified Public Accountants (AICPA)

Your business must eventually rely on a certified public accountant (CPA) to help maintain accurate and acceptable financial records for commercial and tax purposes. When that time comes, you can benefit from the services of the American Institute of Certified Public Accountants. The AICPA was established to help CPAs, from internal company staff members to outside specialists, maintain high professional standards and exchange information about accounting procedures, practices, and ethics. The AICPA communicates regularly with businesses of all types and sizes, informing those who inquire about the benefits of using CPAs for corporate accounting and the keeping of adequate records.

The AICPA distributes informational booklets and reports at no cost on a variety of pertinent topics. Of special interest to small-business executives are those relating to financial planning, taxes, bookkeeping, annual reports, loans, and commercial documents.

American Society of Women Accountants

This nonprofit association of over 6,500 women in accounting advises with the general public. Many of the society's members are in small businesses themselves or have clients who are the owners and/or managers of small and home-based businesses and who are familiar with many levels and fields of accounting and finance. You also can refer to the association's newsletter, published eight times a year, which covers topics pertinent to accounting.

Institute of Certified Financial Planners (ICFP)

The Institute of Certified Financial Planners can refer you to specialists who are concerned with developing standards of ethical conduct and procedure, providing services to consumers, and disseminating information about the role of financial planning in the matter of investments and other personal economic programs. The ICFP holds continuing educational seminars for professionals and businesses and financial-planning orientations for consumers. It also publishes a bimonthly newsletter that presents digests of issues affecting business, the profession and public.

Internal Revenue Service (IRS)

The Internal Revenue Service maintains a volunteer and education branch that provides, at no cost, professional counseling on accounting procedures. It can help you avoid tax-related accounting errors and develop bookkeeping methods to minimize tax liability.

Small Business Administration (SBA)

The Small Business Administration provides current, down-to-earth information and counsel on accounting procedures and practices, as well as all other aspects of small business operations. Its Service Corps of Retired Executives (SCORE) is a nationwide program of some 12,000 volunteers, one or more of whom can be matched with you to assist you as long as there is a need.

Another valuable SBA resource is the Small Business Institute (SBI), which provides counseling from qualified business-school students working under the guidance of faculty members. It provides detailed reports on the steps to take to improve accounting methods and operations.

Small Business Development Centers (SBDCs), sponsored by the SBA in coordination with local governments, provide assistance, counseling, and research on many areas of operations, including accounting and financial functions.

U.S. Department of Commerce Office of Business Liaison

The Office of Business Liaison provides an outreach to the business community and can guide small businesses through the complex, and sometimes baffling, government channels related to accounting and financial matters.

Understanding Budgets

A budget, according to the Encyclopedic Dictionary of Business Terms, is "a formal document prepared in detail, listing the past financial history and estimating expenses and income, credits and debits, and related figures for a specified period, generally the calendar year." A conventional budget consists of a projected income statement, balance sheet, and cash budget.

The budget serves two basic purposes. At the beginning of the time period projected (generally monthly, quarterly, semiannually, or annually), the budget is a *pattern,* an anticipation of economic situations and conditions. At the end of the period, it serves as a *control measure* to help management compare its actual performance with the intended plan.

HOW TO WRITE A BUDGET

1. *Separate your budget into two categories: operating and financial.* The operating budget focuses on company operating decisions and consists of the following elements:

- Sales budget,
- Production budget,
- Direct materials budget,
- Direct labor budget,
- Factory overhead budget,
- Selling budget,
- Administrative expense budget, and
- Pro forma income statement.

The financial budget focuses on the financial decisions of management and consists of the following elements:

- Cash budget and
- Pro forma balance sheet.

2. *Compose a realistic sales forecast.* Base your forecast on past records, ongoing organizational and operational changes, and an evaluation of existing and projected market conditions.

3. *Ascertain your expected volume of production.* This is based on sales forecasts and the processing that will be required.

4. *Calculate manufacturing costs that relate to the forecast sales and production requirements.* Account for expected increases in the prices for supplies and charges for labor.

5. *Compute cash flow and other financial circumstances that will affect your operations.*

6. *Draft projected financial statements.*

Many small businesses use computer software to set up models for budgeting, making it much easier and faster to create budgets. Suitable software programs are widely available at modest costs from suppliers in the field of financial planning and administration.

Tip Sheet
Calculating Cash Flow

All businesses function on cash and the orderly flow (use) of that cash. A *cash flow projection,* also referred to as a *cash forecast,* is a necessary tool for financial planning and management. Because a projection shows all of the money entering and exiting your business, its most constructive function is pinpointing potential danger spots. To make a projection, follow the following steps from month to month:

1. List your business's cash balance at the beginning of the month.
2. Add outstanding receipts.
3. Subtract any disbursements.
4. Calculate the balance.
5. Indicate a surplus (+) or shortage (−).

The degree of detail produced by this method depends on several components, including the size of your company, amount of financial activity during the period in question, and kinds of items that you decide qualify as disbursements and receipts. Sales figures alone, as an example, can be misleading if your company extends credit, since the payments for sales may not be received within the time frame being calculated. You can reduce errors by checking earlier cash flow records to adjust the calculations for your type of business.

If your business is seasonal, or if receipts and disbursements vary considerably from month to month, adjust your projections accordingly. Seasonal fluctuations show up well in advance of seasonal peaks and valleys, and it is essential for you to ascertain the time lags between income you receive and disbursements you have to make to maintain your operations. The timing of purchases, for example, depends on such matters as the delivery schedules of suppliers, availability of supplies, production time, and proportions of inventories essential to your business.

Another crucial factor in projecting your cash flow is the kind of payment arrangements you make with vendors. The figures entered into your books from month to month should accurately reflect such agreements. For instance, record whether vendors require full or partial payment before orders are processed or sell on credit.

Cash flow projections should cover major items such as salaries, distribution, marketing, and utilities, as well as payroll taxes, sales taxes, income taxes, and emergency commitments. Disbursements that occur infrequently can be too easily overlooked in a monthly calculation of cash flow. Examples of some of the strays that result in cash flow pitfalls are insurance premiums, business gifts, entertainment, dues, and professional fees.

Tip Sheet
How to Draw Up a Balance Sheet and Financial Statement

Balance sheets are statements of the assets, liabilities, and capital of a business, usually computed over a predetermined period of time or on a specific date. Think of them as all of the elements on your company books that have to be balanced for you to know where your business stands financially. By comparing today's balance sheets with those of the past month, or six months ago, you can more readily see where you stand. A typical balance sheet contains four sections:

1. *Current assets* include cash, accounts receivable, inventory, notes receivable, and marketable securities.
2. *Fixed assets* include real estate, equipment, long-term investments, and miscellaneous assets.
3. *Current liabilities* include taxes, notes payable, accounts payable, and accrued liabilities.
4. *Long-term liabilities* include mortgages payable, bonds payable, and notes payable.

For an example, see the balance sheet in the SBA business plan guide on pages 60–61.

A financial statement is defined by the American Banking Association as any supporting statement in accounting procedures that provides data about a company's financial condition. The usual components of a financial statement are the *income and expense statement* and the *balance sheet;* both are prepared periodically.

Before preparing your company's financial statement, construct a trial balance; be certain total debits equal total credits. If a particular trial balance shows that certain items are losing value as a result of age and use, then this loss, called *depreciation,* must be calculated and recorded prior to preparing the statements. Since depreciation lessens the value of assets and increases expenses, you must post a depreciation entry in the general journal. Another expense to be recorded before financial statements are prepared is the value of office supplies that have been used, as well as insurance, interest, and any other prepaid expenses. Other entries are bad debts, unpaid taxes, salary payments that are overdue or not yet recorded, inventory losses, and damages.

Your income and expense statement reports any change in the owners' equity as a result of current operations, and shows the net income your company has earned in the interval since your financial statements were last prepared.

RECOMMENDED READING

Carmichael, Douglas R., *Accountants' Handbook-1997 Supplement* (New York: Wiley, 1997). Comprehensive but understandable to the layperson.

Livingstone, John Leslie, *Portable MBA in Finance and Accounting,* 2d ed. (New York: Wiley, 1997). Overview of finance and accounting methods taught in top business schools. Discusses financial statements, budgeting, and evaluating potential acquisitions.

Martin, Thomas, *Cash Flow for Small Business* (New York: Wiley, 1993). Basic and clear. Defines and explains cash flow, a frequently misunderstood term.

Shim, Joe, *Encyclopedic Dictionary of Accounting and Finance* (New York: Fine Communication, 1996). An in-depth guide to accounting, including hundreds of solved examples, explained step-by-step.

Tracy, John, *The Fast-Forward MBA in Finance* (New York: Wiley, 1996). Excellent, highly practical guide to financial statements and how to use them to manage a business. Other relevant and useful titles in the Fast Forward MBA series include *The Fast Forward MBA in Business* by Virginia O'Brien and Paul A. Argenti, *The Fast Forward MBA in Marketing* by Dallas Murphy and Alexander Hiam, and *The Fast Forward MBA Pocket Reference* by Paul A. Argenti.

Compensation
and Benefits

 INTRODUCTION

Any business that employs more than a sole proprietor must deal with various forms of remuneration other than wages. Benefits can be expensive and their administration complex; but at the same time, they can improve the lives of your employees and make your business an attractive place to work. Take the attitude that benefits represent money well spent since they help you to recruit better employees, keep them loyal, and encourage them to stay with your company. Statistics show that the absence of such programs can hamper the ability of a company to attract and retain top-level employees. Types of compensation and benefits that are attractive to employees include:

1. *Competitive salaries:* Pay is all-important to typical job seekers at the start, and only later do they begin assessing the value of other forms of compensation, which are the incentives that keep them in your employment.

2. *Incentive and bonus packages:* These include stock-option plans, health insurance, dental plans, life insurance, retirement plans, disability policies, tuition and educational benefits, and pensions.

3. *Pensions, 401(k)s, and Keoghs:* Seventy percent of all employees in America retire before the age of 65. One of the major reasons is that Social Security benefits, when combined with pension and retirement plans, provide enough freedom for people with long records of service to quit their jobs and seek less demanding lifestyles. Companies offer appealing

retirement benefits to employees they would like to retain. Common retirement programs include:

- *Pensions,* in which the employees contribute a specified amount periodically that is then matched by the employer.

- *401(k)s* make it possible for employees to place a portion of their compensation into profit sharing efforts, stock bonuses, or pensions in which they can defer income tax until the money is actually withdrawn.

- *Keoghs* are for employees of unincorporated businesses or people who are self-employed. The maximum that may be invested in this kind of pension depends on the participant's income and can be as high as $30,000.

4. *Severance packages:* Termination policies require owners and managers of a business to exercise tact as well as financial insight, especially if they concern unfavorable circumstances, such as firing for cause, forced early retirement, plant shutdowns, or business failures. In such cases, employees being terminated are almost always owed some form of severance pay or disbursements over a period of years. Even when employees are fired for cause, management must be careful not to violate the employees' rights. Managers who anticipate a downward trend in their respective business fields promote early retirement and offer lump-sum benefits or other compensation to employees who take this option.

 ## Sources of Information

Council on Employee Benefits

The Council on Employee Benefits advises business owners and/or managers with respect to offering the right benefits to attract and hold employees. It also provides information on how to finance those benefits and integrate them into your budget. Membership would be valuable for small companies large enough to have a number of employee benefit programs, but it is not necessary as an initial step in contacting the council. The council publishes a newsletter, the *Reporter,* a quarterly review of news about benefit programs.

Employee Benefit Research Institute (EBRI)

The Employee Benefit Research Institute was founded in 1978 to contribute to the development of effective and responsible public policy in the field of employee benefits. Of interest to small-business owners and managers are the EBRI's educational programs, seminars, publications, research, and counsel related to employee benefits. The EBRI publishes the *EBRI Issues Briefs, EBRI Quarterly Pension Investment Report, Benefit Outlook,* and *Employee Benefit Notes.*

International Foundation of Employee Benefit Plans (IFEBP)

The International Foundation of Employee Benefit Plans is a source for employee-benefits education and information. While the association is primarily geared toward continuing education for benefits professionals, it offers a broad spectrum of publications and video- and audiotapes. It also maintains an information center, where five full-time specialists research topics for the foundation's members. About forty educational programs, covering various areas in the employee-benefits field, are offered each year.

The IFEBP's monthly publications are the *Employee Benefits Digest* and the *Legal-Legislative Reporter* (a newsletter), which provides updates on legislative developments, court cases, arbitration awards, and benefits-related decisions in Congress and other legislative bodies. Two quarterly publications are the *Employee Benefits Basics* and *Employee Benefits Practices.* Visit the foundation's online database at:

www.ifebp.org

Service Corps of Retired Executives (SCORE)

Many members of SCORE, which has centers in all 50 states, are experts in employee compensation and fringe benefits. SCORE can offer—for free—specific help on employee matters and problems.

U.S. Department of Commerce Office of Business Liaison (OBL)

This department is an excellent resource for small businesses; it is particularly useful in guiding business owners and personnel managers in all matters related to employee compensation and benefits. Specialists at OBL can answer questions regarding government policies and regulations, and can provide instructions to assist you in instituting and maintaining workable fringe benefit programs.

For further information on employee compensation and benefits, read this chapter's Tip Sheets on retirement plans, health insurance plans, and your responsibilities under the Equal Opportunity Act.

Tip Sheet

Retirement Plans

The nature and extent of the retirement plans and options your business offers depends on a number of factors, including the size and composition of your company, length of time you have been—and will be—in business, and amount of money you are able to allocate for that purpose. If you fall under the category of a self-employed person, your qualifications for retirement plans are different than if you were classed as an employee; also, you will have different tax and deferral benefits. Because of the complexity of retirement plans and their preciseness in meeting certain qualifications, it is important to consult with an expert to ensure you are not overstepping any legal or tax exemption boundaries.

The Keogh Plan, available to unincorporated individuals and partnerships, is a popular retirement package aimed at tax saving. The maximum contribution is $30,000 or 25 percent of annual compensation, whichever is less. The most common type is a profit-sharing plan that permits you to determine contribution amounts based on business profits.

An Individual Retirement Account (IRA) is an investment for retirement that has short-term and long-term tax benefits. Since IRAs allow income tax deferrals until the employee retires, they accumulate compounded interest over the years. After retirement, income from IRAs is taxed at a lower rate.

You also have a choice of corporate pension plans, real estate tax shelters, and other ways of setting aside retirement funds and paying minimum taxes. To be sure you select the best plan—and one within the lowest possible tax bracket—for your business, consult a CPA or any other financial specialist who is familiar with your field and whom you trust.

Tip Sheet

Finding Health Care Information on the Web

You can locate information on business-related health care through several sources; one of the best is HealthNet Connection, which provides links primarily in Wisconsin but also has links to government agencies and health care associations within the nation and worldwide. Find information on health and health insurance at the HealthNet Connection at www.healthnetconnect.net/widatal.html.

McMaster University Health Sciences Library in Hamilton, Ontario, provides a massive amount of information and links page at www.mcmaster.ca/. Health care concerns are categorized logically and their respective pages are readily accessible.

Tip Sheet
Health Insurance Plans

Small-business owners who establish medical programs for their employees are governed by a number of restrictions and regulations concerning such matters as employee eligibility, cost, and coverage. The U.S. Chamber of Commerce reports that "faulty medical-history information can lead to rejection, or incur higher rates for health, disability, and life insurance for business owners and their employees."

TYPES OF HEALTH CARE PLANS

If you are a sole proprietorship, partnership, or S corporation, it is important that you establish your company's medical plan to qualify for an income tax deduction of a percentage of the cost of health insurance for yourself, your spouse, or your dependents. (Check with your accountant to determine how this allowance will apply to you.)

In a company with employees, this deduction is allowed only if you provide health insurance for *all* your employees on an equal basis. Although that cost is 100-percent deductible as a business expense for your company, the IRS has established nondiscrimination requirements to define who is—and who is not—an employee for prospective health insurance participation.

Compiling data on individuals for health insurance policies is a highly complex process, handled largely through an organization called the Medical Information Bureau (MIB), located in Westwood, Massachusetts. MIB is a nonprofit organization with some 680 member insurance companies accounting for most of the life, health, and disability policies in the United States and Canada. The bureau, which functions under regulations by the Federal Trade Commission, collects data from insurance companies and then furnishes that information for the processing of insurance applications. A business's health insurance costs and premiums are determined in part by (a) an evaluation of the company's records regarding number and amount of medical claims each year, and (b) insurance company statistics for other businesses of similar size and type.

Health care plans fall into three categories:

1. Fee-for service plans provide employees with the services of hospitals and/or practitioners with partial or total reimbursement (depending on the insurer). A common practice is for the insurance company to pay 80 percent of billing amounts, while employees pay the remaining 20 percent. Employees are free to choose doctors and services, but there are limitations as to what is defined in the plan as medically essential.

2. Managed-care plans, which Health Maintenance Organizations (HMOs) provide, offer a range of benefits to employees at a fixed annual charge. The respective proportions of these charges paid by the company and its employees depend on the specific plan selected. HMOs usually specify which practitioners and facilities are to be used, but some provide certain options for out-of-network services and permit the use of doctors or hospitals outside the plan in the event of extreme emergencies or medical needs.

3. There are plans available that include elements characteristic of each of the two concepts listed above. There are certain restrictions involved to control the cost and frequency of managed care and to specify fees for service. For example, a cooperative payment plan might require employees to pay $10, or so, per hospital or doctor visit and the insurance company to pay the outstanding amount.

TIPS FOR ESTABLISHING YOUR COMPANY HEALTH INSURANCE PLAN

-   Set up your plan with the understanding that any plan, no matter how sound it seems, will fail unless it is properly administered.
-   Review a number of workable plans and determine which insurers can most assist your business with the administration of the plans.
-   Query the prospective insurance representatives about all aspects of the plans, particularly any options that would apply to your particular business and its employees.
-   Ask for realistic examples of claims and how they were processed and resolved.
-   Talk to owners of other small businesses similar to yours; inquire of their plans and get their opinions.
-   Review government regulations that require businesses to continue such plans for employees even after they have been terminated. For example, the Consolidated Omnibus Reconciliation Act (COBRA) mandates this extension for any firm with 20 or more full-time employees.

- Obtain an estimate of changes likely to take place within a year or two following the start of the plan, such as increases in premiums or reductions in coverage.
- Once you settle on a plan and an insurer, notify all employees (and future ones as they are hired) about their benefits and costs to prevent possible claims of ignorance about the existing provisions.

 ## RECOMMENDED READING

Arthur, Diane, *Managing Human Resources in Small and Mid-Sized Companies* (New York: Amacom, 1995). Specific advice, many examples.

Brown, Charles, James Hamilton, and James Medoff, *Employers Large and Small* (Cambridge, Massachusetts: Harvard University Press, 1990). Case histories and discussion of compensation, benefits, and personnel issues, among other topics.

Chapman, Larry S., *Affordable Employee Health Care: Options for a Model Benefit Plan* (New York: Amacom, 1991). Chapman presents a basic model health plan that small businesses may adapt to their own needs. Includes discussions of basic care, preventive medicine, and mental health programs.

Combe, Cynthia M., and Gerald J. Talbot, *Employee Benefits Answer Book: Forms* J. Talbot, 3rd ed. (New York: Pauel Publishers). Helps employers follow federal regulations. Includes information on the Americans with Disabilities Act of 1990, the Family and Medical Leave Act of 1993, and the Age Discrimination and Employment Act.

Fundamentals of Employee Benefit Programs 5th ed. (Employee Benefit Research Institute, 1997). A comprehensive and popular guide. Recent update focuses on legislative, regulatory, and tax policy changes that have swept benefit programs. Topics covered include health insurance, managed care, retirement plans, life insurance, and pensions.

Basics of
Business Management

 INTRODUCTION

Defined in its briefest form as the art and science of getting things done
through other people, management is a highly complex function that requires individuals to take charge in five crucial areas:

1. *Planning* requires visualizing today what is necessary, expedient,
and promising for tomorrow. Planning includes the genesis of ideas and
conception of events that will make goals and objectives possible, realistic,
and favorable. Successful managers emphasize that a good plan, even if executed poorly, will serve a company well, but the absence of plans—both
long-range and short-range—will breed economic disaster.

2. *Organizing* involves allocating assignments to employees; matching
tasks with skills, facilities, and tools; and establishing goals and timetables. Organization is comprised of many elements: employees, departments
or divisions, time, function, products or services, customers or clients, economics, and administration.

3. *Staffing* requires evaluating area demographics, assessing company
needs and requirements, recruiting, interviewing, testing, screening, hiring, orientating and training, and maintaining a loyal and dedicated workforce. Staff management is one of the most sensitive areas of management
and administration, requiring charisma in dealing with people, judgment in
evaluating character, and tact in relationships with labor unions and community officials.

4. *Leading and motivating* and inducing others to follow are skills that are both inborn and acquired. Effective leadership is achieved by those managers who are strongly motivated and who, in turn, are able to earn personal respect and motivate others by instilling in them the conviction that they can achieve their individual goals and realize their dreams. There are almost as many styles of leadership as there are leaders, the most common classifications being autocratic, democratic, charismatic, exemplary, militaristic, and low-key. No single style is best, since the results greatly depend on the nature of the business, its location, and disposition of its employees.

5. *Exercising control* involves keeping the troops (employees) on course in the manner intended. Positive control demands four management accomplishments: (1) setting standards of performance, (2) measuring performance against those standards, (3) taking immediate corrective action when the standards are not met, and (4) providing ongoing incentives and rewards for achievement. Control is characterized by productivity and quality, tempered by a realistic adherence to schedules and time frames.

Since the beginning of the 1980s, management in business and industry has moved away from the traditional corporate administrative structure, delegating more planning and authority to line managers and others who supervise operations at lower levels. In many instances, managerial decision making at the top level has depended to a great extent on the counsel and decisions of managers down the line who are specialists or have acknowledged expertise in certain fields.

 SOURCES OF INFORMATION

American Business Association (ABA)

The American Business Association's membership includes owners of businesses, as well as individuals in executive, managerial, and sales capacities; membership is limited to businesses with fewer than 35 employees. ABA provides information on management and administration and offers a number of benefits to its members, including financial services, loans, group travel packages, insurance, and discounts. The ABA publishes a quarterly business brief, which includes information valuable to business owners.

American Institute of Management (AIM)

The American Institute of Management is a research and educational organization comprised of executives interested in developing better management concepts and job performance. AIM conducts professional development correspondence courses and management audits for its members. Also, the Institute publishes *American Institute of Management Digest,* as well as continuing reports and monographs on management.

American Management Association (AMA)

The American Management Association provides educational forums on business management and administration for executives at all levels and in all sizes and types of businesses. Membership (dues for which are on a sliding scale according to the size and nature of member companies) is recommended for small-business owners and managers who would wish to participate in seminars and workshops held throughout the United States and abroad. Membership is not necessary for businesspeople who merely want to take advantage of AMA's publishing program, which offers many of the association's books, cassettes, and other professional tools on the open market.

Center for Entrepreneurial Management, Inc. (CEM)

The Center for Entrepreneurial Management is a nonprofit organization whose mission is to assist entrepreneurs in the communication of ideas through publications, lectures, and individual exchanges of information. CEM has a membership of 3,000 and a mailing list of more than 100,000, the latter composed of entrepreneurs and small-business managers who do not desire membership but wish to take advantage of the information and references made available by the center. CEM offers nonmembers books and periodicals at discounts, and its members receive free subscriptions to business periodicals such as *Inc.* and *Success* magazines, discounts on books and tapes, low-cost insurance, and special rates on travel.

Center for Family Business (CFB)

The Center for Family Business may be an excellent supportive organization for you to join if, like some 5,000 current members, you are the owner, manager, or inheritor of a family-owned business or an independent, private, or closely held company. Membership in CFB provides such benefits as educational programs in business management and management succession, professional consultation covering specific concerns of your business, product research, administration, advertising and merchandising assistance, and the creation of public relations programs to enhance family businesses. The center publishes a monthly newsletter and several books, including *Beyond Survival, Outside Director In the Family Business,* and *Inside the Family Business.*

Center for Management Effectiveness (CME)

The Center for Management Effectiveness was established for directors of training and management development, many from small- and middle-rank companies. CME conducts programs on business- and management-related subjects; topics include problem solving, risk taking, and resolving partnership disagreements. The center also publishes guidebooks on such topics as resolving management conflicts, decision making, managing strategies, and the administration of training programs.

Council of Independent Managers (CIM)

The Council of Independent Managers is composed of owner-operator officers and partners of small- and medium-sized companies (from 5 to 500 employees). CIM provides opportunities for members to exchange experiences and ideas with those who face similar problems. It also publishes the *CIM Directory* annually.

The Entrepreneurship Institute

The Entrepreneurship Institute serves entrepreneurs involved in planning, creating, managing, or growing small businesses. Areas of expertise include small-business-related matters such as administration and management; financial advice; legal assistance; the use of computer programs; and consultation on accounting, management, marketing, advertising, public relations, and selling. Membership is not required.

National Association for Business Organizations (NAFBO)

The National Association for Business Organizations is small-business oriented; it particularly supports those businesses with the capabilities to expand from local enterprises to those that are regional or countrywide. If you find your business growing or changing, need management assistance, and have any thoughts about the possibilities of a joint venture, merger, or other affiliation, NAFBO can be a source of information or referral to appropriate sources and resources. The association also represents the interests of small business in legislatures, monitoring laws that affect small business, and promotes a code of ethics.

National Association of Private Enterprise (NAPE)

The National Association of Private Enterprise consists of 5,000 people who are owners, managers, and/or employees of small businesses. While NAPE furnishes useful information and offers small-business literature either free or at a reasonable cost, full membership provides benefits including management counseling. The association sponsors business seminars and courses and brings together members for interactive discussions on administrative problems and solutions. In a broader sense, NAPE lobbies extensively on behalf of private enterprise, channeling the power of its collective membership into legislation promotion and issues beneficial to small business in general.

National Association for the Self-Employed (NASE)

The National Association for the Self-Employed can be a helpful organization for small businesses, since its membership is largely comprised of owners generally having fewer than five employees. Membership provides opportunities for discussing small-business management concerns and issues during meetings with other members who have similar needs and objectives. Many of the association's members have joined because of the material benefits offered, which include discounted business equipment and supplies; a toll-free business consulting hotline; health, dental, and disability insurance; low-cost travel programs; and career-oriented seminars. The NASE publishes *Self-Employed America,* a bimonthly newsletter and a variety of business forms that help owners and/or managers facilitate day-to-day business operations.

National Business Incubator Association (NBIA)

Business incubators are business assistance programs for start-up firms, and the National Business Incubator Association is the only national association exclusively devoted to the growing incubator field. It offers information, referrals, networking, newsletters, research, and information resources. NBIA also sponsors conferences and training seminars. While primarily an association for operators of business incubators, the association also maintains a list of 750 member-proprietors of business incubators. NBIA publishes a monthly newsletter, the *NBIA Review,* and has an extensive publications catalog.

National Business Owners Association (NBOA)

The National Business Owners Association was founded to promote the interests of small business and the efforts of entrepreneurs. Members have access to a variety of benefits, including management workshops; information on buying from, and selling to, the government; computer services and Internet hotlines; and periodic reports from Capitol Hill on legislation affecting small businesses.

Small Business Administration (SBA)

For information, counsel, and assistance in all matters relating to management, administration, organization, motivation, and leadership, your best government resource is the SBA. The following organizations, all administered by the SBA directly or in collaboration with federal and local agencies, can be particularly useful:

Business Information Centers
Export Assistance Centers
Management and Technical Assistance Program
Office of Women's Business Ownership
Service Corps of Retired Executives
Small Business Development Centers
Small Business Institutes
Small Business Investment Companies
Veterans Entrepreneurial Training
Women's Network for Entrepreneurial Training

Small Business Foundation of America (SBFA)

The Small Business Foundation of America is an advocate of emerging companies and can be an excellent resource for any small business starting to take hold and grow. SBFA's hotline, 800-243-7232, is available between 9:00 A.M. and 5:00 P.M. (Eastern standard time). Leave a message (or send a fax to 202-628-8392), and the people at SBFA will answer your questions about many topics of concern to small-business owners, including market research, sales, exporting, product development, consumer demographics, distribution, market conditions in foreign and domestic locations, joint ventures, research, employee benefits, government restrictions, and suggestions for additional sources of information and resources.

Tip Sheet
The Danger of Growing Too Quickly

Few entrepreneurs dream that a future management or administrative problem may involve a business that has grown too quickly. While it is natural for a well planned and well executed new business to grow, some small companies are allowed to grow too quickly when management becomes flushed with early success. Impatient owners might launch new product lines or services, expand into unfamiliar fields, hire too many employees, and acquire expensive facilities. Here are some of the indications of growth that is too rapid, as cited by National Small Business United:

- The decision to expand is based more on impulse than on sound financial evaluation, market studies, or economic analysis.
- Loans acquired for expansion are so large that servicing them consumes the company's earlier established cash flow.
- The owner and other principals find themselves growing out of touch with the key employees on whom they must rely.
- Management becomes so involved with trying to administer all of the new operations acquired that it loses track of the essential business functions.
- Mounting overhead begins pinching other vital expenses.
- The expansions prove to be producing more personal satisfaction for the owner than net profit.
- Bureaucracy rears its head in the form of more memos, meetings, and buck passing, along with a consequent dilution of decision making and service.
- Customer complaints increase and satisfactory servicing becomes a problem.

External Factors Affecting Growth

The SBA suggests that owners of growing small businesses keep their eye on 10 key demographic and business factors that may affect the healthy growth of their ventures:

- The state of the industry or field in which the business functions;
- Reliable government and private forecasts for the future of the industry;
- Condition of the national economy;
- Condition of the local economy;
- Growth or decline in the ranks of prospective customers, patrons, and clients;
- Availability of prospective employees who are reliable and experienced in relevant areas of expansion;
- Scientific, technological, or other specialized developments that might affect future business;
- Political conditions and events that could impact future growth; and
- Your own expectations and plans with regard to the future of the business and your continuing participation in it.

Time Management in a Nutshell

Ten suggestions for making more effective use of your time:

1. Create a daily planner, with prominent listings for the projects—and portions of projects—you intend to complete each working day. Assess your own abilities so you schedule different types of work, say, creative versus reflective, in accordance with your own biological clock.
2. Review each assignment to make certain it rates top attention and realistically can be executed in the allotted time.
3. Assign priorities to each project or assignment, labeling them alphabetically or numerically, with deadlines. Be strict with yourself and expedite the least pleasant tasks to get them out of the way.
4. Prepare yourself in advance, preferably the day before, by locating all materials you will need to complete the selected assignments (e.g., notes, data, office supplies, and reference guides).

5. Anticipate any interruptions, such as telephone calls, business visitors, and deliveries of mail or supplies, and decide how you will deal with each to minimize wasted time.

6. List supplementary tasks related to the projects at hand so that you can switch activities logically if, for example, you need a break or have to clear your mind before trying to fine-tune the wording of a presentation that is giving you trouble.

7. Focus your thoughts well ahead of time and plot the route you will follow in developing and completing the assignments to which you have given priority.

8. Constantly keep your targets in sight and get back on track if you wander from the path.

9. Allow 15 or 20 minutes at the end of the day to re-evaluate what you intended to accomplish and what you actually did. Jot down what should be done to improve your time management on future projects.

10. Focus on what you have accomplished each day and not on what you haven't done. You will achieve more and continue to improve your working habits and style if you accentuate the positive and don't lament the negative.

Tip Sheet
Expense Accounts

Few functions in the business world have been subjected to more fraud, deceit, misunderstanding, and mismanagement than the personal expense account. You can avoid much of this by keeping your guidelines simple, records accurate, and enforcement of rules and restrictions clear and effective. When establishing expense accounts, clarify the following situations and issues, and present them in writing to all personnel:

• Specify which employees (such as salespeople in the field) will receive cash advances.

• Specify which employees will be reimbursed for out-of-pocket expenses paid.

• List the expenses to be covered by the company in the above cases, and which will not.

• Pinpoint the maximum amounts permissible for each type of expense.

• Provide expense report forms and detailed guidelines for reporting all expenses.

- Distribute to participating employees reprints of passages from the IRS and other tax bureaus (if applicable) describing deductible expenses and their obligations in reporting business expenditures and reimbursements.
- Establish policies limiting the type and amount of expenses (meals and entertainment, for example) employees can accept from outside people with whom they conduct business.
- Maintain accurate records for all expense account transactions, including receipts, bills, credit-card printouts, or other acceptable documentation of amounts, dates, and recipients. One rule of thumb is to insist that such documents be of a type that would be acceptable to the IRS if submitted with tax records.

Tip Sheet
Reducing Theft and Loss

As a business grows, there is often an increase in petty theft, larceny, embezzlement, shoplifting, employee pilferage, or record falsifications. There may be violent crimes of robbery and burglary, too. The National Burglar and Fire Alarm Association suggests the following for small businesses to protect themselves:

- Notify employees that taking small, inexpensive items like office pencils and pens has to be curtailed, since this seemingly minor practice often leads to larger and larger thefts.
- Assign two people with nonmonetary duties to check any functions related to the handling of money and valuables.
- Establish policies and procedures to follow whenever employees are charged with serious crimes like burglary or break-ins.
- Train employees to be alert and keep an eye on strangers who might be in a position to remove valuables in an office, a workshop, or other location.
- Establish a system that offers access to offices and work areas only through entrances that are properly staffed and supervised.
- Hire people whose employment records can be checked, and make it known to them, from the start, that honesty and trust are vital in your business.
- Keep accurate, tamperproof financial records in accordance with acceptable accounting procedures.
- Establish effective supervision in all areas related to shipping and receiving operations.

- Make sure that all cash disbursements have the approval of a trusted supervisor.
- Maintain control over the issuance and storage of keys, and allow keys to be given only to personnel who need them for specific duties.
- Install effective security and alarm systems in all company facilities.
- For all valuables, purchase only top-quality safes and other containers that have been documented as tamperproof and fireproof.
- Provide adequate illumination for any interior and exterior locations that could be subject to breaking and entering.

Tip Sheet
Writing a Procedures Manual

A formal procedures manual is imperative for any business. It need not be complicated or couched in formal rhetoric or legalese; its most important features are clarity; attention to detail; and accessibility to laypersons, professionals, and technicians alike. The manual must have the approval of management and usually should be cleared by an attorney, especially if it will affect large numbers of employees. This section discusses elements that are standard for a typical procedures manual.

TITLE PAGE

One page should be devoted to the title, under the heading "Office Procedures Manual," listing the name of the business, its mailing address, the manual's effective date of publication, and the name and title of the person to whom related inquiries should be made. Telephone and fax numbers are optional.

☐ Statement of Responsibility

The name of the committee or other group or party responsible for delineating the office procedures should be listed on the title page. If pertinent, the basis for its authority to do so should be included.

STATEMENT OF PURPOSE

The approved, stated objective of the publication should be brief and affirmative, printed either on a page by itself or at the top of the Contents page. The following is an example:

This statement of office procedures for the American Distribution Corporation has been prepared and approved by management as an expression of the company's policies and practices in regard to the establishment of offices, office space, and office occupancy by designated employees and/or other company representatives. This document is not a legal instrument, but rather an official expression of management's desires and plans for the use of office space and the establishment of a sound and productive working environment for its personnel. As such, this concept of office procedures is subject to change at any time that may be deemed necessary and replaced with an updated and revised expression of policy and procedure.

CONTENTS PAGE

List the categories of procedures germane to your business operations. Group the subject areas either by priority (importance) or the order in which they most logically might be considered in the overall structure of your company.

REVIEW OF PROCEDURES

Cover each procedure descriptively, as briefly as possible, but without omitting significant details. Gear the review toward your audience—the readers and users of the manual—to determine the language and style most acceptable. Some procedures are more complicated or extensive than others and will need more space for your summary. But most should require no more than 100 words. Here is a typical 100-word entry:

> *Procedures for supervision:* It shall be the responsibility of the personnel committee, appointed by the office management board, to supervise all clerical work and the employees who perform it. This responsibility includes regular coordination with the company's headquarters management, as well as with related departmental units, such as personnel administration and the business department. Whenever deficiencies are noted that are deemed serious enough to warrant formal investigation or disciplinary actions, they first shall be recounted and referred to the office management board. The board will then determine what further steps to take to correct the situation and will so inform the personnel committee.

MANUAL DESIGN

In some cases, the descriptions of office procedures can be enhanced and more successfully depicted to the reader by using sketches or graphs. Your manual's section on design and decor, for example, might benefit from line drawings of desks, chairs, and other furniture; swatches to depict acceptable color schemes; and floor plans to show the most effective uses of space. The section on personnel supervision might include a chart showing employee groups and chains of command, and the section on communications might display symbols representing the types of equipment in use in the locations described.

PUBLICATION AND DISTRIBUTION

Procedures manuals range from simple photocopies of the subjects covered, with pages stapled sequentially, to booklets resembling miniature annual reports in quality and design. The latter are rare, appropriate only for large corporations that place strong emphasis on office procedures and use the manuals for orientation and training purposes as well as for management documentation.

Procedures manuals have limited distribution. They are usually given to top management, members of the active office management board or committee, legal and business departments, and key supervisors and divisional managers.

 ## RECOMMENDED READING

Berryman-Fink, Cynthia, and Charles B. Fink, *Manager's Desk Reference* 2d ed. (New York: Amacom, 1996). Following an A-to-Z format, the authors provide an in-depth guide to managerial responsibilities, including ethics, AIDS in the workplace, preventing violence, and other issues that arise in the office.

Cross, Wilbur, *Growing Your Small Business Made Simple* (Garden City, NY: Doubleday Made Simple, 1993). Fundamental, bottom-line information.

Culligan, Matthew J., *Management 101: The Best Back-to-Basics Techniques* (Englewood Cliffs, NJ: Prentice-Hall, 1993). Covers critical topics for the manager: communication, developing a marketing plan, sales policy, and others.

Kline, Ruth, *Manage Your Time—Market Your Business: The Time-Marketing Equation* (New York: Amacom, 1995). How to maximize time and profits. Includes useful lists and real-life examples.

Sherman, Andrew J., *The Complete Guide to Running and Growing Your Business* (New York: Times Books, Random House, 1997). Sherman, an adviser to over 200 businesses, provides a comprehensive guide to the financial, strategic, and legal aspects of growing a business. Excellent coverage of such sensitive management topics as drug testing, dealing with HIV and AIDS in the workplace, and sexual harassment. Also included are discussions of how to negotiate contracts and manage relationships with partners, cofounders, and financial institutions.

Human Resource Management

 INTRODUCTION

Formerly referred to as *personnel,* the term *human resources* has replaced its narrower counterpart. *Human resources* refers to those resources in an organization that consist of people and their problems, ambitions, and development, rather than facilities or equipment. Resources are evaluated in terms of skills and proficiencies, experience, and availability, as well as the relationships between an organization and its employees.

A major component of human resources is *human resources planning,* a responsibility of top management, to help upgrade functions such as the recruiting and placing employees in the right jobs, anticipating employment problems, motivating employees, and reducing the turnover rate. Human resource planning is made up of the following activities:

- *Inventory:* An appraisal of employees, their job titles, salaries, qualifications, and experience, and determining which employees have matured on the job and which have not.

- *Profile of growth:* Charting changes in growth and development throughout the company that have taken place, seem to be taking place, and will probably take place in the future.

- *Matching people with actions:* Recording which employees have been associated with certain areas of growth, and which are likely to be part of future patterns of change.

- *Turnover:* Charting the rate at which employee turnover has harmed business in the past and may harm it in the future.

- *Education:* Planning courses of training for new and existing employees and for workers moving from one position to another.
- *Salary management:* Improving plans to make employees aware of where they stand with regard to wages, salaries, bonuses, and benefits (with projections into the future).

 SOURCES OF INFORMATION

American Business Women's Association (ABWA)

Many women who own or operate their own enterprises have found it beneficial to join the American Business Women's Association, which was founded to help women executives, particularly in small businesses and in the professions. Benefits of membership include participation in leadership training seminars, networking programs with others in similar administrative positions, business workshops, credit cards, insurance coverage, and a service that provides members with discounts. ABWA publishes *Connect,* a bimonthly newsletter as well as training materials.

Center for Family Business (CFB)

The Center for Family Business may be an appropriate supportive organization to join if, like some 5,000 current members, you are the owner, manager, or inheritor of a family-owned business or an independent, private, or closely held company. Membership in CFB provides such benefits as educational programs in human resources and management, professional consultation covering specific concerns of your business and product research, advertising and merchandising assistance, and the creation of public relations programs to enhance family business in general and your business in particular.

Deaf and Hard of Hearing Entrepreneurs Council (DHHEC)

Many small businesses are owned and/or operated by the deaf and hard of hearing. The Council was founded as a support program to aid people who otherwise might never have undertaken self-employment. DHHEC programs include educating the deaf and hard of hearing in starting a business, teaching the suddenly impaired how to cope with their disability and continue a business already in operation, and encouraging local communities to support businesses run by the deaf and hard of hearing. If you or any of your business associates have hearing deficiencies that you feel are adversely affecting your business, it would be well worth contacting DHHEC, not only to see how you could be helped, but also to participate in some of the educational and support programs yourself.

DHHEC publishes *Deaf and Hard of Hearing, Entrepreneurs Council Quarterly,* and a newsletter containing information on meetings, classes, networking opportunities, legislation, and business tips.

Disabled Businesspersons Association (DBA)

If you are disabled, or if you hire or wish to hire employees with disabilities, the Disabled Businesspersons Association can provide useful guidelines and information about resources and assistance in planning and implementing constructive small-business programs. Currently serving more than 3,000 members, the DBA is recognized as the nation's largest authority on the employment and self-employment of people with disabilities. Whether you elect to join depends on the extent of your interest and involvement, as well as your need for ongoing programs and counsel. The DBA provides educational programs, counseling, and research services to individuals, companies, and organizations. One workshop of interest is the "Disabled Entrepreneur Program," which addresses how people have overcome disabilities to operate their own businesses successfully. The DBA also provides a periodic research study, "Entrepreneurs with Disabilities."

The DBA publishes the *DBA Advisor, DBA International Network Directory,* and the *National Disabled Veterans Business Enterprise Directory.*

Equal Opportunity Employment Commission (EEOC)

The Equal Employment Opportunity Commission is a federal agency responsible for ensuring that people on the job are treated fairly and equally, regardless of race, color, creed, sex, age, or other personal characteristics. Business owners should be in touch with EEOC to keep abreast of regulations and laws governing hiring, firing, promoting, training, and other activities related to human resources.

The Human Resource Planning Society (HRPS)

The Human Resource Planning Society is an association of human resource professionals whose goal is to improve the functions of a company through the application of better personnel management practices. Although HRPS members are typically professionals in large companies, small businesses can tap the resources of this society to obtain useful information. For example, you can find information about regional human resource data, changing trends in personnel recruitment, and development of training programs. The Society publishes *Human Resource Planning,* a quarterly that includes "Current Practices," a column dedicated to the exchange of new ideas and information.

Independent Small Business Employers of America (ISBE)

The mission of the Independent Small Business Employers of America is to help small businesses with five or more employees to grow, increase their earnings, and maintain good employee relations. ISBE accomplishes this in a number of ways. One is to bring its members—small-business employers—together for interactive group discussions about mutual problems and solutions. These meetings also offer orientation sessions and talks by guest speakers who are specialists in personnel administration and management. ISBE also can help interested members to set up regional think-tank sessions to discuss small-business problems in their areas, and advise small-business owners on local sources and resources available to them.

Institute for International Human Resources (IIHR)

The Institute for International Human Resources serves as a clearing house on international concerns and issues for businesses with operations outside of the United States. IIHC publishes a newsletter, a reference guide, and *Worldlink,* a quarterly.

Minority Business Development Agency (MBDA)

The Minority Business Development Agency, a branch of the U.S. Department of Commerce, promotes national economic growth by fostering minority entrepreneurship in the United States. MBDA offers an array of services in a number of fields of operation, including human resources, administration, marketing, finance, law, government, training, and technology.

National Association of Black Women Entrepreneurs (NABWE)

Membership of the National Association of Black Women Entrepreneurs is composed of black women who own and operate businesses, who are interested in starting new enterprises, or who may be taking over family enterprises. The association acts as a support system for these entrepreneurs, fosters educational programs, contacts legislators in a position to improve small-business legislation and ethics, maintains a speakers' bureau, and offers workshops and forums of interest to this small-business group.

NABWE publishes a bimonthly newsletter.

National Association of Temporary and Staffing Services (NATSS)

The National Association of Temporary and Staffing Services is a professional association, not one that a small-business owner or entrepreneur is likely to want to join. However, it can provide inquirers with valuable information about temporary help and staffing, particularly regarding legal, legislative, regulatory, and related matters. If you rely on temporary employees and part-time help and are concerned about laws, standards, and your obligations to them, this association may be of assistance.

NATSS offers its *Resource Guide,* a catalog that features hundreds of products and publications, including books and manuals about temporary help and placement services, professional employer organizations, and general business books.

National Association of Women Business Owners (NAWBO)

Women who own and operate companies have a voice in the National Association of Women Business Owners, which was established to encourage mutual support programs, exchange ideas, and fight discrimination in the business world. The association sponsors workshops and seminars, not only on subjects relating to bias in business, but also on such topics as marketing, management, financing, recruiting, and personnel administration. In these respects, NAWBO can be helpful to women business owners who join as members, but it can also furnish information and reports about issues of concern to nonmembers as well.

NAWBO publishes a newsletter and reports on public issues of particular concern to women.

National Council on Alcoholism (NCA), American Council on Alcoholism (ACA), and National Clearinghouse for Alcohol and Drug Abuse (NCADA)

These three organizations can provide information at no cost to any business confronting problems of employee substance abuse, and can help institute an active program to curb abuse in the workplace. The National Council on Alcoholism, American Council on Alcoholism, and National Clearinghouse for Alcohol and Drug Abuse actively solicit inquiries from businesses whose functions are being affected by drug- or alcohol-related problems, as well as from their employees. All three have divisions that are active in counseling business owners and managers about treatment for employees that allows the workers to continue working and obtain help for their drinking problems. Special attention also is focused on the formation of training programs and the assignment of counselors in the business environment to assist employees and eliminate or lessen the effect of alcoholism on company functions and operations.

National Family Business Council (NFBC)

The National Family Business Council serves as a human resource center for family-owned businesses, many of them small and local in their operations. For persons operating a family business, membership in NFBC offers the following benefits: access to a resource center on family-owned businesses; consultation on financial, legal, and managerial issues; a speaker's bureau and library; and regional seminars on problems characteristic of those in family-run businesses. Some services are available to nonmembers.

NFBC publishes the *Family Business Newsletter* and *Resource Guide to Family Business.*

National Institutes of Health (NIH)

The National Institutes of Health serve as clearinghouses for reports on major diseases and the health resources available to prevent, diagnose, and treat these disorders.

The NIH maintains the following toll-free numbers employers can call to obtain information on substance abuse and mental health issues:

National Alcohol and Drug Treatment Routing Service
    800-662-4357
Center for Substance Abuse Prevention's Workplace Help Line
    800-WORK-PLA (800-967-5752)
National Clearinghouse for Alcohol and Drug Information
    800-729-6686

National Institute of Mental Health Depression Information Line
    800-421-4211
Panic Information Line
    800-64-PANIC (800-647-2642)

Office of Small and Disadvantaged Business Utilization (OSDBU)

The Office of Small and Disadvantaged Business Utilization, under the guidance of the U.S. Department of Commerce, is a small-business advocacy and advisory office. The agency's mission is to increase and improve suitable opportunities for all employers who fit this classification to ensure that they receive equal treatment on the job. Most important for business owners is the fact that OSDBU also takes steps to see that businesses owned by the disadvantaged receive a fair share of government contracts and subcontracts.

Office of Women's Business Ownership (OWBO)

Established under the Small Business Administration, the Office of Women's Business Ownership assists women-owned businesses by providing long-term education and counseling in all aspects of owning or managing a business, assists them in obtaining prequalifications for SBA loan guarantees, and runs periodic demonstration training programs owners and managers can attend. A new mentor program, "Women Helping Women Achieve Entrepreneurial Success," makes it possible for women owners to tap into the knowledge, experience, and one-on-one support needed to help their businesses grow.

Tip Sheet
HIV/AIDS in the Workplace

HIV/AIDS can cause business as well as personal tragedy, and despite the prevalence of the virus, few businesses make advance policies and preparations to deal with it. The Centers for Disease Control (CDC) can help businesses develop workplace HIV/AIDS prevention and education programs. Call the CDD Business and Labor Resource Service toll-free at 800-458-5231. The Resource Service offers a manager's kit with step-by-step information on how to set up a comprehensive workplace program.

CCH publishes books and newsletters about small and home offices and provides a customizable HIV/AIDS policy book on its Web site:

www.toolkit.cch.com/default.htm

Author Andrew Sherman, in his book *Running and Growing Your Business,* provides an excellent primer on dealing with HIV/AIDS in the workplace. It is reprinted with permission here.

DEALING WITH HIV AND AIDS IN THE WORKPLACE

The human immunodeficiency virus (HIV), the virus that causes acquired immunodeficiency syndrome (AIDS), has led to great concern in the workplace in recent years. The majority of people infected with HIV and AIDS are between the ages of 20 and 45 and are employed, many by small- and medium-size businesses. This raises questions regarding the measures an employer must take to accommodate these employees. Despite the ramifications of HIV/AIDS in the workplace, few companies have an established policy to guide their response to this issue.

☐ Federal and State Legislation

At the federal level, two principal laws protect individuals with HIV/AIDS: the Rehabilitation Act and the Americans with Disabilities Act. When making decisions about hiring or promotion, you may not discriminate against an individual who is believed to be infected with HIV/AIDS. In a recent case, a New York State administrative agency found that the law firm of Baker & McKenzie (the world's largest law firm) discriminated against an associate attorney with AIDS when it terminated his employment, and the agency awarded the associate's estate $500,000 in compensatory damages. The award-winning film *Philadelphia* also dramatized the plight of an attorney, played by Tom Hanks, whose services were terminated once it was discovered that he was afflicted with AIDS.

The ADA also prohibits discrimination in places of public accommodation. This means that businesses such as restaurants and hotels may not deny goods or services to a person believed to be HIV- or AIDS-infected. Many states and local jurisdictions have passed laws similar to those on the federal level prohibiting discrimination against people with disabilities. A majority of these laws also include within the definition of "disabled" people who have tested positive for HIV/AIDS. For example, in Minnesota a dentist was found to have violated the state's Human Rights Act (similar to the ADA) for refusing to treat a patient who had tested positive for HIV.

☐ HIV Testing as a Condition of Employment

Several states prohibit HIV/AIDS testing as a condition of employment, although others permit HIV/AIDS testing when the employer can show a legitimate reason. But merely suspecting that an employee is a homosexual or a drug user would not be a legitimate reason. To establish a legitimate reason, there must be some connection between HIV/AIDS and job performance or safety. This connection may exist when the job involves a risk of transmitting the disease. An employer who tests for HIV/AIDS without a legitimate reason may be liable for a claim of invasion of privacy.

☐ Rights of Coworkers

Certain federal laws allow employees to discontinue working when they have a reasonable belief that their working conditions are unsafe. However, given the consensus in the medical profession that HIV/AIDS cannot be transmitted through casual contact, it would be difficult for an employee to refuse to work with an HIV/AIDS-infected coworker on such grounds. The reasonableness of the employee's demand may depend on how the employer has educated employees about HIV/AIDS. If the employees have been taught that HIV/AIDS cannot be transmitted through casual contact, their refusal to work may be found to be "unreasonable," and they could be discharged.

☐ Accommodations for HIV/AIDS Employees

An issue has arisen with respect to whether an employer must make reasonable accommodations for an HIV/AIDS-infected employee. Federal legislation not only prohibits discrimination against handicapped persons but also requires employers to make reasonable efforts to accommodate handicapped applicants and employees where obstacles exist that would restrict their employment opportunities.

In addition, if your company is covered by the Rehabilitation Act and an employee has HIV/AIDS or develops it, you must make reasonable accommodations that permit the employee to continue working. Such accommodations can include leave policies, flexible work schedules, reassignment to vacant positions, and part-time employment. The criteria used to determine whether an employer is making reasonable accommodations for an HIV/AIDS-infected employee include the cost of the accommodations, the size of the business, and the nature of the employee's work.

☐ Guidelines to Consider

Through advance education and preparation, an employer can avoid many of the problems associated with an employee infected with HIV. In 1987, the U.S.

Surgeon General suggested that, when dealing with HIV issues, employers should do the following:

- Adopt an up-to-date HIV/AIDS education program that discusses how HIV is transmitted and explains the company's policies regarding employees with HIV/AIDS.
- Treat HIV/AIDS-infected employees in the same manner as other employees suffering from disabilities or illnesses are treated under company health plans and policies.
- Allow HIV/AIDS-infected employees to continue working as long as they are able to perform their jobs satisfactorily and their continued employment does not pose a threat to their own safety or that of other employees or customers.
- Make reasonable efforts to accommodate HIV/AIDS-infected employees by providing them with flexible work hours and assignments.
- Protect all information regarding an HIV/AIDS-infected employee's condition.

An employer must consider a broad range of legal issues when formulating practices and responses regarding HIV/AIDS. By educating your employees, you may be able to reduce work disruption, legal implications, financial implications, and other effects that HIV/AIDS can have on your business. Because of the complexity and changing nature of HIV/AIDS, an employer should always examine the applicable laws and consult an attorney when handling HIV/AIDS issues in the workplace.

Tip Sheet
When to Employ Temporary Workers

As a small business grows and more employees are hired to meet the demands, many owners and administrators consider hiring temporary workers (temps). In fact, the market for temps is booming: Employment of temporaries has ballooned roughly four times what it was 10 years ago. Temporary workers today account for about 2 percent of all jobs. According to *The New York Times*, growth in temporary employment is probably due, in part, to the rise in the number and size of temporary employment agencies, employer demand for high-technology specialists, and employees whose duties lend themselves to short-term assignments with varied tasks that revolve around a particular technological application.

You can obtain information on temporary employment firms from The National Association of Temporary and Staffing Services, which publishes a directory of member firms and the *Manager's Guide to Employment Law.*

To decide whether to hire temporary help, carefully weigh your situation, asking the following questions:

- Do we have a rush order that simply cannot be completed on time with our present personnel?
- If a key employee is ill and I, as manager, have been asked for a temporary fill-in, have we realistically judged how long the illness will last?
- Have we allocated vacation times properly so we don't have to hire temps during employee absences?
- Can we solve work overloads by offering permanent employees overtime?
- Can we afford the hourly wage rate for temporaries?
- Have we been using temps often enough in the past so we should consider hiring an additional full-time employee to meet the workload demand?

Tip Sheet
Trends in Small-Business Personnel

According to the SBA, the number of small businesses in the United States increased almost 50 percent in the decade prior to 1995. By the mid-1990s, there were approximately 21.5 million non-farm businesses, of which 99 percent were small by the size standards category established by the SBA. These include sole proprietorships, corporations, S corporations, and partnerships, about two-thirds of which operate full-time. Under a broad definition that includes not only persons running a business full-time but also those part-time, about 15 million American sole proprietors are engaged in some entrepreneurial activity. These 15 million entrepreneurs represent about 13 percent of all non-agricultural workers in the United States.

The number of new small businesses has increased steadily during the past 30 years. In 1993, new business corporations reached a record 706,540, or 18 percent more than had been recorded a decade earlier. In addition, part-time entrepreneurs have increased five-fold in recent years. The most recent statistics indicate financial gains for most small businesses. For example, the earnings of sole proprietors and partners increased 7.2 percent, well above the 3.6 percent increase in big-business wage-and-salary earnings during the same period.

Small businesses employ 54 percent of the private workforce, contribute 52 percent of all sales in the country, and are responsible for 50 percent of the private gross domestic product. In addition, they produce more than 70 percent of the new jobs created.

Data on women- and minority-owned businesses at the start of the 1990s reveal that these businesses fared well and that the number of women-owned businesses rose about 58 percent in a single decade. The total receipts of women-owned businesses—some $5.5 billion—nearly tripled during this time period, and the number of black-owned small businesses rose by 38 percent, while their receipts more than doubled. In terms of numbers of businesses, Hispanic-owned businesses have proved to be one of the fastest growing segments of the U.S. business population, with a steady annual growth record of almost 10 percent. Similar increases in numbers and earnings were documented for other small-business minority groups.

Tip Sheet

Crafting an Employee Handbook

Employers and employees can benefit from a publication that provides guidelines relating to jobs, benefits, goals; the organization's history and policies; the community personnel services; and the like. Here's a list of some points to cover in your employee handbook, as recommended by the SBA:

Absence from work

Benefits

Bonuses

Coffee breaks

Community benefits

Company policies

Complaints

Education and training

Equal employment opportunities

Future plans for expansion

Goals and objectives

Health and fitness programs

History and background

Holidays

Insurance

Meals, snacks, and beverages

Medical assistance

Military leave

Old-age benefits

Parking and transportation

Past and present growth

Pay periods

Profit sharing

Publications

Recreational periods

Rest facilities

Retirement

Social Security

Sports programs

Substance abuse

Telephone usage

Unemployment compensation

Vacations

Work facilities

Working hours

Job Analysis Checklist

One of the best ways to avoid personnel problems, such as absenteeism and low morale, is to make certain that all employees you hire have a clear image of the jobs they are to perform. The SBA suggests the following checklist as a starting point for evaluating each position as you wish to define it. (This may include re-defining currently existing positions.) Add other items to the list in accordance with your own expectations:

1. Make a working file of all of the information relating to the duties, quali-fications, and responsibilities of the job.

2. Evaluate these standards and list them in writing, clearly and in order of priority.

3. Prepare a job analysis definition to help you organize your thoughts and outline your expectations for the assignment.

4. Ask employees who now hold the same job, or parts of it, to list the du-ties, responsibilities, and qualifications they themselves believe are nec-essary for good performance.

5. Review these essentials with the person who supervises the job, for sim-ilar input.

6. Keep in mind the ultimate goals of the analysis: to simplify employee re-cruitment, improve employee performance, develop training programs to maintain standards of performance, and evaluate jobs so proper wage scales can be confirmed.

Tip Sheet
Your Responsibilities under Equal Opportunity

The Equal Employment Opportunity Commission (EEOC) has specific expecta-tions of employers large and small. The EEOC was created under the Civil Rights Act, which was written to eliminate discrimination based on race, color, sex, reli-gion, or ethnic origin. The EEOC enforces antidiscrimination law in all business personnel matters, including recruiting, evaluating, hiring, promoting, compen-sating, training, and firing. The Commission maintains field offices in all states and encourages and assists voluntary action by employers, unions, and employ-ment agencies in the effort to end discrimination.

Under EEOC regulations, an employer must post notices explaining federal laws that prohibit job discrimination based on race, color, sex, national origin, religion, age, and disability, as well as describing the provisions of the Equal Pay Act. The EEOC provides literature and a poster summarizing applicable laws and procedures for filing complaints.

Complying with the letter and spirit of EEOC regulations is critical to small business for at least two basic reasons: First, compliance establishes a company's reputation for fairness and impartiality, which directly affects the organization's image in the minds of customers, suppliers, and the community at large. This, in turn, is a strong factor in recruiting and keeping desirable employees. Second, compliance minimizes the possibility that the company will be charged with discrimination and face lengthy litigation and costly settlements.

Employee rights under EEOC policies fall into three categories: the right to job security, the right to fair treatment by the employer, and the right to fair treatment in the workplace. You can obtain free copies of the regulations, posters, and fact sheets by contacting the Equal Employment Opportunity Commission, 1800 L Street Northwest, Washington, DC 20507 (Phone: 202-663-4900 or 800-USA-EEOC).

Tip Sheet
Job Orientation Checklist

The following are suggestions and thought stimulators to help determine what points should be covered when interviewing or introducing a new employee to the company:

- Company's status.
- Company's goals.
- Description of job.
- Related jobs.
- Tie-ins, if any, to those jobs.
- Explanation of pertinent facilities.
- Areas in building to tour with new employee.
- Headquarters office.
- Plant.
- Laboratory.
- Cafeteria.
- Computer facilities.
- Transportation area.

- Employee facilities.
- Accounting and business department.
- Other.
- Review of duties and responsibilities.
- Review of compensation and benefits.
- Introduction to other employees.
- Questions and answers.

Tip Sheet
Hiring the Disabled

Many people who are physically handicapped or who have bodily disabilities have proven to be excellent workers when placed in positions that do not tax their particular impediments. There are even some who suffer mental and psychological disorders, but are not psychopathic or progressive, who hold steady jobs and are admirable performers in their limited employment fields. It is important to give such candidates full and fair consideration. Indeed, you might follow in the footsteps of some small-business leaders who have encouraged the hiring of handicapped and disabled persons, benefited from their steady work habits and loyalty, and earned the respect of their communities.

For more information, contact one of several resources in this subject area, such as the Disabled Businesspersons Association or the Deaf and Hard-of-Hearing Entrepreneurs Council.

 RECOMMENDED READING

ASTD Buyer's Guide and Consultant Directory: Torchlight: The ASTD Buyer's Guide and Consultant Directory on CD-ROM. Both publications, printed and on CD-ROM, list over 700 suppliers and consultants to meet training and professional development needs. The sources are indexed by alphabet, but specialization, category, and industry focused. The CD-ROM allows streamlined searching.

Brattina, Anita F., *Diary of a Small Business Owner: A Personal Account of How I Built a Profitable Business* (New York: Amacom, 1995). Brattina's 10-year diary tracking her small business's growth into a million dollar enterprise; useful sections on dealing with employees.

Cook, Mary F., *Complete Do-It-Yourself Personnel Department* (Prentice-Hall, 1997). Includes model forms, checklists, and sample manuals.

Handbook for Employers: Instructions for Completing Form 1-9. The Immigration Reform and Control Act of 1986 requires U.S. employers to complete Form 1-9, a document verifying immigration status, and obtain documentation of eligibility for work from all employees hired since November 6, 1986. You can obtain instructions on this process in the handbook, available by calling the INS Forms Request Line at 800-870-3676. The automated service will ask you to record your name, phone number, and forms requested.

Lane, Byron, *Managing People: A Practical Guide* (Grants Pass, Oregon: Oasis, 1996). Cuts through self-help rhetoric and gives clear suggestions for delegating responsibility and motivating employees.

Sachs, Randi Toler, *Productive Performance Appraisals* (New York: Amacom, 1992). Lays out a three-part process for approaching employee appraisals that relies on collaboration and appraisal meetings.

Weiss, Donald H., *Fair, Square and Legal: Safe Hiring, Managing, and Firing Practices to Keep You and Your Company out of Court* (New York: Amacom, 1995). Avoiding legalese, Weiss explains the do's and don'ts of employee relations. Includes a discussion of the Civil Rights Act of 1991 and the Family and Medical Leave Act.

Yate, Martin, *Hiring the Best: A Manager's Guide to Effective Interviewing* (Seattle: Adams, 1993). Useful guide for choosing personnel. Current edition includes updated information on the Americans with Disabilities Act.

Hiring the Right
Legal Services

 INTRODUCTION

Small businesses require the services of a law firm or independent attorney to handle the legal requirements facing any enterprise, large or small. The purpose of this chapter is to outline the basic functions and operations that require attention by an attorney.

Business law involves the formation, operation, and termination of a business firm—almost every aspect from the company's birth to its death. The legal system regulates the way a firm is founded and organized, the character of its transactions with other firms, management-personnel relationships, environmental health, responsibilities to consumers, and obligations to society. Specific subjects in the field of business law cover contracts, sales, affiliates, bankruptcy, insurance, negotiable documents, and industrial structures.

One of the most active instruments covered by law is the *commercial contract,* a vehicle by which managers establish rules to govern a particular enterprise. Another cornerstone of business law is *agency law,* concerned primarily with the legal relationships of agents to companies and their principals.

Business law covers many aspects of marketing and sales, particularly through the Uniform Commercial Code (UCC), which puts forth regulations governing merchandising, selling, and commercial paper. *Sales contracts* specify the dual obligations of both buyer and seller. The seller's obligation is to put proper goods at the buyer's disposition and give suitable notice. If the contract obliges the seller to deliver the goods to the buyer, the seller must do so, obtaining the necessary documents and delivering them to the buyer.

In the conduct of buying and selling, an important legal instrument is the *warranty,* a written guarantee by a seller that the goods will be of a certain quality. If they are below that quality, the buyer may sue for the difference in value.

The effect of these UCC warranties is to negate the old doctrine of *caveat emptor* ("let the buyer beware") by requiring that the goods be of suitable quality or that the buyer be warned that the goods may not be up to standard.

Another important field of business law involves insolvency and *bankruptcy,* methods by which debtors may be discharged from claims held by creditors. In a typical bankruptcy proceeding, the bankrupt party lists all assets and debts, and the creditors are then paid on a pro rata basis out of the debtor's available assets.

Last, business law is directly concerned with the manner in which a commercial enterprise is formulated and made into a legal entity: as a *sole proprietorship, partnership,* or *corporation.*

 ## SOURCES OF INFORMATION

American Arbitration Association (AAA)

Complex disputes occur frequently in small business, particularly when dealing with vendors, contractors, or labor organizations. The American Arbitration Association is a public service, nonprofit organization, specializing in arbitrating and resolving dissension, many of them relating to small-business and professional problems. The association conducts fact-finding field studies, maintains contacts with attorneys and arbitration specialists, and invites inquiries from small companies; AAA often helps to resolve disputes without having to go to court.

American Bar Association (ABA) and National
Bar Association (NBA)

Both the American Bar Association and the National Bar Association administer programs to assist businesses and entrepreneurs with legal problems, support community groups that provide low-cost legal services to employees who may need help, and offer educational workshops on problems that especially concern business owners and managers and their employees. These include personnel issues, health, pensions, discrimination, retirement plans, and other individual rights. The ABA and NBA also provide referral services and publications to help businesses, as well as individuals, locate counseling and assistance. You can contact either association directly or through an attorney.

American Insurance Services Group (AISG)

The American Insurance Services Group specializes in property casualty insurance. Of special interest to small businesses are the group's studies determining better ways to develop claim settlement techniques, fight frauds, estimate casualty losses, and evaluate situations relating to claims regarding fire, construction, environmental problems, product safety, and crime prevention. The AISG distributes booklets, at no cost, on the topics just listed and many others.

American Society for Industrial Security (ASIS)

A growing fear expressed by the owners of small businesses is that, unlike most large corporations, they can be crippled by a single act of violence, vandalism, or burglary. The American Society for Industrial Security, the largest global organization for security professionals, has as its mission protecting the employees, property, and assets of businesses. ASIS can be a valuable source of data for you if you feel a need to tighten your security programs or otherwise protect your business from threats to property or personnel. You do not have to be a member to turn to ASIS for security literature, referrals to security professionals, and facts about programs and personnel to meet specific needs. For example, ASIS can help determine how much and what kind of security a particular business needs and will furnish lists of experienced security firms in local areas.

Citizens for a Better Environment (CBE)

Environmental programs are often associated with legal procedures; it is worthwhile to have a pipeline to one or more organizations that can provide counsel on this subject. Citizens for a Better Environment is an excellent source. It is a nonprofit organization established by people concerned about air and water pollution and other factors that unfavorably affect our ecology. CBE offers environmental studies, provides information to small businesses, and engages in civil suits to protect the environment.

The CBE maintains an environmental library and distributes fact sheets and booklets on environmental issues to business owners, as well as the general public.

Copyright Clearance Center (CCC)

The Copyright Clearance Center provides a simplified mechanism for businesspeople to understand copyright law and obtain clearances for copyrighted material. Among other resources, the center provides a channel for large and small businesses to obtain the rights to reuse copyrighted material and aids firms in licensing the use of visuals. The CCC was established by authors, publishers, and users as the not-for-profit Reproduction Rights Organization (RRO) for the United States. CCC operates collective licensing systems that facilitate compliance with the copyright law.

Available books and pamphlets dealing with copyright law also are listed on the CCC's Web site. Visit the site at:

www.copyright.com/

Environmental Protection Agency (EPA)

The Environmental Protection Agency, through its central or regional offices (listed in Part Three) can help you assure that your business is in compliance with environmental laws, rules, and regulations. Also, the EPA posts the full text of its regulations at:

www.epa.gov/epahome/rules.html

Insurance Information Institute (III)

A good way to obtain objective information about all forms of coverage—without being bombarded by sales agents—is to contact the Insurance Information Institute. Small businesses find the Institute to be a valuable source of data about wide ranges of commercial coverage, such as policies relating to fire, theft, vandalism, natural disasters, and liability. III also can provide background information and specific details on policies involving such matters as health, long-term care, dentistry, hospitalization, retirement plans, and other forms of coverage of special interest to employees. The Institute distributes free booklets on many insurance topics upon request, including *The Fact Book,* a useful annual containing more than 150 pages of detailed information, such as statistics on all types of casualties and losses.

Useful for almost any business owner is *Insuring Your Business,* by Sean Mooney. Chapters specifically address the needs of manufacturers, truckers, restaurateurs, professionals such as lawyers and accountants, and other types of business owners. It also covers topics like workers' compensation and insuring company vehicles.

The Institute also can supply pertinent information about state insurance commissioners. It is essential that you contact such sources because of the wide variations in insurance laws, practices, restrictions, and procedures from state to state and sometimes from county to county.

National Recycling Coalition (NRC)

The National Recycling Coalition is a nonprofit organization committed to maximizing recycling as an integral part of solid waste and resource management. Members include businesses, recycling and environmental organizations, and state and local governments. NRC provides technical assistance, shapes public policy, and operates programs that foster recycling to conserve resources and reduce waste. It serves as a prime source of information and counsel for any small business with recycling demands or problems. NRC has a number of publications, including the *Buy Recycled Business Alliance Newsline* and the *Market Development Newslink.* Also available are fact sheets and industry-specific guidebooks such as *Beyond Bags,* for grocers, and *Building for Tomorrow,* for the construction industry.

Office of Business Liaison (OBL)

The Office of Business Liaison serves as a point of contact between the government and the business community. Among its objectives are to help companies keep abreast of federal regulations and restrictions. Make it a point to be forewarned about operating your business in a way that complies with the law. OBL makes itself available at all times to field your questions on governmental policies, statutes, and regulatory trends.

Office of Consumer Affairs (OCA)

Although the Office of Consumer Affairs is usually considered as an agency that sides with consumers, its responsibility is actually two-sided. OCA can be an ally for any small business that manufactures or distributes products. The agency also functions as a valuable resource for producers and sellers of consumer products who need assistance and counsel in avoiding situations that might result in complaints from the public.

Patent and Trademark Office (PTO)

The Patent and Trademark Office administers the patent and trademark laws of the country, registers trademarks, and reviews applications from firms seeking protection for their inventions and innovations. The PTO also maintains one or more libraries in each state to provide businesses with trademark collections and related data so that you can research the feasibility of using certain symbols and marks legally and without risk of protest.

Small Business Administration (SBA)

Through the Small Business Administration, you can stay informed about legislative and legal matters and gain access to pertinent resources that will provide data and services relating to such concerns as government regulations and laws, patents, copyrights, labor relations, environmental compliance, liability, and licensing. For more information, read the following Tip Sheets: *Legal and Tax Structures for Businesses, Laws That Can Affect Business, Licensing,* and *Trademarks, Copyrights, and Patents.*

Tip Sheet
Legal and Tax Structures for Business

There are four distinct legal structures for establishing a commercial organization, all of which can be considered for a small business. The office of the Management and Legal Counsel of the Small Business Administration advises that you obtain the services of an attorney to help you decide which structure is best and handle the necessary legal paperwork. Representatives from SCORE also can furnish helpful advice. Your choice of a business structure is critical because the correct structure can help you reduce taxes, avoid personal liability, and tie in better with local regulations and licensing fees. Your four choices are: (1) sole proprietorship, (2) partnership, (3) corporation, and (4) S corporation.

SOLE PROPRIETORSHIP

A sole proprietorship is the simplest and most common business. If you are the single owner, you are automatically a sole proprietor if you do not establish yourself in another structure, and you can start your business after obtaining whatever licenses are required for local enterprises. The advantage of a sole proprietorship is that it offers relative freedom from government control and special assessments, and you can be your own boss. The disadvantages are that you are fully and personally responsible for taxes that could adversely affect income tax obligations if not properly handled. Also, all of your personal assets are subject to any legal liabilities you might encounter while operating the business. Therefore, to guard against potential lawsuits from your customers, you should secure liability insurance.

PARTNERSHIP

A partnership is defined as an association of two or more principals who serve as partners under a legal contract and whose objective is to make a profit. The advantages are that a partnership offers relative freedom from government control and special taxation. The disadvantages are that the entire firm can be bound by the acts of one of the partners and negatively affected in cases of fraud, misunderstanding, or mismanagement. For obvious reasons, choosing the right partner(s) is one of the most important steps you would have to take in this kind of venture. A clear-cut division and understanding of duties and responsibilities also is imperative. Agreements on partnerships may be oral but should be in writing, and can be recorded on agreement forms available in most stationery stores. There are various types of partnerships, such as a limited partnership, which you will find described in any library guidebook on the subject.

CORPORATION

By far the most complex of the four business structures, the corporation is a legal entity, distinct from the individuals who own or administer it. If you intend to form your business as a conventional corporation, you must engage the services of an attorney—and preferably one who is experienced in this field.

The advantages of a corporation are that it exists as a separate entity, with a more impressive image, and that officers, managers, and employees generally are not personally responsible for tax obligations or liabilities. (However, this does not guarantee personal blanket immunity from liability, civil or criminal, for the conduct of your corporation.) The disadvantages are that tax reporting is complicated and can eat into profits if the corporation is not properly managed. Since corporations are affected by more kinds of taxes, regulations, and restrictions than sole proprietorships or partnerships, management has more burdensome decisions to make regarding the operations, staffing, goals, and policies of the company.

S CORPORATION

The S corporation option is available even to a one-person or home-based organization. The advantages are that, as an individual, you are less liable for any tax delinquencies, as well as obligations and losses suffered by your business. An S corporation can be established only under certain restrictions; for example, it must be a domestic company (though it can do business abroad as well), can issue only one class of stock, and can have no more than 35 shareholders.

Tip Sheet
Licensing

The best time to check out requirements for licensing, as well as the complex paperwork sometimes required, is well before the business is started. In rare cases, the money and time required may make you think twice about the viability of the business. Most licensing arrangements do have reasonable intent, such as to protect the general public, preserve the environment, uphold zoning restrictions, or avoid fraud and deceit. Failure to obtain the necessary papers could subject you and your business to additional fees and penalties.

To avoid problems by obtaining pertinent information on the local requirements, contact your local city hall and explain which field of operation with which you are concerned (e.g., waste disposal, recycling, trucking in restricted zones, or parking lot construction). You also can obtain this kind of information from your nearest Small Business Development Center, or check your local Chamber of Commerce if you cannot find an SBDC.

Other kinds of credentials you might require are:

- *Business licensing,* generally a local permit to conduct business within the municipal borders. If you conduct business in more than one municipality, you may need two or more such licenses.

- *Specialized operating permits,* usually for a business that has some degree of hazard or environmental restriction.
- *Sales impost,* which in effect taxes a business on the basis of the sales volume within a certain geographical area.
- *Zoning deposit,* a sum that is held in escrow in the event that any fine is imposed for zoning deviations or variances.
- *County license,* similar to the town license but imposed for doing business in one or more locations within a county, especially within an unincorporated area of the county.
- *Fictitious business name statement,* a fee for sole proprietors and partnerships choosing to operate under a fictitious name.
- *State licenses,* mainly in the form of an occupational permit for persons engaged in certain vocations, such as electricians, mechanics, and insurance agents, that require the passing of state examinations before they can conduct business.
- *Federal licenses,* required for certain professions whose activities fall under the jurisdiction of the Federal Trade Commission.
- *Structural permits,* often at county and state levels as well as local, to ensure compliance with the appearance and safety of all structures owned or used by a business.
- *Seller's permit,* required in some states before manufacturers or wholesalers will sell you products and materials at wholesale prices.

Tip Sheet
Trademarks, Copyrights, and Patents

According to the International Trademark Association, a *trademark* is a "distinguishing brand name, symbol, mark, emblem, or fanciful initials that identifies a product or company, and which has been protected through registration with the United States Patent Office." A trademark differs from a *copyright* and a *patent* in that it protects the symbol that distinguishes products, materials, or services, and not those commodities themselves.

Unprotected trademarks often become generic terms, as in the case of the word, "refrigerator," and can then no longer belong to any particular manufacturer or supplier. Trademarks exist in a number of categories, the most common of which are: (1) technical trademarks, which identify the derivation of a product or service; (2) descriptive marks, which feature the nature of the items being protected; (3) certification marks, which authenticate the quality or origin of products and materials; (4) collective marks, which associate the marketer with a trade association or union; and (5) service marks, which are used in the sale or advertising of services.

A *copyright* is defined as "the legal right of ownership in any published or artistic creation, which is specified in a legal instrument and viable for a designated period of time." Copyrights can be applied to articles, books, musical scores, computer programs, and many other types of creative works of a kind not protected by a patent.

A *patent* is "the exclusive right, protected by government decree, granted to an inventor or group to enjoy any profits or benefits derived from an invention, and proscribing that anyone who makes, uses, or sells something patented without the consent of the patentee is liable for damages and possible lawsuits." In the United States, only certain classes of inventions are patentable, including machinery, manufactured articles, production processes, creative designs, and computer software programs. Patent applications require comprehensive information; exacting details, specifications; sketches, if applicable; and descriptions of the invention and its applications and uses. Patent rights may be transferred to others by written agreement, as well as by licensing, but are generally valid only in the country of origin or within certain geographical and political limits.

RECOMMENDED READING

Fishman, Stephen, *The Copyright Handbook* (Berkeley: Nolo, 1994). Plain-English guide.

Friedman, Robert, *The Complete Small Business Legal Guide* (Deaborn, 1993). Offers crucial information about the legal concerns of small businesses while explaining the complexities of legal transactions. Written in language understandable by the layreader. Sections on buying and selling a business, franchise, and employees.

Lane, Byron, *Legal Handbook for Small Business* (New York: Amacom, 1989). General overview, geared for small firms.

Williamson, John H., *Handbook of the Law of Small Business Enterprises* (Argyle, 1996). Comprehensive and easy-to-access.

Finding Knowledgeable Consultants

 ## INTRODUCTION

A consultant is an independent specialist who provides expert evaluations and advice to clients under the terms of a long-range retainer or on an hourly or per diem basis. Consultants are classified under two headings: as *specialists* or *generalists*. A specialist is a professional in such fields as banking, law, accounting, advertising, medicine and health, or education. A generalist is a consultant whose expertise is more sociological or theoretical, such as members of community organizations, government leaders, clergy, librarians, or even customers and clients.

Consulting directories, of which there are several that are published annually, list more than 20,000 consultants and consulting organizations in North America. You can search the lists for candidates geographically, professionally, and economically appropriate in a business library, through your Chamber of Commerce, or on the Internet. Recommendations from associates are useful, as is information from the resources discussed in this chapter.

 ## SOURCES OF INFORMATION

Association of Small Business Development Centers (ASBDC)

The Association of Small Business Development Centers was instituted to provide assistance and training in development centers that are located in all 50 states, the District of Columbia, and several U.S. territories. These centers are local resources established specifically to help businesses succeed and provide counsel and assistance to small businesses or to entrepreneurs planning such ventures. Membership is not required for small-business owners and managers seeking information and assistance. Since the centers are partially funded by the SBA—and partially by state programs—most of the services are at little or no cost. Counseling, for example, is provided free; if you decide to take a training class, there may be a small charge. SBDCs do not assist in financing, but they can steer you in the right direction with regard to your objectives and options. Some examples of how ASBDCs can help include the following:

- A *feasibility study* before you even embark on a venture, to assess your readiness and preparedness to go into business.
- *Market research,* to diagnose your company's strengths and weaknesses and intensify marketing plans for the future.
- *Accounting analysis,* to improve your selection and use of bookkeeping systems for the financial management of your company.
- *Review of structuring options,* to help you decide which entity is best: sole proprietorship, partnership, corporation, or S corporation.
- *Cash flow analysis,* to examine and, if necessary, revise your cash flow procedures and business operations forecasting.
- *Procurement assistance,* to determine whether your company can qualify for government contracts and help you place bids.

Center for Management Technology (CMT)

The Center for Management Technology's membership consists of management consultants who help companies improve business operations and profitability. If this is an operational function in which you need outside assistance, request a list of members in your region who would be qualified to serve as consultants to meet your needs.

Council of Consulting Organizations (CCO)

The Council of Consulting Organizations, the parent for several consulting associations, maintains a membership directory that is periodically updated. Ask for suggestions with regard to CCO members in your region who might fit the categories and qualifications your require.

Industry Specialists-International Trade Administration, U.S. Department of Commerce

The International Trade Administration has industry specialists for almost every conceivable industry. They will provide market, product, and statistical information for U.S. and international markets. A complete listing, with individual telephone numbers, is in Part Three.

International Executive Service Corps (IESC)

The International Executive Service Corps may be a source of assistance for questions about foreign markets. It was established in the mid-1960s by American business leaders to assist private enterprise, particularly small businesses, in the developing countries of Latin America, the Middle East, Africa, Asia, and Central and Eastern Europe. The IESC provides managerial and technical assistance on a temporary basis to individual small- and medium-sized enterprises engaged in a wide range of operations and services in developing countries. Except for travel and related costs, these services are free to small-business owners and managers.

National Executive Service Corps (NESC)

The National Executive Service Corps is a nonprofit organization that provides management consulting assistance to small businesses and nonprofit organizations. Its members are volunteers, largely retirees, with experience as executives and managers. Membership is not required to benefit from NESC's services.

Service Corps of Retired Executives (SCORE)

The Service Corps of Retired Executives provides invaluable consulting services for small businesses. It is a nationwide program of some 12,000 volunteers, each with an average of 35 years of business experience. SCORE provides one-on-one consulting by seasoned professionals. Since the backgrounds of SCORE volunteers in your region are public record, you have the opportunity to match up a consultant with your needs. You can set up an appointment by calling your local SBA office.

Small Business Development Centers (SBDCs)

Small Business Development Centers, generally located on college campuses, were formed as cooperative efforts among the academic world, small businesses, and local governments. Centers have been established in all 50 states, with a total of more than 700 sub-centers. Each is qualified to provide counseling, training, and research assistance on financial, marketing, production, management, and technical questions. Some examples include (1) a feasibility study to determine your readiness to start a new business; (2) advice as to whether you should organize your business as a sole proprietorship, partnership, corporation, or S corporation; (3) a diagnosis of your marketing plans; (4) how to qualify for government contracts and place bids; and (5) determining the advisability of diversifying or undertaking a merger.

Small Business Institutes (SBIs)

Small Business Institutes can provide intensive management counseling from qualified undergraduate and graduate business school students who are studying under the guidance of expert faculty members. They can provide a number of valuable guidelines, including written proposals and oral presentations on actions you need to take to improve your procedures and operations. Local SBA district offices can provide you with information about the SBI nearest you.

Tip Sheet
Locating the Right Consultant

Here is a step-by-step guide to finding a consultant:

1. First, decide whether you want a consultant who is a generalist, providing expertise in the fields that are basic to small business, or a specialist, whose capabilities are narrower but more in-depth in a given area.

2. Consider whether you want to deal with a large firm that may assure a greater range of coverage, or a small firm that may be more limited but will provide personal service.

3. Consult a directory and list the firms that are within reach and that seem to cover the subject areas of concern. Send for literature that describes their services, and ask about rates and contracts.

4. Obtain objective outside information about the candidates you have selected.

5. Narrow the field to two or three and set up interviews at a mutually convenient location. Bring along a third party, such as your attorney or CPA, if you feel more comfortable.

6. For decisions of far-reaching significance, consider getting a second opinion.

7. Ask a prospective consultant for a proposal with the specifics of what the firm can do to help you; this should be in the form of a written presentation.

8. Find out which individuals would be servicing your account and request their resumes and a chance to meet them. Make sure you can switch later, if you so desire.

9. Determine how you will be billed, and how often. Insist on clear, understandable invoicing procedures.

10. Get full disclosure of potential conflicts of interest relating to your competitors or service providers.

11. Make sure your adviser is knowledgeable in the areas in which you need help.

12. Use advisers for what they can supply in their own fields of expertise, not in yours. They should be experienced, not only in your industry, but also in emerging fields.

13. Think long-term. Pick advisers who will stay current on relevant issues and state-of-the-art equipment when your company expands and/or diversifies.

Tip Sheet

Ten Tips for Getting the Best Service from Your Consultant

1. Select competent accountants and lawyers who can also serve as business advisers. Get referrals from other business owners, interview

several candidates, and settle on the person with the right background, with whom you can communicate most easily.

2. Involve them early and thoroughly in your business activities. The quality of their advice often depends on how much they know about your company and its functions and missions.

3. Anticipate the level of accessibility and the approximate amount of time you will need to get the kind of advice you seek.

4. Agree on exactly whom you will be dealing with in the firm, how you can switch to someone else if you so desire, and how and when your company will be billed. Insist on clear, understandable invoicing procedures.

5. For decisions of critical import, select standby professionals on whom you can count for second opinions.

6. Insist on full disclosures of any potential conflicts of interest with your competitors or service providers.

7. Ascertain in advance that your advisers are knowledgeable in areas in which you need help.

8. Select advisers for what they can supply in their own areas of expertise—not just in yours—particularly in fields into which your business may move.

9. Choose ones who can do this for the long-term, when your business has grown and/or diversified.

10. Be sure there is adequate backup or contingency plans in case your consultant changes jobs, becomes ill, or goes on vacation.

 ## RECOMMENDED READING

Carmichael, Douglas, *Guide to Business Consulting Engagements* (Practitioners Publishing, 1988). A view from the side of the consultant; valuable for understanding the field and the practitioners.

Cohen, William, *How to Make It Big as a Consultant* (New York: Amacom, 1993). As the title implies, a book for would-be consultants, but also a very valuable insight into how the profession functions.

Consultants and Consulting Organizations Directory (Gale Research, 1996). Available in most major libraries, these books list thousands of consultants and outline their fields of expertise.

Directory of Management Consultants (Kennedy Publications, Annual). Over 1,500 firm listings, 6,000 individual management consultants, and nearly 5,000 offices worldwide. Detailed firm descriptions, including functional and industry specialties. Full contact information, including e-mail and Web addresses. Introductory material on working with consulting firms.

O'Shea, James, and Charles Madigan, *Dangerous Company: The Consulting Powerhouses and the Businesses They Save and Ruin* (New York: Times Books/ Random House, 1997; Penguin, 1998). An expose by two *Chicago Tribune* journalists. While the book primarily focuses on the big consulting companies and the clients with whom they work, the book provides insights and lessons for small businesses. Especially useful are the authors' insights into how you, as a small-business manager, need to keep a firm rein on consultants to make sure they are serving the needs of your business.

Bringing Your Corporate Values to Life

 INTRODUCTION

In business and industry, the term *ethics* can be defined as the observance of principles that individuals and companies morally owe to the public and to all concerned, directly or indirectly, with the business and its operations. Today's concept of ethics is based on numerous previous philosophies going back to ancient times regarding studies and evaluations of human conduct in light of moral principles and the individual's standard of conduct in the matter of social obligations and responsibilities. According to Dr. Robert C. Solomon, an authority on business ethics:

> Business is an ethical activity. . . . The search for excellence, whatever else it may be, begins with ethics. In fact, the ethics of business and the moral code of our society are inseparable, sometimes indistinguishable. Our daily concern with efficiency, fair exchange, and the work ethic—getting what we pay for, earning our keep, being paid what we're worth—is the very heart of business ethics.

One of the basic tests of the ethical nature of any operation or policy for your company is to imagine yourself in the shoes of those people outside the company—customers, clients, suppliers, agents, and others—who will be affected by what you do and how you do it. Note that the public is increasingly intolerant of businesses that behave in unethical ways, and negative publicity regarding ethical transgressions of your business can be crippling. Understanding ethics, or even drawing up a code of ethics, will not guarantee a path free of trouble, but at least all members of your organization can have a toolbox of ideas and concepts with which to evaluate tough business calls.

 ## SOURCES OF INFORMATION

Environmental Protection Agency (EPA)

A 1996 study by the SBA reported that many ethical problems and infractions in the world of small business were related to pollution. Often because of increasing costs of complying with restrictions, business owners and managers tend to look the other way when it comes to such violations as disposing of waste improperly, allowing liquid pollutants to seep into nearby bodies of water; failing to install devices to prevent air pollution; and the like. Businesspeople concerned with such matters should maintain contact with the Small Business Ombudsman (SBO) of the EPA. The SBO serves as a liaison for small businesses, helping them to understand and comply with new and ever-changing requirements, and to make the point that while a single company's violations may seem minor and inconsequential, the undesirable accumulation from hundreds of small businesses can be devastating.

For more information about ethics in business, see the following Tip Sheets: *Are You Acting Ethically?* and *The Seven Deadly Sins of Business.*

Institute for Global Ethics (IGE)

The Institute for Global Ethics, headquartered in Camden, Maine, is a think tank that provides practical seminars on business ethics. IGE has consulted for many large corporations and state and federal government agencies. Members of the Institute receive a magazine that features articles and columns about business ethics.

Society for Business Ethics (SBE)

The Society for Business Ethics is largely academic but can help you understand the nature of, and need for, ethics in your business dealings, employment, management, and company policies.

SBE publishes an ethics newsletter and a quarterly and can suggest books that relate to business ethics.

Tip Sheet
Are You Acting Ethically?

If you are about to take an action or establish a company policy and are not certain whether it is ethical, ask yourself these questions:

Have I accurately defined the problems?

How did these problems evolve and where does the blame lie?

What would be the position of an adversary, or someone outside looking in?

Whom are we really serving—where is our loyalty?

Which individuals or organizations will my action injure?

Will my decision seem like the right one a year from now, five years from now?

Should I be making a compromise or settlement?

If I were asked to describe my action to a board of directors or a local community group, would I have to hedge on my summary, or perhaps even fabricate my description?

Would I flinch from telling the truth to family members or business friends outside the company?

What self-interest motives may have guided my action? Conversely, did I have any altruistic motives?

Tip Sheet
The Seven Deadly Sins of Business

An editorial in *Business and Society Review* listed the following seven deadly sins committed by businesses in the United States:

1. Ignoring social problems and issues in products sold, services rendered, or dealings in the communities in which the company does business.
2. Placing the blame for an offense on some other organization or individual.
3. Discrediting outside critics whose opinions are basically accurate.
4. Firing employees who cause dissension in the company or in the eyes of the public, but who have legitimate beefs.
5. Suppressing information that is true but might damage the company's reputation.

6. Spending an inordinate amount on public relations or an advertising campaign to counter honest complaints by the press, or by those who work for or do business with the company.

7. Denying charges that are relevant and factual.

 ## RECOMMENDED READING

Childs, James M., Jr., *Ethics in Business: Faith at Work* (Philadelphia: Fortress, 1995). Ethicist Childs argues that core Christian values can inject responsibility and character into the business world. Discusses competitiveness, leadership, discrimination, and conflict resolution, among other business topics.

Michalos, Alex C., *Pragmatic Approach to Business Ethics* (Sage, 1995). Primarily consists of articles from various journals, this book considers the boundary between rational and ethical decisions, honesty in advertising, and a company's responsibilities to employees.

Solomon, Robert C., and Kristine R. Handson, *It's Good Business* (Harper-Collins, 1989). Discussion of good business practices and values.

Velasquez, Manuel G., *Business Ethics: Cases and Concepts* (Prentice-Hall, 1992). Business ethics are weighed and judged, using many real-life examples.

Leasing Office
and Storage Space

 INTRODUCTION

Many small-business owners do not realize that a lease can be subjected to bargaining—and sometimes the terms can be lowered substantially. The first step is to do some homework and study the kinds of leases typically used in your area and for your type of business. Second, make yourself familiar with all the terms in your proposed lease. Finally, you should prepare a checklist of the points you want to cover with the owner of the property, or the agent, before you sign any kind of agreement. Here are a few of the essentials to ask about:

- History of the premises.
- Approval to make any building alterations you desire.
- Dates on which the lease begins and ends.
- Clearance by police and fire departments.
- Any assessments for which you would be liable.
- Sufficiency of power supply and electrical boxes.
- Insurance coverage in effect or needed.
- Parking space availability for exclusive use.
- Access roads and footpaths.
- Boundaries and description of neighboring properties.
- Environmental or health problems.

- Map and detailed written description of the property.
- Maintenance fees.
- Nature and capabilities of all utilities.
- Signage restrictions.
- Zoning laws that pertain to the property.
- Lease renewal terms, if desired.
- Vulnerability to flooding and other natural problems.
- Crime rate and history in the area and on site.
- Security systems and protection.
- Proximity of police and fire departments.
- Proximity of medical and emergency facilities.

SOURCES OF INFORMATION

American Society of Appraisers (ASA)

Although the American Society of Appraisers is a nonprofit independent organization whose members are professionals in the real estate field, you may find it helpful to contact the ASA for information and referrals if you want to appraise land or buildings you are considering for business use.

National Association of Realtors (NAR)

The National Association of Realtors can provide referrals in your area for help in the purchase or sale of business property. The association works on behalf of property owners and provides facilities for research, education, and the exchange of information.

Property Management Association (PMA)

The Property Management Association represents the commercial and residential leasing and management industry. It conducts seminars, distributes publications and reports, and provides a medium for the exchange of ideas on methods of managing property. Contact PMA for information or referrals in connection with the buying and selling or leasing of business property of any kind.

Small Business Development Centers (SBDCs)

The SBA recommends Small Business Development Centers as the most likely source of information and counsel on matters relating to commercial real estate, leasing, and the administration of property of all kinds used for business purposes. Through 56 SBDCs in the United States, small-business owners and managers can obtain services in more than 900 locations. Many of these are located in colleges and universities, where faculty members and graduate students in business are qualified to provide management guidance and technical assistance. These centers also work in liaison with more than 30 BICs that specialize in providing state-of-the-art reports in the fields of communications, data processing, and high-tech hardware useful in property administration and management.

Warehousing Education and Research Council (WERC)

If you require assistance in solving storage and warehousing problems, try contacting the Warehousing Education and Research Council for reference to a member near you who will be available for consultation. The WERC, composed of specialists in this field, conducts research and provides reports on improved methods for storage and warehousing. Another organization to try for information of storage problems is the Storage Council.

Tip Sheet
Choosing the Right Location

When starting a new business—especially one that depends upon a flow of customers, patrons, or clients—location is an essential ingredient in its success or failure. Even when the business is such that its principals and employees are on the road and there is little customer traffic flow on the premises, location can be vital to attaining necessary services and supplies in good time and at reasonable cost, as well as to minimizing commuting or travel time.

Manufacturers, too, have to take location into consideration, staying close to essential sources of supply in an area that will be cost efficient, easily accessible, and zoned for industrial production.

The formula for analyzing a location is known in business jargon as *trade area analysis,* which calls for analysis of two key factors: (1) deciding on the most promising community from a list of all those that are likely candidates, and (2) targeting a favorable site within that community.

The *trade area* is divided into three distinct zones of influence:

1. The primary trading area is the geographic zone within the community where you can expect the most business leverage. In the case of a retailer, this might influence 75 percent of total sales. In the case of a manufacturer or service company, the trade area might reduce costs by as much as 25 percent, as well as expediting transportation and communication.
2. The secondary trading area is the zone immediately beyond the primary one. This customarily accounts for as much as 20 percent of sales.
3. The tertiary trading area, third in line, can be important because it generates business from customers who do not reside in the area but still patronize the business, buying its products or using its services.

To conduct a productive trade area analysis, the American Marketing Association advises that you ask yourself the following questions:

- Is the population base near the site large enough to support my business?
- Does the community have a stable economic past and present that promises to provide a healthy commercial environment for my business?
- Is the demography—the nature of the population—compatible with the market I wish to serve?
- Are the community attitudes, outlooks, and culture likely to be harmonious in regard to my products or services and business policies?
- Will the location provide everything I need in the way of transportation and communication?
- Will the site maximize my ability to obtain sufficient internal and external help, at the same time minimizing commuting time and trouble?
- From a financial viewpoint, is the community acceptable to me in terms of taxes, assessments, and restrictions that might entail extra costs?

RECOMMENDED READING

Harris, Jack C., and Jack P. Friedman, *Real Estate Handbook* (Woodbury, New York: Barron's, 1993). Explains about 2,000 real estate terms and includes legal forms and financial tables.

Burstiner, Irving, *Small Business Handbook: A Comprehensive Guide to Starting and Running Your Own Business* (New York: Fireside, 1997). Well-organized advice for a wide range of business solutions.

Pickle, Hal B., and Royce L. Abrahamson, *Small Business Management* (New York: Wiley, 1990). Comprehensive and easy-to-understand guide.

Product Testing and Research

INTRODUCTION

One of the most vital fields of commercial research is directed at the design and manufacture of products and parts. Production engineering is devoted to the physical and mechanical means of perfecting products to meet market demands, satisfy purchasers, and turn a substantial profit for the manufacturer. Like all forms of research, this field of investigation, experimentation, and study depends upon a close working knowledge of new technologies and state-of-the-art procedures. Small businesses are often based on one great idea—one product, a better mousetrap, that leads business to their door.

In addition to a mousetrap, a new product developer needs people to buy the device. Essential is demographic product research, the in-depth analysis of people and populations. This field of study looks at a population from the standpoint of age, race, gender, marital and family status, income, ethnic background, faith, employment, nationality, and other personal characteristics, then attempts to associate these data with economic factors, such as consumer needs and demands, buying habits, discretionary spending, brand loyalty, and the like.

SOURCES OF INFORMATION

Advertising Research Foundation (ARF)

The Advertising Research Foundation was established for the purpose of advancing advertising, marketing, and media research, but it also is concerned with matters related to product testing and research to improve products and merchandise to meet the needs of consumers. Most small-business owners would not be likely to join this foundation, but they can turn to it for information on product research, literature in this subject area, and occasional reports on pertinent ARF workshops and conferences.

Consumer Product Safety Commission (CPSC)

Any manufacturer of products or materials should maintain regular contact with the Consumer Product Safety Commission, the independent federal regulatory agency created to administer the Consumer Product Safety Act, which protects the public against unreasonable risks of injuries and deaths associated with consumer products. The CPSC develops safety standards, enforces these standards, and bans products that do not meet them. This agency can be helpful if you have products in research and need to determine, in advance, whether they will meet CPSC standards before you invest needless time and expense in their development.

Inventors Workshop International Education Foundation (IWIEF)

The Inventors Workshop International Education Foundation was formed by volunteer inventors for the purpose of assisting inventors and entrepreneurs trying to create unique and marketable new products. The IWIEF provides members with a detailed evaluation that either encourages them to proceed with the development of ideas or suggests abandonment if the idea's potential does not warrant investment of further time and money. If you have one or more inventors on your staff—or if you are working with freelance inventors to perfect new products or materials—ask IWIEF how it can provide educational materials, include your people in seminars and workshops, or otherwise help your company.

National Institute of Standards and Technology (NIST)

The National Institute of Standards and Technology assists businesses, large and small, in applying new technologies that lead to greater productivity, higher quality, and more competitive products. It also provides seed money to help businesses conduct product research and testing.

Patent and Trademark Office (PTO)

Under the authority of the U.S. Department of Commerce, the Patent and Trademark Office administers U.S. patent and trademark laws. After reviewing applications, PTO grants protection to qualified inventions and the marks and symbols associated with them. If you need such protection or are creating new or redesigned products and need technological information before proceeding, contact this office for assistance.

Trademark Research Corporation (TRC)

Hand in hand with product research goes research to protect the names, symbols, and phrases that will promote them in the marketplace. If you are creating and selling new products, the Trademark Research Corporation can be a valuable resource to help protect the identity of your merchandise and avoid infringing on the commodities of other businesses. TRC is one of a number of professional organizations specializing in trademark-search services to determine the availability of a trademark and monitor the marketplace to detect infringements of their use. Searches are inexpensive and can be valuable in preventing legal hassles and large expenditures to revise designs when an ineligible mark has been used.

Tip Sheet
Research and Development for the Small Business

Research and development is an expensive process, and often out of the reach of small business. But small businesses definitely can benefit from R&D. In particular, you may become involved in:

- Remodeling your manufacturing capabilities (production engineering).
- Improving products to meet those of your competitors (product research).
- Streamlining your operations (operations research).
- Upgrading your training programs and job assignments (personnel research).
- Defining your markets and market potential more accurately (market research).

- Characterizing the population of your area (demographic research).
- Making your advertising more effective (advertising effectiveness studies).

There are more than 10,000 nonprofit R&D companies in the United States and Canada, along with government facilities, that may be able to provide information and referrals. Your closest and quickest taps of information about R&D resources are likely to be SCORE, Small Business Development Centers. You also can expect help from the Marketing Research Association, the Small Business Administration, the National Technical Information Service of the U.S. Department of Commerce, and the Office of Technology Utilization of the U.S. Department of Energy.

 ## RECOMMENDED READING

Gold, Robert J., *Eureka! The Inventor's Guide to Developing, Protecting, and Profiting from Your Ideas* (Prentice-Hall, 1994). Explores the particulars of inventing: researching, protecting your ideas, finding a patent attorney, and other issues. Includes sample letters and forms.

Nuese, Charles J., *Building the Right Things Right: A New Model for Technology Development* (Quality Resources, 1995). Presents a five-step process for planning, producing, and marketing a product.

Locating Sources
of Supply

 INTRODUCTION

Having the right office supplies on hand at the right time can considerably streamline the workday. Logical filing systems can prevent confusion and the expense of re-creating lost stores of information. Also, properly designed equipment can prevent injuries brought on by repetitive stress placed on vulnerable joints and muscles.

All this is part and parcel of designing a proper office system. Office systems vary extensively in type, complexity, and magnitude, depending on the size and nature of the business and many other factors. The term *office system* encompasses those functions involved in the operation of an office that are fundamental to the efficiency and productivity of a business, regardless of its field of operation. A productive office system is one that keeps the paperwork under control and avoids clutter, obsolescence, and confusion in that part of the business responsible for record keeping, facts, documentation, and presentations.

The establishment of an office system is an extension of good management. Like any sort of management function, office procedures, and policies are:

- Realistic and workable;
- Uniform throughout the company;

- Clear-cut and easily communicated to all levels of management and employees;
- In line with equal opportunity and other impartial and unbiased standards;
- Subject to review and revision whenever functional or operational changes occur that might affect them; and
- A direct responsibility of office management.

Office management implies planning, administration, and professional responsibility in the formulation of the structure and avenues of communication for all office systems, procedures, and related realms of performance. Office procedures are integral elements in any organization plan, whether for a commercial enterprise or a nonprofit institution. The management of an effective office system also includes:

- Supervising all clerical work and the personnel who perform it.
- Drawing up specifications for all standard office accessories, such as desks, filing cabinets, chairs, typewriters, calculators, reference books, copiers, electronic equipment, and stationery supplies.
- Administering all communications systems and policies, including those involving telephones, telegraph equipment, answering systems, mail processors, facsimile (fax) machines, electronic mail facilities, and other information transmissions.
- Planning, implementing, and monitoring bookkeeping functions, filing, and other forms of record keeping; specifying the physical and aesthetic designs and configurations of offices in the matter of furniture, fabrics, furnishings, heat, air conditioning, and lighting.
- Planning special events, such as seminars, training programs, and public tours that require the use of selected office space and systems for short-term occupancy; and monitoring quality control, which includes the installation of standards of design and decor, additions and renovation, and general compatibility with the rest of the physical environment.

Competent office management implies initial and continuing responsibilities for the effectiveness of these procedures.

SOURCES OF INFORMATION

Association for Corporate Growth (ACG)

The focus of the Association for Corporate Growth is largely on forums in which members exchange ideas for improving profits and growth, including mergers, acquisitions, and joint ventures for small firms. However, since many of the member firms are manufacturers of products and supplies used by businesses, special attention is paid to improved logistical methods for ordering supplies, controlling inventories, and making certain that supplies are adequate to meet changing demands, but never top-heavy. If you have supply problems, consider the ACG as a good resource for helping you solve them.

National Association of Purchasing Management (NAPM)

The National Association of Purchasing Management focuses its activities primarily on research and education in the fields of supply purchasing and equipment services, there is little incentive for you to join. However, NAPM is an excellent resource for information on how to better plan for controlling your supplies and equipment.

National Executive Service Corps (NESC)

The National Executive Service Corps is a nonprofit organization that provides management consulting assistance to small businesses (in much the same way that SCORE does). Its members are volunteers, largely retirees who have experience as executives and managers with corporations, in the education field or as professionals. They can assist you with problems relating to many small-business functions, including supply and materials management. You can benefit from the counseling and services of NESC at little or no cost, and with no membership requirements.

Small Business Foundation of America (SBFA)

Small businesses that have recently matured past the formation stage and are beginning to take hold and grow have an ally in the Small Business Foundation of America, which has become known as an advocate of emerging companies. The SBFA is a private, nonprofit organization that can advise you, among other things, on better ways to handle supply problems of all kinds. You do not need to hold a membership to obtain SBFA research benefits. The SBFA maintains a hotline that provides relevant information immediately and at no charge.

Support Services Alliance (SSA)

The Support Services Alliance is an organization of 12,500 self-employed people and business owners, primarily concentrated in New York (but gradually spreading into other states). The SSA was established to provide small businesses (with 1 to 50 employees) with direct access to low-cost supplies through group purchasing programs; educational seminars; and business services, such as office management, job placement, self-help manuals, and group health, dental, and life insurance coverage. Membership is required, but fees are moderate and based on a sliding scale according to the size of each member's organizational affiliation.

Office Supply Checklist

Maintaining the right level of supplies takes some planning. While running out of supplies is disruptive, being overstocked is expensive and a waste of storage space. Use the following checklist as a planning document. Delete items you don't use and add others you do, then list beside each the quantity you expend over the period of time for which you want to keep stocks in hand. Use this as your guide in anticipating needs and ordering replenishments:

Accordion files

Adhesives

Art supplies

Bank checks and forms

Binders

Business cards

Calendars

Cartons and shipping materials

Charts and graphs

Cleaning supplies

Computer accessories (types and specifications)

Correction fluid

Envelopes (style and size)

File folders

File labels and tabs

Forms (type and size)

Index cards

Invoices	Postage stamps
Labels	Printer, ink cartridges, paper
Light bulbs	Rubber bands
Notebooks and note pads	Stamp pads and inks
Paper (bond, copy, fax, carbon, etc.)	Staples
	Stationery, letterheads
Paper clips, fasteners	Tapes (types, sizes)
Pens, pencils, markers	Typewriter (and other) ribbons

Tip Sheet

Resources for Researching Your Purchases

With so much of your money at stake, it is wise to do all the homework you can before buying. Here are some options:

BUYERS LABORATORY

Since its inception over 35 years ago, more than 100,000 organizations have turned to Buyers Laboratory for reports on a wide variety of office products and services—from furniture to fax machines, from multifunctional devices to copiers. These extensive reports, which are the results of months of exhaustive testing, provide you with the good and the bad of such features as copy quality, reliability/downtime, cost per copy, maintenance, ease of use, throughput speeds, and more. For information, you can call Buyers Laboratory at 201-488-0404 or visit its Web site at:

www.buyers-lab.com

BUYER'S ZONE

An outstanding Web site called "The Buyer's Zone" lists information about a huge variety of office equipment, including copiers and fax machines. A key feature of this site is the Buyer's Forum, where you can get feedback from people who have already bought certain brands of equipment. Visit the Zone at:

www.buyerszone.com

CONSUMER REPORTS

Consumer Reports makes it product reviews available to America On Line members. Go keyword CONSUMERREPORTS.

RECOMMENDED READING

Attard, Janet, *The Home Office: Solutions for the Most Frequently Asked Questions about Starting and Running Home Offices and Small Businesses* (New York: Holt, 1993). Detailed guide to working at home or starting a small business. Written in clear, first-person narrative. Covers finding customers, pricing, insurance, choosing and "800" numbers. Appendices list business ideas, a glossary, resources, and state tax department addresses and telephone numbers.

Toth, Al, *Office Supply Buying Guide: How to Save 20 Percent to 60 Percent on the Cost of Office Supplies* (PBM Publishing, 1992). Practical advise; easy-to-follow ideas that are surprisingly workable. Will leave you wondering why you didn't think of these ideas yourself.

Manufacturing and Processing

 ## INTRODUCTION

Small manufacturers of products or processors of materials feel competitively threatened by large producers who have the capital and manpower to take advantage of computer-aided design, popularly known as CAD, and computer-aided manufacturing (CAM).

But during the 1990s, the margin of the small versus big handicap began dwindling markedly, thanks to galloping advances in desktop computer systems and huge price slashes for software and hardware. If you feel that you are not yet taking advantage of new technological advances available to manufacturing operations in the small to medium range, you need education and counsel—both readily available through private and government resources.

 ## SOURCES OF INFORMATION

National Association of Manufacturers (NAM)

Membership in the National Association of Manufacturers is recommended for small businesses engaged in the production of products, parts, or materials. NAM is involved in technological research, government regulations, industrial relations, taxation, logistics, legal matters affecting industry, and contacts with legislators to present manufacturers' viewpoints on laws and issues affecting their businesses. As a member, you also will have access to seminars, workshops, and literature on all phases of production, manufacturing, and processing.

National Institute of Standards and Technology (NIST)

The National Institute of Standards and Technology is the only federal technology agency with the primary mission of helping American industry strengthen its competitiveness against foreign companies. The NIST assists manufacturers of all sizes and types to achieve greater productivity, higher quality, and new and improved products and services. You may even be eligible for participation in ongoing manufacturing engineering research projects at the Institute's laboratories in Maryland and Colorado. Other NIST research involves chemicals production, electronics, computers, and materials.

U.S. Department of Commerce Technology Administration

As a branch of the U.S. Department of Commerce, this agency provides a focal point for small businesses concerned with the creation, production, and commercial success of technology-based American goods and services. An internal unit, the Office of Technology Policy, operates a variety of programs that reach out to business executives, professionals, and production managers with essential information and timely reports on such topics as automated manufacturing, research and development, technology commercialization, and government policies that affect manufacturing at all levels.

Tip Sheet
Manufacturing Engineering

Producers of products or materials should be familiar with the term *manufacturing engineering*. Also referred to as *production engineering*, this is the scope of operations that fits into the manufacturing sequence between product design and full-scale production. It encompasses the following:

- *Process engineering*, which develops the logical sequence of manufacturing operations for each product or part;
- *Tool engineering*, the adaptation of existing tools and the creation of new ones for the particular job(s) on hand and scheduled;

- *Materials handling,* the physical movement of materials and parts from one part of a plant or assembly line to another;
- *Plant engineering,* the designing of plant layouts to locate tools, equipment, personnel, and supplies so they can be processed in the most efficient and economical manner; and
- *Standards and methods,* a quality-control function which assures that each product or component complies with the exact specifications, and that working methods and practices support the specified procedures.

The purpose of manufacturing (or production) engineering is to design the product to overcome any problems foreseen in its eventual manufacture. One of the major responsibilities of a production manager in a small- to medium-size manufacturing company is to determine whether (a) to manufacture a product in toto or contract with another producer to do so, (b) let out contracts for some of the parts of a product, making the rest and handling the assembly, or (c) obtain all of the parts from an outside producer and be involved solely with assembly. The decision rests on many factors, including:

- Demand for the product, whether short- or long-term;
- Permanency of the product, whether it will virtually remain the same over the next few years or require substantial changes to avoid technological obsolescence;
- Competitive advantages gained by choice of product design or production equipment;
- Integration with other products, materials, and services offered by the company;
- Suitability of present manpower and equipment in regard to the end product;
- Effect on quality of the product;
- Cost of operating and maintaining the production equipment; and
- Source and availability of capital for each option.

 ## Recommended Reading

Dunac, William, *Manufacturing 2000* (New York: Amacom, 1994). Evaluates technological trends to help businesses getting ahead. Written by the director of material management for Macdonnell Douglas.

Jha, Nand K., *Handbook of Flexible Manufacturing Systems* (New York: Academic, 1991). Reviews steps in factory automation: planning, construction, and using software for simulation models.

Lottner, Bruno, *Manufacturing Assembly Handbook* (Butterwork-Heinemann, 1990). How to reduce costs in the manufacture of precision and electrical engineering products.

Thomas Register of American Manufacturers, 1997 (87th Ed) (Thomas Register, 1997). Comprehensive sourcebook.

Todd, Robert H., Dell K. Allen, and Leo Alting, *Fundamental Principles of Manufacturing Processes* (Industrial Allen, 1994). General discussion of 10 manufacturing processes including mass-reducing, joining, and surface treatment. Good illustrations.

Woodgate, Ralph, *Managing the Manufacturing Process: A Pattern for Excellence* (New York: Wiley, 1991). A practical guide that avoids theory and considers the technical side of successful manufacturing as well as the human element involved. Also considers questions of design, engineering, and buying materials.

Sales and Marketing

 INTRODUCTION

The term *marketing* involves the economic system by which goods and materials are sold and purchased and services are promoted. The process ranges from simple acts of buying and selling to highly sophisticated programs whereby goods are moved from suppliers to consumers.

Simple marketing activities began with the development of local trade, even barter, with goods being transported by individuals, caravans, and ships. A century ago, almost all marketing enterprises could have been classified as small businesses. Village markets, seasonal fairs, and peddlers all were involved in primitive marketing activities, followed by the birth of the general store and much later by supermarkets, chain stores, and the like.

Modern Marketing and Market Research

Modern marketing has evolved into a complex and sophisticated field with many interactions in related fields, such as sales, advertising, merchandising, promotion, publicity, retailing, wholesaling, discounting, transportation, distribution, and consumer research. Research has a major impact on marketing because an obvious objective is to acquire, retain, and satisfy customers. Typically, marketers begin by identifying the market for their product, then tailor their efforts to meet the needs and desires of customers within that market. Customers range from individuals to wholesale and retail chains, other companies, warehousers, and any organization—large or small—that might be interested in merchandise and services offered.

The Costs and Roles of Marketing

Marketing requires a substantial investment; its costs average at least half of the total expenditure of producing consumer goods. Marketing costs typically include product design, market research, consumer testing, distribution, credit plans, and warranties.

There is no limit to the types of organizations that require sound marketing techniques—even governments, nonprofit institutions, colleges, and political parties, to name a few.

Marketing in the United States has been greatly complicated by exterior forces over which marketers have little control, such as federal, state, and local government regulations; consumer movements on behalf of product safety; truth-in-advertising campaigns; unpredicted changes in taxation; and the increasing inroads of foreign marketers.

Global Trends in Marketing

With the growth of multinational corporations, marketing has greatly expanded its range and scope. For many modern companies, the whole world is their marketplace. It is not at all rare to see a major manufacturer introducing a product line simultaneously in a dozen or more countries, with advertising campaigns in as many different languages. Managers of such global marketing activities must take into account the multitudes of international differences in customs, business practices, protocol, and even the sensitivity of certain words, expressions, and viewpoints. This can be a problem for the small businessperson as well; growing internationalism has compelled many businesses to market globally.

 SOURCES OF INFORMATION

American Mailorder Association (AMOA)

The American Mailorder Association was established to assist organizations that use mail-order or direct mail marketing, many of them small or home-based businesses. AMOA can be helpful in a number of ways, whether for distributing your products more quickly and thriftily, receiving basic supplies on time, or both. And it can keep you posted on forthcoming changes in postal rates, packaging restrictions, foreign consignments, and the advantages of alternative shipment methods. Membership can be helpful to companies in the mail-order business, but is not necessary for business owners and managers seeking occasional information about mailings. The association distributes information on news and trends relating to business mailings, issues warnings about mail-order frauds, and provides data to legislators, particularly in a continuing effort to remove unnecessary restrictions and improve mail services.

American Marketing Association (AMA)

The American Marketing Association is a professional association of marketers, including many who are engaged in the management of small businesses. Dues are on a sliding scale, depending on the size and financial status of member companies. However, AMA also can be a useful source of information for non-members who simply want to keep abreast of marketing trends, practices, and case histories through AMA publications and reports, rather than internal programs and seminars.

A useful directory published by the AMA is *Marketing Information: A Professional Reference Guide, Third Edition,* by Hiram C. Barksdale and Jac L. Goldstucker (Eds.). The directory provides addresses, contacts, and telephone and fax numbers for the many associations, businesses, agencies, and other organizations involved in the marketing field. Other useful AMA publications include *Marketing Management* and *Marketing News.*

American Telemarketing Association (ATA)

Formed to assist businesses involved in telephone marketing sales, the American Telemarketing Association provides information and orientation, and takes action to prevent fraud and dissimilation in an industry that has had more than its share of problems. If you are engaged in telemarketing, which unfortunately has attracted many questionable operators, you may benefit from being in touch with an association that can provide useful guidelines and advice.

ATA publications include the *Journal of the American Telemarketing Association* and *Industry Reports.*

Association of Incentive Marketing

If your business engages in the use of incentives—the buying and selling of merchandise to be used as consumer premiums and for trade promotions—consider membership in the Association of Incentive Marketing. The group is composed of small-business owners and professionals in the field of incentive sales and marketing. Although membership is beneficial for incentive marketers who want to be actively involved in professional discussion groups, non-members can turn to the association for facts and statistics about the use of premiums in small-business merchandising ventures. You might discover that you are currently buying or making products that could be marketed as premiums, or that your company itself could profit by using premiums as customer incentives.

Association for Innovative Marketing (AIM)

Consider membership in the Association for Innovative Marketing if you need continuing, in-depth guidance about marketing—especially if you face unconventional marketing situations. If you have occasional need for innovative marketing ideas, you can contact AIM for the names of members who might be likely candidates to work with you as a consultant. Such a liaison could be productive, for example, if you are about to market a new product that requires unique or specialized merchandising techniques, or plan a new kind of technical service and must sell the idea to prospective clients in scientific fields of business.

For its members, AIM operates workshops and schedules meetings and seminars during which participants share and exchange marketing ideas.

Direct Marketing Association (DMA)

The Direct Marketing Association's interests and activities are aimed at helping companies that sell directly to customers, rather than through retail and wholesale outlets or outside salespersons. Included, for example, are catalog distributors, telemarketers, financial services, book and magazine publishers, music clubs, and other types of direct-selling businesses, many of them small or moderate in size. If you are engaged in direct marketing, membership could be beneficial. If you are not, but are considering such ventures, contact DMA for information about its services and resources.

The DMA publishes many useful books and research reports on direct marketing.

Direct Selling Association (DSA)

Direct Selling Association members are in the business of direct sales. If you are not in the business of direct sales but think it may be a marketing channel which will benefit your business, the DSA can provide you with information to help you analyze potential opportunities.

The DSA publishes a newsletter and reports on direct-selling activities. It also maintains lists of firms seeking retirees interested in becoming direct sales representatives.

Government Contracting Program of the Small Business Administration

One of the lesser known services of the SBA is its Government Contracting Program, which, among other operations, counsels small businesses on marketing their products in quantity to the U.S. government. This program increases small-business opportunities in the federal acquisition process by identifying sales and marketing needs and counseling business owners and managers on doing business with the government.

Marketing Research Association (MRA)

The mission of the Marketing Research Association is to upgrade marketing research and improve the quality of marketing and merchandising for companies of all sizes and in many fields. Although the association's membership is largely composed of professionals engaged in the planning and administration of market research, non-members can obtain information and reports about trends and techniques in marketing, including those that affect small businesses.

Minority Business Development Agency (MBDA)

The Minority Business Development Agency promotes economic growth by fostering minority entrepreneurship in the United States. Minority-owned businesses can obtain information and appropriate counsel and services in such areas as marketing, merchandising, retailing, wholesaling, and sales. Your easiest contact would be with one of the many Minority Enterprise Growth Assistance Centers, which are located across the United States.

MLMIA: The Association for Network Marketing

The MLMIA was founded as a trade organization for everyone involved in network marketing. The name refers to "Multi-Level (Network) Marketing," which has experienced unprecedented growth in recent years. MLMIA plays an active role in building better relationships between the marketing industry and regulators and others who impact and affect the operation of its members.

MLMIA publications include *MLM Magic, Network Marketing Windows of Opportunity, MLM Laws in All 50 States,* and *How to Build a Large Successful MLM Organization.*

National Retail Federation (NRF)

The National Retail Federation is an association for small businesses involved with retail. Its mission is to help retailers increase their traffic, improve their sales, and keep abreast of trends in merchandising and marketing. The Federation conducts research on retail trends and markets, provides training and educational opportunities for its members, and represents members' interests in federal, state, and local legislation. Although non-members cannot take advantage of NRF's primary services, they can turn to the Federation for reports on current issues and references to other sources of retail information.

The NRF has an active publications program that includes *Stores,* a monthly on retailing, and books titles such as the following:

Practical Merchandising Math

Credit Card Marketing

National Retail Federation Combined Financial, Merchandising & Coopers & Lybrand Software Directory for Retailers, Fifth Edition

Management of Retail Buying, Third Edition

1997 Annual Specialty Store Wage & Benefit Survey

Small Store Survival

Loss Prevention Guide for Retail Businesses

Value Retailing in the 1990's: Off-Pricers, Factory Outlets, and Close-out Stores

Retail Store Planning and Design Manual

Packaged Facts: The Electronic Retailing Market

Specialty Shop Retailing: How to Run Your Own Store

Masterminding the Store: Advertising, Sales Promotion, and the New Marketing Reality

National Telecommunications and Information Administration (NTIA)

For useful information and counsel on telecommunications as a marketing tool, contact the National Telecommunications and Information Administration, which is a division of the U.S. Department of Commerce.

For additional information about marketing for small business, read the following Tip Sheets: *Telemarketing, Distribution,* and *Collection Letter Techniques.*

Office of Consumer Affairs (OCA)

A branch of the U.S. Department of Commerce, the Office of Consumer Affairs provides consultation and technical and professional assistance to businesses that encounter customer-related problems. Contact with OCA is a good starting point for a company compiling data with the objective of making marketing plans for future growth.

Society of Competitive Intelligence Professionals (SCIP)

The Society of Competitive Intelligence Professionals is an organization of specialists who have the experience and ability to evaluate competitive business situations and counsel executives on methods to hone their competitive skills. As such, it is an association that only a handful of small-business owners might consider joining. Yet, you can turn to SCIP for professional referrals and literature if you are having serious problems with your competition and procedures for maintaining a competitive position in the marketplace.

U.S. Census Bureau

The U.S. Census Bureau (Web site: www.census.gov) is a tremendously useful research tool. The site contains data so specific about the 1990 census that you can find out how many people in your town took the bus to work when the census was taken. The Census offers downloadable software to utilize its information. Also on the Web site is an A-to-Z subject list that ranges from age statistics to zip codes. The site serves as a comprehensive demographic index. Current information, besides 1990 Census information also is available.

Telemarketing

Telemarketing is a direct-marketing program in which salespersons phone prospective purchasers, selected from prepared lists, and deliver sales pitches followed by requests for orders. The good news is that telemarketing is often profitable. The bad news is that the field is replete with scams and frauds, so much so that a Washington-based affiliation of more than 70 groups, called the Alliance Against Fraud in Telemarketing (AAFT), has been formed to protect consumers.

The AAFT advises that small businesses with telemarketing programs make certain that they are abiding by both the spirit and substance of the law, that they provide prospective customers with complete information about themselves and what they are selling, and that they avoid aggressive selling and overstated product or service claims. If you launch a telemarketing campaign, make it straightforward and consumer oriented, and spell out the details clearly.

When properly planned and initiated, telemarketing can provide you with a productive complement to your overall marketing program. It offers the following advantages:

- Quick, direct communication with prospects.
- A means of judging the listener's degree of interest and needs.
- The opportunity to add information about your product or service that meshes with the listener's own expressed personal interests.
- Obtaining the names of new prospects once an interested listener has been reached.
- Providing a more personal approach that often pays off better than an impersonal mailing. Personal feedback is useful in test marketing because you can obtain many reactions to your offer, promptly and distinctly.

Business owners also can lease telecommunications services offered by AT&T, MCI, Sprint, and others, and can acquire temporary 800 numbers. Since costs and services vary widely, comparison shop before undertaking any telemarketing campaign.

Marketing Information Online

There are many excellent resources available to Web surfers interested in marketing. Some of the information is free; in other cases, you can investigate and purchase services via the companies' Web sites. CACI Marketing Systems sells data, on diskette and CD-ROM, that help businesspeople reach consumers in particular areas of interest. Data are formatted for use with report generation and mapping software. The cost of data depends on the geographic area and the number of items you select on the Web site. You can get an online quotation at:

demographics.caci.com/data.html

FIND/SVP says it is the largest information services provider of its type in the United States, with sales of more than $25 million in research and consulting services. FIND/SVP performs custom research assignments including surveys, focus groups, and intelligence gathering. Find out more by visiting its Web site:

etrg.findsvp.com/etrginfo/fsvpinfo.html

The J. Paul Leonard Library home page provides an outstanding array of resources. Some are only available within the library at San Francisco State University, but others are electronic sources you can download. Categories of information in this easy-to-navigate site include marketing, industry surveys, consumer surveys, market statistics, advertising expenditures, and costs:

www.library.sfsu.edu/Instruction/guides/marketing.19.html

Standard Rate and Data Services is a major provider of media rates and data for the advertising industry. Its compilations of rates are available in major libraries, but an enormous amount of information is available at the SRDS Web site. There is a fee for services, but at the time this book went to press, SRDS offered a free trial period:

www.srds.com/index.html

Simmons Market Research provides marketing resource information on its Web site. The site lists over 7,000 full-service organizations, focus facilities, test kitchens, field services, malls, WATShouses, Moderators, transcribers, recruiters, and tab houses. Listings are for the United States and 75 other countries. Basic listings in the laboratory and on the Web site are free:

www.marketsresearch.com/index.html

Distribution

Distribution is essentially moving merchandise from the producer to the consumer directly, through various middlemen, or through retail points of sale. For the small-business operation, the appropriate type or types of distribution depend largely on the size of your market and the nature of the industry with which you are associated. The most common channels of distribution are:

- *Manufacturer's representatives,* salespersons who belong to agencies who handle many products, most of them in the same field, and who can distribute merchandise more effectively then the producer.
- *Wholesaler distributors,* who receive the items for sale from the producer and disburse them in turn to retailers.
- *Brokers,* third-party distributors who purchase items (often large in size and price) from producers or wholesalers and sell them to end users.
- *Direct sales,* the most proficient distribution channel, if the producer's plan is to market products directly to consumers.
- *Direct mail,* a form of direct sales with shipments going through the postal service or commercial carriers.
- *Retail distributors,* the channel opted by many small businesses when the end users are consumers.

Before selecting any method(s) of distribution, contact small-business associations and other sources for information, and also make a careful study of what your competitors are doing.

Tip Sheet
Collection Letter Techniques

People hate to write letters, hate to dun others, and hate to risk losing customers. Combine these three factors, and you can understand why the owners of a business are likely to be ineffective when writing collection letters. Passing the chore along to someone else only aggravates the situation, according to the National Association for Credit Management, which suggests that you establish your collection procedures and policies in a businesslike manner, stick to the point, and keep your cool. When writing a collection letter, for example, try this calculated sequence:

Letter 1: State the facts precisely and briefly, and request a timely response.

Letter 2: When a response is lacking after a reasonable time, refer to the first letter, request proper action, and enclose a duplicate bill or other necessary documentation.

Letter 3: Include a photocopy of the previous letter and express surprise or bafflement at the addressee's silence.

Letter 4: In a blunt, but restrained manner, refer to third-party action—a collection agency in the case of an unpaid bill, an attorney when a credit agreement is the problem, or some other professional known to take a no-nonsense position. Be prepared, however, to take the action that you spell out.

Tip Sheet
Retailing

The National Retail Federation asserts that the success of a retail operation depends on a number of key factors, including the following (not necessarily in order of priority):

- Nature of the competition.
- Demography of the local population.
- Proximity to a place of ongoing public interest.
- Parking facilities.
- Safety and security of the area.
- Volume of traffic.
- Availability of public transportation.
- Compatibility of neighboring shops and services.
- Attractiveness of the architecture and environment.
- Storefront and layout of the building.
- Ample merchandise display space.
- Sufficient space for storage and work rooms.
- Inventory and quick availability of back order goods.
- Courtesy, knowledge, and training of the clerks.
- Location where the economy is on the upswing.

 ## RECOMMENDED READING

American Demographics is a magazine focusing on business and the population trends that drive business. The magazine also features columns on subjects such as "Tomorrow's Markets," "Trend Cop," "Lifestyles," and "Current Conditions." The magazine is available on newsstands, and current issue and selected back issues are available from its Web site: www.demographics.com/publications.

Fuld, Leonard M., *The New Competitor Intelligence: Complete Resource for Finding, Analyzing, and Using Information about Your Competitor* (New York: Wiley,

1994). A guide to resources that will help business owners learn more about their competitors. Most useful for scouting American Companies.

Gerson, Richard F., *Marketing Strategies for Small Businesses* (Crisp, 1996). Over 225 low-cost ideas for marketing small businesses of almost any type.

Hodgson, Richard S., *Greatest Direct Mail Sales Letters of All Time* (Darnetell, 1986). Clear, concise approach to direct mail, offering many examples of how to effectively apply direct-mail principles.

Holtz, Herman, *Priced to Sell: Complete Guide to More Profitable Pricing* (Upstart, 1996). Setting prices for maximum profit for small-business people, consultants, and freelancers.

Keeler, Len L., *Cybermarketing: E-mail, CD-Rom Online Services* (New York: Amacom, 1995). This 332-page guide explains how to use new technology for marketing and is divided into three sections: cybertools, cybertasks, and cyberopportunities. The book includes illustrations and lists of useful resources.

Levinson, Jay Conrad, & Charles Rubin, *Guerrilla Marketing Online: The Entrepreneur's Guide to Earning Profits on the Internet* (Houghton Mifflin, 1995). Accessible guide specially written for small- and medium-size businesses, showing how to profit from the 'Net and Web.

Ramicitte, David F., *Do-It-Yourself Marketing* (New York: Amacom, 1994). Defines the basics of marketing for the novice. Includes chapters on target marketing, choosing a name, and designing a logo.

Shiffman, Stephan, *Cold Calling Techniques That Really Work* (Adams, 1991). In its third edition, this popular book now includes sections on reading decision makers and saving "lost" calls.

The *Survey of Current Business* is a monthly journal published by the U.S. Department of Commerce; it contains estimates and analyses of U.S. economic activity and includes the "Business Situation," a review of current economic developments, as well as regular and special articles pertaining to the national, regional, and international economic accounts. Also, the survey features current quarterly estimates of the national income and a "Business Cycle Indicators" section, which consists of tables for about 270 series and charts for about 130 series that are widely used in analyzing current cyclical developments. Each journal costs $9 and is available through the Government Printing Office, Ordering & Inquiry, North Capitol & G Streets, Northwest, Washington, DC 20401 (Phone: 202-783-3238).

Public Relations and Advertising

 INTRODUCTION

The terms *public relations* and *advertising* are often misunderstood and sometimes confused with one another. That is probably natural because there is much overlap between the functions, and the same firms and professionals often handle duties that straddle each field. This chapter provides definitions and explanations of the two.

Public Relations

Public relations (PR) is a broad term, but as it applies to most small-business owners, PR basically involves:

- *Promoting good will:* Businesses and individuals use public relations techniques to enhance their reputation and standing within the community.
- *Gaining favorable publicity, especially through the news media:* Positive exposure in the news is inherently valuable because people give greater credence to news than to advertising.
- *Dealing with the news media:* There are specialized techniques for attempting to line up news coverage, such as writing press releases in a style similar to professionally written news copy. Also, people involved in small business often answer inquiries from the press, including specialized publications covering the company's field. Sometimes, your interaction with the news media will involve

counteracting negative publicity or putting the best possible spin on an unfavorable development.

- *Reaching customers and potential customers through your own media:* Newsletters are a relatively inexpensive but highly effective method of maintaining a loyal customer base. Web pages can accomplish the same purpose if your customers are techno-savvy.

Public relations is fundamentally different from advertising, although advertising professionals and agencies do routinely handle public relations. Advertising almost always refers to messages placed on media for a fee. Advertising is space in a publication, time on a broadcast station, or a message on a billboard; in these examples, the content is solely determined by the advertiser, and the media are paid directly for time or space.

You don't pay for PR-generated news exposure, although the process of making the news can be expensive because it often involves hiring writers, mass-mailing of press releases, or staging of events. You also do not have strict control over the message because it will be reshaped by a reporter or editor.

PR techniques are relatively simple and easily learned by anyone with good language skills and common sense. You can build your business by:

1. *Sending regular press releases about your particular business:* Business editors need news, and if you can provide them with information that has legitimate news value, everyone can benefit. For example, a computer-store owner might make the news by providing the business editor with a well-written press release explaining how small businesses can set up a Web page for under $500. While most editors will not run the release verbatim, they will use such material as the skeleton of a story.

2. *Appearing on local radio and talk shows:* A financial services consultant might offer his or her services to explain the new varieties of retirement plans. You also can create positive publicity by appearing in person before civic groups with a similar message.

3. *Starting a newsletter or Web page:* One cigar store owner has boosted business considerably by mailing a monthly newsletter that carries interesting features about cigars and lists of specials targeted toward his customers.

4. *Staging an event:* A private-practice physical therapist in a small town recently mounted a 10K race on a Sunday afternoon. This brought

him media attention, community good will, and (apparently not coinciden-tally) some new patients on Monday morning.

5. *Cultivating media contacts:* A new computer database or an old Rolodex can be a superb promotional tool. By keeping track of who is oc-cupying which media position, you can cultivate a working professional relationship with that person. Send regular press releases and make an oc-casional phone call just to keep in contact. (People in media jobs change positions frequently, and simply by knowing the correct name and title of the person, you have already distinguished yourself from the pack.) This practice often results in a reporter calling *you* when needing a comment or looking for story sources.

Advertising

Many small-business owners think of advertising in a limited way, visual-izing local campaigns in terms of newspaper ads, radio commercials, brief television spots, billboards, and promotional literature. But advertising is a much more complex medium of communications to prospective consumers than most people realize. Newspapers, magazines, broadcasting, outdoor advertising, mailings, and graphics are but a few of the many elements.

The American Association of Advertising Agencies and the American Advertising Federation view advertising as being composed of three major elements, the first of which is probably the most familiar to you:

1. A form of communications, delivered to audiences large or small, gen-eralized or specialized, that is distinguished from other means of com-munication, such as PR or editorial matter, in that the advertiser pays the medium to deliver the message.

2. As a means of financing the mass media, in effect, providing as much as 75 percent of total revenues of newspapers and magazines and 95 per-cent of the revenues of radio and television stations.

3. As a component of our free-enterprise system, in which consumer pref-erences dictate what goods will be produced and what services will be available; in other words, a means whereby you and other businesses have benchmarks to determine what will sell best in the marketplace.

Advertising can be successfully geared to small, home-based businesses as well as to megacorporations. There are many forms of advertising that are inexpensive, easy to prepare and expedite, and bring in customers. Among them are the following:

- *Point-of-sale items,* such as posters, leaflets, business cards, and order blanks.
- *Classified ads,* in newspapers, periodicals, or newsletters. Start your campaign with small test ads, then gradually expand them as they pay off.
- *Shopper ads,* which are cheap, published in free tabloids distributed locally in shopping malls and other outlets.
- *Direct mail,* which gives you the advantage of reaching only a selective group of prospective buyers of your products or services. To avoid losing money, however, you must usually evaluate the potential results by starting with limited, low-cost test mailings.
- *Spot radio commercials,* which can be easily and inexpensively run in local markets, with quick results.

Many types of businesses can sometimes sidestep advertising costs by developing publicity, public relations campaigns, and press releases that are interesting and timely enough for the media to use at no charge.

 ## Sources of Information

American Advertising Federation (AAF)

If you are seeking information to help you plan and develop advertising campaigns for your products or services, you can probably obtain what you need locally by contacting several ad agencies in your area and getting estimates and proposals. But if you need broader information, or are not satisfied with what can be obtained locally, you can turn to the American Advertising Federation for assistance. You do not need to be a member unless your company has an active advertising department and you want to be regularly involved with professional issues and orientation. Since AAF works with advertisers to contest state and local threats to advertising interests and freedoms and protect advertisers from excessive government intervention, you can enlist its aid in seeking to eliminate local restrictions or constraints you feel are detrimental to your advertising campaigns.

American Association of Advertising Agencies (AAAA)

Like the American Advertising Federation, the "Four A's" can help entrepreneurs in a number of ways. The Association can be particularly useful, for example, for businesses seeking an ad agency to best serve their needs. Because the American Association of Advertising Agencies was formed to improve the advertising industry by setting standards of operation and monitoring advertising practices in all media, it can advise you about the kinds of ad campaigns that are effective, yet in good taste. If you have questions about the ethics of certain kinds of advertising, or grievances about competitors whose ads are misleading, the AAAA and the AAF are resources to which you can turn. If you are actively interested in knowing more about advertising as a tool for your business, inquire about becoming an affiliate member through your company's advertising agency. AAAA is divided into three regions with bureaus in New York, Chicago, and Los Angeles.

Association of Area Business Publications (AABP)

The Association of Area Business Publications members welcome regional news and reports and can be quite useful for small businesses trying to publicize products and services. A list of publications is contained in Part Three of this book.

City and Regional Magazine Association (CRMA)

The City and Regional Magazine Association can be helpful in locating magazines that carry news or advertising about your firm. The CRMA can help locate which magazines are published in the areas in which you sell products or services and which have readerships likely to be interested in news about you. CRMA is the only national association exclusively devoted to city and regional magazines, providing opportunities for its 60-some members to exchange up-to-date information and ideas.

Editorial Freelancers Association (EFA)

The Editorial Freelancers Association is a national, nonprofit professional organization comprising writers, editors, indexers, proofreaders, researchers, translators, and other self-employed workers in the publishing industry. EFA members are a source of writing talent for marketing and PR campaigns, or in working with staff members to compose articles and books for publication. The annual membership directory lists members by skill, specialty, and geographic locations; it is distributed to all members and circulates widely in the publishing industry.

International Association of Business Communicators (IABC)

The International Association of Business Communicators is an association of public relations, public affairs, marketing, advertising, employee communications, community relations, corporate relations, and investor relations professionals. If your business is on a growth path and you want to learn to expand your communications channels, contact the IABC for information about potential resources and options to consider. IABC has 117 chapters in the United States, Canada, the United Kingdom, Australia, Belgium, Hong Kong, Ireland, the Philippines, Mexico, New Zealand, and South Africa, with offices in San Francisco and Toronto.

Public Relations Society of America (PRSA)

Many small companies belong to the Public Relations Society of America, the world's largest organization for PR professionals. The Society's more than 17,000 members—many of whom include businesses with less than 20 employees—represent business, industry, counseling firms, government, hospitals, schools, professional services, and nonprofit organizations, among others. If you do not choose to join, you still can obtain information and publications to assist you in planning your own promotional campaigns. The PRSA Information Center, open to non-members, contains a large collection of public relations manuals, articles, reference books, and other materials, with information available on more than 1,000 subjects. The Center also conducts research via four electronic databases: DataTimes, Nexis, Dialog, and NewsNet.

PRSA publications include *Public Relations Tactics, Public Relations Strategist,* and the *Cyberspace PR Report.*

Tip Sheet
How to Choose an Advertising Agency

If you need only a small amount of advertising for your business, such as occasional newspaper ads, infrequent radio commercials, banners and signs, and a few items of sales literature, you can probably handle the job yourself. Newspaper advertising sales managers, broadcast stations, graphic arts studios, and printers are all at your service when they solicit your business. But if you have more complex needs, want to run special promotional campaigns, need help with market research, or could use some practical guidance when it comes to targeting the most likely prospects, an ad agency may be the answer.

Here are some tips on choosing an agency from the owner of a moderate-size agency, many of whose clients are small businesses:

1. Contact the AAAA to obtain a list of its members in your area, but don't overlook word-of-mouth suggestions from business people you know who have had experience with agencies.

2. Select several that seem likely, from the standpoint of their size, location, and current campaigns, and ask them for lists of their clients.

3. Study these lists and focus on those agencies that seem to have a preponderance of small businesses as their clients.

4. Call for appointments and interview representatives of the potential agencies to learn what services they offer organizations similar to your type and size.

5. Discuss finances candidly. Ad agencies traditionally make a large percent of their income through discounts from the media in which they place advertising, and thus charge you no more than you would pay when buying print space or broadcast time directly. However, they do charge fees and commissions for such services as graphic design, art, and photography; writing copy for ads and scripts for commercials; conducting consumer surveys; undertaking product research; and testing advertising in the field.

6. Ask which fees, commissions, and other charges are negotiable, particularly for those services you may need regularly. Most of these expenses can be negotiated, the amounts depending a great deal on how large or regular a client you may be, and how much advertising you intend to place in the future.

7. If you find that fees quoted by agencies or other advertising resources are too rich for your budget, seek out individuals who are professionals in advertising, graphics, or communications and who might be able to provide what you need at bargain rates, since they themselves have low overhead.

8. Talk to other clients, whom you know or whose businesses are somewhat similar in size and need to yours, and get their opinions of the agencies they use.

9. If there are no AAAA member agencies convenient to you, or if the ones you visit do not seem compatible with your objectives, stop by your local

Chamber of Commerce and ask for facts and suggestions. In areas not large enough, or commercial enough, to have accredited advertising agencies, such services are often handled, in a limited way, by graphic designers, printers, newspapers and periodicals, or other local media.

Tip Sheet
Letterheads and Stationery

The lettering, colors, and composition of letterheads and stationery can make as deep and powerful a point as the words written on them. Design elements are extensions of you and your company—as important as the way you dress, speak, and introduce yourself to potential customers or clients. Many people who are meticulous about the way they dress, and the quality of the clothes they purchase for business or professional wear, completely ignore the kind of impression they impart when it comes to printed communications.

"If you are in business of any kind that requires even a minimal amount of correspondence," advises the American Institute of Graphic Arts (AIGA), "a suitable letterhead is essential." It should not be treated as a routine necessity, says AIGA, as much as a PR tool. When properly designed and used on the right occasions, letters, business cards, and even imprinted memos or postcards, can upgrade your professional image and help to generate business. Your stationery supplies and letterheads need not be engraved, expensive, or elegant. More importantly, they should have style and class and reflect the kind of image you would like to implant in the mind of the recipient. It is acceptable to reproduce your company's logo on your letterheads, but it should be low key, moderate in size, and not give any blatant impression that you are in love with the colors and design.

The same graphic design standards hold true for business cards. The Graphic Artists Guild in New York has a collection of cards that are virtually unbelievable, with samples looking as though they had been printed on birch bark, colored every hue of the rainbow, cut in the shapes of diamonds and animals, fluorescent, edged in velvet, and conspicuous with cartoons.

Forget these stretches of the imagination. You are more likely to elicit the favorable response you want if you stick to tradition. The standard card is 3½ by 2 inches, and yours should not differ in size or shape unless you have an appropriate reason for the variation. The imprint should be limited to your name in the center, your title and company name in the lower left-hand corner, and the address and phone number(s) in the lower right-hand corner. A conservative style of type is preferable, such as block or roman, engraved in black on quality parchment or white card stock. A trademark or emblem is quite acceptable, if not too large, but a business slogan should not be imprinted, unless it is very short and customarily associated with the company's mark. If there is a reason for a brief message, such as the announcement of "50 Years of Community Service" or a listing of local affiliates, it should be on the back of the card.

When planning and ordering business cards, letterheads, and all other items of communication, advises AIGA, adhere to a uniform design throughout to build your company identity. If you must be thrifty, print simplified black-and-white stationery for internal use and a modest supply of more deluxe papers for clients and others you want to impress.

Tip Sheet
Demographics

Demographics has been described as "data that has been compiled and computed to present statistics about the makeup of population segments, specifically in regard to age, sex, education, location, income, ethnic background, and religious faith. Demography is the scientific study of the size, distribution, and composition of human populations . . . a branch of sociology that uses birth and death rates and related statistics to determine the character of a population, discover patterns of change, and make predictions."

Only in recent years has there been so much emphasis on the various demographic categories, a phenomenon that has occurred because of a number of meaningful factors that include:

- The growth of the senior citizens and retirement populations, particularly in regard to their regional orientations.
- Increased emphasis on minority groups and their expanding desires for ethnic products and services.
- The rise in the number of double-income families, in which both spouses bring home substantial salaries, while at the same time often requiring full-time child care facilities.

Although the growth of these and other demographic segments of the population has not always been large, the significant fact is that their voices have grown louder and more compelling in the marketplace. The producers and marketers of merchandise, goods, and services can no longer ignore them. The situation has been complicated, too, by the extremes in some of the population shifts from coast to coast, and most importantly in the relocation of marketing locales. One of the most significant shifts—and often disruptive to small businesses and local retailers—has been the shift of sales outlets and services from Main Street to suburban shopping malls. This has been devastating to the economic health and image of central areas of many towns and villages, where store fronts have been boarded up and litter is not removed, creating an atmosphere that discourages shopping anywhere in the vicinity.

All of these demographic factors should be taken into account by business owners who are making location and marketing plans. Fortunately, you'll find a wealth of demographic data in books and periodicals that address themselves specifically to this subject.

 ## RECOMMENDED READING

Baker, Kim, and Sunny Baker, *How to Promote, Publicize, and Advertise Your Growing Business: Getting the Word Out Without Spending a Fortune* (New York: Wiley, 1994). Specific techniques for low-budget PR. Several sections on staging events and displays at trade shows.

Cutlip, Scott (ed.), *Effective Public Relations* (Prentice-Hall, 1994). The bible of PR. A textbook, but well written and practical. Many examples from small business.

Hausman, Carl, and Philip Benoit, *Positive Public Relations* (Macmillan, 1990). This book is specifically written for one-person and small businesses. It includes major sections on writing press releases and dealing with the media.

Lant, Jeffrey, *The Unabashed Self-Promoter's Guide: What Every Man, Woman, Child, and Organization Needs to Know about Getting Ahead by Exploiting the Media* (JLA Press, in press). Take-no-prisoners advice from someone who's done it all.

O'Dwyer's Directory of PR Firms (J. R. O'Dwyer, updated yearly). Listings on 1,400 PR firms and 14,000 clients. Full contact information.

CHAPTER

21

Training and
Continuing Education

INTRODUCTION

According to a study by the National Federation of Independent Business, the most commonly mentioned problem of concern to small business was the need for "far more employee training than had been anticipated." A typical example is a financial manager whose department usually required six hours to prepare a monthly report, but was spending almost triple that amount of time when "aided" by a new computer system because of inadequate training on the computer.

Setting up a Training Program

Your first step in devising better training is to study programs in effect in other small companies that are similar to yours. If necessary, consider hiring an education consultant or contacting a training firm; and ask yourself the following questions when planning training and orientation programs:

- What is our short-term goal, our long-term goal?
- What does each participant need to learn?
- What type of training is necessary?
- What kind of training is likely to be most effective?
- How will the successful completion of a training program benefit on-the-job performances of our employees?

192

- What physical facilities will we need that are not already available?
- What cost factors are important, and how much will they add to our overall training budget?
- Can we obtain any kind of government funding for the curricula we have in mind, perhaps through the SBA?
- Will participants need job substitutes while they are enrolled, or can we integrate classes into normal work schedules?
- What about the timing and length of the training program?
- Which of our employees should be selected and how should they be screened as qualifiers?
- What controls, or checks, should we use to make certain our target objectives remain valid and clear?
- Should our program be publicized internally and promoted, and if so, how?

Career Counseling

Owners of larger firms, say 50 employees or more, can benefit from taking courses in career management, or appointing a training expert to handle training and career counseling duties. Career counseling is an essential role in the development of any growing small business. A major purpose of such personnel counseling has been to solve some of the increasing educational/occupational problems that afflict young people coming into the job market. Such problems include school dropouts, graduates, and near-graduates leaving high school without marketable skills or ambitions and with foggy personal goals. It has become evident, too, that far too many high school graduates aim at college-degree programs that would provide few job-seeking capabilities, and shun vocational or technical schooling that might be far better roads to satisfying and remunerative employment.

The purpose of career management is not only to attempt to place the right people in the right positions, but also to undertake a number of personnel evaluations that include:

Assessing skills, abilities, interests, and attitudes;

Determining qualifications needed for different occupations and assignments;

Defining career goals and plans for attaining them;

Identifying educational and training opportunities;

Isolating factors that might impair career development; and

Pinpointing resources, both internal and external, where additional help is available.

 ## SOURCES OF INFORMATION

American Society for Training and Development (ASTD)

The American Society for Training and Development is an association of professionals in the field of employee training and as such, is not an organization that would be helpful for many small-business owners to join. However, it can provide literature at little or no cost on instructional programs for the workforce, give you cost estimates, and provide the names of training firms and professionals in this field.

As noted in the listing in Part Three, ASTD publishes a directory of training professionals, listing them by speciality and geographic region. The directory also is available on CD-ROM.

American Women's Economic Development Corporation (AWED)

The American Women's Economic Development Corporation was formed to assist women who owned or planned to start small businesses. It sponsors training and technical assistance programs and counsels women entrepreneurs through volunteer advisors knowledgeable in specific problem areas.

AWED's publications include "In Business," a bimonthly newsletter.

Business Schools

Business schools have specialized entrepreneurship programs; many are of recent vintage but some—notably Babson College—are of long-standing. Babson, especially, is known for the breadth and depth of its entrepreneurship programs. Many of these schools have executive education programs and some will tailor a program specifically for your company. Part Three contains a list of the major graduate schools of business.

Center for Creative Leadership

The Center for Creative Leadership is an excellent source of management and leadership programs for senior people in large and small companies. It publishes the *Journal of Management Consulting.*

Center for Workforce Preparation (CWP)

The chances are that your business, like some 70 percent of small businesses in the United States, are a member of your local Chamber of Commerce and can avail yourself of its programs and benefits. Yet many business owners are not familiar with a useful affiliation of the Chamber, the Center for Workforce Preparation. The CWP focuses on small businesses, with the goal of helping them compete with larger competitors. The Center provides employee instruction programs that are beyond the capability or budget of local companies, collaborates on recruitment programs to attract skilled workers to smaller shops, provides training equipment too costly for purchase by small businesses, and hosts school-to-work transition programs to reduce the exodus of young people to the big cities and large corporations.

You can obtain from CWP a number of publications with an educational slant, such as training for positions in small businesses, bridging the literacy gap, community efforts to achieve national education goals, and business glossaries.

Institute of Lifetime Learning (ILL)

The Institute of Lifetime Learning was founded more than 30 years ago as a pioneer in continuing education courses for adults, and has extended its programs to encourage small companies to interest their employees in courses that might enhance their careers. ILL also provides technical assistance to small businesses, such as teaching aids, computer programming, software, and a directory of educational centers. If your company could benefit by motivating your employees to sign up for courses, contact the Institute to find out what curricula are available that would fit your company's needs. There are no initial fees or dues.

National Institute for Occupational Safety and Health (NIOSH)

The National Institute for Occupational Safety and Health is an excellent source of information about safety laws and regulations that are mandatory in the workplace. The Institute can provide useful literature on safety and emergency programs and can steer you to other sources of information on training and orientation in this field.

National Safety Council

This voluntary nongovernmental organization offers extensive programs in safety training, home-study safety courses, a research library, and a wealth of literature on safety programs for just about every kind of job and every category of business and industry you could name. Membership is not required.

National Safe Workplace Institute (NSWI)

The National Safe Workplace Institute provides educational programs, literature, and research on issues related to occupational health and safety. As a small-business owner or manager, you can contact the Institute for constructive recommendations and sources relating to safety practices and on-the-job training.

National Speakers Association (NSA)

The National Speakers Association has 3,500 professional members and provides speakers to businesses and nonprofit organizations on a wide variety of topics, including competitiveness, customer service, retailing, salesmanship, improving productivity, management, communications, public relations, new technologies, economics, the environment and pollution, selling to the government, motivating employees, taxes, and personnel administration. NSA publishes a 400-page *Guide to Professional Speakers,* and also will record the texts of speeches when requested by clients. Books and other publications by its speakers are available.

Office of Business Education and Management, Small Business Administration (OBEM)

Through its Office of Business Education and Management, the SBA works with technical experts, resource specialists, and professionals from educational institutions, SCORE, and the private sector to provide management and technical training and educational programs to small businesses. OBEM also supplies publications, workbooks, audiotapes, videotapes, and other media for training purposes, and lists sites on the Internet for obtaining similar educational materials via computer.

Small Business Resource Centers

Small Business Resource Centers are located across the United States, functioning in association with local Chambers of Commerce. They can be of invaluable help to the owners and managers of small and home-based businesses because they not only steer them to local sources and resources, but also provide information about business-related educational programs, such as marketing workshops, seminars, business-to-business expositions, conferences, public speakers covering educational topics, and orientation liaison projects between business and government. (See also the entry for Association of Small Business Development Centers.)

U.S. Department of Education National Institute on Postsecondary Education, Libraries, and Lifelong Learning (USDE)

You might find it useful to contact one of the divisions of USDE—the National Institute of Postsecondary Education, Libraries, and Lifelong Learning—for assistance with employee instruction and training. The Institute conducts research and develops procedures to expand the training of adults in a variety of settings, including the workplace. In this respect, it can guide small businesses into improved curricula to enhance and supplement on-the-job orientation programs.

For additional information, read the following Tip Sheets on Video and Online Sources of Continuing Education and Business Information Centers on the Web.

U.S. Department of Education Office of Educational Research and Improvement (OERI)

The Office of Educational Research and Improvement serves as the principal adviser to the Secretary of Education on educational research, statistics, and practice, as well as on the dissemination of information to improve the quality of education. OERI assists in developing and implementing federally supported educational research and improvement efforts. Although the functions of OERI are broad, a number of its divisions are potential resources for the owners and managers of small and home-based businesses who are seeking ideas and assistance for orientation programs, training, and continuing education.

Tip Sheet

Video and Online Sources of Continuing Education

You can take courses by video and computer/modem. An excellent resource for locating Web-based courses is the Global Network Academy, which lists contacts for hundreds of Web-based courses, at:

www.gnacademy.org:8001/uu-gna/index.html

The U.S. Chamber of Commerce provides satellite television courses to hundreds of locations around the nation. Call the Chamber (202-659-6000) or visit its Web site:

www.uschamber.org/index.html

Tip Sheet

Business Information Centers on the Web

One of the more recent additions to the services offered by the SBA is the nationwide chain of Business Information Centers (BICs). BICs allow entrepreneurs to educate themselves about the market, business practices, technology, and financial planning, and a variety of technology is available to facilitate such, including computers, graphic workstations, CD-ROMs, and videotape players. Each BIC is stocked with reference materials, software, videotapes, and interactive tutorials. You can find out more about BICs by accessing its Web site:

gopher://gopher.sbaonline.sba.gov

See the sample site on page 199.

 RECOMMENDED READING

Culligan, Matthew J., *Management 101: The Best Back-to-Basics Techniques* (Prentice-Hall, 1993). Good sections on motivating and training employees, as well as much other practical advice.

Hansen, Mark Victor, and Joe Batten, *The Master Motivator* (Lexington, MA: Heath, 1995). Explains secrets of motivation and training, showing links between the two functions.

The Portable MBA Series is a multivolume set of books that provides overviews, written in plain English, of the courses offered by the typical MBA program. Titles include: *The Portable MBA Desk Reference: An Essential Business Companion, The Portable MBA in Economics, The Portable MBA in Entrepreneurship, The Portable MBA in Entrepreneurship Case Studies, The Portable MBA in Finance and Accounting, The Portable MBA in Investment, The Portable MBA in Management, The Portable MBA in Marketing,* and *The Portable MBA in Strategy.* All are published by John Wiley & Sons, Inc.

Trainer's Handbook: The AMA Guide to Effective Training (New York: Amacom, 1998). First-hand reports from the trenches. Authoritative.

Mergers, Acquisitions, and Joint Ventures

 INTRODUCTION

Mergers and joint ventures, in business jargon, can make one and one equal three. In other words, adding the talents and capabilities of two organizations can ignite a spark that makes the business take off—producing a whole that is greater than the sum of its parts. This could be accomplished through a formal merger of the two companies, by joint ventures on certain projects, or the acquisition of a complementary business. But a merger, joint venture, or acquisition is not a sure-fire solution to a business's problems, nor is success guaranteed. Before entering into what can be a complex arrangement, ask yourself the following questions, focusing on whether you can fix your internal problems before looking elsewhere:

- Do you have a written plan setting out the goals you want to achieve in the next five years? Has it been revised recently?

- Can you prove that you have made progress toward the goals with hard numbers?

- Can you generate a cash flow without having to suffer through too many dry spells?

- Does your accountant prepare and thoroughly explain reports other than tax returns, such as monthly profit-and-loss statements and balance sheets?

- Have you consulted experts recently about financial or marketing strategy?

- Have you talked about your business with your bank's loan officer, even though a loan wasn't the object right then?

- Do you know your break-even point and whether you are on target for reaching it?

- Do you know how much it actually costs to make each sale?

- Do you know how much inventory you have on hand?

- Do you belong to a trade association for your industry or profession?

- Do you read the same publications that your competitors and customers read?

- Do you consistently study your competitors' ads and read their sales literature?

- Do you talk regularly about business-related topics with other small-business owners?

- Do you get regular feedback from your customers and follow their suggestions?

- Do you have periodic training sessions and regular motivational workshops for your employees?

If the business is still foundering despite honest affirmative answers, be as sure as you can that the operations of the target company complement yours and that the other firm can counter your weak points. The ultimate point is that there's little to be gained by mating two foundering companies that essentially perform the same functions. Look for complementary areas where a match-up can multiply, rather than just add, your company's capabilities. This issue is addressed in the Tip Sheet "The Pluses and Minuses of Mergers and Joint Ventures."

 ## SOURCES OF INFORMATION

Institute of Certified Business Counselors (ICBC)

The Institute of Certified Business Counselors is a nationwide network. Its membership consists largely of professional accountants, attorneys, brokers, appraisers, and consultants, all involved in the valuation, acquisition, sale, or transfer of businesses. Businesspeople who are in none of those categories can turn to the Institute for information and sources when having serious thoughts about mergers and acquisitions. ICBC, either directly or through its membership, offers training and advice on how to buy and sell a business, including suggestions on what to look for in any prospective proposal.

MicroLoan Demonstration Program of the Small Business Administration

The MicroLoan Demonstration Program is an ongoing entity under the Small Business Act that authorizes the SBA to guarantee loans up to $25,000 to small businesses that cannot obtain financing on reasonable terms through normal lending channels. Proceeds cannot be used to pay debts, but one of the valid uses is for expansion, such as an acquisition or a joint venture. Similar programs are available specifically for small businesses run by women, minorities, or the disabled.

For additional information, see the following Tip Sheets: "Buying a Business" and "The Pluses and Minuses of Mergers and Joint Ventures."

The National Business Association (NBA)

The overall mission of the National Business Association is to assist small- and home-based business owners and managers in achieving their personal, commercial, and professional goals. Most importantly, it maintains close working relationships with the SBA and other organizations throughout the nation that assist small businesses. Membership is worth considering because NBA offers an array of benefits and services and holds seminars and workshops that make it possible for you to discuss such subjects as mergers, acquisitions, and other crucial changes in your business operations on a one-on-one basis with other small-business owners.

National Federation of Independent Business (NFIB)

Of the many associations that have been formed to represent entrepreneurs, the National Federation of Independent Business is by far the largest, with offices in all 50 states and some 600,000 members. As such, it has accumulated a wealth of information and research studies on such matters as mergers, acquisitions, and joint ventures of all kinds. You do not have to be a member to take advantage of the Federation's activities on your behalf or to obtain reports and suggestions about issues of this kind that affect small business.

National Small Business United (NSBU)

The National Small Business United is one of the most popular emissaries of small business in America, with 65,000 members representing every facet of the small-business world. Many members are leaders in programs and activities designed to develop and improve small-business operations, locally and nationally. NSBU conducts research in all sectors of small business, including mergers, acquisitions, and joint ventures, and makes surveys of its members on economic and operational issues. The results of these surveys and studies can be useful if you decide to join NSBU. The association also hosts seminars and workshops on starting, administering, and growing small businesses, and serves as a liaison with government agencies in business and industrial fields. NSBU also does research in many other areas, including advertising, marketing, training, recruitment, and labor relations.

Tip Sheet
Buying a Business

Many entrepreneurs who do not have the know-how to build a business from scratch or expand their existing business into unfamiliar areas buy an existing firm. There are advantages to buying an established firm. According to the Association of Small Business Development Centers, buying an existing business can save time and avoid many of the errors that you might make in developing your own business from ground zero. Everything is in place: from facilities and customers, to a credit line at the bank.

The American Small Businesses Association notes some other advantages to buying an existing business:

- You can enjoy successful involvement much sooner.
- You don't have to wait so long to see profits.
- The return on your investment will be in hand long before it would have been had you started from the ground up.
- You can easily visualize what is taking place, given an established customer or client register, reliable suppliers, and employees who have had training and experience.
- Your investment in the purchase of the business represents the total, and you don't have to lie awake nights wondering how much equipment and initial supplies are going to cost.
- Financing for future growth or diversification will be less a headache because the business already has a credit rating and performance record.

- The previous owner, if cooperative, will be a good consultant.
- The track record is already in the books for examination and evaluation.

But there are perils and drawbacks to buying a business. To name a few:

- The equipment, though adequate at the time of purchase, may be obsolescent and in need of change.
- The company image in the community may not be all that the owners imply and difficult to change.
- The location may be downgrading, either demographically, economically, or both.
- There may be hidden reasons why the owner wants to sell the business. A fundamental reason for putting the business on the block may be that it is about to fail, for reasons that might not be apparent on the surface.
- The business may be undercapitalized, so that what you pay for its purchase is not really enough to maintain it in good economic health.
- The business may have liens or lawsuits pending that are not yet evident to an outsider.
- The appraised value of the business may be too high because of misrepresentation.
- There may be new competition entering the marketplace of which you are not aware.
- There may be hidden loans, overdue loan payments, or other obligations not readily apparent.

Do some sleuthing before making a bid for a business. Among other steps: (1) Determine the company's record of bill payments, and be suspicious if they often run over 60 days; (2) gauge the cash flow to determine whether the business is properly capitalized by examining its bank statements; and (3) run a credit check on the company through the local credit bureau, determining whether the business experiences cycles or is seasonal. Be mindful of false impressions of its average degree of business activity.

Tip Sheet

The Pluses and Minuses of
Mergers and Joint Ventures

If you have been considering a merger or joint venture, you must project yourself into the company with which you intend to merge. Ask yourself these questions:

Do I have firm reasons for wanting a merger and can justify the benefits so derived?

Will this kind of partnership add strength to areas in which my company is weak? Will it fill strategic gaps?

Will the merger give me access to new markets, funds, and management strength without forcing me to risk untried ventures or seek new capital?

Have I carefully calculated the costs, not only in money, but in terms of our resources and personnel?

Would the merger entail any conflicts of interest, or even potential liabilities?

Have I established good communications with the company with which I would like to merge? Have we discussed our mutual expectations and responsibilities, and can we grow together in new geographic areas or markets targeted for the future?

What kind of alliance would be most compatible—an informal partnership, a temporary consortium, or a formal joint venture?

According to the Association of Small Business Investment Companies, the most common type of merger is that of the small, relatively young company with special qualities but limited resources with a larger, more experienced corporation that offers marketing, production, or managerial know-how, and often special facilities, equipment, or technology. Whether merged for a single project, for a limited time, or for a continuing relationship, a joint venture stands a better chance of achievement if both parties have a clear understanding of their mutual goals and future prospects together.

 ## RECOMMENDED READING

Bloom, Martin H., *Business Buying Basics: Your Step-by-Step Guide to Buying a Business* (Erdman, 1992). Very specific, lots of examples.

Robb, Russel, *Buying Your Own Business* (Adams, 1995). Notable for its good coverage of financing these deals.

Snowden, Richard W., *Complete Guide to Buying a Business* (New York: American Management Association, 1994). Highly recommended. Includes self-assessment guides and exceptionally concrete directions for searching out, pricing, and purchasing a business.

Getting Connected: Computers, the Internet, and the World Wide Web

INTRODUCTION

In the past, businesspeople associated computer systems more with large corporations and government agencies than with small business. But today, the trend is actually reversed; it is the small business that relies on the computer as its most valuable means of competing with mid-size and large companies.

The National Federation of Independent Business reported that computer use by small companies increased at a rate of more than 10 percent a year, on average, during the 1990s. This statistic can be attributed to the following key factors:

1. The dramatically decreasing cost of computer hardware.
2. The rapidly escalating production of software programs in every conceivable subject field.
3. The substantial and continuing increase in online services by major communications corporations.
4. The increasing familiarity with computers on the part of small-business leaders.
5. The widespread sophistication of employees in computer functions and programming.

6. The extensive availability of computer courses for laypersons, at reasonable tuition fees.

Many suppliers of computers and related products for business use offer reliable orientation, and even consultation, at no charge. In addition, reports the SBA, these companies provide a useful source of information on general descriptions of particular management techniques, as well as help on specific management problems.

 ## SOURCES OF INFORMATION

Business Technology Association (BTA)

Membership of the Business Technology Association is comprised of mainly dealers, technical systems integrators, manufacturers, and distributors of high-tech communications networks, computers, copiers, facsimiles, scanners, dictation equipment, telephone installations, document imaging systems, and multifunctional devices. However, it can be a useful source of information for small businesses that rely on data-processing equipment and state-of-the-art communications systems and products for their operations. BTA sponsors educational programs and publishes reports on new products that can give a company a competitive edge in its technical field.

BTA publishes *Business Technology Solutions,* a monthly magazine that features articles from industry experts and new product updates; and a membership directory.

The Small Business Administration Home Page

The SBA publishes an "Internet Business Resource Sampler" to provide online services geared especially for small businesses to help them compete with companies much larger in size and with far greater communications budgets. The SBA regards the Internet as a valuable business tool and notes that the 'Net provides endless opportunities for establishing business contacts.

You can obtain an "Internet Business Resource Sampler" from the SBA, which will provide you with many possible sources for business intelligence and contacts, along with the appropriate Internet numbers. Your Internet contacts include such institutions as the U.S. Bureau of Labor, business schools and journals, marketing organizations, public information centers, and the SBA itself.

www.sbaonline.sba.gov/

The SBA's home page offers simple menus, extensive information on a wide variety of business topics, and contacts to other government organizations. There are extensive sections on starting and financing your own business. More to the point for this chapter, the SBA home page also features many entries on computerization and an extensive software library. Access also is available to SBA On-Line, a bulletin board linking you to others in small business.

For additional information, refer to the following Tip Sheets: "Alleviating Inventory Woes" and "Crash Courses on Computers and the Internet."

Tip Sheet
Alleviating Inventory Woes

One of the least attractive chores in business, according to a survey taken in the mid-1990s by the American Federation of Small Business, is keeping track of inventory. But accurate inventory-keeping is vital since many businesses have substantial proportions of their budgets allocated to the storing and maintenance of products, goods, materials, and operational supplies. Inventory trailing, which can mean the difference between profit and loss in a small business, is not simply a matter of counting products in the stock room or warehouse; it affects many other areas of business, including:

- The timing of purchases.
- The entire marketing and sales program.
- The calculation of taxable income and deductions.
- Security procedures and protection from thefts.

The first requisite for sound inventory control and tracking is to establish a computerized system that will improve accuracy, as well as lighten the burden of keeping track of items. The second requisite is competent purchasing of all items, whether for distribution and sale or for company functions and operations. Such purchasing must take into account seasonal variations, business growth or decline, and the possibility of emergencies that could affect business if certain commodities were out of stock.

Computer inventory is clearly superior to hand tracking because of the ease with which items can be entered into the database and sorted by category. Also, bar-coding devices can label and enter the items into inventory with the swipe of an electronic bar code reading pen.

When taking an inventory, follow these steps:

1. Check all items precisely against invoices to determine whether the quantities are correct.
2. Make sure the prices, quoted and listed, are what they should be.
3. Check the totals against original orders to be sure the types and quantities agree with the specifications.
4. Check incoming items for damage, improper packaging, or (in the case of perishables) proper shelf life.
5. List and report any and all discrepancies immediately to the supplier, transporter, or agent.

Inventory control is often faulty because of laxity in inspection and record keeping. In many businesses, record keeping and the actual handling of inventory items are supervised in different locations and under different supervisors. Therefore, both coordination and computerization are essential to effective inventory control.

Tip Sheet

Crash Course on Computers and the Internet*

Computers mystify some and terrify others. While computers can be complex, and the programs they run mulish and arcane, the basic concepts really are not that complicated. And understanding the basics de-mystifies the business of computers considerably.

Let's begin with an explanation of the binary code that runs computers. Binary means "two," and binary functions have been around for a long time. For example, looms in the 1700s were automated with punch cards. If a wire finger felt a hole in a punch card, it would use one color thread; no hole, a different color. Stacks of punch cards could be used to automate an intricate pattern.

It didn't take long for people involved in the business of counting to embrace this new on-and-off technology. One application: In the 1880s, the population in the United States was growing so quickly that it was difficult to count. James Burke, an historian of technology, writes that it took eight years to tabulate the results of the 1880 census. Why was this so difficult? In addition to counting the raw

---

* *Source:* Adapted from *The Connected World,* by Carl Hausman (St. Martin's Press, 1998).

number of people in the country, census takers needed to correlate the results, mixing various figures to produce specific results (e.g., how many people who *own their own homes* also *have children?* How many *veterans* are *unemployed?*).

In the late 1800s, an official of the census ordered a young engineer named Hollerith to use this evolving on-and-off technology to solve the problem. Hollerith used cards the size of a dollar bill (so he could take advantage of machinery already built to handle dollars) and punched holes corresponding to the various bits of information that needed to be sorted. This allowed his machine not only to count but also *manipulate* the information.

The secret to the computer's speed and reliability is the simplicity of this on-and-off system, known as the binary system.

You can move around a lot of information using a binary system. For example, the software program used to write this book represents the letter a as: off-on-off-off-off-off-off-off-on,—or numerically, with 1 standing for "on"— 010000001.

These eight "bits" of binary information represent what is called one "byte." A byte is not a particularly handy way to measure the size of a binary file because you quickly would find yourself having to use huge numbers. Therefore, it is easier to measure by kilobytes (one thousand bites) or megabytes (one thousand kilobytes), or gigabytes (one thousand megabytes).

A page of double-spaced manuscript uses about 1.25K (kilobytes) of binary information, or 1,250 bytes, or—since each byte is eight ones and zeros—8 × 1,250 = 10,000 digits.*

If you had a lot of ambition and an unusual amount of time on your hands, you could punch those 10,000 digits into cards and automate word processing by building a mechanical typewriter that works like an automated loom, pounding out the same page time after time. But you would soon long for the flexibility of an electronic computer that could move those strings of bits along at literally light speed. (Electricity and light both move at 186,000 miles per second.)

So instead of mechanical devices for counting and manipulating bits, scientists in the 1940s and 1950s came to use sophisticated series of vacuum tubes. These tubes allow us to amplify, move, and redirect streams of electricity that carry on-and-off digital information. What is usually thought of as the first modern computer, the UNIVAC, used thousands of these tubes. But tube technology has built-in limitations. Tubes need a lot of power and room, and as a result, there is a built-in cap on computing power. UNIVAC took up a whole room and

---

* These numbers are close but not exact because a computer counts in exponents of 2 and can't actually multiply to exactly a thousand when calculating its own number of bits and bytes. The closest it can come is 1,024. Because humans count in multiples of 10, we are more comfortable rounding off the numbers. This only applies to the computer's generation of bits and bytes and does not affect the ability of a computer to handle math. The level of the calculations we see have been rounded off for us.

used as much electricity as an electric stove with all its burners on, and couldn't do as much as today's hand-held calculator.

The answer to this problem was the solid-state circuit. Small pieces of mineral substances can perform roughly the same function as electron tubes. One such devise, the transistor, became common in small radios. The computer industry still needed to overcome the difficulty of wiring thousands of transistors together on a board and turned to a photographic process, where a large layout of the electronic pathways is reproduced on a small chip of mineral. The substance that proved most adaptable was silicon, and the center of the computer industry became a low-lying area known, at first in jest, as Silicon Valley.

The silicon chip enables computation using an enormous amount of digits "put through" the computer brain at high speed. This, in turn, allows the throughput of enough digits to reproduce text, sound, and pictures. In other words, media passing through the so-called "Information Highway."

The Information Highway is an imprecise term, and aside from providing reporters with endless opportunities to create metaphors ("road kill along the . . . ", "stuck on the on-ramp to the . . . "), it probably does little to help our understanding of the digital world. There is, for starters, no one discrete *highway* along which the information travels. In fact, it is the ability of digitized transmissions to take *side roads* that makes the process revolutionary.

A more accurate term is *digital infrastructure.* An infrastructure is the broad, over-arching arrangement and design of a system. It is the worldwide availability of computers, digital transmission pathways (wires or transmission through the air), and links among those lines that allows you to tap into the flow on the figurative highway. Upgrading this infrastructure will allow:

- One source of entertainment, news, and communication that mates your PC, television, and telephone. Media will converge, meaning "come together in one pathway."

- The ability to tap into a sea of digitized information: online libraries; government collections of data, catalogs, magazines and newspapers; and so forth. Above and beyond that, the capability to search among these options for the specific information or programming we seek.

- Two-way video communication used in business conferencing and education.

- Virtually infinite choice of programs. While we may not see "500 channel TV" it is likely that we will have significantly more program offerings and the ability to "demand" (and pay for) special programming at will.

The concept of a digital infrastructure is not synonymous with the Internet, the World Wide Web, or multimedia. Each of these is a component of the digital infrastructure.

The Internet is a collection of digital transmission lines and host computers, a web originally woven by the government. It allows computers to share information and information pathways. The Internet began as a project of the U.S. Department of Defense; the Defense Advanced Research Projects Agency (DARPA) wanted to develop a system that could link various military sites in a "headless" network. Lore has it that the motivation was to produce a network that could not be knocked out by one missile strike, though some accounts dispute such. In any event, the intent was to produce a system of communications that could make its own path, bouncing from New York to Washington, DC or, if necessary, from New York to London, Alaska, California, and Washington, DC.

This early form of the Internet, called the DARPANET, overcame the initial problem of computer-to-computer transmission, the fact that files of digital information, transmitted as a big chunk, would clog the system. Researches then developed what is called TCP/IP software (TCP stands for *transmission control protocol;* IP stands for *Internet protocol*). *Protocol* means a standard system laid out step by step.

The TCP breaks a message into pieces small enough to scatter over the Internet. All the pieces bear an address, and the IP guides the pieces to their destination. The message-pieces simply bounce from computer to computer, taking whatever route is available. While many messages take a direct route, it takes only a fraction of a second (literally) for messages to go by a different route, even if it is around the earth. Delays in the Internet (which do happen) result from overloaded computers relaying the messages, not from the distance the messages are sent.

Where is the Internet? The real answer is *everywhere,* because it is a network of networks. Some people locate the Internet's backbone along the path of a large cross-country fiberoptic cable owned by the National Science Foundation. Around this backbone were clustered powerful host computers belonging to government, business, and education. The host computers receive the information and sent it toward its final destination according to whichever pathways are open at the time. If you think about it, you realize why the Internet experienced such initial growth: Any time a host computer joins the system it actually *adds* to the capacity of the Internet, because it becomes one of the tools to sort and propel the message bits. This is not to say that the capacity of the Internet is limitless, though, and some experts say it is likely that we will see overloads of computers and cables as people begin to send fatter files containing more information.

Logging directly on to the Internet requires some technical expertise, so many users choose to use commercial online services, such as America Online, Compuserve, and Prodigy. The online service takes care of the Internet connection and provides users with an easy system with which to log on and navigate.

The services also provide various types of content, including online magazines, live events, and chat rooms.

It is interesting to note that commercial online services have become viable but are not now great money makers. They have, however, attracted many new users to the previously mysterious worlds of e-mail and online text of publications.

Equally mysterious—and alluring—is the World Wide Web. The Web is part of the Internet that features graphic displays. It uses a computer language known as hypertext markup language (HTML); hypertext is a system for jumping between cross-referenced items. The absurdly long addresses for Web sites, which are known as Uniform Resource Locators, or URLs, begin with HTTP, which stands for "hypertext transfer protocol," a system for enabling this cross-referencing link. A Web page usually features several of these links. The page is simply a graphic display stored in computer memory. Clicking on a highlighted item connects you to other relevant pages. Designers of this site or other sites program the links.

LEARNING ABOUT THE WEB ON THE WEB

The Online Education Web page, at www.web-action.com/remottr.html, is an enormously useful tool that offers any and all Internet information you could ever need. The page contains free links to the following categories: Connections to Online Journals, Elements of Web Page Design, Remote Education, Learn About Search Engines, Links to Other Pages about Remote Education, and Attracting Users to Your Site and Enticing Them to Return. Other topics include Books on How to Use Library Sources & Rational for Sources Mounted on the Internet and Webliography: Meta Data, Meta Tags, and the Dublin Core. Under these topics, you can find specific and detailed instructions for using World Wide Web search engines and Gopher search engines, over 20 links to Internet guides and tutorials, and tips on how to keep your Web site user-friendly, plus links to an extremely wide variety of guides and resources, like Learn on the 'Net and Internet Web Text, that all offer free Internet training and assistance.

 RECOMMENDED READING

Freedman, Alan, *Computer Glossary: The Complete Illustrated Desk Reference* (New York: Amacom, 1994). Defines 6,000 computer terms, includes profiles of computer firms, and has 200 black-and-white illustrations, along with an accompanying glossary on disk for DOS and Windows.

Glister, Paul, *Internet Navigator* (New York: Wiley, 1994). Avoiding technical language, Glister provides a clear, in-depth guide to this rapidly growing resource. Includes a list of resources.

Gralla, Preston, Joshua Eddings, and Sarah Ishida, *How the Internet Works* (Ill.), (Ziff-Davis, 1996). Stylish, highly illustrated introduction to the Internet, its history, and how to access what's out there. Beautifully illustrated.

Juliussen, Karen Petska, and Egil Juliussen, *The 8th Annual Computer Industry Almanac* (Computer Industry Almanac, 1996). Almost 800 pages of facts, figures, and contacts. In addition to entries of various computer companies and associations, there are many rankings of companies, people, and products.

Keeler, Len L., *Cybermarketing: Internet E-mail CD-ROM Online Services* (New York: Amacom, 1995). This 332-page guide explains how to use new technology for marketing and is divided into three sections: cybertools, cybertask, cyberopportunities. Includes illustrations and resources.

Minasi, Mark, *The Complete PC Upgrade and Maintenance Guide* (Berkeley: Sybex, 1996). Reassuring to those who worry about probing the guts of their computer. It's not as hard as it seems.

Importing and Exporting

 ## INTRODUCTION

The reasons to explore foreign markets for your product or service are "numerous and tempting," reports the National Foreign Trade Council. "Selling overseas broadens your market, forces you to be more competitive, and might well reduce your per-unit cost of production. It can help to hedge against recession or a change in demand at home. Foreign marketing may even extend the life of a good product that is beginning to lose ground at home, perhaps because a competitor has arrived on the scene. In short, 'going foreign' might boost your bottom line."

But exporting is not a universal solution for all small businesses; for example, it is not an easy way to dump excess inventory. The ups and downs of the dollar can make pricing a nightmare, and exporters may be faced with knotty and unfamiliar local laws, regulations, and customs.

Importing offers another set of opportunities and difficulties. Merchandise can be obtained at enormous discounts overseas, and therefore sold at large markups in the United States, but you must run a gauntlet of import restrictions and deal with suppliers who are sometimes unreliable and often speak a foreign language. You are less likely to receive help from the U.S. government when importing as opposed to exporting, because it is the export of goods that feeds the U.S. economy.

SOURCES OF INFORMATION

Center for International Private Enterprise (CIPE)

Membership in the Center for International Private Enterprise could be beneficial for any firm that has foreign affiliates or markets in other countries, or is considering international expansions. The CIPE, which is affiliated with the U.S. Chamber of Commerce, encourages active participation in political and legislative programs abroad that serve to stabilize American business operations and government relationships. One of the goals of CIPE abroad is to help establish local organizations similar to Chambers of Commerce that can go to bat for their members to overcome local trade restrictions.

International Council for Small Business (ICSB)

The mission of the International Council for Small Business is to foster the discussion and implementation of issues relating to the development and improvement of small-business management worldwide. If you have business overseas—or intend to—ICSB can be of assistance, since it provides research materials and reports, sponsors an annual conference, and encourages discussion groups on small-business administration and operations abroad.

International Executive Service Corps (IESC)

The International Executive Service Corps was established in the mid-1960s by American business leaders to assist private enterprise, particularly small businesses in developing countries in Latin America, the Middle East, Africa, Asia, and Central and Eastern Europe. Working much like SCORE, volunteers, largely retired executives, provide managerial and technical assistance to small- and mid-size businesses. Except for travel and related costs, these services are free. The IESC publishes *IESC News,* a bimonthly.

International Trade Council (ITC)

International Trade Council membership is made up of small and large companies that import and export products. The ITC promotes free trade and the elimination of trade barriers around the globe. It provides information on some 300 industries. Small businesses will find the ITC an excellent ally in finding overseas markets and in lending assistance in minimizing trade barriers.

National Foreign Trade Council (NFTC)

The National Foreign Trade Council is a leading advocate on behalf of the export/import business and opposes government policies that constrain competitiveness, such as foreign policy sanctions. The NFTC is the only broad-based trade association dealing exclusively with U.S. public policy affecting international trade and investment. It enjoys a high degree of credibility because it has a first-class constituency and speaks not for a single industry, but rather on behalf of a cross-section of American companies concerned with international economic policy issues.

Small Business Exporters Association (SBEA)

The Small Business Exporters Association promotes the interests of small-to mid-size North American exporters. Its members are manufacturers, trading companies, export/import management companies, and services companies, both public and private. Among other activities, the Association monitors and influences public policy and issues as they relate to exporting and international competitiveness. SBEA also sponsors spring and fall membership meetings, during which discussions and workshops are held on topics like the Export-Import Bank, customs duties, overseas shipping, and unfair international competition.

SBEA publishes a newsletter and informative bulletins, as well as research studies on small business in the export/import field. It also publishes a newsletter and informative bulletins, as well as research studies in many areas of concern to those in the export-import business.

U.S. Department of Commerce

The U.S. Department of Commerce is a source of valuable information about importing and exporting. The following departments within the agency can provide you with almost everything you need to know about doing business abroad. The Commerce Department will fax you information on export markets in Eastern Europe, Russia, Latin America, Japan, the rest of Asia, Africa, and Northern Ireland; call 800-872-8723. You can also talk to area specialists by calling the same number.

U.S. Department of Commerce Bureau of Economic Analysis (BEA)

The Bureau of Economic Analysis is part of the U.S. Commerce Department's Economic and Statistics Administration. The BEA serves as the nation's accountant and provides an accurate picture of the U.S. economy. The BEA Web site is available at www.bea.doc.gov and features detailed documents and articles relating directly to the nation's economic status, as well as survey statistics and industry and wealth data. The site is broken into three categories: national, international, and regional. Each category has links to the various fields of information. The site also contains links to an overview of the U.S. economy, BEA news releases, and related publications.

U.S. Department of Commerce Bureau of Export Administration (BXA)

The Bureau of Export Administration is the central U.S. agency for coordinating and administering programs related to the export/import business. The agency is responsible for matters pertinent to business abroad, such as licensing, enforcing export/import regulations, overseeing fair trade practices, and maintaining information systems and communications for businesses of all sizes that engage in business overseas.

U.S. Department of Commerce Export Assistance Centers (Office of Domestic Operations)

Since 1993, the Office of Domestic Operations (ODO) has successfully transformed itself into an organization that is more responsive to the needs of its clients—U.S. exporters. As one of the key export promotion agencies of the federal government, the Commercial Service's Office of Domestic Operations continually strives to assist American businesses in expanding their exports to markets around the globe.

ODO provides export counseling and marketing assistance to the U.S. business community through its Export Assistance Centers (EACs). The EACs work closely with the Office of International Operations' overseas posts to facilitate export transactions by linking U.S. suppliers with international buyers. The two field networks operate in unison to provide U.S. exporters with the best international trade support the U.S. government can offer.

The ODO operates the Export Assistance Center Network with 19 U.S. Export Assistance Centers (USEACs) connecting 100 EACs in a hub-and-spoke network. The mission of the EAC network is to deliver a comprehensive array of export counseling and trade finance services to U.S. firms, particularly small- and medium-size enterprises. As client-driven, bottom-line oriented offices that integrate the export marketing know-how of the U.S. Department of Commerce, with the trade finance expertise of the SBA and Export-Import Bank, EACs have the look and feel of private-sector export consulting firms. They have gone beyond being simply a federal partnership by also incorporating the resources of state and local export promotion organizations.

EACs focus on service to U.S. business clients. They provide in-depth, value-added counseling to U.S. firms seeking to expand their international activities and to those companies that are just beginning to venture overseas. EAC trade specialists help firms enter new markets and increase market share by:

- Identifying the best markets for their products;
- Developing an effective market-entry strategy aided by information generated from U.S. overseas offices;
- Facilitating the implementation of these plans by advising clients on distribution channels, market-entry strategies, exporting operational procedures. Export Promotion Services (EPS) programs and services, relevant trade shows, missions, and so on; and
- Assisting with trade finance programs that are available through federal, state, and local (public and private sector) entities.

EAC trade professionals counsel clients on relevant program information and market research as a standard part of their operations. Additionally, they facilitate communications between clients and overseas contacts through the most expedient technologies available, such as the Internet and e-mail, phone and fax. The trade specialists are mobile, equipped with laptops, modems, and cellular phones that allow them to deliver export services at the client's place of business wherever and whenever is most convenient for the client. (A complete list of Export Assistance Centers can be found in Part Three.)

U.S. Department of Commerce International Trade Administration (ITA)

Firms that encounter problems doing business overseas can contact the International Trade Administration, which is an indispensable champion of small firms affected by foreign economic policies, trade development, and global commercial services. The ITA maintains an Advocacy Center whose mission is to promote and protect American economic health, by assisting businesses in their marketing and servicing operations in other countries.

U.S. Department of Commerce Trade Adjustment Assistance Program (TAAP)

Contact the Trade Adjustment Assistance Program, part of the U.S. Department of Commerce, if you are in the export/import business—or otherwise engaged in trade outside of America—and feel you have been adversely affected by foreign competition. Today, there are hundreds of small businesses in the United States that face measurable and unfair foreign competition. The goal of the TAAP is to provide these firms with workable, cost-effective strategies to enable them to compete with foreign producers and marketers.

For additional information, see the following Tip Sheet, "Checklist to Determine If Your Product Is Exportable."

Tip Sheet
Ten-Question Checklist to Determine If Your Product Is Exportable

1. Is our product special and of high quality? It's tough to try to sell cheap merchandise abroad.
2. Are we flexible? Moving into an international market means catering to the tastes and needs of people whose cultures and tastes are different from those of Americans and you have to evaluate the differences carefully.

3. Do we have the capabilities to translate brochures and product manuals into foreign languages? You have to be exacting in providing instructions and could be liable if you make errors in providing operating data.

4. If we intend to sell electronic products, are they suitable for electrical current differentiations abroad?

5. Are product names acceptable? Some names may have unfavorable meanings or connotations in other countries.

6. Are we personally committed to exporting? Commitment must be more than a buzzword. You also have to have immeasurable patience, since preparations and clearances can take many months before you make a single initial shipment.

7. Are we willing to invest the money needed to expedite a foreign business? Getting organized can involve little cost, but once you get underway, costs—especially unexpected ones—can mount up.

8. Have we evaluated these cost potentials? You may, for example, have to make product modifications, pay extra production costs, provide translation services for your sales personnel, face greatly expanded telephone and other communication bills, and make plans to visit the countries in which you plan to market your product(s).

9. Can we sell at a competitive price abroad? Price differentials that are acceptable in the domestic market may not hold true in other countries.

10. Do we know what our competitors are doing? Foreign companies competing with you in the United States often can be a good sign that the same kinds of products are in demand globally.

 ## RECOMMENDED READING

Axtell, Roger E., *Do's & Taboos of International Trade: Small Business Primer* (New York: Wiley, 1994). Reviews the basics of international protocol, from planning the first trip to overseas communications.

Basic Guide to Exporting, U.S. Department of Commerce (Passport Books, 1989). A government guide to the basics of export for small businesses new to export sales. Divided into three sections, the book offers advice before, during, and after a sale. Includes glossary of export terms and lists of contacts in major overseas markets.

Basic Guide to Importing, by U.S. Customers Service Department of the Treasury (NTC Businesses Books, 1995). A guide for new importers, including sections on the entry process, paying duty, foreign trade zones, and transportation.

Directory of United States Importers. Directory of United States Exporters (Journal of Commerce, 1997). Comprehensive volumes indexed under many categories, including products, consulates, embassies, banks, company listings, customs information, and foreign consulates in the United States. Also available on CD-ROM. (Call 800-222-0356 for information.)

Export Yellow Pages. Each year, The Office of Export Trading Company Affairs (OETCA) compiles a database designed to match U.S. trade intermediaries with U.S. manufacturers of exportable goods. The data are then released in a publication called *The Export Yellow Pages* that are available through local U.S. Department of Commerce Export Assistance Centers. The database also is accessible on the Internet on the STAT.USA Export & International Trade Web site: www.stat-usa.gov/BEN/subject/trade.html. A $150 annual or a $50 quarterly fee is required.

Transportation
and Relocation

 ## INTRODUCTION

Companies that plan to relocate their business direct most of their planning efforts at locating the right space, making sure they can recruit the right kinds of employees, and settling in a community where the taxes and assessments are reasonable. Too often, however, they ignore the issue of transportation.

Many factors come into play when evaluating the transportation network surrounding your new business site, including the shipment of goods and ease of employees and visitors reaching your business. Traffic is an obvious consideration but one often overlooked; for example, many entrepreneurs have been chagrined to find that their location is boxed in by snarled traffic during afternoon rush hour, or when a nearby school lets out, or after their street becomes a bypass when a year-long construction project begins on a nearby major artery. Access to airports, and the quality of transportation provided by those airports, also are critical factors to consider.

A Tip Sheet later in this chapter provides a checklist for evaluating transportation in new locations.

 ## SOURCES OF INFORMATION

Air Transport Association of America

The Air Transport Association of America is the major trade association for the principal U.S. airlines and is the one to which you can turn for information and advice about your air transportation needs, whether for company travel, air shipments, or related functions. This is not a contact for day-to-day questions about flights and fares, but for professional help when you are making long-range business plans and establishing transportation procedures.

American Automobile Association (AAA)

Like many motorists, you probably think of the American Automobile Association as basically an emergency highway and travel service for individuals and families. However, AAA also can be an important transportation resource for small businesses whose representatives are frequently on the road. Many, though not all, AAA clubs offer businesses group memberships and travel discounts that apply to food, accommodations, automotive supplies, and other requisites associated with highway travel. Membership is obligatory, but rates are reasonable.

American Trucking Association (ATA)

The American Trucking Association includes 51 affiliated trucking associations located in every state and the District of Columbia, representing all types and classes of motor carriers. If you need information about short- or long-range commercial haulage, or logistical help during relocation, contact ATA prior to your planning sessions for information and counsel.

Council of Logistics Management (CLM)

Though highly specialized and probably not a likely association for most entrepreneurs to join, the Council of Logistics Management can help non-members with information about the improvement of logistics and distribution skills. CLM sponsors research and educational programs about logistics systems and functions, and can refer you to an appropriate member should you desire consultation.

National Highway Traffic Safety Administration

This agency, a division of the U.S. Department of Transportation, maintains a 7-day, 24-hour hotline (800-424-9393) from which you can receive information and report traffic and vehicle safety violations you feel are in any way a threat to your business or employees.

National Vehicle Leasing Association (NVLA)

When your transportation plans include the use of leased vehicles, you can contact the National Vehicle Leasing Association for recommendations on leasing services in the region in which you do business. One of the basic functions of the NVLA is to encourage sound business practices among its members for the good of its customers and the public. If you have complaints about rates or services, you may be able to resolve them through the NVLA.

U.S. Department of Transportation

A small business involved with trucking and interstate commerce should be on the U.S. Department of Transportation's mailing list for changes and forecasts regarding vehicular laws and restrictions as far in advance as possible.

Tip Sheet
How to Evaluate Transportation Options in a New Location

Look at a map, and . . .

1. Mark the sources of your raw materials, products, or other commodities and plot the distance between your proposed new location and existing suppliers.
2. Mark the locations of your competitors and see whether they would then have any transportation advantages over you.
3. Note whether you would have to invest too heavily to provide the kind of transportation facilities you would need.
4. Find out whether you would cross any township, county, or state lines that would change your status regarding business regulations, as well as taxes.
5. Ask yourself whether the cost of supplies from your present sources would increase substantially with your move.

6. Check out the transportation facilities and mileage for personnel if you have many employees who commute.

7. Determine how accessible your facilities are to potential clients or customers.

8. Note the locations and distances of emergency services that might be needed, such as police precincts, fire stations, or first aid and ambulance assistance.

Tip Sheet
Finding Cheap Flights via the Internet

The Internet offers more opportunities to book flights than there are destinations. Search engines like Yahoo! (www.yahoo.com), and Webcrawler (www.webcrawler.com) have their own travel services that provide search forms including time, date, destination, preferred airline, and preferred price range. You can submit the completed forms, view the choices of available flights, and then book your selection. Search engines also offer links to other travel sites. Another option is the variety of competing travel agencies offering web booking. Preview Travel (www.previewtravel.com) offers assistance in booking flights at its site and provides a rate finder that aids in the location of available flights at the appropriate price. Www.vacationrez.com offers discount rates either through the site or telephone number 800-650-4329. Www.vactionweb.com offers drastically discounted round-trip and one-way fares. If you feel more comfortable booking with major airlines, American Airlines (www.americanair.com), Delta Airlines (www.delta-air.com), Northwest Airlines (www.nwa.com), TWA (www.twa.com), United Airlines (www.ual.com), and US Air (www.usair.com) each provide Web sites with varying levels of options and services.

 ## RECOMMENDED READING

Branch, Alan E., *Economics of Shipping Practice and Management*, 2nd ed. (Chapman and Hall, 1988).

PART THREE

A to Z Listings

**Air Transport Association
of America**
1301 Pennsylvania Avenue, NW, Suite 1100
Washington, DC. 20004
(202) 626-4000
FAX: (202) 626-4181
www.air-transport.org
Contacts: Carol Hallett, President & CEO,
and Christopher Chiames, Managing
Director, Public Relations

American Advertising Federation
1101 Vermont Avenue NW,
Suite 500
Washington, DC 20005
(202) 898-0089 FAX: (202) 898-0159
www.aaf.org
E-mail: aaf@aaf.org
Contact: Wally Snyder, President

American Arbitration Association
140 West 51st Street
New York, NY 10020
(212) 484-4000 FAX: (212) 765-4874
www.adv.org
Contact: Toni L. Griffin, Director,
Public Relations

Following is a listing of regional
offices of the AAA:

ARIZONA
Phoenix (85012-2365) - Harry Kaminsky
333 East Osborn Road, Suite 310
(602) 234-0950/230-2151 (Fax)

CALIFORNIA
Irvine (92714-7240) - P. Jean Baker
2030 Main Street, Suite 1650
(714) 474-5090/474-5087 (Fax)

Los Angeles (90010-1108) - Kelvin Chin
3055 Wilshire Boulevard, Floor 7
(213) 385-6516/386-2251 (Fax)
San Diego (92101-4584) - Dennis Sharp
600 B. Street, Suite 1450
(619) 239-3051/239-3807 (Fax)
**San Francisco (94104-4207) - Stephen
  P. Van Liere**
225 Bush Street, Floor 18
(415) 981-3901/781-8426 (Fax)

COLORADO
**Denver (80264-2101) - D. Breckenridge
  Grover**
1660 Lincoln Street, Suite 2150
(303) 831-0823/832-3626 (Fax)

CONNECTICUT
**East Hartford (06108-3256) - Karen
  M. Jallrut**
111 Founders Plaza, Floor 17
(860) 289-3993/282-0459 (Fax)

DISTRICT OF COLUMBIA
**Washington, DC (20036-4104) - Steven
  G. Gallagher**
1150 Connecticut Avenue, NW, Floor 6
(202) 296-8510/872-9574 (Fax)

FLORIDA
Miami (33131-2808) - René Grafuls
799 Brickell Plaza, Suite 600
(305) 358-7777/358-4931 (Fax)
**Orlando (32801-2742) - Mark
  Sholander**
201 East Pine Street, Suite 800
(407) 648-1185/649-8668 (Fax)

GEORGIA
Atlanta (30345-3203) - India Johnson
1975 Century Boulevard, NE, Suite 1
(404) 325-0101/325-8034 (Fax)

HAWAII
**Honolulu (96813-4714) - Lance
  K. Tanaka**
810 Richards Street, Suite 641
(808) 531-0541/533-2306 (Fax)
In Guam, (671) 477-1845/477-3178 (Fax)

ILLINOIS
Chicago (60601-7601) - Scott Carfello
225 North Michigan Avenue, Suite 2527
(312) 616-6560/819-0404 (Fax)

LOUISIANA
**New Orleans (70163-2810) - Glen
  H. Spencer**
2810 Energy Centre, 1100 Poydras Street
(504) 522-8781/561-8041 (Fax)

MARYLAND
**Baltimore (21201-2930) - Steven
  G. Gallagher**
10 Hopkins Plaza
(410) 837-0087/783-2797 (Fax)

MASSACHUSETTS
**Boston (02110-1703) - Christina
  L. Newhall**
133 Federal Street
(617) 451-6600/451-0765 (Fax)

MICHIGAN
**Southfield (68076-3728) - Mary
  A. Bedidan**
One Towne Square, Suite 1600
(810) 352-3300/352-3147 (Fax)

MINNESOTA
**Minneapolis (55402-1092) - James
  R. Doye**
514 Nicollet Mall, Floor 6
(612) 332-6545/342-2334 (Fax)

MISSOURI
**Kansas City (84184-2110) - Lori
  A. Madden**
1101 Walnut Street, Suite 903
(816) 221-6401/471-5264 (Fax)
**St. Louis (63101-1614) - Neil
  Moldenhauer**
One Mercantile Center, Suite 2512
(314) 621-7175/621-3730 (Fax)

NEVADA
Las Vegas (89102-8719) - Laura Camp
4425 Spring Mountain Road, Suite 310
(702) 252-4071/252-4073 (Fax)
From Reno, (702) 786-5566

NEW JERSEY
Somerset (08873-4120) - Philip Levine
265 Davidson Avenue, Suite 140
(908) 560-9560/560-8850 (Fax)

NEW YORK
Garden City (11530-2004) - Mark
A. Resnick
666 Old Country Road, Suite 603
(516) 222-1660/745-6447 (Fax)
New York (10020-1203) - Agnes
J. Wilson
140 West 51st Street
(212) 484-3266/307-4387 (Fax)
Syracuse (13202-1376) - Deborah
A. Brown
205 South Salina Street
(515) 472-5483/472-0966 (Fax)
White Plains (10603-1916) - Marion
J. Zinman
399 Knollwood Road, Suite 116
(914) 946-1119/946-2661 (Fax)

NORTH CAROLINA
Charlotte (28202-2431) - Debi Miller
Moore
428 East Fourth Street, Suite 300
(704) 347-0200/347-2804 (Fax)

OHIO
Cincinnati (45202-2973) - Eileen
B. Vernon
441 Vine Street, Suite 3308
(513) 241-8434/241-8437 (Fax)
Cleveland (44130-3490) - Eileen
B. Vernon
17900 Jefferson Park, Suite 101
(216) 891-4741/891-4740 (Fax)

PENNSYLVANIA
Philadelphia (19102-4106) - Kenneth
Egger
230 South Broad Street, Floor 6
(215) 732-5260/732-5002 (Fax)
Pittsburgh (15222-1207) - John
F. Schano
Four Gateway Center, Room 419
(412) 261-3617/261-6055 (Fax)

TENNESSEE
Nashville (37219-1823) - Judy
C. Johnson
211 Seventh Avenue North, Suite 300
(615) 256-5857/244-8570 (Fax)

TEXAS
Dallas (75240-6620) - Helmut O. Wolff
13455 Noel Road, Suite 1440
(972) 702-8222/490-9006 (Fax)
Houston (77002-6708) - Glen H. Spencer
1001 Fannin Street, Suite 1005
(713) 739-1302/739-1702 (Fax)

UTAH
Salt Lake City (84111-3834) - Diane
Abegglen
645 South 200 East, Suite 203
(801) 531-9748/323-9624 (Fax)

VIRGINIA
McLean (22102) - Steven G. Gallagher
8201 Greensboro Drive, Suite 610
(703) 760-4820/760-4847 (Fax)
Richmond (23219-2803) - Betty Starks
707 East Main Street, Suite 1610
(804) 649-4838/643-6340 (Fax)

WASHINGTON
Seattle (98101-2511) - Sheri L. Raders
1325 Fourth Avenue, Suite 1414
(206) 622-6435/343-5679 (Fax)

American Association of Advertising Agencies
405 Lexington Avenue, 18th Floor
New York, NY 10174
(212) 682-2500
FAX: (212) 953-5665
www.commercepark.com/AAA
/member.htm

American Automobile Association
1000 AAA Drive
Heathrow, FL 32746
(407) 444-7000
FAX: (407) 444-7380
www.aaa.com

American Bankers Association
1120 Connecticut Avenue, NW
Washington, DC 20006
(202) 663-5000
FAX: (202) 828-4535

American Bar Association
750 Lakeshore Drive
Chicago, IL 60611
(312) 988-5000
abanet.org
E-mail: info@abanct.org

American Business Association
292 Madison Avenue
New York, NY 10017
(212) 949-5900
FAX: (212) 949-5910
Contact: Pat Arden, Executive
  Director

**American Business Women's
  Association**
9100 Ward Parkway
Kansas City, MO 64114
(816) 361-6621
FAX: (816) 361-4991
www.majesticweb.com/abwa/pages
  /home.html
Contact: Carolyn B. Elman,
  Executive Director

American Council on Alcoholism
2522 St. Paul Street
Baltimore, MD 21218
(410) 889-0100
www.chamd.org/acq.html

**American Financial Services
  Association**
919 18th Street, NW
Washington, DC 20006
(202) 296-5544
FAX: (202) 223-0321
www.americanfinsvcs.org
Contact: Lynne Strang, Director,
  Communications

**American Institute of Certified
  Public Accountants**
1211 Avenue of the Americas
New York, NY 10036
(212) 596-6200
FAX: (212) 596-6213
www.aicpa.org

**American Institute of
  Management**
P.O. Box 7039
Quincy, MA 02269
(617) 472-0277
Contact: Barbara C. Doll,
  President

**American Insurance Services
  Group**
85 John Street
New York, NY 10038
(212) 669-0455
www.aisg.org
Contact: Director,
  Communications

**American Management
  Association**
1601 Broadway
New York, NY 10019-7420
(212) 586-8100
FAX: (212) 903-8168
www.amanet.com

American Marketing Association
250 South Wacker Drive, Suite 200
Chicago, IL 60606
(312) 648-0536
FAX: (312) 993-7542
www.ama.com
Contact: Ginny Shipe, Director,
    Member Services

American Small Businesses
    Association
1800 North Kent Street, Suite 910
Arlington, VA 22209
(800) 235-3298
FAX: (703) 522-9789
www.asba.net/index.htm
Contact: Vernon Castle, Executive
    Director

American Society of Appraisers
555 Herndon Parkway, Suite 125
Herndon, VA 20170
(800) ASA-VALU
appraisers.org/asa/default.asp
E-mail: tbaker@appraisers.org
Contact: Edwin W. Baker,
    Executive Director

American Society of
    Industrial Security
1625 Prince Street
Alexandria, VA 22314
(703) 519-6200
www.asionline.org
E-mail: info@asionline.org

American Society of Journalists
    and Authors
1501 Broadway, Suite 302
New York, NY 10036
(212) 997-0947
FAX: (212) 768-7414
www.asja.org
Dial-A-Writer Service:
    (212) 398-1934

American Society for Training
    and Development
1640 King Street
Alexandria, VA 22313
(703) 683-8100
FAX: (703) 683-8103
www.ASTD.org
E-mail: jgilde@ASTD.org
Contact: Scott Cheney

American Society of Women
    Accountants
1255 Lynnfield Road, Suite 257
Memphis, TN 38119
(901) 680-0470
FAX: (901) 680-0505
www.aswa.org
Contacts: Allison Conte, CAE,
    Executive Director; Patricia
    Ware, Membership
    Administrator; and Penny Flynn,
    Communications Coordinator

American Telemarketing
    Association
4605 Lankershim Boulevard,
    Suite 824
North Hollywood, CA 91602-1891
(818) 766-5324
www.ataconnect. org

American Trucking Association
2200 Mill Road
Alexandria, VA 22314-4677
(703) 838-1700
FAX: (703) 548-1841

**American Women's Economic
    Development Corporation**
71 Vanderbilt Avenue, 3rd Floor
New York, NY 10169
(212) 692-9100
FAX: (212) 692-9296
Contact: Rosalind Paaswell, CEO

**Associated Business Writers
    of America**
1450 South Havana Street,
    Suite 424
Aurora, CO 80012
(303) 751-7844
FAX: (303) 751-8593
Contact: Sandy Whelchel, Director

**Association of Area
    Business Publications**
5820 Wilshire Boulevard, No. 500
Los Angeles, CA 90036
(213) 937-5514
FAX: (213) 937-0959
www.bizpubs.org/about.htm

AABP member publications
include:

ALABAMA
**Birmingham (35205) - Tina Verciglio
    Savas**
Birmingham Business Journal
Birmingham Business Journal, Inc.
2101 Magnolia Avenue South, #400
(205) 322-0000/322-0040 (Fax)

ALASKA
Anchorage (99516) - Terri Newsom
The Alaska Journal of Commerce
4220 B Street, Suite 210
(907) 762-1416/907/563-4744 (Fax)

ARIZONA
Phoenix (85004) - Stephanie Pressly
Arizona Business Gazette
Phoenix Newspapers, Inc.
120 East Van Buren
(602) 271-7300/444-4277 (Fax)
Tucson (85706) - Stephan Jewett
Inside Tucson Business
Territorial Newspapers
3280 East Hemisphere Loop, #174
(520) 294-1200/294-4040 (Fax)

ARKANSAS
Little Rock (72203) - Jeff Hankins
Arkansas Business
Arkansas Writer's Project
201 East Markham, #200
(501) 372-1443/375-0933 (Fax)

CALIFORNIA
Fresno (93721) - Gordon Webster, Jr.
The Business Journal Serving Fresno &
    the Central San Joaquin Valley
Webster Publishing, Inc.
1315 Van Ness, Suite 200
(209) 490-3400/237-3540 (Fax)
Los Angeles (90036) - Matt Toledo
Los Angeles Business Journal
CBJ Associates, Inc.
5700 Wilshire Boulevard, #170
(213) 549-5225/549-5255 (Fax)
San Diego (92101) - Ms. Sara Wilensky
San Diego Transcript
San Diego Daily Transcript
2131 Third Avenue
(619) 232-4381/239-5716 (Fax)
San Jose (95112) - Armon Mills
Business Journal Serving San Jose & the
    Silicon Valley
American City Business Journals
96 North Third Street, #100
(408) 295-3800/295-5028 (Fax)
Santa Rosa (95403) - Ken Clark
The Business Journal Serving Sonoma &
    Marin Counties
Sloan Publications
5510 Skylane Boulevard, #201
(707) 579-2900/579-8475 (Fax)

COLORADO
Englewood (80112) - Jackie Kilfoyle
Colorado Business
Wiesner, Inc.
7009 South Potomac
(303) 397-7600/397-7619

CONNECTICUT
Hartford (06106) - Joseph Zwiebel
Hartford Business Journal
Worcester Publishing Ltd.
56 Arbor Street
(860) 236-9998/236-9561

FLORIDA
St. Petersburg (33701) - Lynda Keever
Florida Trend
Times Publishing Company
490 First Avenue South
(813) 821-5800/822-5083 (Fax)

HAWAII
Honolulu (96814) - Kim Jacobsen
Hawaii Business
Hawaii Business Publishing Co.
P.O. Box 913
(808) 537-9500/537-6455 (Fax)
Honolulu (96813) - Mary Winpenny
Island Business
Honolulu Publishing Co.
36 Merchant Street
(808) 524-7400/531-2306 (Fax)

IDAHO
Boise (83707) - Carl A. Miller
The Idaho Business Review
The Idaho Business Review, Inc.
4301 West Franklin, PO Box 8866
(208) 336-3768/336-3768 (Fax)

ILLINOIS
Chicago (60611) - Gloria Scoby
Crain's Chicago Business
Crain Communications, Inc.
740 Rush Street
(312) 649-5371/649-5415 (Fax)
Oak Brook (60521-8814) - James E. Elsener
Business Ledger
Ledger Publications, Inc.
709 Enterprise Drive
(630) 571-8911/571-4053 (Fax)

INDIANA
Indianapolis (46204) - Chris Katterjohn
Indianapolis Business Journal
IBJ Corp.
41 East Washington, Suite 200
(317) 634-6200/263-5060 (Fax)

IOWA
Des Moines (50309) - Connie Wimer
Des Moines Business Record
Business Publications Corp.
100 Fourth Street
(515) 288-3336/288-0309 (Fax)

KANSAS
Overland Park (66212) - Stephen Rose
Johnson County Business Times
7373 West 107th Street
(913) 649-8778/381-3889 (Fax)

KENTUCKY
Lexington (40507) - Ed G. Lane
Lane Report
Lane Consultants, Inc.
269 West Main Street, 4th Floor
(606) 244-3522/244-3544 (Fax)

LOUISIANA
Baton Rouge (70808) - Julio Melara
Baton Rouge Business Report
Louisiana Business, Inc.
5757 Corporate Boulevard, #402
(504) 928-1700/923-3448 (Fax)
Metairie (70005) - William M. Metcalf, Jr.
New Orleans City Business
New Orleans Publishing Group
111 Veterans Boulevard, #1810
(504) 834-9292/837-2258 (Fax)

MARYLAND
Baltimore (21202) - Christopher Eddings
Daily Record (Warfields)
The Daily Record Co.
11 East Saratoga Street
(410) 752-1717/752-2894 (Fax)

MASSACHUSETTS
Worcester (01604) - Peter Stanton
Worcester Business Journal
Worcester Publishing Ltd.
172 Shrewsbury Street
(508) 755-8004/755-8860 (Fax)

MICHIGAN
Brighton (48116) - Jim Mason
Insider Business Journal
Suburban Communication, Corp.
9947 East Grandiver
(810) 220-1800/220-5320 (Fax)
Detroit (48207-3187) - Mary Kramer
Crain's Detroit Business
Crain Communications Inc.
1400 Woodbridge
(313) 446-6000/393-0997
**Grand Rapids (49503) - John
  H. Zwarensteyn**
Grand Rapids Business Journal
Gemini Publications
549 Ottawa Avenue Northwest
(616) 459-4545/459-4800 (Fax)
Traverse City (49686) - Michael L. Dow
The Business News
800 Hastings Street, Suite E
(616) 929-7919/929-7914 (Fax)

MINNESOTA
**Minneapolis (55402-1207) - Craig
  Wessel**
Corporate Report Minnesota
CityMedia Inc.
105 South Fifth Street, #100
(612) 338-4288/373-0195 (Fax)
**Minneapolis (55402-1302) - Lisa
  Bornaster**
Minneapolis/St. Paul City Business
CityMedia, Inc.
527 Marquette Avenue, #300
(612) 288-2100/288-2121 (Fax)
Minneapolis (55402-4507) - Tom Mason
Twin Cities Business Monthly
MSP Communications
220 South Sixth Street, #500
(612) 339-7571/339-5806 (Fax)

MISSISSIPPI
Jackson (39206-4308) - Joe D. Jones
Mississippi Business Journal
Venture Publications, Inc.
5120 Galaxie Drive
(601) 364-1000/364-1007 (Fax)

MISSOURI
Kansas City (64108) - Joe Sweeney
Ingram's
Show-Me Publishing, Inc.
306 East 12th Street, Suite 1014
(816) 842-9994/474-1111 (Fax)
Springfield (65801) - Dianne Elizabeth
Springfield Business Journal
Springfield Business Journal, Inc.
P.O. Box 1365
(417) 831-3238/831-5478 (Fax)

NEVADA
**Las Vegas (89102-8218) - Bruce
  Spotelson**
Las Vegas Business Press
Wick Communications, Inc.
3335 Wynn Road
(702) 871-5579/871-3740 (Fax)

NEW JERSEY
New Brunswick (08901) - Jean Taber
Business News New Jersey
391 George Street
(732) 246-7677/249-8886 (Fax)

NEW MEXICO
Albuquerque (87102) - Joe Houston
New Mexico Business
Starlight Publishing
600 First Street
(505) 768-7008/768-0890 (Fax)

NEW YORK
New York (10017) - Alair Townsend
Crain's New York Business
Crain Communications, Inc.
220 East 42nd Street
(212) 210-0100/210-0499 (Fax)
Rochester (14604) - Susan R. Holliday
Rochester Business Journal
Rochester Business Journal, Inc.
55 St. Paul Street
(716) 546-8303/546-3398 (Fax)
Ronkonkoma (11779) - Terry Townsend
Long Island Business News
Long Island Commercial Review, Inc.
2150 Smithtown Avenue
(516) 737-1700/737-1890 (Fax)

NORTH CAROLINA
Charlotte (28217) - David Kinney
Business North Carolina
The News & Observer Publishing
    Company
5435 Seventy-Seven Center Drive, #50
(704) 523-6987/523-4211 (Fax)

OHIO
Cleveland (44113) - Brian Tucker
Crain's Cleveland Business
Crain Communications, Inc.
700 West St. Clair Avenue, #310
(216) 522-1383/694-4264 (Fax)

OREGON
Eugene (97401-3449) - Lee White
Business News
326 West 12th Avenue
(541) 343-6636/343-0177 (Fax)

PENNSYLVANIA
Bethlehem (18018) - Larry Jalowiec
Eastern Pennsylvania Business Journal
Press Enterprise
65 East Elizabeth Street, Suite 700
(610) 807-9619/807-9612 (Fax)
Harrisburg (17104) - David
    A. Schankweiler
Central Penn Business Journal
Journal Publications, Inc.
409 South Second Street, #3D
(717) 236-4300/236-6803 (Fax)
Kingston (18704) - Karen Nocerine
The Northeast Pennsylvania Business
    Journal
Press Enterprise Inc.
403 Third Avenue
(717) 283-9271/283-9307 (Fax)
Philadelphia (19106) - Lyn Kremer
Philadephia Business Journal
CityMedia, Inc.
400 Market Street, Suite 300
(215) 238-1450/238-1466 (Fax)
State College (16801) - Thomas D. King
Pennsylvania Business Central
2011-201 Cato Avenue
(814) 867-2222/234-4487 (Fax)

SOUTH CAROLINA
Charleston (29401) - Bill Settlmyer
Charleston Regional Business Journal
145 Market Street, Suite 310
(803) 723-7702/723-7060 (Fax)

TENNESSEE
Memphis (38103) - Stuart Chamblin III
Memphis Business Journal
Mid-South Communications, Inc.
88 Union, Suite 102
(901) 523-1000/526-5240 (Fax)
Nashville (37201) - Kevin Lorance
Nashville Business Journal
Mid South Communications
222 Second Avenue North, #610
(615) 248-2222/248-6246 (Fax)

TEXAS
Dallas (75206) - Stephani Kompus
Texas Business
Empower Media Group, LLC
5910 North Central Expressway,
    Suite 1580
(214) 265-2496/739-1421 (Fax)

VIRGINIA
Richmond (23220) - Michael Abernathy
Inside Business
Landmark Communications
1113 West Main Street
(804) 358-5500/355-8183 (Fax)
Richmond (23219) - James A. Bacon
Virginia Business
Media General Business Publications Inc.
411 East Franklin Street, Suite 105
(804) 649-6999

WASHINGTON
Spokane (99202) - Greg Beven
Journal of Business (Spokane)
112 East First Avenue
(509) 456-5257/456-0624 (Fax)

WEST VIRGINIA
Charleston (25301) - Robert C. Payne
State Journal
904 Virginia Street, East
(304) 344-1630/345-2721 (Fax)

WISCONSIN
Milwaukee (53202) - Dan Meyer
Small Business Times
1123 North Water Street
(414) 277-8181/277-8191 (Fax)

BRITISH COLUMBIA, CANADA
Vancouver (V6E-2P4) - George Mleczko
Business in Vancouver
BIV Publications, Ltd.
1155 Pender Street, West, #500
(604) 688-2398/688-1963 (Fax)

ONTARIO, CANADA
Ottawa (K1R5T8) - Mark Sutcliffe
Ottawa Business Journal
The Business Press Group, Inc.
424 Catherine Street
(613) 230-8699/230-9606 (Fax)
Sudbury (P3E3N5) - John Thompson
Northern Ontario Business
Laurentian Publishing Company
158 Elgin Street
(750) 673-5705/673-9542 (Fax)

POLAND
Warsaw (00-789) - Russ Havens
Warsaw Business Journal
New World Publishing
UL SLONECZNA 29
(48-22) 646-0575/646-0576 (Fax)

Association for Corporate Growth

4350 DiPaolo Center, Suite C
Dearlove Road
Glenview, IL 60025
(847) 699-1331
www.acg.org/mission
Contact: Carl A. Wangman,
   Executive Director

Association of Incentive Marketing

1620 Route 22 East
Union, NJ 07083
(908) 687-3090
FAX: (908) 687-0977
Contact: Howard C. Henry, CIP,
   Executive Director

Association for Innovative Marketing

34 Summit Avenue
Sharon, MA 02067
(800) 729-1747
FAX: (617) 237-7112
Contact: Alan Rosenspan,
   President

Association of Small Business Development Centers

1300 Chain Bridge Road, Suite 201
McLean, VA 22101
(703) 448-6124
FAX: (703) 448-6124

BUSINESS INFORMATION CENTERS

CALIFORNIA
Chula Vista (91910) - Ken Clark
Business Information Center
Southwestern College
900 Otay Lake Road, Building 1600
(619) 482-6393/482-6402 (Fax)
Los Angeles (90010) - Ken Davis
U.S. Small Business Administration
Business Information Center
3600 Wilshire Boulevard, Suite L100
(213) 251-7253/251-7255 (Fax)
San Diego (92101-3540) - Ron Serafine
U.S. Small Business Administration
San Diego District Office
550 West C Street, Suite 550
(619) 557-7250 ext. 1126/557-5894 (Fax)
San Francisco (94105-2420) - Kathleen Butler-Tom
The Entrepreneur Center
U.S. Small Business Administration
455 Market Street, 6th Floor
(415) 744-4242/744-6812 (Fax)

COLORADO
Denver (80202-2599) - Jeanette DeHerara
U.S. Small Business Administration
Denver District Office
721 19th Street, Suite 426
(303) 844-3986/844-6490 (Fax)

CONNECTICUT
Hartford (06103) - Greta Johanson
Connecticut Small Business-Key to the
　　Future, Inc.
Hartford Civic Center
1 Civic Center Plaza, Suite 301
(860) 251-7000/251-7006 (Fax)

DELAWARE
Wilmington (19801) - Kai Brunswick
Delaware Small Business Resource &
　　Information Center
1318 North Market Street
(302) 571-5225/571-5222 (Fax)

DISTRICT OF COLUMBIA
Washington, DC (20043-4500) - Joyce
　　Howard
SBA/Bell Atlantic
Business Information Center
1110 Vermont Avenue Northwest,
　　Suite 900
(202) 606-4000 ext. 266/606-4225 (Fax)

FLORIDA
Miami (33128) - Terry Stubblefield
U.S. Small Business Administration
NationsBank/MBDA/Bell South
49 Northwest Fifth Street
(305) 374-1899/374-1882 (Fax)

GEORGIA
Atlanta (30303) - Annette Rodriquez
U.S. Small Business Administration
Atlanta District Office
270 Peachtree Stree, NW, Suite 140
(404) 529-9808/529-9853 (Fax)

HAWAII
Honolulu (96813) - Jane Sawyer
Hawaii Business Information and
　　Conseling Center
1111 Bishop Street, Suite 204
(808) 522-8130/522-8135 (Fax)

IDAHO
Boise (83702-5745) - Sherrie Sugden
U.S. Small Business Administration
Boise District Office
1020 Main Street, Suite 290
(208) 334-1696 ext. 236/334-9353 (Fax)

ILLINOIS
Chicago (60661-2511) - Phyllis Scott
U.S. Small Business Administration
Chicago District Office
500 West Madison Street, Suite 1250
(312) 353-1825/886-5688 (Fax)

MAINE
Lewiston (04240) - Bonnie Erickson
Business Information Center of Maine
The Bates Mill Complex
35 Canal Street
(207) 783-2770/783-7745 (Fax)

MARYLAND
Baltimore (21201) - Rachel Howard
SBA/NationsBank/MBDA/Bell Atlantic
Small Business Resource Center
3 West Baltimore Street
(410) 605-0990/605-0995 (Fax)

MASSACHUSETTS
Boston (02222-1093) - Andrea Ross
U.S. Small Business Administration
Boston District Office
10 Causeway Street, Room 265
(617) 565-5590/565-5598 (Fax)

MISSOURI
Kansas City (64105) - Kim Malcolm
U.S. Small Business Administration
Kansas City District Office
323 West 8th Street, Suite 104
(816) 374-6675/374-6692 (Fax)
St. Louis (63101) - Maureen Brinkley
Business Information Center
815 Olive Street, Suite 208
(314) 539-6970/539-3785 (Fax)

MONTANA
Helena (59626) - Robert Much
U.S. Small Business Administration
Business Information Center
301 South Park, Room 334
(406) 441-1081/441-1090 (Fax)

NEBRASKA
Omaha (68154) - Jan Allen
U.S. Small Business Administration
Business Information Center
11141 Mill Valley Road
(402) 221-3606/221-3680 (Fax)

NEW JERSEY
Camden (08102-1102) - Joe Fernicola
Business Information Center
Camden County College
200 Broadway Avenue, Room 513
(609) 338-1817 ext. 3162/756-0497 (Fax)
Newark (07102) - Bobby Sepolen
Business Information Center
U.S. Small Business Administration
2 Gateway Center, 4th Floor
(201) 645-3968/645-6265 (Fax)

NEW MEXICO
Albuquerque (87106) - Chevo Contreras
ATVI/Workforce Training Center -
   UNIM
University of New Mexico, 3rd Floor
801 University Boulevard East, Suite 300
(505) 272-7980/272-7979 (Fax)

NEW YORK
Albany (12205) - Daniel O'Connell
The Capital Resource Center
1 Computer Drive South
(518) 446-1118 ext. 231/446-1228 (Fax)

NORTH CAROLINA
Charlotte (28202-2137) - Eileen Joyce
U.S. Small Business Administration
NationsBank/MBDA/Bell South
Small Business Resource Center
200 North College Street, Suite A2015
(704) 344-9797/344-9990 (Fax)

OKLAHOMA
**Oklahoma City (73102) - Maria
   Barnaba-Moore**
U.S. Small Business Administration
UCO Small Business Development Center
115 Park Avenue
(405) 232-2376/232-1967 (Fax)

OREGON
Chiloquin (97624) - Ed Case
SBA/The Klamath Tribes
34005 Highway 97 North
P.O. Box 436
(503) 783-2472/783-3406 (Fax)

**Grand Ronde (97347) - Audrey
   Campbell**
SBA/Confederated Tribes of the Grand
   Ronde Community
Salmon River Highway
9615 Grand Ronde Road
(503) 879-5211/879-2479 (Fax)
E-mail: ctgremoore@maanet.com
Warm Springs (97761) - David Dona
SBA/Confederated Tribes of the
   Warm Springs
Economic Development Office
2102 Wasco Street
P.O. Box 945
(541) 553-3592/553-3593 (Fax)

RHODE ISLAND
Providence (02907) - Patricia O'Rourke
Enterprise Community Center
550 Broad Street
(401) 272-1083/272-1186 (Fax)
Providence (02903) - Jaime Aguayo
U.S. Small Business Administration
Business Information Center
380 Westminister Mall, Room 511
(401) 528-4688/528-4539 (Fax)

SOUTH CAROLINA
Charleston (29401) - Luder Messervy
SBA/NationsBank/MBDA
BellSouth/College of Charleston
Small Business Resource Center
284 King Street
(803) 853-3900/853-2529 (Fax)

TENNESSEE
Nashville (37203) - Lillie Taylor
SBA/NationsBank/MBDA
Small Business Resource Center
3401 West End Avenue, Suite 110
(615) 749-4000/749-3685 (Fax)

TEXAS
El Paso (79901) - Minda Villarreal
SBA/Greater El Paso Chamber of
   Commerce
Business Information Center
10 Civic Center Plaza
(915) 534-0531/534-0513 (Fax)

Fort Worth (76102) - Adrienne Hudson
U.S. Small Business Administration/Fort
   Worth Business Assistance Center
100 East 15th Street, Suite 400
(817) 871-6001/871-6031 (Fax)
Houston (77074-1591) - Steve Curry
U.S. Small Business Administration
Houston District Office
9301 Southwest Freeway, Suite 365
(713) 773-6542/773-6550 (Fax)

UTAH
**Salt Lake City (84111) - Suzan
   Yoshimura**
Business Information Center
169 East 100 South
(801) 741-4253/741-4265 (Fax)

VERMONT
Burlington (05401) - Vallerie Rogers
Burlington Business Information Center
149 Bank Street
(802) 660-4580
**Randolph Center (05061) - Vallerie
   Rogers**
Business Information Center
Vermont Technical College
Hartness Library
(802) 828-4518/728-1506 (Fax)

WASHINGTON
Seattle (98101-1128) - Bettina Bradley
U.S. Small Business Administration
Seattle District Office
1200 Sixth Avenue, Suite 1700
(206) 553-7317/553-7099 (Fax)
Spokane (99201) - Coralie Myers
SBA/Spokane Chamber of Commerce
Business Information Center
1020 West Riverside
(509) 353-2800/353-2600 (Fax)

WEST VIRGINIA
Fairmont (26554) - Nick Lambernedis
SBA/WVHTC Foundation
Business Information Center
1000 Technology Drive, Suite 111
(304) 368-0023/367-2717 (Fax)

Business Technology Association
12411 Wornall Road
Kansas City, MO 64145
(816) 941-3100/(800) 247-2176
FAX: (913) 941-2829
www.cais.com/ata/index.html
Contacts: Keith Anderson,
   Executive Director, and Kathy
   Logli, Director, Member
   Services
Other Locations: Eastern
   Region—Rochester, NY; Mid-
   America—Grand Blanc, MI;
   Southeastern Region—Largo,
   FL; and Western Region—Los
   Angeles, CA.

MAJOR GRADUATE
SCHOOLS OF BUSINESS

Babson College
Graduate School of Business
Babson Park, MA 02157-0310
(617) 239-4542
FAX: (617) 239-6148
Contact: Office of Dr. Robert
   E. Holmes, Dean

Carnegie Mellon University
Graduate School of Industrial
   Administration
500 Forbes Avenue, Pittsburgh,
   PA 15213
(412) 268-2265
Contact: Office of Dr. Robert
   S. Sullivan, Dean

Columbia University
Graduate School of Business
New York, NY 10027
(212) 854-6083
FAX: (212) 932-0545
Contact: Office of Dr. Meyer
   Feldberg, Dean

Cornell University
Johnson Graduate School of
   Management
Ithaca, NY 14853
(607) 255-6418
Contact: Office of Dr. Alan
   G. Merten, Dean

Dartmouth College
Amos Truck School of Business
   Administration
Hanover, NH 03755
(603) 646-2460
FAX: (603) 646-1308
Contact: Office of Dr. Colin
   C. Blaydon, Interim Dean

Duke University
Fuqua School of Business
Durham, NC 27706
(919) 660-7703
FAX: (919) 681-8026
Contact: Office of Dr. Wesley
   A. Magat, Senior Associate Dean

Harvard University
Graduate School of Business
   Administration
Boston, MA 02163
(617) 495-6000
Contact: Office of Dr. Kim
   B. Clark, Dean

Indiana State University
Graduate School of Business
Terra Haute, IN 47809-1401
(812) 237-2000
Contact: Office of Dr. Herbert
   Ross, Dean

**Massachusetts Institute of
   Technology**
Sloan School of Management
Cambridge, MA 02142
(617) 253-6615
FAX: (617) 258-6617
Contact: Office of Dr. Glenn
   L. Urban, Dean

New York University
Leonard N. Stern School of
   Business
New York, NY 10012
(212) 998-0900
FAX: (914) 323-5333
Contact: Office of Dr. George
   D. Daly, Dean

Northwestern University
J. L. Kellogg Graduate School
   of Management
Evanston, IL 60208
(847) 491-3300
Contact: Office of Dr. Donald
   P. Jacobs, Dean

Purdue University
Krannert Graduate School of
   Management
1310 Krannert Building
West Lafayette, IN 47907-1310
(765) 494-4366
Contact: Office of Dr. Dennis
   J. Weidenaar, Dean

Stanford University
Graduate School of Business
Stanford, CA 94305-5015
(415) 723-2766
FAX: (650) 725-7831
Contact: Office of Dr. A. Michael
   Spence, Dean

University of California at Berkeley
Haas School of Business
545 Student Services Building, #1900
Berkeley, CA 94720
(510) 642-1425
Contact: Office of Dr. William A. Hasler, Dean

University of California at Los Angeles
John E. Anderson Graduate School of Management
Los Angeles, CA 90024
(310) 825-6121
Contact: Office of Dr. William P. Pierskalla, Dean

University of Chicago
Graduate School of Business
Chicago, IL 60637
(773) 702-7121
FAX: (773) 702-9085
Contact: Office of Dr. Robert S. Hamada, Dean

University of Michigan
School of Business Administration
Ann Arbor, MI 48109
(313) 764-2343
Contact: Office of Dr. B. Joseph White, Dean

University of North Carolina
Joseph M. Bryan School of Business and Economics
Greensboro, NC 27412
(910) 334-5338
Contact: Office of Dr. James K. Weeks, Dean

University of Pennsylvania
The Wharton School
Philadelphia, PA 19104
(215) 898-3430
Contact: Office of Dr. Thomas P. Gerrity, Dean

University of Pittsburgh
Joseph M. Katz Graduate School of Business
Pittsburgh, PA 15260
(412) 648-1556
FAX: (412) 648-1552
Contact: Office of Dr. Frederick W. Winter, Dean

University of Rochester
William E. Simon Graduate School of Business
Rochester, NY 14627
(716) 275-3533
FAX: (716) 271-3907
Contact: Office of Dr. Charles Plosser, Dean

University of Southern California
Graduate School of Business Administration
Los Angeles, CA 90089
(213) 740-7846
Contact: Office of Dr. Randolph Westerfield, Dean

University of Texas
College of Business Administration
Austin, TX 78712
(512) 471-5921
Contact: Dr. Robert G. May, Acting Dean

University of Virginia
Darden Graduate School of
  Business Administration
Charlottesville, VA 22903
(804) 924-7481
Contact: Office of Dr. Leo
  I. Higdon, Jr., Dean

Vanderbilt University
Owen Graduate School of
  Management
401 21st Avenue South
Nashville, TN 37203
(615) 322-2534
FAX: (615) 343-7110
Contact: Office of Dr. Martin
  S. Geisel, Dean

Yale University
School of Management
135 Prospect Street
New Haven, CT 06511
(203) 432-6035
Contact: Office of Dr. Jeffrey
  E. Garten, Dean

ENTREPRENEURSHIP
CENTERS

Babson College
Center for Entrepreneurial Studies
Babson Park, MA 02157-0310
Entrepreneurial Division
(617) 239-4567
Contact: Office of Dr. William
  Bygrave, Director

Center for Creative Leadership
P.O. Box 26300
Greensboro, NC 27438-6300
(910) 288-7210
FAX: (910) 288-3999
www.ccl.org
Contact: Walter F. Ulmer Jr.,
  President

Center for Family Business
P.O. Box 24219
Cleveland, OH 44124
(216) 442-0800
FAX: (216) 442-0178
Contact: Leon A. Danco Ph.D.,
  President

**Center for International Private
Enterprise**
1615 H Street, NW
Washington, DC 20062
(202) 463-5901
FAX: (202) 887-3447
www.cipe.org
Contact: Wally Workman, Vice
  President

**Center for Management
Effectiveness**
427 Beirut Avenue
Pacific Palisades, CA 90272
(310) 459-6052
FAX: (310) 459-9307
Contact: Herbert S. Kindler Ph.D.,
  Director

**Center for Workforce
Preparation**
1615 H Street, NW
Washington, DC 20062-2000
(202) 463-5525
FAX: (202) 463-5730
Contact: Michelle Griffin,
  Communications Director

**Citizens for a Better
Environment**
407 South Dearborn, Suite 175
Chicago, IL 60605
(312) 939-1530
FAX: (312) 939-2536
www.cbemu.org
Contact: Jennifer Li, Program
  Assistant

**Citizens for a Better
Environment**
3255 Hennepin Avenue South
Minneapolis, MN 55331
(612) 824-8637
www.cbemw.org

**City and Regional Magazine
Association**
5820 Wilshire Boulevard, #500
Los Angeles, CA 90036
(213) 937-5514
FAX: (213) 937-0959
Contact: Jim Dowden, Executive
Director

**Commercial Service Posts
Abroad (U.S. Foreign and
Commercial Service)**
For a complete listing see entry under
U.S. Department of Commerce

Consumer Alert
1001 Connecticut Avenue,
Northwest, Suite 1128
Washington, DC. 20036
(202) 467-5809

**Consumers Union of the
United States**
101 Truman Avenue
Yonkers, NY 10703
(914) 378-2000
www.consumerreports.org

Copyright Clearance Center
222 Rosewood Drive
Danvers, MA 01923
(978) 750-8400
FAX: (978) 750-4744
www.copyright.com
Contact: Jospeh S. Alen,
President/CEO (Ed. Alen,
One 'N') info@copyright.com

**Council of Better Business
Bureaus**
4200 Wilson Boulevard, Suite 800
Arlington, VA 22203
(703) 276-0100
FAX: (703) 525-8277
www.bbb.org.sitemap/index.html

**Council of Consulting
Organizations**
521 Fifth Avenue, 35th Floor
New York, NY 10175-3598
(212) 697-9693
FAX: (212) 949-6571

Council on Employee Benefits
1144 East Market Street
Akron, OH 44316
(216) 796-4008
FAX: (216) 824-0446
Contact: Carl S. Lazaroff,
Secretary-Treasurer

**Council of Independent
Managers**
11512 North Port Washington Road
Mequon, WI 53092
(414) 241-8560
FAX: (414) 241-9493
Contact: Donna Kitlan, Executive
Secretary

**Council of Logistics
Management**
2803 Butterfield Road, Suite 380
Oak Brook, IL 60521
(708) 574-0985
FAX: (708) 574-0989
www.clm1.org

**Deaf and Hard of Hearing
Entrepreneurs Council**
814 Thayer Avenue, Suite 301
Silver Spring, MD 20910-4500
(301) 587-8596
FAX: (301) 587-5997
Contact: Louis J. Schwartz, President

**Direct Marketing Association,
Inc.**
1120 Avenue of the Americas
New York, NY 10036-6700
(212) 768-7277
FAX: (212) 768-4547
www.the-dma.org/
Contact: Chet Dalzell, Director of
Communications

Direct Selling Association
1666 K Street, NW, Suite 1010
Washington, DC 20006-2808
(202) 293-5760
FAX: (202) 463-4569
Contact: Liz Doherty, Director of
Communications

**Disabled Businesspersons
Association**
9625 Black Mountain Road,
Suite 207
San Diego, CA 92126-4564
(619) 586-1199
FAX: (619) 578-0637
www.web-link.com/dba.htm
Contact: Urban Miyares, President
(himself disabled)

**Employee Benefit Research
Institute**
2121 K Street, Northwest,
Suite 600
Washington, DC 20037
(202) 659-0670
FAX: (202) 775-6312
www.ebri.org

Entrepreneur Magazine Group
2392 Morse Avenue
Irvine, CA 92714-9440
(800) 421-2300
FAX: (714) 755-4211

The Entrepreneurship Institute
3892 Corporate Drive, Suite 101
Columbus, OH 43231
(614) 895-1153
FAX: (614) 895-1473
www.tsti.com/tei/
Contact: Jan W. Zupnick,
Executive Officer

University of Charleston
Tate Center for Entrepreneurship
School of Business and Economics
66 George Street
Charleston, SC 29424
(803) 953-6596

Wichita State University
Center for Entrepreneurship
1845 North Fairmount Street
Wichita, KA 67260-0147
(316) 978-3000
FAX: (316) 978-3687

EXPORT ASSISTANCE CENTERS,
U.S. DEPARTMENT OF COMMERCE

Web site addresses for the
Commercial Service State (home
pages for the Export Assistance
Centers are www.ita.doc.gov
/uscs/** [** is the 2 letter state
abbreviation]):

ALABAMA
**Birmingham (35203) - George Norton,
Director**
950 22nd Street North, Room 707
(205) 731-1331/731-0076 (Fax)
OBirming@doc.gov

ALASKA
Anchorage (99503) - Charles Becker, Director
3601 C Street, Suite 700
(907) 271-6237/271-6242 (Fax)
OAnchora@doc.gov

ARIZONA
Phoenix (85012) - Frank Woods, Director
2901 North Central Avenue, Suite 970
(602) 640-2513/640-2518 (Fax)
OPhoenix@doc.gov

ARKANSAS
Little Rock (72201) - Lon J. Hardin, Director
425 West Capitol Avenue, Suite 700
(501) 324-5794/324-7380 (Fax)
OLittleR@doc.gov

CALIFORNIA
Clovis (93611) - Arlene Mayeda, Manager
390-B Fir Avenue
(209) 325-1619/325-1647 (Fax)
OFresno@doc.gov
Downtown Los Angeles (90071) - Jim Cunningham, Manager
350 South Figueroa Street, Suite 172
(213) 894-8784/894-8790 (Fax)
jcunning@doc.gov
Inland Empire (91764) - Fred Latuperissa, Director
2940 Inland Empire Boulevard, Suite 121
(909) 466-4134/466-4140 (Fax)
OOntario@doc.gov
Long Beach (90831) - Joe Sachs, Director; US&FCS Director, Mary Delmege
Long Beach U.S. Export Assistance Center
One World Trade Center, Suite 1670
(310) 980-4550/980-4561 (Fax)
OLongBea@doc.gov
Los Angeles (90024) - Sherwin Chen, Manager
11000 Wilshire Boulevard, Room 9200
(310) 235-7104/235-7220 (Fax)
OLosAnge@doc.gov

Monterey (93940) - Dao Le, Manager
c/o Center for Trade & Commercial Diplomacy
411 Pacific Street, Suite 200
(408) 641-9850/641-9849 (Fax)
OMontere@doc.gov
Newport Beach (92660) - Paul Tambakis, Director
3300 Irvine Avenue, Suite 305
(714) 660-1688/660-8039 (Fax)
ONewport@doc.gov
Novato (94949) - Elizabeth Krauth, Manager
330 Ignacio Boulevard, Suite 102
(415) 883-1966/833-2711 (Fax)
ONorthBa@doc.gov
Oakland (94607) - Raj Shea, Manager
530 Water Street, Suite 740
(510) 273-7350/251-7352 (Fax)
OOakland@doc.gov
Oxnard (93030) - Gerald Vaughn, Manager
300 Esplanade Drive, Suite 2090
(805) 981-8150/981-1855 (Fax)
OOxnard@doc.gov
Sacramento (95814) - Brooks Ohlson, Manager
917 7th Street, 2nd Floor
(916) 498-5155/498-5923 (Fax)
OSacrame@doc.gov
San Diego (92122) - Matt Andersen, Manager
6363 Greenwich Drive, Suite 230
(619) 557-5395/557-6176 (Fax)
OSanDieg@doc.gov
San Francisco (94104) - Vacant, Manager
250 Montgomery Street, 14th Floor
(415) 705-2300/705-2297 (Fax)
OSanFran@doc.gov
San Francisco (94104) - Stephan Crawford
World Trade Center
345 California Street, 7th Floor
(415) 705-1053/705-1054 (Fax)
OWTCente@doc.gov
San Jose (95113) - James S. Kennedy, Director
U.S. Export Assistance Center
101 Park Center Plaza, Suite 1001
(408) 271-7300/271-7307 (Fax)
OSanJosx@doc.gov

**Santa Clara (95054) - James
C. Rigassio, Manager**
5201 Great American Parkway, #456
(408) 970-4610/970-4618 (Fax)
OSantaCl@doc.gov

COLORADO
**Denver (80202) - Nancy Charles-
Parker, Director**
U.S. Export Assistance Center
1625 Broadway, Suite 680
(303) 844-6622/844-5651 (Fax)
ODenver@doc.gov

CONNECTICUT
**Middletown (06457-3346) - Carl
Jacobsen, Director**
213 Court Street, Suite 903
(860) 638-6950/638-6970 (Fax)
OHartfor@doc.gov

DELAWARE
Served by the Philadelphia, Pennsylvania
    U.S. Export Assistance Center
OPhilade@doc.gov

FLORIDA
**Clearwater (34615) - George Martinez,
Manager**
1130 Cleveland Street
(813) 461-0011/449-2889 (Fax)
OClearwa@doc.gov
**Miami (33159) - Karl Koslowski,
Acting Director**
U.S. Export Assistance Center
P.O. Box 590570
5600 Northwest 36th Street, Suite 617
(305) 526-7425/526-7434 (Fax)
OMiami@doc.gov
**Orlando (32801) - Philip A. Ouzts,
Manager**
200 East Robinson Street, Suite 1270
(407) 648-6235/648-6756
OOrlando@doc.gov
**Tallahassee (32399-0001) - Michael
Higgins, Manager**
The Capitol, Suite 2001
(904) 488-6469/921-5395 (Fax)
OTallaha@doc.gov

GEORGIA
**Atlanta (30303-1229) - Samuel Troy,
Director**
U.S. Export Assistance Center
285 Peachtree Center Avenue, NE,
    Suite 200
(404) 657-1900/657-1970 (Fax)
OAtlanta@doc.gov
**Savannah (31405) - Barbara Prieto,
Manager**
6001 Chatham Center Drive, Suite 100
(912) 652-4204/652-4241 (Fax)
OSavanna@doc.gov

HAWAII
**Honolulu (96850) - Amer Kayani,
Manager**
P.O. Box 50026
300 Ala Moana Boulevard, Room 4106
(808) 541-1782/541-3435 (Fax)
OHonolul@doc.gov

IDAHO
**Boise (83720) - Steve Thompson,
Manager**
700 West State Street, 2nd Floor
(208) 334-3857/334-2783 (Fax)
OBoise@doc.gov

ILLINOIS
Chicago (60603) - Mary Joyce, Director
U.S. Export Assistance Center
55 West Monroe Street, Suite 2440
(312) 353-8045/353-8120 (Fax)
OCHICAGO@doc.gov
**Highland Park (60035) - Robin
F. Mugford, Manager**
610 Central Avenue, Suite 150
(847) 681-8010/681-8012 (Fax)
OHighlan@doc.gov
**Rockford (61110) - James Mied,
Manager**
515 North Court Street
(815) 987-8123/963-7943 (Fax)
ORockfor@doc.gov
Wheaton (60187) - Roy Dube, Manager
c/o Illinois Institute of Technology
201 East Loop Road
(312) 353-4332/353-4336 (Fax)
OWheaton@doc.gov

INDIANA
Indianapolis (46032) - Dan Swart, Manager
11405 North Pennsylvania Street, Suite 106
(317) 582-2300/582-2301 (Fax)
OIndiana@doc.gov

IOWA
Des Moines (50309) - Allen Patch, Manager
210 Walnut Street, Room 817
(515) 284-4222/284-4021 (Fax)
ODesMoin@doc.gov

KANSAS
Wichita (67214) George D. Lavid, Manager
151 North Volutsia
(316) 269-6160/683-7326 (Fax)
OWichita@doc.gov

KENTUCKY
Louisville (40202) - John Austin, Director
601 West Broadway, Room 634B
(502) 582-5066/582-6573 (Fax)
OLouisvi@doc.gov
Somerset (42501) - Sara Melton, Manager
2292 South Highway 27, Suite 320
(606) 677-6160/677-6161
OSomerse@doc.gov

LOUISIANA
New Orleans (70130) - David Spann, Director
Delta U.S. Export Assistance Center
365 Canal Street, Suite 2150
(504) 589-6546/589-2337 (Fax)
ONewOrle@doc.gov
Shreveport (71109) - Norbert O. Gannon, Manager
5210 Hollywood Avenue Annex
(318) 676-3064/676-3063 (Fax)
OShrevep@doc.gov

MAINE
Portland (04101) - Jeffrey Porter, Manager
c/o Maine International Trade Center
511 Congress Street
(207) 541-7430/541-7420 (Fax)
JPorter1@doc.gov

MARYLAND
Baltimore (21202) - Michael Keavney, Director
U.S. Export Assistance Center
World Trade Center, Suite 2432
401 East Pratt Street
(410) 962-4539/962-4529 (Fax)
OBaltimo@doc.gov

MASSACHUSETTS
Boston (02210) - Frank J. O'Connor, Director
U.S. Export Assistance Center
164 Northern Avenue
World Trade Center, Suite 307
(617) 424-5990/424-5992 (Fax)
OBoston@doc.gov
Marlborough (01752) - William Davis, Manager
100 Granger Boulevard, Unit 102
(508) 624-6000/624-7145
OMarlbor@doc.gov

MICHIGAN
Ann Arbor (48104) - Paul Litton, Manager
425 South Main Street, Suite 103
(313) 741-2430/741-2432 (Fax)
OAnnArbo@doc.gov
Detroit (48226) - Neil Hesse, Director
U.S. Export Assistance Center
211 West Fort Street, Suite 2220
(313) 226-3650/226-3657 (Fax)
ODetroit@doc.gov
Grand Rapids (49504) - Thomas Maguire, Manager
301 West Fulton Street, Suite 718-S
(616) 458-3564/458-3872 (Fax)
OGrandRa@doc.gov

Pontiac (48341) - Richard Corson, Manager
Oakland Pointe Office Building
250 Elizabeth Lake Road
(810) 975-9600/975-9606 (Fax)
OPontiac@doc.gov

MINNESOTA
Minneapolis (55401) - Ronald E. Kramer, Director
U.S. Export Assistance Center
110 South 4th Street, Room 108
(612) 348-1638/348-1650 (Fax)
OMinneap@doc.gov

MISSISSIPPI
Jackson (39201) - Harrison Ford, Director
201 West Capitol Street, Suite 310
(601) 965-4388/965-5386 (Fax)
OJackson@doc.gov

MISSOURI
Kansas City (64106) - Thomas Strauss, Director
601 East 12th Street, Room 635
(816) 426-3141/426-3140 (Fax)
OKansasC@doc.gov
St Louis (63105) - Randall J. LaBounty, Director
U.S. Export Assistance Center
8182 Maryland Avenue, Suite 303
(314) 425-3302/425-3381 (Fax)
OStLouis@doc.gov

MONTANA
Served by the Boise, Idaho Export
  Assistance Center
OBoise@doc.gov

NEBRASKA
Omaha (68137) - Meredith Bond, Acting Manager
11135 "O" Street
(402) 221-3664/221-3668 (Fax)
OOmaha@doc.gov

NEVADA
Reno (89502) - Jere Dabbs, Manager
1755 East Plumb Lane, Suite 152
(702) 784-5203/784-5343 (Fax)
OReno@doc.gov

NEW HAMPSHIRE
Portsmouth (03801-2838) - Susan Berry, Manager
17 New Hampshire Avenue
(603) 334-6074/334-6110 (Fax)
OPortsmo@doc.gov

NEW JERSEY
Newark (07102) - Tom Rosengren, Manager
One Gateway Center, 9th Floor
(201) 645-4682/645-4783 (Fax)
ONewark@doc.gov
Trenton (08648) - Rod Stuart, Director
3131 Princeton Pike, Building #6,
  Suite 100
(609) 989-2100/989-2395 (Fax)
OTrenton@doc.gov

NEW MEXICO
Santa Fe (87504-5003) - Sandra Necessary, Manager
c/o New Mexico Department of Economic
  Development
P.O. Box 20003
1100 St. Francis Drive
(505) 827-0350/827-0263 (Fax)
OSantaFe@doc.gov

NEW YORK
Buffalo (14202) - George Buchanan, Director
111 West Huron Street, Room 1304
(716) 551-4191/551-5290 (Fax)
OBuffalo@doc.gov
Harlem (10027) - K. L. Fredericks, Manager
163 West 125th Street, Suite 904
(212) 860-6200/860-6203 (Fax)
OHarlem@doc.gov
Long Island (11501) - George Soteros, Manager
1550 Franklin Avenue, Room 207
(516) 739-1765/739-3310 (Fax)
OLongIsl@doc.gov
New York (10048) - Joel W. Barkan, Acting Director
U.S. Export Assistance Center
6 World Trade Center, Room 635
(212) 466-5222/264-1356 (Fax)
ONewYork@doc.gov

Rochester (14604) - James C. Mariano, Manager
111 East Avenue, Suite 220
(716) 263-6480/325-6505 (Fax)
ORochest@doc.gov
Westchester (10604) - William Spitler, Director
707 West Chester Avenue
(914) 682-6218/682-6698 (Fax)
OWestche@doc.gov

NORTH CAROLINA
Charlotte (28202) - Roger Fortner, Director
Carolinas U.S. Export Assistance Center
521 East Morehead Street, Suite 435
(704) 333-4886/332-2681 (Fax)
OCharlot@doc.gov
Greensboro (27401) - Samuel P. Troy, Director
400 West Market Street, Suite 400
(910) 333-5345/333-5158 (Fax)
OGreensb@doc.gov

NORTH DAKOTA
Served by the Minneapolis, Minnesota
Export Assistance Center
OMinneap@doc.gov

OHIO
Cincinnati (45202) - Michael Miller, Director
36 East 7th Street, Suite 2650
(513) 684-2944/684-3227 (Fax)
OCincinn@doc.gov
Cleveland (44114) - John McCartney, Director
U.S. Export Assistance Center
600 Superior Avenue East, Suite 700
(216) 522-4750/522-2235 (Fax)
OClevela@doc.gov
Columbus (43215) - Mary Beth Double, Manager
37 North High Street, 4th Floor
(614) 365-9510/365-9598 (Fax)
OColumbo@doc.gov
Toledo (43604) - Robert Abrahams, Manager
300 Madison Avenue
(419) 241-0683/241-0684 (Fax)
OToledo@doc.gov

OKLAHOMA
Oklahoma City (73116) - Ronald L. Wilson, Director
301 Northwest 63rd Street, Suite 330
(405) 231-5302/231-4211
OOklahom@doc.gov
Tulsa (74106) - Vacant, Manager
700 North Greenwood Avenue, Suite 1400
(918) 581-7650/594-8413
OTulsa@doc.gov

OREGON
Eugene (97401-4003) - Pamela Ward, Manager
1445 Willamette Street, Suite 13
(541) 465-6575/465-6704 (Fax)
OEugene@doc.gov
Portland (97204) - Scott Goddin, Director
U.S. Export Assistance Center
One World Trade Center, Suite 242
121 Southwest Salmon Street
(503) 326-3001/326-6351 (Fax)
OPortlan@doc.gov

PENNSYLVANIA
Harrisburg (17101) - Deborah Doherty, Manager
One Commerce Square
417 Walnut Street, 3rd Floor
(717) 232-0051/232-0054 (Fax)
OHarrisb@doc.gov
Moosic (18507) - Henry LaBlanc, Manager
One Montage Mountain Road, Suite B
(717) 969-2530/969-2539 (Fax)
OScranto@doc.gov
Philadelphia (19106) - Maria Galindo, Director
U.S. Export Assistance Center
615 Chestnut Street, Suite 1501
(215) 597-6101/597-6123 (Fax)
OPhilade@doc.gov
Pittsburgh (15222) - Ted Arnn, Manager
2002 Federal Building
100 Liberty Avenue
(412) 395-5050/395-4875 (Fax)
OPittsbu@doc.gov

RHODE ISLAND
Providence (02903) - Raimond
  Meerbach, Manager
One West Exchange Street
(401) 528-5104/528-5067 (Fax)
OProvide@doc.gov

SOUTH CAROLINA
Charleston (29403) - David Kuhlmeier,
  Manager
P.O. Box 975
81 Mary Street
(803) 727-4051/727-4052 (Fax)
OCharlSC@doc.gov
Columbia (29201) - Ann Watts,
  Director
1835 Assembly Street, Suite 172
(803) 765-5345/253-3614 (Fax)
OColumbi@doc.gov
Greenville (29607) - Denis Csizmadia,
  Manager
Park Central Office Park, Building 1,
  Suite 109
555 North Pleasantburg Drive
(864) 271-1976/271-4171 (Fax)
OGreenvi@doc.gov

SOUTH DAKOTA
Sioux Falls (57197) - Harvey
  Timberlake, Manager
Augustana College, 2001 South Summit
  Avenue
Room SS-29A
(605) 330-4264/330-4266 (Fax)
OSiouxFa@doc.gov

TENNESSEE
Knoxville (37915) - Thomas McGinty,
  Manager
301 East Church Avenue
(423) 545-4637/545-4435 (Fax)
OKnoxvil@doc.gov
Memphis (38103) - Ree Russell, Manager
22 North Front Street, Suite 200
(901) 544-4137/544-3646 (Fax)
OMemphis@doc.gov
Nashville (37219) - Michael Speck,
  Director
Parkway Towers, Suite 114
404 James Robertson Parkway
(615) 736-5161/736-2454 (Fax)
ONashvil@doc.gov

TEXAS
Austin (78711) - Karen Parker,
  Manager
1700 Congress, 2nd Floor
P.O. Box 12728
(512) 916-5939/916-5940 (Fax)
OAustin@doc.gov
Dallas (75342-0069) - Bill Schrage,
  Director
U.S. Export Assistance Center
P.O. Box 420069
2050 North Stemmons Freeway, Suite 170
(214) 767-0542/767-8240 (Fax)
ODallas@doc.gov
Fort Worth (76102) - Vavie Sellschopp,
  Manager
711 Houston Street
(817) 212-2673/978-0178 (Fax)
OFortWor@doc.gov
Houston (77002) - James D. Cook,
  Director
500 Dallas, Suite 1160
(713) 718-3062/718-3060 (Fax)
OHouston@doc.gov
San Antonio (78212) - Mitchel
  Auerbach, Manager
1222 North Main, Suite 450
(210) 228-9878/228-9874 (Fax)
OSanAnto@doc.gov

UTAH
Salt Lake City (84111) - Stephen
  P. Smoot, Director
324 South State Street, Suite 221
(801) 524-5116/524-5886 (Fax)
OSalLak@doc.gov

VERMONT
Montpelier (05609) - James Cox,
  Manager
109 State Street, 4th Floor
(802) 828-4508/828-3258 (Fax)
OMontpel@doc.gov

VIRGINIA
Richmond (23219) William Davis
  Coale, Jr., Director
704 East Franklin Street, Suite 550
(804) 771-2246/771-2390 (Fax)
ORichmon@doc.gov

WASHINGTON
Seattle (98121) - Lisa Kjaer-Schade, Director
U.S. Export Assistance Center
2001 6th Avenue, Suite 650
(206) 553-5615/553-7253 (Fax)
OSeattle@doc.gov
Spokane (99201) - James K. Hellwig, Manager
c/o Greater Spokane Chamber of Commerce
1020 West Riverside
(509) 353-2625/353-2449
OSpokane@doc.gov

WEST VIRGINIA
Charleston (25301) - Martha Butwin, Acting Director
405 Capitol Street, Suite 807
(304) 347-5123/347-5408
OCharlWV@doc.gov
Wheeling (26003) - Martha Butwin, Manager
1310 Market Street, 2nd Floor
(304) 233-7472/233-7492 (Fax)
OWheelin@doc.gov

WISCONSIN
Milwaukee (53202) - Paul D. Churchill, Director
517 East Wisconsin Avenue, Room 596
(414) 297-3473/297-3470 (Fax)
OMilwauk@doc.gov

WYOMING
Served by the Denver, Colorado U.S. Export Assistance Center
ODenver@doc.gov

PUERTO RICO
San Juan (00918) - J. Enrique Vilella, Director
525 F.D. Roosevelt Avenue, Suite 905
(787) 766-5555/766-5692 (Fax)
OSanJuan@doc.gov

EXPORT ASSISTANCE CENTERS
For a complete listing, see the entry for the U.S. Department of Commerce.

Editorial Freelancers Association
71 West 23rd Street, Suite 1504
New York, NY 10010
(212) 929-5400
FAX: (212) 929-5439

The Human Resource Planning Society
317 Madison Avenue, Suite 1509
New York, NY 10017
(212) 490-6387
FAX: (212) 682-6851
www.aevans.com/frames/hrps/html/member.htm
Contact: Beverly B. Pinzon, Director of Communications

Independent Small Business Employers of America
520 South Pierce Street, Suite 224
Mason City, IA 50401
(515) 424-3187
FAX: (703) 548-6216

INDUSTRY SPECIALISTS - INTERNATIONAL TRADE ADMINISTRATION, U.S. DEPARTMENT OF COMMERCE

Industry	Contact	Phone
Abrasive Products	Graylin Presbury	202-482-5158
Accounting	J. Marc Chittum	202-482-0345

Industry	Contact	Phone
Adhesives/Sealants	Raimundo Prat	202-482-0810
Advanced Materials	Lauren Brosler	202-482-4431
Advertising	Bruce Harsh	202-482-4582
Aerospace Financing Issues	Jon Montgomery	202-482-6234
Aerospace Industry Analysis	Frederick Elliott	202-482-1233
Aerospace Industry Data	Ronald Green	202-482-3068
Aerospace Information & Analysis	Ronald Green	202-482-3068
Aerospace Market Development	Tony Largay	202-482-6236
Aerospace Market Promo	Tony Largay	202-482-6236
Aerospace-Space Market Support	Kim Farner	202-482-2232
Aerospace Marketing Support	Heather Pederson	202-482-6239
Aerospace Office of	Sally H. Bath	202-482-1229
Aerospace-Space Programs	Kim Farner	202-482-2232
Aerospace Trade Policy	Fred Elliott	202-482-1233
Aerospace (Trade Promo)	Tony Largay	202-482-6236
Agricultural Chemicals	Michael Kelly	202-482-0811
Agricultural Machinery	Mary Wiening	202-482-4708
Air Couriers	Eugene Alford	202-482-5071
Air Conditioning Eqmt	Eugene Shaw	202-482-3494
Air, Gas Compressors	Leonard Heimowitz	202-482-0552
Air, Gas Compressors (Trade Promo)	George Zanetakos	202-482-0558
Air Pollution Control Eqmt	Eric Fredell	202-482-0343
Aircraft & Aircraft Engines (Market Support)	Heather Pederson	202-482-6239
Aircraft Auxiliary Eqmt	Heather Pederson	202-482-6239
Aircraft Parts (Market Support)	Shannon Ballard	202-482-3786
Airlines	Eugene Alford	202-482-5071
Airport Equipment	Shannon Ballard	202-482-3786
Airport (Major Proj)	Mike Thompson	202-482-5126
Air Traffic Control Eqmt	Shannon Ballard	202-482-3786
Air Transport Services	Eugene Alford	202-482-5071
Alcoholic Beverages	Donald Hodgen	202-482-3346
Aluminum	David Cammarota	202-482-5157
Aluminum Oxide	Graylin Presbury	202-482-5158
Analytical Instruments	George Litman	202-482-3411
Analytical & Scientific Instruments (Trade Promo)	Franc Manzolillo	202-482-2991
Apparel	Joanne Tucker	202-482-4058
Apparel (Trade Promo)	Ferenc Molnar	202-482-5153
Artificial Intelligence	Mike Diaz	202-482-0397
Asbestos/Cement Prod	Charles Pitcher	202-482-0385
Audio Visual Services	John Siegmund	202-482-4781
Auto Industry Affairs	Henry Misisco	202-482-0554
Auto Industry (Trade Promo)	John C. White	202-482-0671

Industry	Contact	Phone
Auto Parts & Suppliers	Robert O. Reck	202-482-1418
Aviation Services	Eugene Alford	202-482-5071
Avionics Marketing	Heather Pederson	202-482-2835
Bakery Products	Donald Hodgen	202-482-3346
Ball Bearings	Richard Reise	202-482-3489
Banking Services	John Shuman	202-482-3050
Basic Paper & Board Mfg	Gary Stanley	202-482-0375
Bauxite, Alumina, Prim Alum	David Cammarota	202-482-5157
Beer	Donald Hodgen	202-482-3346
Belting & Hose	Raimundo Prat	202-482-0128
Beryllium	Barbara Males	202-482-0606
Beverages	Donald Hodgen	202-482-3346
Bicycles	John Vanderwolf	202-482-0348
Biomass Energy Equipment	Les Garden	202-482-0556
Biotechnology	Emily Arakaki	202-482-0130
Boats, Pleasure	John Vanderwolf	202-482-0348
Books	William S. Lofquist	202-482-0379
Breakfast Cereal	Donald Hodgen	202-482-3346
Bridges (Major Proj)	Michael Thompson	202-482-5126
Broadcasting Equipment	Krysten Jenci	202-482-2952
Brooms & Brushes	John M. Harris	202-482-1178
Building Materials & Construction	Charles B. Pitcher	202-482-0385
Business Eqmt (Trade Promo)	Judy Fogg	202-482-4936
Business Forms	Rose Marie Bratland	202-482-0380
CAD/CAM/CAE Software	Vera A. Swann	202-482-0396
Canned Food Products	Donald Hodgen	202-482-3346
Carbon Black	Raimundo Prat	202-482-0128
Cellular Radio Telephone Eqmt	Richard Paddock	202-482-5235
Cement	Charles Pitcher	202-482-0385
Cement Plants (Major Proj)	Wally Haraguchi	202-482-4877
Chemical Industries Machinery (Trade Promo)	Eugene Shaw	202-482-3494
Chemical Plants (Major Proj)	Wally Haraguchi	202-482-4877
Chemicals & Allied Products	Michael J. Kelly	202-482-0128
Chinaware	Rose Marie Bratland	202-482-0380
Chromium	Graylin Presbury	202-482-5158
Civil Aircraft Agreement	Fred Elliott	202-482-1233
Civil Aviation Policy	Eugene Alford	202-482-5071
Coal Exports	John Rasmussen	202-482-1466
Cobalt	Graylin Presbury	202-482-5158
Columbium	Graylin Presbury	202-482-5158
Commercial Lighting Fixtures	Tony Vandermuhll	202-482-2390
Commercial/Indus Refrig Eqmt	Eugene Shaw	202-482-3494

Industry	Contact	Phone
Commercial Printing	William S. Lofquist	202-482-0379
Commercialization of Space (Market)	Kim Farner	202-482-4222
Computer Consulting	Jennifer Tallarico	202-482-5820
Computer and DP Services	Jennifer Tallarico	202-482-5820
Computer Software	Heidi Hijikata	202-482-0571
Computers, Systems (Hardware)	Timothy Miles	202-482-2990
Computer, Large Scale	Wayne Ebenfeld	202-482-1987
Computers, Personal/Portables	R. Clay Woods	202-482-3013
Computers Trade Promo	Judy A. Fogg	202-482-4936
Computers, Workstations	R. Clay Woods	202-482-3013
Confectionery Products	Donald Hodgen	202-482-3346
Construction Machinery, Large Off Road	Leonard Heimowitz	202-482-0558
Construction Services	Wally Haraguchi	202-482-4877
Construction Statistics	Patrick MacAuley	202-482-0132
Consumer Electronics	Laureen Daly	202-482-3360
Consumer Goods		202-482-0338
Conveyors/Conveying Eqmt	Mary Weining	202-482-4708
Copper	Barbara Males	202-482-0606
Containers & Packaging		202-482-0132
Cosmetics (Overseas Trade Show Recruitment)	Edward Kimmel	202-482-3640
Countertrade Services	Paula Mitchell	202-482-4471
	Pompiliu Verzariu	202-482-4434
Cutlery	Rose Marie Bratland	202-482-0380
Dairy Products	Donald Hodgen	202-482-3346
Data Base Services	Jennifer Tallarico	202-482-5820
Data Processing Services	Jennifer Tallarico	202-482-5820
Dental Equipment (Devices and Supplies)	Duaine Priestley	202-482-2410
Dental Equipment (Trade Promo)	George Keen	202-482-2010
Desalination/Water Reuse	Frederica Wheeler	202-482-3509
Desalination (Major Proj)	William Holroyd	202-482-6168
Diamonds, Industrial	Graylin Presbury	202-482-5158
Direct Marketing	Bruce Harsh	202-482-4582
Disk Storage	Daniel Valverde	202-482-0573
Distilled Spirits	Donald Hodgen	202-482-3346
Dolls	Jonathan Freilich	202-482-5783
Drugs	William Hurt	202-482-0128
Durable Consumer Goods	Kevin Ellis	202-482-1176
Education Svcs/Manpower Training (Trade Promo)	J. Marc Chittum	202-482-0345
Electric Industrial Apparatus Nec	Julie Fouque	202-482-2390

Industry	Contact	Phone
Elec/Power Gen/Transmission & Dist Eqmt (Trade Promo)	Andy Collier	202-482-0680
Electrical Power Plants (Major Proj)	Andy Collier	202-482-0680
Electrical Test & Measuring	Michael Andrews	202-482-2795
Electricity	Andy Collier	202-482-0680
ElectroOptical Instruments (Trade Promo)	Franc Manzolillo	202-482-2991
Electronic Components (Director)	Margaret Donnelly	202-482-5466
Electronic Components	Marleen Ruffin	202-482-0570
Electronics (Printed Circuit Boards)	Jodee Mussehl-Aziz	202-482-3360
Electronic Database Services	Jennifer Tallarico	202-482-5820
Elevators, Moving Stairways	Mary Wiening	202-482-4708
Employment Services (Trade Promo)	J. Marc Chittum	202-482-0345
Energy	Helen Bourroughs	202-482-1466
Energy, Renewable	Les Garden	202-482-0556
Energy, Renewable (Tech & Eqmt)	Les Garden	202-482-0556
Engineering/Construction Services	Jay Smith	202-482-4642
Entertainment Industries	John Siegmund	202-482-4781
Entertainment Services	Wray O. Candilis	202-482-0339
Environmental Technologies	(Main Number)	202-482-5225
Equipment, Used	John Bodson	202-482-0681
Explosives	Mike Kelly	202-482-0811
Export Trading Companies	W. Dawn Busby	202-482-5131
Fabricated Metal Construction Materials	Franklin Williams	202-482-0132
Farm Machinery	Mary Wiening	202-482-4708
Fasteners (Industrial)	Richard Reise	202-482-3489
Fats and Oils	Donald Hodgen	202-482-3346
Fencing (Metal)	Franklin Williams	202-482-0132
Ferroalloys Products	Graylin Presbury	202-482-5158
Ferrous Scrap	Charles Bell	202-482-0608
Fertilizers	Mike Kelly	202-482-0811
Fiber Optics	Stuart Sandall	202-482-2006
Filters/Purifying Eqmt	Eric Fredell	202-482-0343
Financial Services	S. Cassin Muir	202-482-0349
Fisheries	National Marine Fisheries Service	202-482-2379
Flexible Mfg Systems	Megan Pilaroscia	202-482-0609
Flour	Donald Hodgen	202-482-3346
Flowers	Donald Hodgen	202-482-3346
Food Processing/Packaging Machinery (Trade Promo)	Eugene Shaw	202-482-3494
Food Products Machinery	Eugene Shaw	202-482-3494

Industry	Contact	Phone
Food Retailing	Donald Hodgen	202-482-3346
Footwear	James E. Byron	202-482-4034
Forest Products	Gary Stanley	202-482-0375
Forest Products, Building Materials	Chris Kristensen	202-482-0384
Forestry/Woodworking Eqmt (Trade Promo)	Ed Abrahams	202-482-0312
Forgings/Semifinished Steel	Charles Bell	202-482-0608
Fossil Fuels	John Rasmussen	202-482-1889
Foundry Industry	Charles Bell	202-482-0608
Fruits	Donald Hodgen	202-482-3346
Frozen Foods Products	Donald Hodgen	202-482-3346
Fur Goods	James E. Byron	202-482-4034
Furniture	Jonathan Freilich	202-482-5783
Gallium	David Cammarota	202-482-5157
Games & Children's Vehicles	Jonathan Freilich	202-482-5783
Gaskets/Gasketing Materials	Richard Reise	202-482-3489
General Aviation Aircraft	Eugene Alford	202-482-5071
Gen Indus Mach Nec, Exc 35691	Raymond Robinson	202-482-0610
Generator Sets/Turbines (Major Proj)	Andy Collier	202-482-0680
Germanium	David Cammarota	202-482-5157
Giftware (Trade Promo)	Les Simon	202-482-0341
Glass, Flat	Franklin Williams	202-482-0132
Glassware (household)	Rose Marie Bratland	202-482-0380
Gloves (work)	James Byron	202-482-4034
Grain Mill Products	Donald Hodgen	202-482-3346
Greeting Cards	Rose Marie Bratland	202-482-0380
Grocery Retailing	Donald Hodgen	202-482-3346
Hand Saws, Saw Blades	Edward Abrahams	202-482-0312
Hand/Edge Tools Ex Mach TI/Saws	Edward Abrahams	202-482-0312
Handbags	James E. Byron	202-482-4034
Hard Surfaced Floor Coverings	Franklin Williams	202-482-0132
Hardware (Export Promo)	Edward Kimmel	202-482-3640
Hazardous Waste	Loretta Jonkers	202-482-0564
Health Care Services	Simon Francis	202-482-2697
Heating Eqmt Ex Furnaces	John Manger	202-482-2732
Helicopters	Ronald Green	202-482-3068
High Tech Trade, U.S. Competitiveness	Victoria L. Hatter	202-482-3895
Hoists, Overhead Cranes	Mary Wiening	202-482-4708
Home Video	Wray O. Candilis	202-482-0339
Hose & Belting	Raimundo Prat	202-482-0128
Hotel and Restaurant Equipment	Edward Kimmel	202-482-3640
Household Appliances	John M. Harris	202-482-1178

Industry	Contact	Phone
Household Appliances (Trade Promo)	Les Simon	202-482-0341
Household Furniture	Jonathan Freilich	202-482-5783
Housewares (Export Promo)	Les Simon	202-482-0341
Housing Construction	Charles Pitcher	202-482-0385
Housing (Manufactured)	Charles Pitcher	202-482-0385
Hydro Power, Plants (Major Proj)	Andrew Collier	202-482-0680
Industrial Chemicals	William Hurt	202-482-0128
Industrial Controls	John Bodson	202-482-0681
Industrial Drives/Gears	Richard Reise	202-482-3489
Industrial Eqmt (Trade Promo)	Eugene Shaw	202-482-3494
Industrial Gases	Antonios Kostalas	202-482-2390
Industrial Organic Chemicals	William Hurt	202-482-0128
Industrial Robots	Megan Pilaroscia	202-482-0609
Industrial Trucks	Mary Wiening	202-482-4608
Information Industries	Jennifer Tallarico	202-482-5820
Information Services	Wray O. Candilis	202-482-0339
Infrastructure (Main Number)	Jay Smith	202-482-4642
Infrastructure/Water	Bill Holroyd	202-482-6168
Inorganic Chemicals	Vincent Kamenicky	202-482-0812
Inorganic Pigments	Vincent Kamenicky	202-482-0812
Insulation	Patrick Macauley	202-482-0134
Insurance	Cass Muir	202-482-0346
Intellectual Property Rights (Services)	John E. Siegmund	202-482-4781
Investment Management	S. Cassin Muir	202-482-0349
Iron	Charles Bell	202-482-0608
Irrigation Equipment	Mary Wiening	202-482-4708
Irrigation (Major Projects)	Jay Smith	202-482-4642
Jams & Jellies	Donald A. Hodgen	202-482-3346
Jewelry	John Harris	202-482-1178
Jewelry (Trade Promo)	Ludene Capone	202-482-2087
Jute Products	Maria Corey	202-482-4058
Kitchen Cabinets	Suzanne Willis	202-482-0577
Laboratory Instruments	George Litman	202-482-3411
Laboratory Instruments (Trade Promo)	Franc Manzolillo	202-482-2991
Lasers/ElectroOptics (Trade Promo)	Franc Manzolillo	202-482-2991
Lawn & Garden Eqmt	John Vanderwolf	202-482-0348
Lead Products	David Larrabee	202-482-0607
Leasing: Eqmt, Vehicles, Services	Elnora Uzzelle	202-482-0351
Leather Apparel	James E. Byron	202-482-4034
Leather Products	James E. Byron	202-482-4034

Industry	Contact	Phone
Leather Tanning	James E. Byron	202-482-4034
Legal Services	J. Marc Chittum	202-482-0345
LNG Plants (Major Proj)	Wally Haraguchi	202-482-4877
Local Area Networks		202-482-0572
Logs, Wood	Gary Stanley	202-482-0375
Luggage	James Byron	202-482-4034
Lumber	Gary Stanley	202-482-0377
Machine Tool Accessories	Megan Pilaroscia	202-482-0609
Magazines	Rose Marie Bratland	202-482-0380
Magnesium	David Cammarota	202-482-5157
Major Projects	Jay Smith	202-482-4642
Management and Research Svcs (Trade Promo)	J. Marc Chittum	202-482-0345
Management Consulting	J. Marc Chittum	202-482-0345
Manifold Business Forms	Rose Marie Bratland	202-482-0380
Manmade Fiber	Joanne Tucker	202-482-4058
Margarine	Donald Hodgen	202-482-3346
Marine Recreational Eqmt (Trade Promo)	Ludene Capone	202-482-2087
Marine Insurance	C. William Johnson	202-482-5012
Marine Port/Shipbuilding Eqmt (Trade Promo)	Ludene Capone	202-482-2087
Marine Port/Shipbuilding (Major Projects)	Mike Thompson	202-482-5126
Maritime Shipping	C. William Johnson	202-482-5012
Materials, Advanced	David Cammarota	202-482-5157
Materials Handling Machinery (Trade Promo)	Mary Wiening	202-482-4708
Meat Products	Donald A. Hodgen	202-482-3346
Mech Power Transmission Eqmt	Richard Reise	202-482-3489
Medical Instruments	Victoria Kader	202-482-4073
Medical Instruments & Eqmt (Trade Promo)	George B. Keen	202-482-2010
Medical Services	Simon Francis	202-482-2697
Mercury	David Larrabee	202-482-0607
Metal Building Products	Franklin Williams	202-482-0132
Metal Cutting Machine Tools	Megan Pilaroscia	202-482-0609
Metal Forming Machine Tools	Megan Pilaroscia	202-482-0609
Metal Powders	David Cammarota	202-482-5157
Metals, Secondary	Charles Bell	202-482-0608
Metalworking	John Mearman	202-482-0315
Metalworking Eqmt Nec	Megan Pilaroscia	202-482-0609
Millwork	Gary Stanley	202-482-0377

Industry	Contact	Phone
Mineral Based Construction Materials (Clay, Concrete, Gypsum, Asphalt, Stone)	Charles Pitcher	202-482-0385
Mining Machinery	Len Heimowitz	202-482-0558
Mining Machinery (Trade Promo)	George Zanetakos	202-482-0552
Mobile Homes		202-482-0132
Molybdenum	David Cammarota	202-482-5157
Monorails (Trade Promo)	Mary Wiening	202-482-4708
Motion Pictures	John Siegmund	202-482-4781
Motor Vehicles	Albert T. Warner	202-482-0669
Motorcycles	John Vanderwolf	202-482-0348
Motors, Electric	John Mearman	202-482-0315
Music (prerecorded)	John Siegmund	202-482-4781
Musical Instruments (Trade Promo)	John Harris	202-482-1178
Multichip Modules	Duaine Priestley	202-482-2410
Mutual Funds	S. Cassin Muir	202-482-0349
Natural Gas	John Rasmussen	202-482-1889
Natural, Synthetic Rubber	Raimundo Prat	202-482-0128
Newspapers	Rose Marie Bratland	202-482-0380
Nickel Products	Graylin Presbury	202-482-0575
Non-alcoholic Beverages	Donald Hodgen	202-482-3346
Noncurrent Carrying Wiring Devices	John Bodson	202-482-0681
Nondurable Goods	Les Simon	202-482-0341
Nonferrous Foundries	David Cammarota	202-482-5157
Nonferrous Metals	David Larrabee	202-482-0607
Nonmetallic Minerals Nec	Robert Shaw	202-482-5124
Nonresidential Constr	Patrick MacAuley	202-482-0132
Nuclear Power Plants/Machinery	Andrew Collier	202-482-0680
Nuclear Power Plants (Major Proj)	Andy Collier	202-482-0680
Numerical Controls for Mach Tools	Megan Pilaroscia	202-482-0609
Nuts, Edible	Donald Hodgen	202-482-3346
Nuts, Bolts, Washers	Richard Reise	202-482-3489
Ocean Shipping	C. William Johnson	202-482-5012
Oil & Gas (Fuels Only)	John Rasmussen	202-482-1889
Oil Field Machinery	John Rasmussen	202-482-1889
Oil Shale (Major Proj)	Wally Haraguchi	202-482-4877
Operations & Maintenance	J. Marc Chittum	202-482-0345
Organic Chemicals	William Hurt	202-482-0128
Outdoor Lighting Fixtures	John Bodson	202-482-0681
Overseas Export Promotion	Edward Kimmel	202-482-3640
Outdoor Power Eqmt (Trade Promo)	Les Simon	202-482-0341
Packaging & Containers	John Bodson	202-482-0681
Packaging Machinery	Eugene Shaw	202-482-3494

Industry	Contact	Phone
Paints/Coatings	Raimundo Prat	202-482-0128
Paper	Gary Stanley	202-482-0375
Paper & Board Packaging	Gary Stanley	202-482-0375
Paper Industries Machinery	Edward Abrahams	202-482-0312
Pasta	Donald Hodgen	202-482-3346
Paving Materials (Asphalt & Concrete)	Charles Pitcher	202-482-0385
Pectin	Donald Hodgen	202-482-3346
Periodicals	Rose Marie Bratland	202-482-0380
Pet Food	Donald Hodgen	202-482-3346
Pet Products	Edward Kimmel	202-482-3640
Petrochem, Cyclic Crudes	William Hurt	202-482-0128
Petrochemicals	William Hurt	202-482-0128
Petrochemicals Plants (Major Proj)	Wally Haraguchi	202-482-4877
Petroleum, Crude & Refined Products	John Rasmussen	202-482-1889
Pharmaceuticals	William Hurt	202-482-0128
Pipelines (Major Proj)	Wally Haraguchi	202-482-4877
Photographic Eqmt & Supplies	Joyce Watson	202-482-0574
Plastic Construction Products (Most)	Franklin Williams	202-482-0132
Plastic Materials/Resins	Raimundo Prat	202-482-0128
Plastic Products	Raimundo Prat	202-482-0128
Plastic Products Machinery	Eugene Shaw	202-482-3494
Plumbing Fixtures & Fittings	Charles Pitcher	202-482-0385
Plywood/Panel Products	Gary Stanley	202-482-0377
Pollution Control Equipment	Loretta Jonkers	202-482-0564
Porcelain Electrical Supplies	Helen Burroughs	202-482-4931
Ports	Michael Thompson	202-482-5126
Potato Chips	Donald Hodgen	202-482-3346
Poultry Products	Donald A. Hodgen	202-482-3346
Power Hand Tools	Edward Abrahams	202-482-0312
Power Generation (Major Projects)	Andy Collier	202-482-0680
Precious Metal Jewelry	John M. Harris	202-482-1178
Prefabricated Buildings (Metal)	Franklin Williams	202-482-0132
Prefabricated Buildings (Wood)		202-482-0132
Prepared Meats	Donald A. Hodgen	202-482-3346
Pretzels	Donald Hodgen	202-482-3346
Primary Commodities	Fred Siesseger	202-482-5124
Printed Circuit Boards	Judee Mussehl	202-482-0429
Printing & Publishing	William S. Lofquist	202-482-0379
Printing Trade Services	Rose Marie Bratland	202-482-0380
Printing Trades Mach/Eqmt	Raymond Robinson	202-482-0610
Process Control Instruments	George Litman	202-482-3411
Process Control Instruments (Trade Promo)	Franc Manzolillo	202-482-2991

Industry	Contact	Phone
Professional Services	Wray O. Candilis	202-482-0339
Pulp and Paper Machinery (Trade Promo)	Edward Abrahams	202-482-0312
Pulp and Paper Mills (Construction and Major Projects)	Wallace Haraguchi	202-482-4877
Pumps, Pumping Eqmt	John Manger	202-482-2732
Pumps, Valves, Compressors (Trade Promo)	George Zanetakos	202-482-0552
Radio & TV Broadcasting	John Siegmund	202-482-4781
Radio & TV Communications Eqmt	Linda Gossack	202-482-4523
Railroad Eqmt (Trade Promo)	Len Heimowitz	202-482-0558
Recorded Music	John Siegmund	202-482-4781
Recreational Eqmt	John Vanderwolf	202-482-0348
Refractory Products	David Cammarota	202-482-5157
Refrigeration Eqmt (Industrial Only)	Charles Pitcher	202-482-0385
Renewable Energy Eqmt	Les Garden	202-482-0556
Residential Lighting Fixtures	John Bodson	202-482-0681
Retail Trade	Aaron Schavey	202-482-4117
Rice Milling	Donald Hodgen	202-482-3346
Roads, Railroads, Mass Trans	Mike Thompson	202-482-5126
Robots/Factory Automation	Megan Pilaroscia	202-482-0609
Roller Bearings	Richard Reise	202-482-3489
Rolling Mill Machinery	Edward Abrahams	202-482-0312
Roofing, Asphalt	Charles Pitcher	202-482-0385
Rubber	Raimundo Prat	202-482-0128
Rubber Products	Raimundo Prat	202-482-0128
Saddlery & Harness Products	James E. Byron	202-482-4034
Safety & Security Eqmt (Trade Promo)	Laureen Daly	202-482-3360
Space Services	Ernest Plock	202-482-5620
Satellites & Space Vehicles (Marketing)	Kim Farner	202-482-2232
Satellites, Communications	Krysten Jenci	202-482-2952
Science & Electronics (Trade Promo)	Bart Maroni	202-482-4125
Scientific Instruments (Trade Promo)	Franc Manzolillo	202-482-2991
Scientific Measurement/Control Eqmt	George Litman	202-482-3411
Screw Machine Products	Richard Reise	202-482-3489
Screws, Washers	Richard Reise	202-482-3489
Security Management Svcs.	J. Marc Chittum	202-482-0345
Security/Safety Eqmt (Trade Promo)	Laureen Daly	202-482-3360
Semiconductor Manufacturing Equipment	Mike Andrews	202-482-2795
Semiconductors	Robin Roark	202-482-3090

Industry	Contact	Phone
Semiconductors, Japan	Laureen Daly	202-482-3360
Services Data Base Development	Jennifer Tallarico	202-482-5820
Shingles (Wood)	Gary Stanley	202-482-0377
Shipbuilding (Projects)	Mike Thompson	202-482-5126
Shipping	Bill Johnson	202-482-5012
Shoes	James E. Bryon	202-482-4034
Silverware	John Harris	202-482-1178
Sisal Products	Jon Manger	202-482-2732
Small Arms, Ammunition	John Vanderwolf	202-482-0348
Small Business	Millie Sjoberg	202-482-4792
Snackfood	Donald Hodgen	202-482-3346
Soaps, Detergents, Cleaners	William Hurt	202-482-0128
Software	Heidi Hijikata	202-482-0571
Software (Trade Promo)	Judy Fogg	202-482-4936
Solar Cells/Photovoltaic Devices	Les Garden	202-482-0556
Solar Equip Ocean/Biomass/ Geothermal	Les Garden	202-482-0556
Soy Products	Donald Hodgen	202-482-2346
Space Commercialization (Equipment)	Kim Farner	202-482-2232
Space Policy Development	Kim Farner	202-482-2232
Special Industry Machinery	Eugene Shaw	202-482-3494
Speed Changers	Richard Reise	202-482-3489
Sporting & Athletic Goods	John Vanderwolf	202-482-0348
Sporting Goods (Trade Promo)	Ludene Capone	202-482-2087
Steel Industry	Charles Bell	202-482-0608
Steel Markets	Charles Bell	202-482-0608
Storage Batteries	David Larrabee	202-482-0607
Sugar Products	Donald Hodgen	202-482-3346
Supercomputers	Wayne Ebenfeld	202-482-1987
Switching	Jason Leuck	202-482-4202
Tea	Donald Hodgen	202-482-3346
Technology Affairs	Edwin B. Shykind	202-482-4694
Telecommunications	Krysten Jenci	202-482-2952
Telecommunications (Cellular technology)	Richard Paddock	202-482-5235
Telecommunications (Major Proj)	Richard Paddock	202-482-5235
Telecommunications (Network Eqmt)	Richard Paddock	202-482-5235
Telecommunications (Wireless)	Linda Gossack	202-482-4523
Telecommunications Services	Jennifer Tallarico	202-482-5820
Telecommunications, Terminal Eqmt	Nathaniel Cadwell	202-482-0399
Telecommunications (Trade Promo)	Alexis Kemper	202-482-1512
Teletext Services	Jennifer Tallarico	202-482-5820

Industry	Contact	Phone
Textile Machinery	John Manger	202-482-2732
Textiles	Joanne Tucker	202-482-4058
Textiles (Trade Promo)	Ferenc Molnar	202-482-5153
Timber Products (Tropical)	Sue Willis	202-482-0577
Tin Products	Jon Manger	202-482-2732
Tires	Raimundo Prat	202-482-0128
Tools/Dies/Jigs/Fixtures	Megan Pilaroscia	202-482-0609
Tourism Services	Scott Johnson	202-482-0140
Toys & Games	Jonathan Freilich	202-482-5783
Transborder Data Flows	Jennifer Tallarico	202-482-5820
Transformers	Julie Fouque	202-482-2390
Transportation Industries	Bill Johnson	202-482-5012
Transportation Svcs (Trade Promo)	Bill Johnson	202-482-5012
Travel Services	Scott Johnson	202-482-0140
Tropical Commodities	Sue Willis	202-482-0577
Trucking Services	Claudia Wolfe	202-482-5086
Trucks, Trailers, Buses (Trade Promo)	John White	202-482-0671
Tungsten Products	Jon Manger	202-482-2732
Turbines, Steam	John Mearman	202-482-0315
Uranium	Andy Collier	202-482-0680
Used, Reconditioned Eqmt		
(Trade Promo)	John Bodson	202-482-0681
Value Added Telecommunications		
Serv	Jennifer Tallarico	202-482-5820
Valves, Pipe Fittings (Except Brass)	Richard Reise	202-482-3489
Vegetables	Donald A. Hodgen	202-482-3346
Video Services	John Siegmund	202-482-4781
Videotex Services	Jennifer Tallarico	202-482-5820
	John Siegmund	202-482-4781
Wallets, Billfolds, Flatgoods	James Byron	202-482-4034
Wastepaper	Gary Stanley	202-482-0375
Watches	John Harris	202-482-1178
Water and Sewerage Treatment		
Plants (Major Proj)	Jay Smith	202-482-4642
Water Resource Eqmt	Denise Carpenter	202-482-1500
Water Supply & Distribution	Denise Carpenter	202-482-1500
Welding/Cutting Apparatus	Edward Abrahams	202-482-0312
Wine	Donald Hodgen	202-482-3346
Windmill Components	Les Garden	202-482-0556
Wire & Wire Products	Charles Bell	202-482-0608
Wire Cloth, Industrial	Richard Reise	202-482-3489
Wire Cloth	Franklin Williams	202-482-0132

Industry	Contact	Phone
Wood Containers	Gary Stanley	202-482-0375
Wood Preserving	Gary Stanley	202-482-0375
Wood Products	Gary Stanley	202-482-0375
Wood Working Machinery	Ed Abrahams	202-482-0312
Yarns (Trade Promo)	Fernec Molnar	202-482-5153
Yeast	Donald Hodgen	202-482-2250

Institute of Certified Business Counselors
P.O. Box 70326
Eugene, Oregon 97401
(503) 345-8064
FAX: (503) 726-2402
www.nust.com/rsrc/cbcjn.htm
Contact: Wally Stabbert, President

Institute of Certified Financial Planners
3801 East Florida Avenue, Suite 708
Denver, CO 80210-2571
(303) 759-4900
www.icfp.org

Institute for International Human Resources
606 North Washington Street
Alexandria, VA 22314
(703) 548-3440
FAX: (703) 836-0367
www.shrm.org/docs/IIHR.html
Contact: D. Patricia Digh, Director

Institute of Lifetime Learning
7852 16th Street, Northwest
Washington, DC 20012
(202) 291-5008

Insurance Information Institute
100 William Street
New York, NY 10038
(212) 669-9200
FAX: (212) 732-1916
www.iii.org/default.htm

Internal Revenue Service
Call 1-800-829-4477 for contact information and location of the office nearest you.
Check its Web site for detailed lists of IRS contacts. You can also download tax forms and regulations. irs.ustreas.gov/

International Association of Business Communicators
One Hallidie Plaza, Suite 600
San Francisco, CA 94102
(415) 433-3400
FAX: (415) 362-8762
ccnet.com/~shel/iabc.html
Contact: Gloria Gordon, vice-president, communication

International Council for Small Business
c/o Jefferson Smurfit Center for Entrepreneurial Studies
St. Louis University
3674 Lindell Boulevard
St. Louis, MO 63108
(314) 977-3628
FAX: (314) 658-3897
www.icsb.org
Contact: Lloyd W. Fernald, Jr.

International Executive Service Corps
333 Ludlow Street
P.O. Box 10005
Stamford, CT 06904
(203) 967-6000
FAX: (203) 324-2531
www.iesc.oncv/
Contact: Hobart C. Gardiner, President

International Foundation of Employee Benefit Plans
18700 West Bluemound Road
P.O. Box 69
Brookfield, WI 53008
(414) 786-6700
FAX: (414) 786-8670
www.ifebp.org/
Contact: John Altobelli, Chief Executive Officer

International Trade Council
3114 Circle Hill Road
Alexandria, VA 22305
(703) 548-1234

Inventor Workshop International Education Foundation
7332 Mason Ave
Canoga Park, CA 91307
(818) 340-4268
FAX: (818) 884-8312
Contact: Alan A. Tratner, President

Marketing Research Association
2189 Silas Deane Highway, Suite 5
Rocky Hill, CT 06067-0230
(860) 257-4008
FAX: (203) 257-3990
Contact: Betsy J. Peterson, Executive Director

MLMIA: The Association for Network Marketing
1101 Dove Street
Newport Beach, CA 92550
(714) 622-0300
FAX: (714) 251-1319
www.mlm-institute.com/mlmia.htm
Contact: Doris Wood, Executive Director

National Association of Black Women Entrepreneurs
P.O. Box 1375
Detroit, MI 48231
(313) 559-9255
FAX: (313) 559-9256
www.nas.edu/cwse/NABWE.html
Contact: Marilyn French-Hubbard, Director

National Association for Business Organizations
P.O. Box 30149
Baltimore, MD 21270
(410) 581-1373
Contact: Rudolph Lewis, President

National Association of Development Companies
4301 North Fairfax Drive, Suite 860
Arlington, VA 22203
(703) 812-9000/(800) 972-2504
Contacts: Christopher Crawford, Executive Director; Leslie Jividen, Office Manager

National Association of Manufacturers
1331 Pennsylvania Avenue, NW, Suite 1500-N
Washington, DC 20004
(202) 637-3000
FAX: (202) 637-3182

National Association of Private Enterprise
P.O. Box 612147
Dallas, TX 75261-2147
(800) 223-6273
FAX: (817) 428-4235
Contact: Laura Squiers, Secretary

National Association of Purchasing Management
2055 East Centennial Circle
P.O. Box 22160
Tempe, AZ 85285-2160
www.napm.org/
Contact: Derrick C. Schnebelt, Public/Media Relations

National Association for the Self-Employed
P.O. Box 612067
Dallas, TX 75261-2067
(800) 232-NASE
www.selfemployed.nase.org/NASE
Contact: Bennie L. Thayer, President

National Association of Small Business Investment Companies
1199 North Fairfax Street, Suite 200
Alexandria, VA 22314
(703) 683-1601
FAX: (703) 683-1605
www.hostlink.com/nasbic
Contact: Jeanette D. Smith, Director, Communications and Marketing

National Association of Temporary Staffing Services
119 St. Asaph Street
Alexandria, VA 22314
(703) 549-6287
FAX: (703) 549-4808
www.natts.org
Contact: Bruce Steinberg, natss

National Association of Women Business Owners
1100 Wayne Avenue, Suite 830
Silver Spring, MD 20910
(301) 608-2590
FAX: (301) 608-2596
Contact: Virginia Littlejohn, Executive Director

National Bar Association
1225 11th Street, NW
Washington, DC 20001
(202) 842-3900
www.melanet.com/nba

The National Business Association
5151 Belt Line Road, #1150
Dallas, TX 75240-7545
(214) 458-0900
FAX: (214) 960-9149
www.kitchenet.com /assocln_bus_as.htm
Contacts: Robert Allen, President; David Hammock, Director of Member Services; Amy Bonney, Director of Marketing and Communications
Other location: A second office is located in Washington, DC

National Business Incubator Association
20 East Circle Drive, Suite 190
Athens, Ohio 45701-3751
(740) 593-4331
FAX: (740) 593-1996
Contact: Dinah Adkins, Executive Director, dadkins
www.nbia.org/homepg.htm

The association's Web site, www.nbia.org/homepg.htm, offers links to the following member sites:

Advanced Technology Development
Center (ATDC), Atlanta, GA

Albany Center for Economic Success,
Inc., Albany, NY

Allen Economic Development Group,
Lima, Ohio

AMIEPAT, Mexico

Appalachian Center for Economic
Networks, Athens, Ohio

Austin Technology Incubator (IC2-ATI),
Austin, TX

Australian Technology Park Incubator
Centre, Sydney, NSW, Australia

The Ben Craig Center, Charlotte, NC

Ben Franklin Technology Center(s), PA

Birmingham Business Assistance Network
(BBAN), Birmingham, AL

Bonner Business Center, ID

Boulder Technology Incubator (BTI),
Longmont, CO

Bryan-College Station Research &
Development Incubator, Bryan, TX

Business Incubator Program - Technology
Incubators - Jerusalem, Israel

Calgary Research & Development
Authority (CRDA), Calgary, AB,
Canada

CALSTART - Project Hatchery Business
Incubator, Burbank, CA

The CASE Center at Syracuse University,
Syracuse, NY

Cass County Business Center, Cassopolis,
MI

Centre d'entreprises et d'innovation de
Montreal, Montreal Canada

The Center for Environmental Enterprise,
Portland, ME

The Center for Technological Innovation,
Charleston, SC

Chattanooga/Hamilton County Business
Development Center, Chattanooga, TN

Chicago Southland Enterprise Center,
Chicago Heights, IL

Colorado Advanced Technology Institute
(CATI), Denver, CO

Colorado Bio/Medical Venture Center
(CBVC), Lakewood, CO

Communications Research Centre's
Innovation Centre, Ottawa, Canada

Communications Technology Cluster-
Oakland, CA

Coopers and Lybrand L.L.P.

Cornell Univ. - Office for Technology
Access and Business Assistance,
Ithaca, NY

Dallas County Community College
District (DCCCD) Business Incubator,
Dallas, TX

Deming (W. Edward) Business Center,
Sioux City, IA

DIO Business Center, Turku, Finland

Dunn Richmond Economic Development
Center, Carbondale, IL

Entergy Arts Business Center, New
Orleans, LA

The Enterprise Development Center,
Newark, NJ

The Environmental Business Cluster,
San Jose, CA

Evanston Business & Technology Center
(EBTC), Evanston, IL

Genesis Business Centers, Ltd.,
Minneapolis, MN

GENESIS Technology Incubator,
Fayetteville, AR

The Golden Triangle Enterprise Center,
Starkville, MS

Greater Hamilton County Technology
Enterprise Centre, Hamilton, Ontario
Canada

Harlem Business Incubator, Harlem, NY

High Technology of Rochester (HTR),
Rochester, NY

HITEC Technology Enterpreneurship
Center Har Hotzvim, Jerusalem, IL

Hong Kong Industrial Technology Centre
Corp., Hong Kong, China

Incubadora de Empresas con Base
Tecnologica, Baja California, MX

Incubadora de Empresas de Base
Tecnologica do IPRJ/UERJ, Rio de
Janeiro, BR

Incubadora de Empresas COPPE/UFRJ,
Rio de Janeiro, BR

Incubadora de Empresas de Innovacion
Tecnologica, Cuernavaca, Mor. MX

Incubadoras - Polos e Parques
Tecnologicos - EBT, BR

Incutech Brunswick Inc. - Technology
Incubation Centre, Fredericton, NB
Canada

The Initiative Center for the Negev, Beer-Sheva, Israel

Instituto de Engenharia de Sistemas e Computadores (INESC), Lisbon, PT

International Business Incubator, San Jose, CA

Kansas Technology Enterprise Corporation (KTEC), Topeka, KS

Laramie County Enterprise Center, Cheyenne, WY

Long Island High Technology Incubator (LIHTI), Stony Brook, NY

Madison Enterprise Center, Madison, WI

Manoa Innovation Center (MIC), Honolulu, HI

Michigan Biotechnology Institute/Bio-Business Incubator of Michigan, Lansing, MI

Mid-America Commercialization Corporation (MACC), Manhattan, KS

New Century Venture Center, Roanoke, VA

North Central Idaho Business Technology Incubator, Moscow, ID

Otaniemi Science Park, Otaniemi, FL

Pontotoc Area Vo-Tech School, Ada, OK

Quebec Biotechnology Innovation Centre, Quebec, Canada

Rensselaer Polytechnic Institute, Troy, NY

The Richmond Business Campus, Dublin, Ireland

Rural Devel. Ctr. Business Enterprise Research Park, Univ. of Maryland, Princess Anne, MD

St. Louis Enterprise Centers, St. Louis, MO

San Jose Software Business Cluster, San Jose, CA

Silicon Valley Business Incubation Alliance, San Jose, CA

Small Business Incubator Facility, Early, TX

Southeastern Technology Center, Augusta, GA

Technology Advancement Program, Clarksville, MD

Technology Commercialization Laboratory (ACES - University of Illinois), Urbana, IL

Technology Enterprise Centre Business Incubator/La Trobe Univ., VIC, Australia

Technology Innovation Center, Milwaukee County Research Park, Wauwatosa, WI

The Technology Innovation Centre, Dartmouth, NS, Canada

Technology Park Malaysia (TPM), Kuala Lumpur, MY

Technology 2020 Information Technology Incubator, Oak Ridge, TN

The Thomas Hill Enterprise Center, Macon, MO

Trenton Business and Technology Center, Trenton, NJ

Tri-Cities Enterprise Association (TEA), Richland, WA

The Turku Technology Center, Turku, FL

UAB Office for the Advancement of Developing Industries, Birmingham, AL

UND Rural Technology Incubator/Center for Innovation, Grand Fork, ND

UNIDO - Business Incubation Systems, Vienna, AT

Unlimited Future, Inc., Huntington, WV

University City Science Center (UCSC), Philadelphia, PA

The Venture Center, Inc., Lansing, MI

Virginia Biotechnology Research Park, Richmond, VA

Western Entrepreneurial Network, Univ. of Colorado at Denver

Western New York Technology Development Center, Inc. (TDC), Amherst, NY

West Virginia High Technology Consortium Foundation, Fairmont, WV

William C. Goodridge Business Resource Center, York, PA

Wine Country Farm Kitchen, Prosser, WA

York Business Opportunity Centre, Toronto, Ontario, Canada

Youngstown Business Incubator, Youngstown, OH

National Business League
1511 K Street, NW, Suite 432
Washington, DC 20005
(202) 737-4430
FAX: (202) 566-5487
www.thenbl.com

**National Business Owners
Association**
1033 North Fairfax Street,
Suite 402
Alexandria, VA 22314
(202) 737-6501
FAX: (202) 737-3909
Contact: J. Drew Hiatt, Executive
Vice President

National Council on Alcoholism
12 West 21st Street
New York, NY 10010
(212) 206-6770

National Executive Service Corps
257 Park Avenue South, 2nd Floor
New York, NY 10010-7304
(212) 529-6660
FAX: (212) 228-3958
www.ncl.org/anr/partners/nexs.htm
Contact: Robert S. Hatfield,
Chairman

**National Family Business
Council**
1640 West Kennedy Road
Lake Forest, IL 60045
(708) 295-1040
FAX: (708) 295-1898
Contact: John E. Messervey,
Director

**National Federation of
Independent Business**
53 Century Boulevard, Suite 300
Nashville, TN 37214
(615) 872-5800
www.asbids.com.av/NFIB
/inbib1.htm
Contact: David Cullen, Vice
President, Public Affairs

National Foreign Trade Council
1625 K Street NW
Washington, DC 20006
(202) 887-0278
FAX: (202) 452-8160
usaengage.org/background
/nftc.html
Contact: Eric Thomas, Public
Relations, (202) 822-9491

National Mailorder Association
207 Polk Street NE
Minneapolis, MN 55418-2954
(612) 788-1637
FAX: (612) 788-1147
E-MAIL:schulte@nmoa.org

National Recycling Coalition
1101 30th Street NW, Suite 305
Washington, DC 20007
(202) 625-6406
www.recycle.net/recycle/assn
/nrc_au.htm
Contacts: Marsha Rhea, Executive
Director, and Linda Shotwell,
Director of Communications

National Retail Federation
325 7th Street, Northwest,
Suite 1000
Washington, DC 20004-2802
(202) 783-7971
FAX: (202) 737-2849
www.nrf.com

National Safety Council
1121 Spring Lake Drive
Itasca, IL 60143
(630) 285-1121
FAX: (630) 285-1315
le/nsc.org/www.nsc.org/memtop.htm
Contacts: Terry Wilkinson,
  Agriculture, (630) 775-2087;
  Dick Tippie, Business &
  Industry, (630) 775-2384; Eve
  Brouwer, Campus Safety, (630)
  775-2026; Eve Brouwer, Chapter
  & Affiliate, (630) 775-2026;
  Mike Taylor, Community Safety,
  (630) 775-2304; Mike Buchet,
  Construction, (630) 775-2531;
  Jan Sutkus, Educational
  Resources, (630) 775-2028; Al
  Lauersdorf, Highway Traffic
  Safety, (630) 775-2385; Mike
  Buchet, Labor, (630) 775-2531;
  Les Sokolowski, Motor
  Transportation, (630) 775-2221;
  Rick Vulpitta, Utilities, (630)
  775-2128; Pat Pulte, Youth,
  (630) 775-2022

Following is a listing of additional
offices to contact:

CALIFORNIA
Redwood City (94065-1409)
Western Region Office
303 Twin Dolphin Drive, Suite 520
(650) 508-8787

DISTRICT OF COLUMBIA (20036)
Environmental Health Center
1025 Connecticut Avenue, NW, Suite 1200
(202) 293-2270
Public Policy
1025 Connecticut Avenue, NW, Suite 1200
(202) 293-2270

GEORGIA
Atlanta (30341-3941)
Southeastern Region
3300 NE Expressway, Suite 7A
(770) 457-5100

ILLINOIS
Itasca (60143-3201)
Foundation for Safety & Health
1121 Spring Lake Drive
(630) 285-1121
Itasca (60143-3201)
Headquarters
1121 Spring Lake Drive
(630) 775-2056/800-621-7619

UNITED KINGDOM
Kent, TN15 8RS
International Safety Council
21 Tilton Road, Borough Green
(44) 1-7321-88-6581/1-732-88-6582
  (Telefax)

**National Safe Workplace
  Institute**
201 Coronation Boulevard,
  Suite 145
Charlotte, NC 28227
(704) 841-1175
FAX: 841-3893
www2.nswi.com/nswi/
E-MAIL: jkinney@nswi.com
Contact: Joseph A. Kinney,
  Executive Director

National Small Business United
1155 15th Street, NW, Suite 710
Washington, DC 20005
(202) 293-8830
FAX: (202) 872-8543
www.nsbu.org

National Speakers Association
1500 South Priest Drive
Tempe, AZ 85281
(602) 968-2552
FAX: (602) 968-0911
www.nasaspeaker.org/index.html

**National Vehicle Leasing
Association**
P.O. Box 281230
San Francisco, CA 94128-1230
(415) 548-9135
FAX: (415) 548-9155

**National Venture Capital
Association**
1655 North Fort Myer Drive,
  Suite 850
Arlington, VA 22209
nvca.com
Contact: Daniel T. Kingsley,
  Executive Director,
  dkingsley@nvca.org

National Writers Association
1450 South Havana Street,
  Suite 424
Aurora, CO 80012
(303) 751-7844
FAX: (303) 751-8593
www.loc.gov/loc/cfbook/coborg
  /nwa.html

**Newsletter Publishers
Association**
1401 Wilson Boulevard, Suite 207
Arlington, VA 22209
(703) 527-2333
FAX: (703) 841-0629
www.newsletters.org/mission.html

Office of Business Initiatives
409 Third Street, SW,
  Suite 6200
Washington, DC 20416
(202) 205-6665
FAX: (202) 205-7416

**Public Relations Society of
America**
33 Irving Place, 3rd Floor
New York, NY 10003-2376
(212) 995-2230
FAX: (212) 995-0757
www.prsa.org

**Service Corps of Retired
Executives**
(Also known as the SCORE
  Association)
409 Third Street, Southwest
Washington, DC 20024
(202) 205-6762
FAX: (202) 205-7636
www.score.org
Contact: W. Kenneth Yancey, Jr.,
  Executive Director

SERVICE CORPS OF RETIRED EXECUTIVES: CHAPTER DIRECTORY

ALABAMA
Anniston (36202)
P.O. Box 1087
(205) 237-5637/237-4338 (Fax)
Birmingham (35294-4552)
1601 11th Avenue South
(205) 934-6868/934-0538 (Fax)
Fairhope (36532)
327 Fairhope Avenue
(334) 928-8799
Florence (35631-1331)
P.O. Box 1331
(205) 764-0244
Mobile (36652)
c/o Mobile Area Chamber of Commerce
P.O. Box 2187
(334) 433-6951
Montgomery (36101-1114)
c/o Montgomery Area Chamber of
  Commerce
41 Commerce Street
P.O. Box 79
(334) 240-9295

Opelika (36803)
P.O. Box 2366
(334) 745-4861
Tuscaloosa (35402)
2200 University Boulevard
(205) 758-7588

ALASKA
Anchorage (99513-7559)
222 West 8th Avenue
(907) 271-4022

ARIZONA
Flagstaff (86001)
Attn: Barbara Haynes
1 West Route 66
(520) 556-7333
Lake Havasu (86405)
P.O. Box 2049
(520) 453-5951
Mesa (85201)
Federal Building, Room #104
26 North MacDonald
(602) 379-3100/379-3143 (Fax)
Phoenix (85004)
2828 North Central Avenue, #800
Central & One Thomas
(602) 640-2329
Prescott (86303)
101 West Goodwin Street
P.O. Building, Suite 307
(520) 778-7438
Tucson (85702)
P.O. Box 2143
(520) 670-5008

ARKANSAS
El Dorado (71730-5803)
201 North Jackson Avenue
(870) 863-6113/863-6115 (Fax)
Fayetteville (72701)
c/o Margaret Parrish
1141 Eastwood Drive
(501) 442-7619
Fort Smith (72901)
#4 Glenn Haven Drive
(501) 783-3556
Hot Springs (71913)
1412 Airport Road, B10
(501) 321-1700

Little Rock (72202-1747)
2120 Riverfront Drive
SBA Room 100
(501) 324-5893/324-5199 (Fax)
Pine Bluff (71611)
P.O. Box 6866
(870) 535-7189/535-1643 (Fax)

CALIFORNIA
Bakersfield (93301)
1706 Chester Avenue, #200
(805) 327-4421
Chico (95926)
1324 Mangrove Street, Suite 114
(916) 342-8932
Fresno (93727-1547)
2719 North Air Fresno Drive, Suite 200
(209) 487-5605/487-5636 (Fax)
Glendale (91203-2304)
330 North Brand Boulevard, Suite 190
(818) 552-3206/552-3323 (Fax)
Hemet (92544-4679)
1700 East Florida Avenue
(909) 652-4390/929-8543 (Fax)
Modesto (95354)
c/o SCEDCO
1012 11th Street, Suite 300
(209) 521-9333
Monterey (93940-1770)
Monterey Peninsula Chamber of
    Commerce
380 Alvarado
(408) 649-1770
Oakland (94612)
519 17th Street
(510) 273-6611/273-6015 (Fax)
Palmdale (93551)
445 West Palmdale Boulevard, Suite N
(805) 265-7733/265-7712 (Fax)
Palm Springs (92264)
555 South Palm Canyon, Room A206
(760) 320-6682/323-9426 (Fax)
Pomona (91769-1457)
c/o Pomona Chamber of Commerce
485 North Garey Avenue
P.O. Box 1457
(909) 622-1256
Redding (96099)
c/o Cascade SBDC
737 Auditorium Drive
(916) 247-8100

Sacramento (95814-2413)
660 J Street, Suite 215
(916) 498-6420/498-6422 (Fax)
San Diego (92101-3500)
550 West C Street, Suite 550
(619) 557-7272/557-5894 (Fax)
San Francisco (94105)
455 Market Street, 6th Floor
(415) 744-6827/744-6812 (Fax)
San Jose (95113)
280 South 1st Street, Room 137
(408) 288-8479/535-5541 (Fax)
San Luis Ibispo (93401)
3566 South Hiquera, #104
(805) 547-0779
Santa Ana (92701)
200 West Santa Ana Boulevard, Suite 700
(714) 550-7369/550-0191 (Fax)
Santa Barbara (93130)
P.O. Box 30291
(805) 563-0084
Santa Maria (93455)
2524 South LaCosta Drive
(805) 934-4146
Santa Rosa (95404)
777 Sonoma Avenue, Room 115E
(707) 571-8342/541-0331 (Fax)
Sonora (95370)
222 South Shepherd Street
(209) 532-4212
Stockton (95202)
401 North San Joaquin Street, Room 215
(209) 946-6293
Ventura (93001)
5700 Ralston Street, Suite 310
(805) 658-2688

COLORADO
Colorado Springs (80903)
2 North Cascade Avenue, Suite 110
(719) 636-3074
Denver (80201-0660)
U.S. Customs House, 4th Floor
721 19th Street
(303) 844-3985/844-6490 (Fax)
Grand Junction (81501)
c/o Chamber of Commerce
360 Grand Avenue
(970) 242-3214

Pueblo (81003)
c/o Chamber of Commerce
302 North Santa Fe
(719) 542-1704/542-1624 (Fax)

CONNECTICUT
Bridgeport (06604)
10 Middle Street, 14th Floor
(203) 335-3800/366-0105 (Fax)
Danbury (06811)
100 Mill Plain Road
(203) 791-3804
Hartford (06106)
330 Main Street
(860) 240-4700
New Haven (06511)
25 Science Park, Building 25/Room 366
(203) 865-7645
Norwalk (06850)
24 Belden Avenue, 5th Floor
(203) 847-7348/849-9308 (Fax)
Old Saybrook (06475)
c/o Chamber of Commerce
146 Main Street
P.O. Box 625
(860) 388-9508

DELAWARE
Wilmington (19801)
824 Market Street, Suite 610
(302) 573-6552/573-6092 (Fax)

DISTRICT OF COLUMBIA
Washington, DC (20043)
1110 Vermont Avenue, NW, 9th Floor
P.O. Box 34346
(202) 606-4000 ext. 287/606-4225 (Fax)

FLORIDA
Clearwater (34622)
Airport Business Center
4707 140th Avenue North, #311
(813) 532-6800/532-6800 (Fax)
Coral Gables (33146)
1320 South Dixie Highway, 3rd Floor
(305) 536-5521/536-5058 (Fax)
Delray Beach (33483)
1050 South Federal Highway, Suite 132
(561) 278-7752/278-0288 (Fax)
Ft. Lauderdale (33301)
229 East Broward Boulevard
Federal Building, Suite 123
(954) 356-7263/356-7145 (Fax)

Fort Myers (33919)
The Renaissance,
8695 College Parkway, Suites 345 & 346
(941) 489-2935
Ft. Pierce (34982)
Professional Center, Suite 2
3220 South US #1
(561) 489-0548
Gainesville (32601)
101 Southeast 2nd Place, Suite 104
(352) 375-8278
Holly Hills (32117)
921 North Nova Road, Suite A
(904) 255-6889/255-0229 (Fax)
Hollywood (33021)
3475 Sheridian Street, Suite 203
(954) 966-8415
Jacksonville (32256)
7825 Baymeadows Way, 100-B
(904) 443-1911
Lakeland (33801)
404 North Ingraham Avenue
(941) 687-4403/687-6225 (Fax)
Melbourne (32935)
Melbourne Professional Complex
1600 Sarno, Suite 205
(407) 254-2288/254-2288 (Fax)
Naples (34112)
Barnett Bank
3285 Tamiami Trail East
(941) 417-1280/417-1281 (Fax)
New Port Richey (34652)
6014 US Highway 19, Suite 302
(813) 842-4638
Ocala (34470)
110 East Silver Spring Boulevard
(352) 629-5959
Orlando (32801)
Federal Building, Room 455
80 North Hughey Avenue
(407) 648-6476/648-6425
Punta Gorda (33950)
Punta Gorda Professional Center
201 West Marion Avenue, #211
(941) 575-1818
Sarasota (34237)
2801 Fruitville Road, Suite 280
(941) 955-1029

Tallahassee (32302)
c/o Leon County Library
200 West Park Avenue
(904) 487-2665
Tampa (33614-6509)
4732 Dale Mabry Highway North,
    Suite 400
(813) 870-0125
Tavares (32778-3810)
First Union National Bank
122 East Main Street
(352) 365-3556
West Palm Beach (33401)
500 Australian Avenue South, Suite 100
(561) 833-1672/833-1712 (Fax)

GEORGIA
Atlanta (30309)
1720 Peachtree Road, NW,
    6th Floor
(404) 347-2442/347-1227 (Fax)
Augusta
106 Pleasant Home Road
LePavillion Center, Suite 2-R
(706) 869-9100
Columbus
1st Union Bank
101 13th Street
(706) 596-8331
Dalton (30722)
P.O. Box 1941
(706) 279-3383
Savannah (31401)
111 East Liberty Street, Suite 103
(912) 652-4335/652-4184 (Fax)
Winterville (30683)
340 Weatherly Woods Drive
(706) 548-5968

HAWAII
Honolulu (96813)
130 Merchant Street, Suite 1030
(808) 522-8130/522-8135 (Fax)
Kihei (96753)
590 East Lipoa Parkway, Suite 227
(808) 875-2380

IDAHO
Boise (83702)
1020 Main Street, #290
(208) 334-1696/334-9353 (Fax)

Idaho Falls (83401)
2300 North Yellowstone, Suite 119
(208) 523-1022/528-7127 (Fax)

ILLINOIS
Aurora (60507)
40 West Downer Place
P.O. Box 277
(630) 897-9214/897-7002 (Fax)
Carbondale (62901)
150 East Pleasant Hill Road
Box 1
(618) 453-6654/453-5040 (Fax)
Chicago (60661)
Northwest Atrium Center
500 West Madison Street, #1250
(312) 353-7724/886-5688 (Fax)
Decatur (62522)
Milliken University
1184 West Main Street
(217) 424-6297/424-3993 (Fax)
Godfrey (62035-2466)
Alden Hall
5800 Godfrey Road
(618) 467-2280/466-8289 (Fax)
Moline (61265)
c/o Chamber of Commerce
622 19th Street
(309) 797-0082/757-5435 (Fax)
Peoria (61602)
c/o Peoria Chamber of Commerce
124 Southwest Adams, Suite 300
(309) 676-0755/676-7534
Quincy (62301)
c/o Chamber of Commerce
300 Civic Center Plaza, Suite 245
(217) 222-8093/222-3033 (Fax)
Rockford (61103)
515 North Court Street
(815) 962-0122/962-0122 (Fax)
Springfield (62704)
511 West Capitol Avenue, Suite 302
(217) 492-4359/492-4867 (Fax)

INDIANA
Anderson (46015)
c/o Chamber of Commerce
205 West 11th
P.O. Box 469
(317) 642-0264

Bloomington (47403)
Star Center
216 West Allen
(812) 335-3744
Columbus (47201)
c/o Chamber of Commerce
500 Franklin Street, Box 29
(812) 379-4457
Elkhart (46515)
418 South Main Street
P.O. Box 428
(219) 293-1531/294-1859 (Fax)
Evansville (47708)
Old Post Office Place
100 Northwest 2nd Street, #300
(812) 421-5879
Fort Wayne (46802)
1300 South Harrison Street
(219) 422-2601/422-2601 (Fax)
Gary (46402)
973 West 6th Avenue, Room 326
(219) 882-3918
Indianapolis (46204-1873)
429 North Pennsylvania Street, Suite 100
(317) 226-7264
Kokomo (46901)
106 North Washington Street
(765) 457-5301/452-4564 (Fax)
Logansport (46947)
Logansport County Chamber of
  Commerce
300 East Broadway, Suite 103
(219) 753-6388
Marion (46952)
215 South Adams
(317) 664-5107
New Albany (47150-9538)
4100 Charleston Road
(812) 945-0266
South Bend (46601)
300 North Michigan Street
(219) 282-4350

IOWA
Burlington (52601)
Federal Building
300 North Main Street
(319) 752-2967

Cedar Rapids (52401-1806)
Lattner Building
215 4th Avenue, SE, #200
(319) 362-6405/362-7861 (Fax)
Clinton (52732)
333 4th Avenue South
(319) 242-5702
Council Bluffs (51502-1565)
Chamber of Commerce
P.O. Box 1565
(712) 325-1000
Cresco (52136)
3404 285th Street
(319) 547-3377
Des Moines (50309-2186)
Federal Building, Room 749
210 Walnut Street
(515) 284-4760
Fort Dodge (50501)
Federal Building, Room 436
205 South 8th Street
(515) 955-2622
Iowa City (52240-1853)
210 Federal Building
P.O. Box 1853
(319) 338-1662
Keokuk (52632)
c/o Keokuk Area Chamber of Commerce
401 Main Street, Pierce Building #1
(319) 524-5055
Marshalltown (50158)
Fisher Community College
709 South Center
(515) 753-6645
Mason City (50401)
15 West State Street
P.O. Box 1128
(515) 423-5724
Ottumwa (52501)
SBDC, Indian Hills Community College
525 Grandview Avenue
(515) 683-5127
Peosta (52068)
c/o Northeast Iowa Community College
10250 Sundown Road
(319) 556-5110
Shenandoah (51601)
Chamber of Commerce
614 West Sheridan, Box 38
(712) 246-3260

Sioux City (51101)
Federal Building
320 6th Street
(712) 277-2324
Spencer (51301)
P.O. Box 7937
122 West 5th Street
(712) 262-3059
Storm Lake (50588)
c/o Storm Lake Chamber of Commerce
119 West 6th Street
(712) 732-3780
Waterloo (50703)
Chamber of Commerce
215 East 4th
(319) 233-8431

KANSAS
Concordia (66901)
130 West 18th
P.O. Box 642
(913) 243-4290
Dodge City (67801)
Dodge City Chamber of Commerce
P.O. Box 939
(316) 227-3119
Emporia (66801)
Chamber of Commerce
719 Commercial
P.O. Box 703
(316) 342-1600
Girard (66743)
P.O. Box 342
(316) 724-6100
Great Bend (67530)
Chamber of Commerce
1307 Williams
(316) 792-2401
Hays (67601)
c/o Emprise Bank NA
P.O. Box 400
(913) 625-6595
Hutchison (67501)
One East Ninth
(316) 665-8468
McPherson (67460)
Chamber of Commerce
306 North Main
(316) 241-3303

Topeka (66621)
1700 College
(913) 231-1010
Wichita (67202)
SBA/100 East English, Suite 510
(316) 269-6273
Winfield (67156)
P.O. Box 314
(316) 221-1617

KENTUCKY
Lexington (40507)
410 West Vine Street, Suite 290, Civic C
(606) 231-9902/253-3190 (Fax)
Louisville (40202)
188 Federal Office Building
600 Dr. Martin Luther King Jr. Place
(502) 582-5976
Paducah (42001)
Federal Office Building, Room B-36
501 Broadway
(502) 442-5685

LOUISIANA
Alexandria (71309)
802 Third Street
P.O. Box 992
(318) 442-6671
Baton Rouge (70801)
564 Laurel Street
P.O. Box 3217
(504) 381-7130/336-4306 (Fax)
Hammond (70404)
P.O. Box 1458
(504) 345-4457/345-4749 (Fax)
Lafayette (70505-1307)
Lafayette Chamber of Commerce
804 St. Mary Boulevard
P.O. Drawer 51307
(318) 233-2705/234-8671 (Fax)
Lake Charles (70601)
120 West Pujo Street
(318) 433-3632
New Orleans (70130)
365 Canal Street, Suite 3100
(504) 589-2356/589-2339 (Fax)
Shreveport (71101)
400 Edwards Street
(318) 677-2536/677-2541 (Fax)

MAINE
Augusta (04330)
40 Western Avenue
(207) 622-8509
Bangor (04401)
Husson College, One College Circle
Peabody Hall, Room 229
(207) 941-9707
Caribou (04736)
NMDC
2 South Main Street
(207) 498-6562
Ellsworth (04605-1105)
Mill Mall
P.O. Box 1105
(207) 667-5800
Lewiston (04240-7764)
BIC of Maine-Bates Mill Complex
35 Canal Street
(207) 782-3708/783-7745 (Fax)
Portland (04101)
66 Pearl Street, Room 210
(207) 772-1147/772-5581 (Fax)
Rumford (04276)
c/o Fleet Bank
108 Congress Street
P.O. Box 400
(207) 364-3735
South Paris (04281)
166 Main Street
(207) 743-0499

MARYLAND
Annapolis (21401)
2525 Riva Road, Suite 110
(410) 266-9553/573-0981 (Fax)
Baltimore (21201)
The City Crescent Building, 6th Floor
10 South Howard Street
(410) 962-2233/962-1805 (Fax)
Easton (21601)
c/o Talbot County Chamber of Commerce
P.O. Box 1366
(410) 822-4606/822-7922 (Fax)
Frederick (21701)
43A South Market Street
(301) 662-8723/846-4427 (Fax)
Hagerstown (21740)
111 West Washington Street
(301) 739-2015/739-1278 (Fax)

Salisbury (21801)
c/o Chamber of Commerce
300 East Main Street
(410) 749-0185/860-9925 (Fax)

MASSACHUSETTS
Boston (02222-1093)
10 Causeway Street, Room 265
(617) 565-5591/565-5598 (Fax)
Brockton (02401)
60 School Street
(508) 587-2673/587-1340 (Fax)
Danvers (01923)
Danvers Savings Bank
1 Conant Street
(508) 777-2200
Hyannis (02601)
Independence Park, Suite 5B
270 Communications Way
(508) 775-4884
Springfield (01103)
1350 Main Street
(413) 785-0314
Worcester (01608)
33 Waldo Street
(508) 753-2929/754-8560 (Fax)

MICHIGAN
Detroit (48226)
477 Michigan Avenue, Room 515
(313) 226-7947/226-3448 (Fax)
Kalamazoo (49007)
128 North Kalamazoo Mall
(616) 381-5382/343-0430 (Fax)
Petoskey (49770)
401 East Mitchell
(616) 347-4150
Sault Ste. Marie (49783)
c/o Chamber of Commerce
2581 I-75 Business Spur
(906) 632-3301
Traverse City (49685-0387)
202 East Grandview Parkway
P.O. Box 387
(616) 947-5075

MINNESOTA
Burnsville (55337)
101 West Burnsville Parkway #150
(612) 898-5645/435-6972 (Fax)

Hermantown (55811)
4879 Adrian Lane
(218) 723-2701/723-2712 (Fax)
Mankato (56001)
112 Riverfront Street
P.O. Box 999
(507) 345-4519/345-4451 (Fax)
Minneapolis (55416)
North Plaza Building, Suite 51
5217 Wayzata Boulevard
(612) 591-0539/544-0436 (Fax)
Rochester (55901)
Rochester Chamber of Commerce
220 South Broadway, Suite 100
(507) 288-1122/282-8960 (Fax)
St. Cloud (56303)
1527 Northway Drive
(320) 240-1332/255-9050 (Fax)
St. Paul (55102)
Lowry Professional Building
350 St. Peter Street, #295
(612) 223-5010/223-5048 (Fax)

MISSISSIPPI
Greenville (38701)
Greenville Chamber/915 Washington A
P.O. Box 933
(601) 378-3141
Gulfport (39501)
One Government Plaza
2909 13th Street, Suite 203
(601) 863-4449
Jackson (39201)
First Jackson Center, Suite 400
101 West Capitol Street
(601) 965-4378

MISSOURI
Camdenton (65020)
University Extension
113 Kansas Street
P.O. Box 1405
(573) 346-2644/346-2694 (Fax)
Columbia (65203)
c/o Milo Dahl
1705 Halsted Court
(573) 874-1132
Cuba (65453)
1102 Oak Hill Road
(573) 885-4954

Kansas City (64105)
323 West 8th Street, Suite 104
(816) 374-6675/374-6759 (Fax)
Kimberling City (65686)
c/o Dwayne Shoemaker
P.O. Box 1148
(417) 739-3041
Neelyville (63954)
c/o James W. Carson, Chair
Route 1, Box 280
(573) 989-3577
St. Charles (63304)
c/o Dennis Dexter
531 Fox Pointe Drive
(314) 928-6153
St. Joseph (64506)
Chamber of Commerce
3003 Frederick Avenue
(816) 232-4461
St. Louis (63101-1569)
815 Olive Street, Room 242
(314) 539-6970/539-3785 (Fax)
St. Peters (63376)
425 Spencer Road
(314) 928-2900/928-2900 (Fax)
Springfield (65802-3200)
620 South Glenstone, #110
(417) 864-7670/864-4108

MONTANA
Billings (59101)
815 South 27th Street
(406) 245-4111
Bozeman (59715)
1205 East Main Street
(406) 586-5421
Butte (59701)
2950 Harrison Avenue
(406) 494-4495
Great Falls (59403)
P.O. Box 2127
(406) 761-4434
Helena (59626-0054)
Federal Building
301 South Park
(406) 449-5381
Kalispell (59901)
2 Main Street
(406) 756-5271

Missoula (59803)
802 Normans Lane
(406) 543-6623

NEBRASKA
Columbus (68601)
c/o Wayne R. Davy
41 Stires Lake
(402) 564-2769
Cozad (69130)
414 East 16th Street
(308) 784-2590
Fremont (68025)
Chamber of Commerce
92 West 5th Street
(402) 721-2641
Hastings (68901)
c/o James Svoboda
1338 West 12th Street
(402) 463-5818
Lincoln (68520)
8800 East O Street
(402) 437-2409
Minatare (69356)
c/o Marvin Harms
150549 CR 30
(308) 632-2133
Norfolk (68701)
504 Pierce Street
(402) 371-0940
Omaha (68154)
11145 Mill Valley Road
(402) 221-3606/221-3680 (Fax)

NEVADA
Las Vegas (89125)
301 East Stewart
Box 7527
(702) 388-6104
Reno (89557-0100)
SBDC
College of Bus. Adm./U of Nevada
(702) 784-4436/784-4337 (Fax)

NEW HAMPSHIRE
Concord (03301)
143 North Main Street, Room 202A
(603) 225-1400
Conway (03818)
P.O. Box 1066
(603) 383-0800

Keene (03431-3421)
34 Mechanic Street
(603) 352-0320
Laconia (03246)
67 Walter Street, Suite 105
(603) 524-9168
Lebanon (03766)
Citizens Bank Building
20 West Park Street, 316 First
(603) 448-3491
Manchester (03103)
275 Chestnut Street, Room 618
(603) 666-7561/666-7925 (Fax)
Portsmouth (03801-3251)
195 Commerce Way, Unit A
(603) 433-0575

NEW JERSEY
Hamburg (07419)
c/o Bob Kopchains, Chair
25 Tannery Hill Drive
(201) 209-8525
Lincroft (07738)
Brookdale Community College Career
    Service
765 Newman Springs Road
(908) 224-2573
Newark (07102)
2 Gateway Center, 4th Floor
(201) 645-3982/645-2375
Paramus (07652)
327 East Ridgewood Avenue
(201) 599-6090
Pennsauken (08109)
c/o United Jersey Bank
4900 Route 70
(609) 486-3421
Princeton (08540)
216 Rockingham Row
Princeton Forrestal Village
(609) 520-1776/520-9107 (Fax)
Somerville (08876)
Paritan Valley Community College
Box 3300
(908) 218-8874
Toms River (08754)
33 Washington Street
(908) 505-6033

NEW MEXICO
Albuquerque (87102)
Silver Square, Suite 330
625 Silver Avenue, SW
(505) 766-1900/766-1833 (Fax)
Las Cruces (88001)
Loretto Towne Center
505 South Main Street, Suite 125
(505) 523-5627
Roswell (88201)
Federal Building, Room 237
(505) 625-2112/623-2545 (Fax)
Santa Fe (87501)
Montoya Federal Building
120 Federal Place, Room 307
(505) 988-6302/988-6300 (Fax)

NEW YORK
Albany (12205)
Albany Chamber of Commerce
1 Computer Drive South
(518) 446-1118/446-1228 (Fax)
Auburn (13021)
c/o Chamber of Commerce
30 South Street
P.O. Box 675
(315) 252-7291
Binghamton (13902)
49 Court Street
P.O. Box 995
Metro Center, 2nd Floor
(607) 772-8860
Buffalo (14202)
Federal Building, Room 1311
111 West Huron Street
(716) 551-4301
www2.pcom.net/score/buf45.html
Elmira (14901)
c/o SBA
333 East Water Street, 4th Floor
(607) 734-3358
Farmingdale (11735)
96 Jerome Drive
(516) 451-6563
Goshen (10924)
Orange County Chamber of Commerce
40 Matthews Street
(914) 294-8080/294-6121 (Fax)

Huntington (11743)
c/o Chamber of Commerce
151 West Carver Street
(516) 423-6100
Ithaca (14850)
c/o Tompkins Chamber of Commerce
904 East Shore Drive
(607) 273-7080
Kew Gardens (11424)
Queens Borough Hall
120-55 Queens Boulevard, Room 333
(718) 263-8961/263-9032
Mineola (11501)
Department of Commerce & Industry
400 County Seat Drive, #140
(516) 571-3303
New York (10278)
26 Federal Plaza, Room 3100
(212) 264-4507/264-4963 (Fax)
Poughkeepsie (12601)
c/o Chamber of Commerce
110 Main Street
(914) 454-1700
Rochester (14614)
601 Keating Federal Building
100 State Street, Room 410
(716) 263-6473/263-3146 (Fax)
Staten Island (10301)
c/o Chamber of Commerce
130 Bay Street
(718) 727-1221
Stone Ridge (12484)
Ulster City Community College
Clinton Building, Room 107
(914) 687-5035/687-5015 (Fax)
Syracuse (13260)
100 South Clinton Street, Room 1073
(315) 448-0422
Utica (13504-3050)
SUNY Institute of Technology
P.O. Box 3050
(315) 792-7553
Watertown (13601)
518 Davidson Street
(315) 788-1200/788-8251 (Fax)
West Hampton Beach (11978)
6 Quantuck Bay Road
(516) 288-6340/288-5715 (Fax)

White Plains (10601)
350 Main Street
(914) 948-3907/948-4645 (Fax)

NORTH CAROLINA
Asheville (28801-5007)
Federal Building, Room 259
151 Patton
(704) 271-4786/271-4009 (Fax)
Chapel Hill (27515)
c/o Chapel Hill/Carboro Chamber of
    Commerce
104 South Estes Drive
P.O. Box 2897
(919) 967-7075/968-6874 (Fax)
Charlotte (28202-2173)
200 North College Street, Suite A2015
(704) 344-6576/344-6769 (Fax)
Durham (27707)
NC Mutual Plaza
411 West Chapel Hill Street
(919) 541-2171
Greensboro (27401-2241)
400 West Market Street, Suite 410
(910) 333-5399
Hendersonville (28792)
Federal Building, Room 108
West 4th Avenue & Church Street
(704) 693-8702
Hickory (28601)
c/o Catawba County Community College
470 Highway Ex-70 Southwest
(704) 328-6111/328-1175
High Point (27262)
High Point Chamber of Commerce
1101 North Main Street
(910) 882-8625/889-9499 (Fax)
Kill Devil Hills (27948)
c/o Outer Banks Chamber of Commerce
P.O. Box 1757
(919) 261-1094/441-0338 (Fax)
New Bern (28560)
c/o Neuse River Council of Governments
312 Tryon Palace Drive, Suite 6
(919) 633-6688/633-9608 (Fax)
Raleigh (27602)
Federal Century Building
300 Fayetteville Street Mall
P.O. Box 406
(919) 856-4739/856-4183 (Fax)

Southern Pines (28387)
c/o Sand Hills Area Chamber of
   Commerce
1480 Highway 15-501
P.O. Box 458
(910) 692-3926/692-0619 (Fax)
Wilmington (28401-3958)
Alton Lennon Federal Building
2 Princess Street, Suite 103
(910) 815-4576/815-4576 (Fax)

NORTH DAKOTA
Bismarck (58502-5509)
P.O. Box 5509
(701) 250-4303
Fargo (58108-3083)
657 2nd Avenue, Room 225
P.O. Box 3086
(701) 239-5677
Grand Forks (58202-8372)
4300 Technology Drive
P.O. Box 8372
(701) 777-3051
Minot (58702-0507)
P.O. Box 507
(701) 852-6883/852-6905 (Fax)

OHIO
Akron (44308)
c/o Regional Dev. Board
One Cascade Plaza, 7th Floor
(330) 379-3163/379-3164 (Fax)
Canton (44702-1720)
116 Cleveland Avenue, NW
Suite 601
(330) 453-6047
Cincinnati (45202)
Ameritrust Building, Room 850
525 Vine Street
(513) 684-2812/684-3251 (Fax)
Cleveland (44114-2507)
Eaton Center
1100 Superior Avenue, Suite 620
(216) 522-4194/522-4844 (Fax)
Columbus (43215-2542)
2 Nationwide Plaza, Suite 1400
(614) 469-2357
Dayton (45402-1430)
Federal Building, Room 505
200 West 2nd Street
(513) 225-2887/225-7667 (Fax)

Mansfield (44902)
Chamber of Commerce
55 North Mulberry Street
(419) 522-3211
Newark (43055)
50 West Locust Street
(614) 345-7458
Toledo (43624)
1946 North 13th Street, Suite 367
(419) 259-7598
Wooster (44691)
377 West Liberty Street
(330) 262-5735/262-5745 (Fax)
Youngstown (44555)
306 Williamson Hall
Youngstown University
(330) 746-2687

OKLAHOMA
Ardmore (73402-1585)
P.O. Box 1585
(405) 223-7765
Grove (74344)
201 South Main
(918) 786-6284/786-9841 (Fax)
Lawton (73505)
Building 100, Suite 107
4500 West Lee Boulevard
(405) 353-8727/250-5677 (Fax)
Oklahoma City (73102)
c/o SBA, Oklahoma Tower Building
210 Park Avenue, #1300
(405) 231-5163/231-4876 (Fax)
Tulsa (74119)
Chamber of Commerce
616 South Boston, Suite 406
(918) 581-7462/581-6908 (Fax)

OREGON
Bend (97701)
c/o Bend Chamber of Commerce
63085 North Highway 97
(541) 382-3221
Eugene (97401-1107)
c/o Chamber of Commerce
1401 Willamette Street
P.O. Box 1107
(541) 465-6600/484-4942 (Fax)
pgr134e@prodigy.com

Medford (97501-0969)
132 West Main
P.O. Box 969
(541) 776-4220
pgr134f@prodigy.com
Portland (97201-5494)
1515 Southwest Fifth Avenue, Suite 1050
(503) 326-3441/326-2501 (Fax)
pgr134a@prodigy.com
Salem (97302-4024)
P.O. Box 4024
(503) 370-2896
pgr134d@prodigy.com

PENNSYLVANIA
Altoona (16601-3493)
c/o Altoona-Blair Chamber of Commerce
1212 12th Avenue
(814) 943-8151
Bethlehem (18015)
Rauch Building 37/Lehigh University
621 Taylor Street
(610) 758-4496/758-5205 (Fax)
Camp Hill (17011)
4211 Trindle Road
(717) 761-4304/761-4315
Chambersburg (17201)
Chambersburg Chamber of Commerce
75 South Second Street
(717) 264-2935
Erie (16501)
120 West 9th Street
(814) 871-5650
Fairless Hills (19030)
c/o Chamber of Commerce
409 Hood Boulevard
(215) 943-8850/943-7404 (Fax)
Jenkintown (19046)
Baederwood Shopping Center
1653 The Fairways, Suite 204
(215) 885-3027
Lancaster (17603)
118 West Chestnut Street
(717) 397-3092
Latrobe (15650-2690)
St. Vincent College
300 Fraser Purchase Road
(412) 539-7505
Monessen (15062)
435 Donner Avenue
(412) 684-4277

Philadelphia (19107)
1315 Walnut Street, Suite 500
(215) 790-5050/790-5016 (Fax)
Pittsburgh (15222)
1000 Liberty Avenue, Room 1122
(412) 395-6560/395-6562 (Fax)
Pottstown (19464)
238 High Street
(610) 327-2673
Reading (19601)
c/o Chamber of Commerce
645 Penn State
(610) 376-6766
Scranton (18503)
Kane Professional Building
116 North Washington Avenue, Suite 2H
(717) 347-4611
State College (16803)
200 Innovation Boulevard, #242-B
(814) 234-9415/238-9686 (Fax)
Stroudsburg (18301)
556 Main Street
(717) 421-4433
Uniontown (15401)
Federal Building
Pittsburg Street
P.O. Box 2065 DTS
(412) 437-4222
Warren (16365)
Warren County Chamber of Commerce
315 Second Avenue
P.O. Box 942
(814) 723-9017
West Chester (19382-4538)
Gov't Svc Center
601 Westtown Road, Suite 281
(610) 344-6910/793-2780 (Fax)
Wilkes-Barre (18702)
20 North Pennsylvania Avenue
(717) 826-6502
Williamsport (17703)
Federal Building, Room 304
240 West 3rd Street
P.O. Box 725
(717) 322-3720/322-1607 (Fax)
York (17404)
Cyber Center
1600 Pennsylvania Avenue
(717) 845-8830/854-9333 (Fax)

RHODE ISLAND
Providence (20903)
380 Westminster Street
(401) 528-4571/528-4539 (Fax)

SOUTH CAROLINA
Charleston (29401)
284 King Street
(803) 727-4778/853-2529 (Fax)
Columbia (29201)
Strom Thurmond Building
1835 Assembly Street, Room 358
(803) 765-5131/765-5962 (Fax)
Greenville (29601)
Federal Building, Room B-02
300 East Washington Street
(864) 271-3638
Myrtle Beach (29578)
P.O. Box 2468
(803) 918-1079

SOUTH DAKOTA
Rapid City (57701)
444 Mt. Rushmore Road, #209
(605) 394-5311
Sioux Falls (57102-1109)
First Financial Center
110 South Phillips Avenue, Suite 200
(605) 330-4231

TENNESSEE
Chattanooga (37402)
Federal Building
900 Georgia Avenue, Room 26
(423) 752-5190/752-5335 (Fax)
Jackson (38302)
c/o Chamber of Commerce
194 Auditorium Street
P.O. Box 190
(901) 423-2200
Johnson City (37601)
1st Tennessee Bank Building
2710 South Roan Street, Suite 584
(423) 929-7686/461-8052 (Fax)
Kingsport (37662)
c/o Chamber of Commerce
151 East Main Street
(423) 392-8805
Knoxville (37902)
Farragot Building
530 South Gay Street, Suite 224
(423) 545-4203

Memphis (38103)
Federal Building
167 North Main Street, Suite 390
(901) 544-3588
Nashville (37228-1500)
50 Vantage Way, Suite 201
(615) 736-7621

TEXAS
Abilene (79601)
2106 Federal Post Office & Court
(915) 677-1857
Austin (78701)
2501 South Congress
(512) 442-7235/442-7528 (Fax)
Beaumont (77704)
P.O. Box 3150
(409) 838-6581/833-6718 (Fax)
Bryan (77802)
Norwest Bank Building
3000 Briarcrest, Suite 302
(409) 776-8876
Corpus Christi (78477)
651 Upper North Broadway, Suite 654
(512) 888-4322/888-3418 (Fax)
Dallas (75214-2619)
Comerica Bank, Second Floor
6260 East Mockingbird
(214) 828-2471/828-2803 (Fax)
El Paso (79935)
10737 Gateway West, Suite 320
(915) 534-0541/540-5155 (Fax)
Ft. Worth (76102)
100 East 15th Street #24
(817) 871-6002/871-6031 (Fax)
Harlingen (78550)
222 East Van Buren, Suite 500
(210) 427-8533/427-8537 (Fax)
Houston (77074)
9301 Southwest Freeway, Suite 550
(713) 773-6565/773-6550 (Fax)
Lubbock (79401)
1611 10th Street, Suite 200
(806) 472-7462/472-7487 (Fax)
San Antonio (78206)
c/o SBA, Federal Building
727 East Durango, Room A527
(210) 472-5931/472-5935 (Fax)
Texarkana (75504)
P.O. Box 1468
(903) 792-7191/793-4304 (Fax)

Tyler (75701)
RTDC
1530 South-Southwest Loop 323, Suite 100
(903) 510-2975
Waco (76701)
401 Franklin Avenue
(254) 754-8898/756-0776 (Fax)
Wichita Falls (76307)
Hamilton Building
P.O. Box 1860
(817) 723-2741

UTAH
Logan (84123)
c/o Cache Valley Chamber of Commerce
160 North Main
(801) 752-2161
Ogden (84401)
324 25th Street 6104
(801) 625-5712
Provo (84604)
1275 North University, Suite 8
(801) 373-5300
St. George (84770)
c/o Dixie College
225 South 700 East
(801) 652-7741
Salt Lake City (84111)
169 East 100 South
(801) 364-1331/364-1310 (Fax)

VERMONT
Essex Junction (05452)
Winston Prouty Federal Building,
    Room 106
11 Lincoln Street
(802) 951-6762
Montpelier (05601)
c/o SBA
87 State Street, Room 205
P.O. Box 605
(802) 828-4422
Rutland (05701-2413)
256 North Main Street
(802) 773-9147
St. Johnsbury (05819)
c/o NCIC/20 Main Street
P.O. Box 904
(802) 748-5101

VIRGINIA
Bristol (24203)
20 Volunteer Parkway
P.O. Box 519
(423) 989-4850
Charlottesville (22903-4878)
918 Emmet Street North, Suite 200
(804) 295-6712/295-7066 (Fax)
Hampton (23666)
c/o Peninsula Chamber of Commerce
6 Manhattan Square
P.O. Box 7269
(804) 766-2000
Hopewell (23860)
c/o Chamber of Commerce
108 North Main Street
(804) 458-5536
Lynchburg (24504-1714)
Federal Building
1100 Main Street
(804) 846-3235
Martinsville (24112-0709)
115 Broad Street
P.O. Box 709
(540) 632-6401
Norfolk (23510)
Federal Building, Room 737
200 Granby Street
(757) 441-3733/441-3733 (Fax)
Prince William (22192)
Prince William Chamber of Commerce
4320 Ridgewood Center Drive
(703) 590-5000
Richmond (23229)
1504 Santa Rosa Road
Dale Building, Suite 200
(804) 771-2400/771-8018 (Fax)
Roanoke (24011)
Federal Building, Room 716
250 Franklin Road
(540) 857-2834/857-2043 (Fax)
Waynesboro (22980)
c/o Waynesboro Chamber of Commerce
301 West Main Street
(540) 949-8203
Williamsburg (23185)
c/o Chamber of Commerce
201 Penniman Road
(757) 229-6511

WASHINGTON
Bellingham (98227)
Fourth Corner, Economic Dev. Group
1203 Cornwall Avenue
P.O. Box 2803
(360) 676-4255/647-9413 (Fax)
Seattle (98101)
1200 6th Avenue, Suite 1700
(206) 553-7320/553-7044 (Fax)
Spokane (99201)
Business Information Center
1020 West Riverside Avenue
(509) 353-2820/353-2600 (Fax)
Tacoma (98402)
1101 Pacific Avenue
(206) 274-1288/274-1289 (Fax)
Vancouver (98668)
1200 Ft. Vancouver Way
P.O. Box 8900
(360) 992-3241
Yakima (98907-1647)
c/o SBDC
P.O. Box 1647
(509) 574-4944/574-4943 (Fax)

WEST VIRGINIA
Charleston (25301)
1116 Smith Street
(304) 347-5463
Fairmont (26555)
1000 Technology Drive, Suite 1111
(304) 363-0486
Huntington (25701-2309)
1101 6th Avenue, Suite 220
(304) 523-4092
Wheeling (26003)
1310 Market Street
(304) 233-2575

WISCONSIN
Appleton (54913)
227 South Walnut Street
P.O. Box 1855
(920) 734-7101 ext. 24/734-7161 (Fax)
Eau Claire (54701)
Federal Building, Room B11
510 South Barstow Street
(715) 834-1573

Fond du Lac (54935)
Fond du Lac Area Association of
  Commerce
207 North Main Street
(920) 921-9500
Green Bay (54304)
835 Potts Avenue
(920) 496-8930/496-6009 (Fax)
Janesville (53545)
51 South Jackson Street
(608) 757-3160
La Crosse (54602-0219)
712 Main Street
P.O. Box 219
(608) 784-4880
Madison (53703)
212 East Washington Avenue, Room 213
(608) 264-5508/264-5541 (Fax)
Middleton (53562)
c/o M & I Bank
7448 Hubbard Avenue
(608) 831-5464
Milwaukee (53203)
310 West Wisconsin Avenue, #425
(414) 297-3942/297-1377 (Fax)
Oshkosh (54901)
120 Jackson Street
(920) 424-7700
Stevens Point (54481)
1224 Lindberg Avenue
(715) 344-7729
Superior (54880)
305 Harborview Parkway
(715) 394-7716/394-3810 (Fax)
Wausau (54402-6190)
300 Third Street, Suite 200
P.O. Box 6190
(715) 845-6231

WYOMING
Casper (82602)
Federal Building, Room 4126
100 East B Street
(307) 261-6529/261-6530 (Fax)

PUERTO RICO
San Juan (00918-2041)
Citibank Towers Plaza
252 Ponce de Leon Avenue, 2nd Floor
(809) 766-5001

Small Business Administration
409 Third Street, Southwest
Washington, DC 20416
(800) 827-5722
www.sba.gov

Following is a listing of SBA local
offices divided by state:

ALABAMA
Birmingham (35203-2398)
2121 8th Avenue North
(205) 731-1344/731-1404 (Fax)

ALASKA
Anchorage (99513-7559)
222 West 8th Avenue
(907) 271-4022/271-4545 (Fax)

ARIZONA
Phoenix (85004-1025)
2828 North Central Avenue
(602) 640-2316/640-2360 (Fax)

ARKANSAS
Little Rock (72202)
2120 Riverfront Drive
(501) 324-5278/324-5199 (Fax)

CALIFORNIA
Fresno (93727-1547)
2719 North Air Fresno Drive, Suite 200
(209) 487-5791/487-5292 (Fax)
Glendale (91203-2304)
330 North Brand Boulevard
(818) 552-3210/552-3260 (Fax)
Sacramento (95814-2413)
660 J Street, Suite 215
(916) 498-6410/498-6422 (Fax)
San Diego (92101)
550 West C Street
(619) 557-7252/557-5894 (Fax)
San Francisco (94105)
455 Market Street, Suite 2200
(415) 744-2118/744-2119 (Fax)
(415) 744-6820/744-6812 (Fax)
Santa Ana (92701)
200 West Santa Ana Boulevard, #700
(714) 550-7420/550/0191 (Fax)

COLORADO
Denver (80202)
721 19th Street
(303) 844-0500/844-0506 (Fax)
(303) 844-3984/844-6468 (Fax)

CONNECTICUT
Hartford (06106)
330 Main Street
(203) 240-4700/240-4659 (Fax)

DELAWARE
Wilmington (19801-3011)
824 North Market Street
(302) 573-6294/573-6060 (Fax)

DISTRICT OF COLUMBIA
Washington, DC (20005)
1110 Vermont Avenue, Northwest
(202) 606-4000/606-4225 (Fax)

FLORIDA
Coral Gables (33146-2911)
1320 South Dixie Highway
(305) 536-5521/536-5058 (Fax)
Jacksonville (32256-7504)
7825 Baymeadows Way
(904) 443-1900/443-1980 (Fax)

GEORGIA
Atlanta (30309-2482)
1720 Peachtree Road, NW
(404) 347-4999/347-2355 (Fax)
(404) 347-4749/347-4745 (Fax)

HAWAII
Honolulu (96850-4981)
300 Ala Moana Boulevard
(808) 541-2990/541-2976 (Fax)

IDAHO
Boise (83702)
1020 Main Street
(208) 334-1696/334-1696 (Fax)

ILLINOIS
Chicago (60661-2511)
500 West Madison Street
(312) 353-5000/353-3426 (Fax)
(312) 353-4528/886-5688 (Fax)
Springfield (62704)
511 West Capitol Avenue
(217) 492-4416/492-4867 (Fax)

INDIANA
Indianapolis (46204-1873)
429 North Pennsylvania
(317) 226-7272/226-7259 (Fax)

IOWA
Cedar Rapids (52401-1806)
215 4th Avenue Road, SE
(319) 362-6405/362-7861 (Fax)
Des Moines (50309)
210 Walnut Street
(515) 284-4422/284-4572 (Fax)

KANSAS
Wichita (67202)
100 East English Street
(316) 269-6616/269-6499 (Fax)

KENTUCKY
Louisville (40202)
600 Dr. M. L. King Jr. Place
(502) 582-5971/582-5009 (Fax)

LOUISIANA
New Orleans (70130)
365 Canal Street
(504) 589-6685/589-2339 (Fax)

MAINE
Augusta (04330)
40 Western Avenue
(207) 622-8378/622-8277 (Fax)

MARYLAND
Baltimore (21201-2525)
10 South Howard Street
(410) 962-4392/962-1805 (Fax)

MASSACHUSETTS
Boston (02222-1093)
10 Causeway Street
(617) 565-8415/565-8420 (Fax)
(617) 565-5590/565-5598 (Fax)
Springfield (01103)
1441 Main Street, Suite 410
(413) 785-0268/785-0267 (Fax)

MICHIGAN
Detroit (48226)
477 Michigan Avenue
(313) 226-6075/226-4769 (Fax)
Marquette (49855)
501 South Front Street
(906) 225-1108/225-1109 (Fax)

MINNESOTA
Minneapolis (55403-1563)
100 North 6th Street
(612) 370-2324/370-2303 (Fax)

MISSISSIPPI
Gulfport (39501-7758)
1 Government Plaza, Suite 203
(601) 863-4449/864-0179 (Fax)
Jackson (39201)
101 West Capitol Street
(601) 965-4378/965-4294 (Fax)

MISSOURI
Kansas City (64105-1500)
323 West 8th Street, Suite 307
(816) 374-6380/374-6339 (Fax)
323 West 8th Street, Suite 501
(816) 374-6708/374-6759 (Fax)
St. Louis (63101)
815 Olive Street
(314) 539-6600/539-3785 (Fax)
Springfield (65802-3200)
620 South Glenstone Street
(417) 864-7670/864-4108 (Fax)

MONTANA
Helena (59626)
301 South Park
(406) 441-1081/441-1090 (Fax)

NEBRASKA
Omaha (68154)
11145 Mill Valley Road
(402) 221-4691/221-3680 (Fax)

NEVADA
Los Vegas (89125-2527)
301 East Stewart Street
(702) 388-6611/388-6469 (Fax)

NEW HAMPSHIRE
Concord (03301)
143 North Main Street
(603) 225-1400/225-1409 (Fax)

NEW JERSEY
Newark (07102)
Two Gateway Center, 4th Floor
(973) 645-2434/645-6265 (Fax)

NEW MEXICO
Albuquerque (87102)
625 Silver Avenue, Southwest
(505) 766-1870/766-1057 (Fax)

NEW YORK
Buffalo (14202)
111 West Huron Street
(716) 551-4301/551-4418 (Fax)
Elmira (14901)
333 East Water Street
(607) 734-8130/733-4656 (Fax)
Melville (11747)
35 Pinelawn Road
(516) 454-0750/454-0769 (Fax)
New York (10278)
26 Federal Plaza
(212) 264-1450/264-0038 (Fax)
(212) 264-2454/264-7751 (Fax)
Rochester (14614)
100 State Street
(716) 263-6700/263-3146 (Fax)
Syracuse (13202)
401 South Salina Street, 5th Floor
(315) 471-9393/471-9288 (Fax)

NORTH CAROLINA
Charlotte (28202-2137)
200 North College Street
(704) 344-6563/344-6644 (Fax)

NORTH DAKOTA
Fargo (58108)
657 2nd Avenue North
(701) 239-5131/239-5645 (Fax)

OHIO
Cincinnati (45202)
525 Vine Street
(513) 684-2814/684-3251 (Fax)
Cleveland (44144-2507)
1111 Superior Avenue
(216) 522-4180/522-2038 (Fax)
Columbus (43215-2592)
2 Nationwide Plaza
(614) 469-6860/469-2391 (Fax)

OKLAHOMA
Oklahoma City (73102)
210 Park Avenue, Suite 1300
(405) 231-5521/231-4876 (Fax)

OREGON
Portland (97201-6695)
1515 SW Fifth Avenue
(503) 326-2682/326-2808 (Fax)

PENNSYLVANIA
Harrisburg (17101)
100 Chestnut Street
(717) 782-3840/782-4839 (Fax)
King of Prussia (19406)
475 Allendale Road
(610) 962-3748/962-3743 (Fax)
(610) 962-3800/962-3795 (Fax)
Pittsburgh (15222-4004)
Federal Building, Room 1128
1000 Liberty Avenue
(412) 395-6560/395-6562 (Fax)
Wilkes-Barre (18701-3589)
20 North Pennsylvania Avenue
(717) 826-6497/826-6287 (Fax)

RHODE ISLAND
Providence (02903)
380 Westminister Mall
(401) 528-4562/528-4539 (Fax)

SOUTH CAROLINA
Columbia (29201)
1835 Assembly Street
(803) 765-5377/765-5962 (Fax)

SOUTH DAKOTA
Sioux Falls (57102)
101 South Main Avenue
(605) 330-4231/330-4215 (Fax)

TENNESSEE
Nashville (37228-1500)
50 Vantage Way
(615) 736-5881/736-7232 (Fax)

TEXAS
Corpus Christi (78476)
606 North Carancahua
(512) 888-3331/888-3418 (Fax)
Dallas/Ft. Worth (76155)
4300 Amon Carter Boulevard
(817) 885-6581/885-6588 (Fax)
(817) 885-6500/885-6516 (Fax)
El Paso (79935)
10737 Gateway West
(915) 540-5676/540-5636 (Fax)
Harlingen (78550)
222 East Van Buren Street
(956) 427-8625/427-8537 (Fax)

Houston (77074-1591)
9301 Southwest Freeway
(713) 773-6500/773-6550 (Fax)
Lubbock (79401-2693)
1611 10th Street
(806) 472-7462/472-7487 (Fax)
San Antonio (78206)
727 East Durango
(210) 472-5900/472-5937 (Fax)

UTAH
Salt Lake City (84138)
125 South State Street
(801) 524-5800/524-4160 (Fax)

VERMONT
Montpelier (05602)
87 State Street
(802) 828-4422/828-4485 (Fax)

VIRGINIA
Richmond (23229)
Dale Building, Suite 200
1504 Santa Rosa Road
(804) 771-2400/771-8018 (Fax)

WASHINGTON
Seattle (98101-1128)
1200 6th Avenue, Suite 1805
(206) 553-5676/553-2872 (Fax)
1200 6th Avenue, Suite 1700
(206) 553-7310/553-7099 (Fax)
Spokane (99204-0317)
West 601 First Avenue
(509) 353-2800/353-2829 (Fax)

WEST VIRGINIA
Charleston (25301)
405 Capitol Street, Suite 412
(304) 347-5220/347-5350 (Fax)
Clarksburg (26301)
168 West Main Street
(304) 623-5631/623-0023 (Fax)

WISCONSIN
Madison (53703)
212 East Washington Avenue
(608) 264-5261/264-5541 (Fax)

Milwaukee (53203)
310 West Wisconsin Avenue
(414) 297-3941/297-1377 (Fax)

WYOMING
Casper (82602)
100 East B Street
(307) 261-5761/261-6535 (Fax)

GUAM
Mongmong (96927)
400 Route 8, Suite 302
(671) 472-7277/472-7365 (Fax)

PUERTO RICO
Hato Rey (00918)
252 Ponce De Leon Avenue
(809) 766-5572/766-5309 (Fax)

VIRGIN ISLANDS
St. Croix (00820)
3013 Golden Rock
(809) 778-5380/778-1102 (Fax)
St. Thomas (00802)
3800 Crown Bay
(809) 774-8530/776-2312 (Fax)

SMALL BUSINESS
DEVELOPMENT CENTERS

ALABAMA
Auburn (36849-5243) - Devron Veasley, Director
Auburn University
108 College of Business
(334) 844-4220/844-4268 (Fax)
veasley@business.auburn.edu
Birmingham (35294-4410) - Ernie Gauld, Associate State Director
1717 11th Avenue South, Suite 419
(205) 934-7260/934-7645 (Fax)
Ernieg@asbdc.asbdc.uab.edu
Birmingham (35294-4410) - Charles Hopson, Procurement Director
Alabama Small Business Procurement System[†]
University of Alabama at Birmingham
1717 Eleventh Avenue South, Suite 419
(205) 934-7260/934-7645 (Fax)
charlesh@asbdc.asbdc.uab.edu

* Lead Small Business Development Center
[†] Specialized Center
[‡] Historical Black College/University

**Birmingham (35294-2180) - Brenda
   Walker, Director**
University of Alabama at Birmingham
1601 11th Avenue South
(205) 934-6760/934-0538 (Fax)
**Birmingham (35294-4410) - John
   Sandefur, State Director**
University of Alabama at Birmingham*
Medical Towers Building
1717 Eleventh Avenue South, Suite 419
(205) 934-7260/934-7645 (Fax)
sandefur@uab.edu
**Florence (35632-0001) - Kerry Gatlin,
   Director**
University of North Alabama
Box 5248, Keller Hall
(205) 760-4629/760-4813 (Fax)
**Huntsville (35804-0168) - Jeff
   Thompson, Director**
Alabama A&M‡ University and the
University of Alabama at Huntsville
P.O. Box 168
225 Church Street, NW
(205) 535-2061/535-2050 (Fax)
jefft@hsv.chamber.org
**Jacksonville (36265) - Pat W. Shaddix,
   Director**
Jacksonville State University
114 Merrill Hall
700 Pelham Road North
(205) 782-5271/782-5179 (Fax)
sbdc@jsucc.jsu.edu
**Livingston (35470) - Paul Garner,
   Director**
University of West Alabama
Station 35
(205) 652-3665/652-3516 (Fax)
**Mobile (36688) - Susan Armour,
   Director**
University of South Alabama
College of Business, Room 8
(334) 460-6004/460-6246 (Fax)
sarmour@usamail.usouthal.edu

**Montgomery (36195) - Lorenzo Patrick,
   Director**
Alabama State University‡
915 South Jackson Street
(334) 229-4138/265-9144 (Fax)
lpatrick@asunet.alasu.edu
**Troy (36082-0001) - Janet Kervin,
   Director**
Troy State University
102 Bibb Graves
(334) 670-3771/670-3636 (Fax)
jkervin@trojan.troyst.edu
**Tuscaloosa (35487-0396) - Brian Davis,
   Director**
Alabama International Trade Center†
University of Alabama
Bidgood Hall, Room 201
(205) 348-7621/348-6974 (Fax)
aitc@aitc.cba.ua.edu
**Tuscaloosa (35487-0396) - Paavo
   Hanninen, Director**
University of Alabama
P.O. Box 870397
Bidgood Hall, Room 250
(205) 348-7011/348-9644 (Fax)
phaninen@ualvm.ua.edu

ALASKA
**Anchorage (99501) - Vern Craig,
   Director**
University of Alaska
Rural Outreach Program
430 West Seventh Avenue, Suite 110
(907) 274-7232/274-9524 (Fax)
**Anchorage (99501) - Jean Wall,
   Director**
University of Alaska Anchorage
430 West Seventh Avenue, Suite 10
(907) 274-7232/274-9524 (Fax)
**Anchorage (99501) - Jan Fredericks,
   State Director**
University of Alaska Anchorage*
430 West Seventh Avenue, Suite 110
(907) 274-7232/274-9524 (Fax)

---

* Lead Small Business Development Center
† Specialized Center
‡ Historical Black College/University

Fairbanks (99701) - Laurie Henderson, Director
University of Alaska Fairbanks
510 Second Avenue, Suite 101
(907) 456-1701/456-1873 (Fax)
Juneau (99801) - Charles Northrip, Director
400 Willoughby Street, Suite 211
(907) 463-3789/463-3929 (Fax)
Kenai (99611) - Clyde Johnson, Director
P.O. Box 3029
(907) 283-3335/283-3913 (Fax)
Wasilla (99654) - Marian Romano, Director
1801 Parks Highway, Suite C-18
(907) 373-7232/373-2560 (Fax)

ARIZONA
Coolidge (85228) - Carol Giordano, Director
Central Arizona College
8470 North Overfield Road
(520) 426-4341/426-4284 (Fax)
Flagstaff (86004) - Mike Lainoff, Director
Coconino County Community College
3000 North 4th Street, Suite 25
(520) 526-5072/526-8693 (Fax)
Holbrook (86025) - Joel Eittreim, Director
Northland Pioneer College
P.O. Box 610
(520) 537-2976/524-2227 (Fax)
Kingman (86401) - Jenn Miles, Director
Mohave Community College
1971 Jagerson Avenue
(520) 757-0894/757-0836 (Fax)
Phoenix (85014)
Maricopa Community College
702 East Osborn Road, Suite 150
(602) 230-7308/230-7989 (Fax)

Prescott (86301) - Richard Senopole, Director
Yavapai College
117 East Gurley Street, Suite 206
East Building
(520) 757-0894/778-3109 (Fax)
Sierra Vista (85635) - Debbie Elver, Director
Cochise College
901 North Colombo, Room 411
(520) 515-5443/515-5478 (Fax)
Tempe (85281) - Michael York, State Director
Maricopa County Community Colleges*
2411 West 14th Street, Suite 132
(602) 731-8722/731-8729 (Fax)
york@maricopa.edu
Thatcher (85552-0769) - Frank Granberg, Director
Eastern Arizona College/Thatcher
622 College Avenue
(520) 428-8590/526-8693 (Fax)
Tucson (85709) - Linda Andrews, Director
Pima Community College
4905-A East Broadway, Suite 101
(520) 748-4906/748-4585 (Fax)
Yuma (85364) - John Lundin, Director
Arizona Western College
281 West 24th Street, #152
(520) 341-1650/726-2636 (Fax)

ARKANSAS
Arkadelphia (71923) - Bill Akin, Director
Henderson State University
P.O. Box 7624
(501) 230-5224/230-5236 (Fax)
Fayetteville (72701) - Jimmie Wilkins, Director
University of Arkansas at Fayetteville
College of Business - BA 106
(501) 575-5148/575-4013 (Fax)

* Lead Small Business Development Center
† Specialized Center
‡ Historical Black College/University

Fort Smith (72901-2067) - Vonnelle Vanzant, Business Specialist
1109 South 16th Street
P.O. Box 2067
(501) 785-1376/785-1964 (Fax)

Harrison (72601-0190) - Bob Penquite, Business Specialist
818 Highway 62-65-412 North
P.O. Box 190
(501) 741-8009/741-1905 (Fax)

Hot Springs (71901) - Richard Evans, Business Specialist
835 Central Avenue, Box 402-D
(501) 624-5448/624-6632 (Fax)

Little Rock (72201) - John Harrison, Business Specialist
University of Arkansas at Little Rock
100 South Main, Suite 401
(501) 324-9043/324-9049 (Fax)

Little Rock (72201) - Janet Nye, State Director
University of Arkansas at Little Rock*
Little Rock Technology Center Building
100 South Main, Suite 401
(501) 324-9043/324-9049 (Fax)

Magnolia (71753) - Lairie Kincaid, Business Specialist
600 Bessie
P.O. Box 767
(501) 234-4030/234-0135 (Fax)

Pine Bluff (71601) - Audrey Long, Business Specialist
Enterprise Center III
400 Main, Suite 117
(501) 536-0654/536-7713 (Fax)

State University (72467) - Herb Lawrence, Director
Arkansas State University
P.O. Box 2650
(501) 972-3517/972-3868 (Fax)

Stuttgart (72160) - Larry Lefler, Business Specialist
301 South Grand, Suite 101
P.O. Box 289
(501) 673-8707/673-8707 (Fax)

West Memphis (72303-2067) - Ronny Brothers, Business Consultant
Mid-South Community College
2000 West Broadway
P.O. Box 2067
(501) 733-6767

CALIFORNIA
Aptos (95003) - Teresa Thomae, Director
6500 Soquel Drive
(408) 479-6136/479-6166 (Fax)

Auburn (95603) - Mary Wollesen, Director
Sierra College
560 Wall Street, Suite J
(916) 885-5488/823-2831 (Fax)
smallbiz@sierra.campus.mci.net

Bakersfield (93301) - Jeffrey Johnson, Director
1706 Chester Avenue, Suite 200
(805) 322-5881/322-5663 (Fax)
weill@lightspeed.net

Chico (95926) - Kay Zimmerlee, Director
Butte College
260 Cohasset Road, Suite A
(916) 895-9017/895-9099 (Fax)
bcsbdc@ben.bcoe.butte.k12.ca.us

Chula Vista (91910) - Mary Wylie, Director
900 Otay Lake Road, Building 1600
(619) 482-6393/482-6402 (Fax)
www.sbditc.org

Chula Vista (91910) - Mary Wylie, Director
International Trade Center[†]
Southwestern College
900 Otay Lakes Road, Building 1600
(619) 482-6393/482-6402 (Fax)

---

* Lead Small Business Development Center
[†] Specialized Center
[‡] Historical Black College/University

Clearlake (95422-4550) - George McQueen, Director
Yuba College
P.O. Box 4550
15145 Lakeshore Drive
(707) 995-3440/995-3605 (Fax)

Concord (94520) - Debra Longwood, Director
2425 Bisso Lane, Suite 200
(510) 646-5377/646-5299 (Fax)
MemoirsInk@aol.com

Crescent City (95531) - Fran Clark, Director
207 Price Mall, Suite 500
(707) 464-2168/465-6008 (Fax)

El Centro (92243) - Debbie Trujillo, Satellite Manager
Town & Country Shopping Center
301 North Imperial Avenue, Suite B
(619) 312-9800/312-9838 (Fax)
ivsbdc@quix.net

El Monte (91731) - Charles Blythe, Manager
10501 Valley Boulevard, Suite 106
(818) 459-4111/443-0463 (Fax)
info@exportsbdc.org

Eureka (95501) - Duff Huettner, Business Counselor
520 E Street
(707) 445-9720/445-9652 (Fax)

Fairfield (94585) - Beth Pratt, Director
424 Executive Court North, Suite C
(707) 864-3382/864-8025 (Fax)

Fresno (93711) - Dennis Winans, Director
3419 West Shaw Avenue, Suite 102
(209) 275-1223/275-1499 (Fax)
sbdc@abrillo.cc.ca.us
www.ccsbdc.org

Gilroy (95020) - Peter Graff, Director
7436 Monterey Street
(408) 847-0373/847-0393 (Fax)
1.nolan@gilroy.com
gilroy.com/sbdc/sbdc.html

Irvine (92715) - Tiffany Haugen, Director
4199 Campus Drive
University Towers, Suite 240
(714) 509-2990/509-2997 (Fax)
www.accelerate.uci.edu

Jackson (95642)
222 North Highway 49
P.O. Box 1077
(209) 223-0351/223-5237 (Fax)

La Jolla (92037) - Hal Lefkowitz, Director
4275 Executive Square, Suite 920
(619) 453-9388/450-1997 (Fax)
www.smallbiz.org

Los Angeles (90022)
5161 East Pomona Boulevard, Suite 212
(213) 262-9797/262-2704 (Fax)

Los Angeles (90037) - Cope Norcross, Satellite Manager
4060 South Figueroa Street
(213) 846-1710/235-1686 (Fax)
sbdcla@ibm.net

Markleeville (96120)
3 Webster Street
P.O. Box 265
(916) 694-2475/694-2478 (Fax)

Marysville (95901)
429 10th Street
(916) 749-0153/749-0152 (Fax)

Merced (95340) - Nick Stavrianoudakis, Satellite Manager
1632 N Street
(209) 725-3800/383-4959 (Fax)

Modesto (95354) - Kelly Bearden, Director
1012 Eleventh Street, Suite 300
(209) 521-6177/521-9373 (Fax)

Napa (94559) - Michael Kauffman, Director
Napa Valley College
1556 First Street, Suite 103
(707) 253-3210/253-3068 (Fax)

---

* Lead Small Business Development Center
† Specialized Center
‡ Historical Black College/University

**Norton Air Force Base (92509) - Chuck
Eason, Incubator Manager**
Building 409
(909) 382-0065/382-8543 (Fax)
**Oakland (94612) - Napoleon Britt,
Interim Director**
519 17th Street, Suite 201
(510) 893-4114/893-5532 (Fax)
sbdc@peralta.cc.ca.us
**Ontario (91761) - John Hernandez,
Trade Manager**
3282 East Guasti Road, Suite 100
(909) 390-8071/390-8077 (Fax)
**Palm Springs (92264) - Brad Mix,
Satellite Manager**
501 South Indian Canyon Drive, Suite 222
(619) 864-1311/864-1319 (Fax)
**Pasadena (91104) - David Ryal,
Satellite Manager**
2061 North Los Robles, Suite 106
(818) 398-9031/398-3059 (Fax)
**Pico Rivera (90660) - Beverly Taylor,
Satellite Director**
9058 East Washington Boulevard
(310) 942-9965/942-9745 (Fax)
Pomona (91766) - Toni Valdez, Director
375 South Main Street, Suite 101
(909) 629-2247/629-8310 (Fax)
**Pomona (91766) - Paul Hischar,
Satellite Manager**
375 South Main Street, Suite 101
(909) 629-2247/629-8310 (Fax)
**Redding (96001) - Carole Enmark,
Director**
737 Auditorium Drive, Suite A
(916) 247-8100/241-1712 (Fax)
cenmark@awwwsome.com
**Riverside (92507) - Teri Corazzini-
Ooms, Director**
2002 Iowa Avenue, Building D,
Suite D-110
(800) 750-2353/(909)
781-2345/781-2353 (Fax)
iesbdc@aol.com
www.commerce.ca.gov/iesbdc

**Sacramento (95825) - Cynthia Steimle,
Director**
1410 Ethan Way
(916) 563-3210/563-3264 (Fax)
sbdc@smallbiz.org
www.losrios,cc.ca.us/oeed/sbdc/sbdc.htm
**Sacramento (95814) - Kim Neri, State
Director**
California Trade and Commerce Agency*
801 K Street, Suite 1700
(916) 324-5068/322-5084 (Fax)
San Andreas (95249)
3 North Main Street
P.O. Box 431
(209) 754-1834/754-4107 (Fax)
**San Francisco (94102) - Tim Sprinkles,
Director**
711 Van Ness, Suite 305
(415) 561-1890/561-1894 (Fax)
sfsbdc@ziplink.net
**Santa Ana (92701) - Gregory Kishel,
Director**
901 East Santa Ana Boulevard, Suite 101
(714) 647-1172/835-9008 (Fax)
**Santa Monica (90405) - Ken Davis,
Administrative Assistant**
3233 Donald Douglas Loop South,
Suite C
(310) 398-8883/398-3024 (Fax)
**Santa Rosa (95401) - Charles Robbins,
Director**
520 Mendocino Avenue, Suite 210
(707) 524-1770/524-1772 (Fax)
robbins@wco.com
www.santarosa.edu/sbdc
Segundo (90245)
222 North Sepulveda, Suite 1690
(310) 606-0166/606-0155 (Fax)
www.exportsbdc.org
**Stockton (95202) - Gillian Murphy,
Director**
814 North Hunter
(209) 474-5089/474-5605 (Fax)
www.inreach.com/sbdc

---

* Lead Small Business Development Center
† Specialized Center
‡ Historical Black College/University

Sunnyvale (94086) - Elza Minor, Director
298 South Sunnyvale Avenue, Suite 204
(408) 736-0680/736-0679 (Fax)
sbdc@best.com
www.siliconvalley-sbdc.org
Torrance (90501) - Susan Hunter,
Director
21221 Western Avenue, Suite 110
(310) 787-6466/782-8607 (Fax)
Ukiah (95482) - Sheilah Rogers,
Director
367 North State Street, Suite 208
(707) 468-3553/468-8945 (Fax)
Van Nuys (91411) - Wilma Berglund,
Interim Director
14540 Victory Boulevard, Suite 101
(818) 373-7092/373-7740 (Fax)
www.VNsbdc@aol.com
Ventura (93003) - Heather Wicka,
Manager
5700 Ralston Street, Suite 310
(805) 644-6191/644-2252 (Fax)
Ventura (93003) - Joe Higgins, Satellite
Manager
5700 Ralston Street, Suite 310
(805) 658-2688/658-2252 (Fax)
Victorville (92392) - Megan Partington,
Business Consultant
15490 Civic Drive, Suite 102
(619) 951-1592/951-8929 (Fax)
Visalia (93277) - Randy Mason,
Satellite Office Director
430 West Caldwell Avenue, Suite D
(209) 625-3051/625-3053 (Fax)

COLORADO
Alamosa (81102) - Mary Hoffman
Adams State College
(719) 589-7372/589-7603 (Fax)
mchoffma@adams.edu
Aurora (80010-2119) - Randy Johnson,
Director
Community College of Aurora[†]
9905 East Colfax Avenue
(303) 341-4849/361-2953 (Fax)
asbdc@henge.com

Boulder (80302) - Marilynn Force,
Director
Boulder Chamber of Commerce
2440 Pearl Street
(303) 442-1475/938-8837 (Fax)
marilynn@chamber.boulder.co.us
Canon City (81212) - Iris Clark,
Director
Pueblo Community College/Canon City
3080 East Main
(719) 275-5335/269-7334 (Fax)
canonsbdc@attmail.com
Castle Rock (80104) - Dennie Kamlet
420 Jerry Street
P.O. Box 282
(303) 814-0936/688-2688 (Fax)
Colorado Springs (80933) - Dawne
Martin, Director
University of Colorado at Colorado
Springs
CITTI Building
1420 Austin Bluffs Parkway
(719) 592-1894/533-0545 (Fax)
sbdc@uccs.edu
Craig (81625) - Ken Farmer, Director
Colorado Northwestern Community
College
50 College Drive
(970) 824-7078/824-1134 (Fax)
cnwcc@attmail.com
Delta (81416) - Bob Marshall, Director
Delta Montrose Vocational School
1765 US Highway 50
(970) 874-8772/874-8796 (Fax)
dmvs@attmail.com
Denver (80202) - Tamela Lee, Director
Community College of Denver[†]
1445 Market Street
(303) 620-8076/534-3200 (Fax)
ccd@attmail.com

---

* Lead Small Business Development Center
[†] Specialized Center
[‡] Historical Black College/University

**Denver (80202) - Cec Ortiz, State
    Director**
Office of Business Development*
1625 Broadway, Suite 1710
(303) 892-3809/892-3848 (Fax)
sbdclcl@attmail.com
www.state.co.us/gov_dir/obd/sbdc.htm
**Durango (81301-3999) - Jim Reser,
    Director**
Fort Lewis College
1000 Rim Drive, 136-G Hesperus Hall
(970) 247-7009/247-7623 (Fax)
RESER_J@fortlewis.edu
www.fortlewis.edu/soba/sbdc
**Fort Collins (80526) - Frank Pryor,
    Director**
Front Range Community College/Ft. Collins[†]
125 South Howes Street, Suite 105
Key Tower Building
(970) 498-9295/221-2811 (Fax)
ftcsbdc@attmail.com
**Fort Morgan (80701) - Dan Simon,
    Director**
Morgan Community College
300 Main Street
(970) 867-3351/867-3352 (Fax)
comcc@attmail.com
**Glenwood Springs (81601) - Susan
    Glenn-James, Director**
215 Ninth Street
(800) 621-1647/(970) 928-0120/945-7279
    (Fax)
lwiltse@coloradomtn.edu
Golden (80401) - Jayne Reiter, Director
Red Rocks Community College[†]
1726 Cole Boulevard, Building 22,
    Suite 310
(303) 277-1840/277-1899 (Fax)
sbdcrrcc@rmii.com
**Grand Junction (81505-1606) - Julie
    Morey, Director**
Mesa State Community College
304 West Main Street
(970) 243-5242/241-0771 (Fax)
mesastate@attmail.com

**Greeley (80631) - Russell Disberger,
    Director**
Aims Community College
902 7th Avenue
(970) 352-3661/352-3572 (Fax)
aimcc@attmail.com
Lamar (81052) - Dan Minor, Director
Lamar Community College
2400 South Main
(719) 336-8141/336-2448 (Fax)
lcc@attmail.com
Pueblo (81004) - Rita Friberg, Director
Pueblo Community College
900 West Orman Avenue
(719) 549-3224/549-3139 (Fax)
friberg@pcc.cccoes.edu
Stratton (80836) - Roni Carr, Director
Morgan Community College/Stratton
P.O. Box 28
(719) 348-5596/348-5887 (Fax)
strsbdc@attmail.com
**Trinidad (81082) - Dennis O'Connor,
    Director**
Trinidad State Junior College
136 West Main Street
(719) 846-5644/846-4550 (Fax)
tsjc@attmail.com
**Westminster (80030) - Leo Giles,
    Acting Director**
Front Range Community College[†]
3645 West 112th Avenue
(303) 460-1032/469-7143 (Fax)
fr_henry@cccs.ccoes.edu

CONNECTICUT
**Bridgeport (06604-4229) - Juan Scotti,
    Director**
10 Middle Street, 14th Floor
(203) 330-4813/366-0105 (Fax)
Bridgeport@ct.sbdc.uconn.edu
Danbury (06810)
72 West Street
(203) 743-5565
Danbury@ct.sbdc.uconn.edu

---

* Lead Small Business Development Center
† Specialized Center
‡ Historical Black College/University

**Danielson (06239-1440) - Roger Doty,
    Director**
Quinebaug Valley Community &
    Technical College
742 Upper Maple Street
(860) 774-1133/774-7768 (Fax)
Danielson@ct.sbdc.uconn.edu
**Groton (06340-6097) - William
    Lockwood, Director**
University of Connecticut
Administration Building, Room 300
1084 Shennecossett Road
(860) 405-9002/445-3415 (Fax)
Groton@ct.sbdc.uconn.edu
**Middletown (06457) - John Serignese,
    Director**
393 Main Street
(860) 344-2158/346-1043 (Fax)
Middletown@ct.sbdc.uconn.edu
**New Haven (06510-2009) - Pete Rivera,
    Regional Director**
195 Church Street
(203) 782-4390 ext. 190/787-6730 (Fax)
NewHaven@ct.sbdc.uconn.edu
**Stamford (06901) - George Ahl,
    Regional Director**
One Landmark Square
(203) 359-3220 ext. 302/967-8294 (Fax)
Stamford@ct.sbdc.uconn.edu
**Storrs (06269-5094) - Zaiga Antonelli,
    Acting State Director; Wanda
    Shapera, Fiscal Manager; Sotiris
    Malas, MIS Manager**
University of Connecticut*
School of Business Administration
2 Bourn Place, U-94
(860) 486-4135/486-1576 (Fax)
Questions@ct.sbdc.uconn.edu
**Waterbury (06702) - Ilene Oppenheim,
    Director**
101 Grand Street, 3rd Floor
(203) 757-8937/756-9077 (Fax)
Waterbury@ct.sbdc.uconn.edu

**West Hartford (06117-2659) - Dennis
    Gruell, Director**
University of Connecticut
1800 Asylum Avenue
(860) 570-9109/241-4907 (Fax)
WestHartford@ct.sbdc.uconn.edu
**Williamantic (06226-2295) - Henry
    Reed, Director**
Eastern Connecticut State University
83 Windham Street
(860) 465-5349/465-5143 (Fax)
Williamantic@ct.sbdc.uconn.edu

DELAWARE
Dover (19901) - Jim Crisfield, Director
Delaware State University
School of Business Economics
1200 North Dupont Highway
(302) 678-1555/739-2333 (Fax)
**Georgetown (19947) - William F. Pfaff,
    Director**
Delaware Technical and Community
    College
Industrial Training Building
P.O. Box 610
(302) 856-1555/856-5779 (Fax)
**Newark (19716-2711) - Clinton Tymes,
    State Director**
University of Delaware*
Purnell Hall, Suite 005
(302) 831-1555/831-1423 (Fax)

DISTRICT OF COLUMBIA
**Washington, DC (20052) - Susan Jones,
    Director**
George Washington University
720 Twentieth Street, Northwest
(202) 994-7463/994-4946 (Fax)
(Legal counseling assistance only)
**Washington, DC (20059) - Terry
    Strong, Acting Regional Director**
Howard University*‡
2600 Sixth Street, Northwest, Room 125
(202) 806-1550/806-1777 (Fax)

---

* Lead Small Business Development Center
† Specialized Center
‡ Historical Black College/University

Washington, DC (20059) - Jose
Hernandez, Director
Howard University Center for Urban
Progress
Howard University Central Region
Subcenter
Fourth & College Streets, Northwest
Annex III, Room 312
(202) 806-4706/806-9556 (Fax)
**Washington, DC - Alesha Ashby, Acting
Director**
Southeastern University
921 Pennsylvania Avenue, Southeast
(202) 547-7933

FLORIDA
**Bartow (33830) - Marcela Stanislaus,
Vice President**
600 North Broadway, Suite 300
(941) 534-4370/533-1247 (Fax)
**Boca Raton (33431) - Nancy Young,
Director**
Florida Atlantic University
P.O. Box 3091, Building T9
(561) 362-5620/362-5623 (Fax)
**Dania (33304) - William Healy,
Regional Manager**
46 Southwest First Avenue
(954) 987-0100/987-0106 (Fax)
**Daytona Beach (32114) - Brenda
Thomas-Ramos, Director**
Daytona Beach Community College
1200 West International Speedway
Boulevard
(904) 947-5463/254-4465 (Fax)
**Fort Lauderdale (33309) - Marty
Zients, Manager**
Florida Atlantic University
Commercial Campus
1515 West Commercial Boulevard,
Room 11
(954) 771-6520/351-4120 (Fax)

Fort Myers (33908-4500)
Florida Gulf Coast University
College of Business
The Midway Center
17595 South Tamiami Trail, Suite 200
(941) 590-7316/590-1010 (Fax)
**Ft. Pierce (34981-5599) - Marsha
L. Thompson, Director**
Indian River Community College
3209 Virginia Avenue, Room 114
(561) 462-4756/462-4796 (Fax)
**Fort Walton Beach (32547) - Walter
Craft, Manager**
Okaloosa-Walton Community College
University of West Florida
1170 Martin Luther King, Jr. Boulevard
(904) 863-6543/863-6564 (Fax)
**Gainesville (32602-2518) - Bill
Stensgaard, Regional Manager**
505 Northwest Second Avenue, Suite D
P.O. Box 2518
(352) 377-5621/377-0288 (Fax)
**Jacksonville (32216) - Dr. Lowell
Salter, Director**
University of North Florida
College of Business
Building 11, Room 2163
4567 St. John's Bluff Road, South
(904) 646-2476/646-2567 (Fax)
**Lynn Haven (32444) - Doug Davis,
Director**
Gulf Coast Community College
2500 Minnesota Avenue
(904) 271-1108/271-1109 (Fax)
**Melbourne (32935) - Victoria Peake,
Manager**
Brevard Community College
3865 North Wickham Road, CM 207
(407) 362-1111 ext. 33201/634-3712
(Fax)

* Lead Small Business Development Center
† Specialized Center
‡ Historical Black College/University

**Miami (33181) - Royland Jarrett,
Regional Manager**
Florida International University
North Miami Campus
Academic Building #1, Room 350
Northeast 151 and Biscayne Boulevard
(305) 919-5790/919-5792 (Fax)
**Miami (33199) - Marvin Nesbit,
Regional Manager**
Florida International University
Trailer MO1 - Tamiami Campus
(305) 348-2272/348-2965 (Fax)
**Miami (33150) - Frederick Bonneau,
Director**
Miami Dade Community College
6300 Northwest Seventh Avenue
(305) 237-1906/237-1908 (Fax)
**Ocala (32670) - Phillip Geist, Regional
Manager**
110 East Silver Springs Boulevard
P.O. Box 1210
(352) 629-8051/629-7651 (Fax)
**Orlando (32816-1530) - Al Polfer,
Director**
University of Central Florida
CBA Suite 309
P.O. Box 161530
(407) 823-5554/823-3073 (Fax)
**Pensacola (32514-5750) - Martha Cobb,
Interim Director**
Procurement Technical Assistance Program[†]
University of West Florida
UFW Downtown Center
19 West Garden Street, Suite 302
(904) 470-4980/470-4987 (Fax)
**Pensacola (32501) - Jerry Cartwright,
State Director**
University of West Florida*
19 West Garden Street, Suite 300
(800) 644-SBDC/(904) 444-2060/
444-2070 (Fax)
**Sanford (32773) - Wayne Hardy,
Regional Manager**
Seminole Community College
100 Weldon Boulevard, Building R
(407) 328-4722 ext. 3341/330-4489 (Fax)

**Tallahassee (32308) - Patricia
McGowan, Director**
Florida A&M University[‡]
1157 East Tennessee Street
(904) 599-3407/561-2049 (Fax)
**Tampa (33607) - Irene Hurst, Interim
Director**
University of South Florida
1111 North Westshore Drive, Annex B
(813) 554-2341/554-2356 (Fax)
**Tampa (33620) - Al Othmer, Program
Manager (Energy); Dick Hardesty,
Program Manager, (DOD)**
University of South Florida
College of Business Administration
4202 East Fowler Avenue, BSN 3403
(813) 974-4371/974-5020 (Fax, Call First)

GEORGIA
**Albany (31701-2885) - Sue Ford,
Assistant State Director**
230 South Jackson Street, Suite 333
(912) 430-4303/430-3933 (Fax)
sbdcwr@uga.cc.uga.edu
**Athens (30602-5412) - Harold Roberts,
Asst. State Director; Nancy Staton,
Area Director**
University of Georgia
1180 East Broad Street
(706) 542-7436/542-6803 (Fax)
**Athens (30602-5412) - Hank Logan,
State Director**
University of Georgia*
Chicopee Complex
1180 East Broad Street
(706) 542-6762/542-6776 (Fax)
sbdcdir@uga.cc.uga.edu
**Atlanta (30303-3083) - Lee
Quarterman, Area Director**
Georgia State University
University Plaza, Box 874
(404) 651-3550/651-1035 (Fax)
sbdcatl@uga.cc.uga.edu

* Lead Small Business Development Center
† Specialized Center
‡ Historical Black College/University

Augusta (30907-3215) - Jeff Sanford, Area Director
1054 Claussen Road, Suite 301
(706) 737-1790/731-7937 (Fax)
sdbcaug@uga.cc.uga.edu

Brunswick (31525-3039) - David Lewis, Area Director
1107 Fountain Lake Drive
(912) 264-7343/262-3095 (Fax)
sbdcbrun@uga.cc.uga.edu

Columbus (31904-6572) - Jerry Copeland, Area Director
North Building, Room 202
928 45th Street
(706) 649-7433/649-1928 (Fax)
sbdccolu@uga.cc.uga.edu

Dalton (30720-3745)
Technical Building, Room 112
213 North College Drive
(706) 272-2707/272-2701 (Fax)
sbdcdal@uga.cc.uga.edu

Decatur (30030-2622) - Eric Bonaparte, Area Director
750 Commerce Drive
(404) 373-6930/687-9684 (Fax)
sbdcdec@uga.cc.uga.edu

Gainesville (30501-3773) - Ron Simmons, Area Director
500 Jesse Jewel Parkway, Suite 304
(770) 531-5681/531-5684 (Fax)
sbdcgain@uga.cc.uga.edu

Kennesaw (30144-5591) - Carlotta Roberts, Area Director
Kennesaw State University
1000 Chastain Road
(770) 423-6450/423-6564 (Fax)
sbdcmar@uga.cc.uga.edu

LaGrange (30240-2955)
601 Broad Street
(706) 812-7353/845-0391 (Fax)

Macon (31208-3212) - David Mills, District Director; Denise Ricketson, Area Director
P.O. Box 13212
(912) 751-6596/751-6607 (Fax)

Morrow (30260) - Bernie Meineke, Area Director
Clayton State College
P.O. Box 285
(770) 961-3440/961-3428 (Fax)
sbdcmorr@uga.cc.uga.edu

Norcross (30093) - Robert Andoh, Area Director
Oakbrook Plaza
1700 Indian Trail Road, Suite 410
(770) 806-2124/806-2129 (Fax)
sbdclaw@uga.cc.uga.edu

Rome (30162-1864) - Drew Tonsmeire, Area Director
P.O. Box 1864
(706) 295-6326/295-6732 (Fax)
sbdcrome@uga.cc.uga.edu

Savannah (31406-4824) - Lynn Vos, Area Director
450 Mall Boulevard, Suite H
(912) 356-2755/353-3033 (Fax)
sbdcsav@uga.cc.uga.edu

Statesboro (30460-8156) - David Lewis, Area Director
Landrum Center
P.O. Box 8156
(912) 681-5194/681-0648 (Fax)
sbdcsav@uga.cc.uga.edu

Valdosta (31602-2782) - Suzanne Barnett, Area Director
Baytree West Professional Offices
1205 Baytree Road, Suite 9
(912) 245-3738/245-3741 (Fax)
sbdcval@uga.cc.uga.edu

Warner Robbins (31088)
151 Osigian Boulevard
(912) 953-9356/953-9376 (Fax)
sbdcwr@uga.cc.uga.edu

HAWAII
Hilo (96720-4091) - Darryl Mleynek, State Director
University of Hawaii at Hilo*
200 West Kawili Street
(808) 933-3515/933-3683 (Fax)
darrylm@interpac.net

---

* Lead Small Business Development Center
† Specialized Center
‡ Historical Black College/University

**Hilo (96720-4091) - Rebecca Winters,
  Center Director**
University of Hawaii at Hilo
200 West Kawili Street
(808) 933-3515/933-3683 (Fax)
winters@interpac.net
**Honolulu (96813) - Laura Noda, Center
  Director**
University of Hawaii at West Oahu
130 Merchant Street, Suite 1030
(808) 522-8131/522-8135 (Fax)
lnoda@aloha.net
**Kihei (96753-6900) - Ruth Corn,
  Library Director**
Maui Community College
Business Research Library (BRL)
590 Lipoa Parkway, Suite 128
(808) 875-2400/875-2452 (Fax)
rcorn@maui.com
**Kihei (96753-6900) - David B. Fisher,
  Center Director**
Maui Community College
Maui Research and Technology Center
590 Lipoa Parkway
(808) 875-2402/875-2452 (Fax)
dfisher@maui.com
**Lihue (96766-9591) - Randy Gingras,
  Center Director**
Kaua'i Community College
3-1901 Kaumalii Highway
(808) 246-1748/245-5102 (Fax)
randyg@aloha.net

IDAHO
**Boise (83725) - Robert Shepard,
  Regional Director**
Boise State University
1910 University Drive
(800) 225-3815 (in Idaho)/
    (208) 385-3875/385-3877 (Fax)
**Boise (83725) - James Hogge, State
  Director**
Boise State University*
College of Business
1910 University Drive
(800) 225-3815 (in Idaho)/
    (208) 385-1640/385-3877 (Fax)

**Idaho Falls (83401) - Betty Capps,
  Regional Director**
Idaho State University
2300 North Yellowstone
(208) 523-1087/523-1049 (Fax)
**Lewiston (83501) - Helen Le Boeuf-
  Binninger, Regional Director**
Lewis-Clark State College
500 Eighth Avenue
(208) 799-2465/799-2878 (Fax)
**McCall (83638) - Larry Smith,
  Associate Business Consultant**
305 East Park Street, Suite 405
(208) 634-2883
**Pocatello (83201) - Paul Cox, Regional
  Director**
Idaho State University
1651 Alvin Ricken Drive
(208) 232-4921/233-0268 (Fax)
**Post Falls (83854) - John Lynn,
  Regional Director**
North Idaho College
525 West Clearwater Loop
(208) 769-3296/769-3223 (Fax)
**Twin Falls (83303) - Cindy Bond,
  Regional Director**
College of Southern Idaho
315 Falls Avenue
P.O. Box 1238
(208) 733-9554 ext. 2450/733-9316 (Fax)

ILLINOIS
**Aurora (60506) - Mike O'Kelley,
  Director**
Waubonsee Community College
Aurora Campus, 5 East Galena Boulevard
(630) 801-7900/892-4668 (Fax)
**Carbondale (62901-6702) - Dennis
  Cody, Director**
Southern Illinois University at
  Carbondale
(618) 536-2424/453-5040 (Fax)
**Centralia (62801) - Richard
  McCullum, Director**
Kaskaskia College
27210 College Road
(618) 532-2049/532-4983 (Fax)

---

* Lead Small Business Development Center
† Specialized Center
‡ Historical Black College/University

**Chicago (60646) - Joon H. Lee,
Director**
6246 North Pulaski Road, Suite 101
(773) 202-0600/202-1007 (Fax)
Chicago (60609) - Bill Przybylski
1751 West 47th Street
(773) 523-4419/254-3525 (Fax)
**Chicago (60601) - Carson Gallagher,
Director**
100 West Randolph, Suite 3-400
(312) 814-6111/814-2807 (Fax)
**Chicago (60608) - Maria Munoz,
Director**
1839 South Carpenter
(312) 733-2270/733-7315 (Fax)
**Chicago (60639) - Paul Petersen,
Director**
4054 West North Avenue
(773) 384-2262/384-3850 (Fax)
**Chicago (60612) - Melvin Eiland,
Director**
2023 West Carroll
(312) 421-3941/421-1871 (Fax)
**Chicago (60647) - Arturo Venecia,
Director**
2539 North Kedzie, Suite 11
(773) 252-5211/252-7065 (Fax)
**Chicago (60618) - Tom Kamykowski,
Director**
2500 West Bradley Place
(773) 588-5855/588-0734 (Fax)
Chicago (60603) - Joyce Wade
8 South Michigan, Suite 400
(312) 853-3477/853-0145 (Fax)
Chicago (60654) - Nancy Berman
350 North Orleans, Suite 1047
(312) 836-1041
Chicago (60651) - Sonja Davis
3709 West Chicago Avenue
(773) 826-4055/826-7375 (Fax)
Chicago (60607)
University of Illinois at Chicago
CUB 601 South Morgan
2231 Utt M/C 075
(773) 996-4057/996-4567 (Fax)

**Crystal Lake (60012-2761) - Susan
Whitfield, Director**
McHenry County College
8900 U.S. Highway 14
(815) 455-6098/455-9319 (Fax)
Danville (61832) - Ed Adrain, Director
Danville Area Community College
28 West North Street
(217) 442-7232/442-6228 (Fax)
**Decatur (62526) - Rick Russell,
Director**
985 West Pershing Road, Suite F-4
(217) 875-8284/875-8288 (Fax)
**Dixon (61021-9110) - John Nelson,
Director**
Sauk Valley Community College
173 Illinois Route 2
(815) 288-5511/288-5958 (Fax)
**East Moline (61244) - Donna Scalf,
Director**
Black Hawk College
301 42nd Avenue
(309) 755-2200 ext. 211/755-9847 (Fax)
East St. Louis (62201) - Robert Ahart
10 Collinsville
(618) 583-2270/583-2274 (Fax)
**Edwardsville (62026) - Alan Hauff,
Director**
Southern Illinois University at
Edwardsville
Campus Box 1107
(618) 692-2929/692-2647 (Fax)
Elgin (60123) - Craig Fowler, Director
Elgin Community College
1700 Spartan Drive
(847) 888-7488/931-3911 (Fax)
**Evanston (60201-3670) - Rick
Holbrook, Director**
1840 Oak Avenue
(847) 866-1817/866-1808 (Fax)
**Glen Ellyn (61832) - David Gay,
Director**
College of DuPage
425 22nd Street
(630) 942-2771/942-3789

---

* Lead Small Business Development Center
† Specialized Center
‡ Historical Black College/University

Godfrey (62035) - Bob Duane, Director
Lewis and Clark Community College
5800 Godfrey Road
(618) 466-3411/466-0810 (Fax)
Grayslake (60030)
College of Lake County
19351 West Washington Street
(847) 223-3633/223-9371 (Fax)
**Harrisburg (62946-2125) - Becky
    Williams, Director**
Southeastern Illinois College
303 South Commercial Street
(618) 252-5001/252-0210 (Fax)
Ina (62846) - Lisa Payne, Director
Rend Lake College
Route 1
(618) 437-5321 ext. 335
    /437-5677 ext. 385 (Fax)
**Joliet (60431) - Denise Mikulski,
    Director**
Joliet Junior College
Renaissance Center, Room 312
214 North Ottawa Street
(815) 727-6544 ext. 1321/722-1895 (Fax)
Kankakee (60901) - Kelly Berry
Kankakee Community College
101 South Schuyler Avenue
(815) 933-0376/933-0380 (Fax)
Macomb (61455) - Dan Voorhis, Director
Western Illinois University
214 Seal Hall
(309) 298-2211/298-2520 (Fax)
**Monmouth (61462-2688) - Carol Cook,
    Director**
620 South Main Street
(309) 734-4664/734-8579 (Fax)
Oglesby (61348) - Boyd Palmer, Director
Illinois Valley Community College
815 North Orlando Smith Avenue,
    Building 11
(815) 223-1740/224-3033 (Fax)
Olney (62450) - John Spitz, Director
Illinois Eastern Community College
401 East Main Street
(618) 395-3011/395-1922 (Fax)

**Palos Hills (60465) - Hilary Gereg,
    Director**
Moraine Valley College
10900 South 88th Avenue
(708) 974-5469/974-0078 (Fax)
**Peoria (61625) - Roger Luman,
    Director**
Bradley University
141 North Jobst Hall, First Floor
(309) 677-3075/677-3386 (Fax)
River Grove (60171) - Lon Bancroft
Triton College
2000 Fifth Avenue
(708) 456-0300 ext. 246/583-3118 (Fax)
**Rockford (61110-1437) - Beverly
    Kingsley, Director**
Rock Valley College
1220 Rock Street
(815) 968-4087/968-4157 (Fax)
Springfield (62703) - Tom Berkshire
2715 South Fourth Street
(217) 525-0398/525-0442 (Fax)
**Springfield (62701) - Jeff Mitchell,
    State Director**
Department of Commerce and
    Community Affairs*
620 East Adams Street, Third Floor
(217) 524-5856/524-0171/785-6328 (Fax)
**Springfield (62703) - Frieda Schreck,
    Director**
Lincoln Land Community College
100 North Eleventh Street
(217) 789-1017/789-0958 (Fax)
Ullin (62992) - Donald Denny, Director
Shawnee Community College
Shawnee College Road
(618) 634-9618/634-9028 (Fax)
**University Park (60466) - Christine
    Cochrane, Director**
Governors State University
College of Business, Room C-3305
(708) 534-4929/534-8457 (Fax)

* Lead Small Business Development Center
† Specialized Center
‡ Historical Black College/University

INDIANA
Bloomington (47403) - David Miller, Director
216 West Allen Street
(812) 339-8937/336-0651 (Fax)
Columbus (47203) - Jack Hess, Director
4920 North Warren Drive
(812) 372-6480/372-0228 (Fax)
Evansville (47708) - Kate Northrup, Director
100 Northwest Second Street, Suite 200
(812) 425-7232/421-5883 (Fax)
Fort Wayne (46803) - A. V. Fleming, Director
1830 Wayne Trace
(219) 426-0040/424-0024 (Fax)
Indianapolis (46204) - Glenn Dunlap, Director
324 North Senate Avenue
(317) 261-3030/261-3053 (Fax)
Kokomo (46901) - Kim Moyers, Director
106 North Washington
(317) 457-5301/452-4564 (Fax)
Lafayette (47901) - Susan Davis, Director
122 North Third
(317) 742-2394/742-6276 (Fax)
Madison (47250) - Rose Marie Roberts, Director
975 Industrial Drive
(812) 265-3127/265-2923 (Fax)
Muncie (47308) - Barbara Armstrong, Director
401 South High Street
(317) 284-8144/741-5489 (Fax)
New Albany (47150) - Gretchen Mahaffey, Director
4100 Charleston Road
(812) 945-0266/948-4664 (Fax)
Portage (46368) Mark McLaughlin, Director
6100 Southport Road
(219) 762-1696

Richmond (47374) Cliff Fry, Director
33 South Seventh Street
(317) 962-2887/966-0882 (Fax)
South Bend (46601) - Carolyn Anderson, Director
300 North Michigan
(219) 282-4350/282-4344 (Fax)
Terre Haute (47809) - William Minnis, Director
ISU School of Business, Room 510
(812) 237-7676/237-7675 (Fax)

KANSAS
Chanute (66720)
Neosho County Community College
1000 South Allen
(316) 431-2820 ext. 219/431-0082 (Fax)
Coffeyville (67337-5064) - Charles Shaver, Director
Coffeyville Community College
11th and Willow Streets
(316) 251-7700/252-7098 (Fax)
Colby (67701) - Robert Selby, Director
Colby Community College
1255 South Range
(913) 462-3984 ext. 239/462-8315 (Fax)
Dodge City (67801)
Dodge City Community College
2501 North 14th Avenue
(316) 227-9247/227-9200 (Fax)
Emporia (66801) - Lisa Brumbaugh, Regional Director
Emporia State University
130 Cremer Hall
(316) 342-7162/341-5418 (Fax)
Fort Scott (66701) - Steve Pammenter, Director
Fort Scott Community College
2108 South Horton
(316) 223-2700/223-6530 (Fax)
Garden City (67846) - Bill Sander, Regional Director
Garden City Community College
801 Campus Drive
(316) 276-9632/276-9630 (Fax)

---

* Lead Small Business Development Center
† Specialized Center
‡ Historical Black College/University

Hays (67601) - Clare Gustin, Regional Director
Fort Hays State University
109 West 10th Street
(913) 628-6786/628-0533 (Fax)
Hutchinson (67501) - Clark Jacobs, Director
Hutchinson Community College
815 North Walnut, Suite 225
(316) 665-4950/665-8354 (Fax)
Independence (67301) - Preston Haddan, Director
Independence Community College
College Avenue and Brookside
P.O. Box 708
(316) 332-1420/331-5344 (Fax)
Iola (66749) - Susan Thompson, Director
Allen County Community College
1801 North Cottonwood
(316) 365-5116/365-3284 (Fax)
Kansas City (66112) - Sue Courtney
Kansas City Kansas Community College
7250 State Avenue
(913) 596-9659/596-9663 (Fax)
Lawrence (66044) - Randee Brady, Regional Director
University of Kansas
734 Vermont Street, Suite 104
(913) 843-8844/843-8878 (Fax)
Liberal (67901) - Dale Reed, Director
Seward County Community College
1801 North Kansas
(316) 624-1951 ext. 150/624-0637 (Fax)
Manhattan (66502-2947) - Fred Rice, Regional Director
Kansas State University
2323 Anderson Avenue, Suite 100
(913) 532-5529/532-5827 (Fax)
Overland Park (66210-1299) - Kathy Nadlman, Regional Director
Johnson County Community College
CEC Building, Room 223
(913) 469-3878/469-4415 (Fax)

Parsons (67357) - Mark Turnbull, Director
Labette Community College
200 South 14th
(316) 421-6700/421-0921 (Fax)
Pittsburg (66762) - Kathryn Richard, Regional Director
Pittsburg State University
Shirk Hall
(316) 235-4920/232-4919 (Fax)
Pratt (67124)
Pratt Community College
Highway 61
(316) 672-5641/672-5288 (Fax)
Salina (67401)
Salina College of Technology
Kansas State University
2409 Scanlan Avenue
(913) 826-2616/826-2630 (Fax)
Topeka (66621) - Dan Kingman, Regional Director
Washburn University
101 Henderson Learning Center
(913) 231-1010 ext. 1305/231-1063 (Fax)
Wichita (67260) - Joann Ard, Regional Director
Wichita State University*
1845 Fairmont
(316) 978-3193/978-3647 (Fax)

KENTUCKY
Ashland (41101) - Kimberly A. Jenkins, Director
Morehead State University/Ashland
1401 Winchester Avenue, Suite 305
(606) 329-8011/324-4570 (Fax)
Bowling Green (42101) - Richard S. Horn, Director
Western Kentucky University
2355 Nashville Road
(502) 745-1905/745-1931 (Fax)
Elizabethtown (42701) - Lou Ann Allen, Director
University of Kentucky
133 West Dixie Avenue
(502) 765-6737/769-5095 (Fax)

* Lead Small Business Development Center
† Specialized Center
‡ Historical Black College/University

Highland Heights (41099-0506) - Sutton Landry, Director
Northern Kentucky University
BEP Center 463
(606) 572-6524/572-6177 (Fax)

Hopkinsville (42240) - Michael Cartner, Director
Murray State University/Hopkinsville
300 Hammond Drive
(502) 889-8666/886-3211 (Fax)

Lexington (40506-0034) - Janet S. Holloway, State Director
University of Kentucky*
225 C.M. Gatton Business and Economics Building
(606) 257-7668/323-1907 (Fax)

Lexington (40507-1376) - Marge Berge, Program Coordinator
University of Kentucky/Lexington
c/o Downtown Public Library
140 East Main Street
(606) 257-7666/257-1751 (Fax)

Louisville (40202) - Thomas Daley, Director
Bellarmine College
School of Business
600 West Main Street, Suite 219
(502) 574-4770/574-4771 (Fax)

Louisville (40292) - Lou Dickie, Director
University of Louisville†
Center for Enterpreneurship & Technology
Room 122 Burhans Hall, Shelby Campus
(502) 852-7854/852-8573 (Fax)

Middlesboro (40965-2265) - Kathleen Moats, Director
Southeast Community College
1300 Chichester Avenue
(606) 242-2145 ext. 2021/242-4514 (Fax)

Morehead (40351) - Wilson Grier, District Director
Morehead State University
CB 309, UPO 2479
(606) 783-2895/783-5020 (Fax)

Murray (42071) - Rosemary Miller, Director
Murray State University
P.O. Box 9
(502) 762-2856/762-3049 (Fax)

Owensboro (42301) - Mickey Johnson, District Director
Murray State University/Owensboro
3860 U.S. Highway 60 West
(502) 926-8085/684-0714 (Fax)

Pikeville (41501) - Michael Morley, Director
Morehed State University/Pikeville
Justice Office Building
Route 7, 110 Village Street
(606) 432-5848/432-8924 (Fax)

Somerset (42501) - Donald R. Snyder, Director
Eastern Kentucky University
2292 South Highway 27, Suite 260
(606) 677-6120/677-6083 (Fax)

LOUISIANA

Alexandria (71301) - Kathey Hunter, Consultant
Hibernia National Bank Building, Suite 510
934 Third Street
(318) 484-2123/484-2126 (Fax)

Baton Rouge (70809) - Gregory Spann, Director
Southern University
9613 Interline Avenue
(504) 922-0998/922-0999 (Fax, Call First)

Hammond (70402) - William Joubert, Director
Southeastern Louisiana University
College of Business Administration
Box 522, SLU Station
(504) 549-3831/549-2127 (Fax)

Lafayette (70504) - Kim Spence, Director
University of Southwestern Louisiana
College of Business Administration
Box 43732
(318) 262-5344/262-5296 (Fax)

---

* Lead Small Business Development Center
† Specialized Center
‡ Historical Black College/University

Lake Charles (70609) - Paul Arnold, Director
McNeese State University
College of Business Administration
(318) 475-5529/475-5012 (Fax)
Monroe (71209) - Dr. Jerry Wall, Director
Louisiana Electronic Assistance Program[†]
Northeast Louisiana University
College of Business Administration
(318) 342-1215/342-1209 (Fax)
Monroe (71209) - Dr. Paul Dunn, Director
Northeast Louisiana University
College of Business Administration
(318) 342-1224/342-1209 (Fax)
Monroe (71209) - Dr. John Baker, State Director
Northeast Louisiana University*
College of Business Administration
Room 2-57
(318) 342-5506/342-5510 (Fax)
Natchitoches (71497) - Mary Lynn Wilkerson, Director
Northwestern State University
College of Business Administration
(318) 357-5611/357-6810 (Fax)
New Orleans (70130) - Ruperto Chavarri, Director
Louisiana International Trade Center[†]
World Trade Center, Suite 2926
2 Canal Street
(504) 568-8222/568-8228 (Fax)
New Orleans (70118) - Ronald Schroeder, Director
Loyola University
College of Business Administration
Box 134
(504) 865-3474/865-3496 (Fax)
New Orleans (70126) - Jon Johnson, Director
Southern University at New Orleans[‡]
College of Business Administration
(504) 286-5308/286-5131 (Fax)

New Orleans (70112) - Norma Grace, Director
University of New Orleans
1600 Canal Street, Suite 620
(504) 539-9292/539-9205 (Fax)
Ruston (71271-0046) - Tracey Jeffers, Director
Louisiana Tech University
College of Business Administration
Box 10318, Tech Station
(318) 257-3537/257-4253 (Fax)
Shreveport (71115) - Peggy K. Connor
Louisiana State University at Shreveport
College of Business Administration
One University Drive
(318) 797-5144/797-5208 (Fax)
pconnor@pilot.lsus.edu
Thibodaux (70310) - Weston Hull, Director
Nicholls State University
College of Business Administration
P.O. Box 2015
(504) 448-4242/448-4922 (Fax)

MAINE
Auburn (04210) - Jane Mickeriz, Counselor
125 Manley Road
(207) 783-9186/783-5211 (Fax)
Augusta (04330) - W. Bradshaw Swanson, Counselor
Tues., Wed., Thurs. - by appointment
Weston Building
7 North Chestnut Street
(207) 621-0245/622-9739 (Fax)
Bangor (04402-2579) - Ron Loyd, Subcenter Director
One Cumberland Place, Suite 300
P.O. Box 2579
(800) 339-6389 (In Maine)/
    (207) 942-6389/942-3548 (Fax)
Belfast (04915)
By appointment - Contact Bangor Office
67 Church Street
(800) 339-6389 (In Maine)/
    (207) 942-6389/942-3548 (Fax)

---

* Lead Small Business Development Center
† Specialized Center
‡ Historical Black College/University

Brunswick (04011)
By appointment - Contact Wiscasset
    Office
8 Lincoln Street
(207) 882-4340/882-4456 (Fax)
Caribou (04736) - Rodney Thompson,
    Subcenter Director
2 South Main Street
P.O. Box 779
(800) 427-8736 (In Maine)/
    (207) 498-8736/493-3108 (Fax)
Dover-Foxcroft Satellite
By appointment - Contact Bangor Office
On-site, at client's place of business
(800) 339-6389 (In Maine)/
    (207) 942-6389/942-3548 (Fax)
East Millinocket (04430)
By appointment - Contact Bangor Office
58 Main Street
(207) 746-5338/746-9535 (Fax)
East Wilton (04234)
By appointment - Contact Auburn Office
Robinhood Plaza
Route 2 & 4
(207) 783-9186/783-5211 (Fax)
Fort Kent (04743)
One day biweekly - by appointment -
    Contact Caribou Office
Corner of Elm and Hall Streets
(800) 427-8736 (In Maine)/
    (207) 493-3108 (Fax)
Houlton (04730)
One day biweekly - by appointment -
    Contact Caribou Office
Superior Court House
Court Street
(800) 427-8736 (In Maine)/
    (207) 498-8736/493-3108 (Fax)
Lewiston (04240)
(Monday & Thursday) - Contact Auburn
    Office
Bates Mill Complex
35 Canal Street
(207) 783-9186/783-5211 (Fax)

Machias (04654) - Diane Tilton,
    Counselor
Washington County Regional Planning
    Commission
63 Main Street
P.O. Box 679
(207) 255-0983/454-2430 (Calais Area)
Portland (04103) - Charles Davis,
    Director
University of Southern Maine*
15 Surrenden Street
(207) 780-4420/780-4810 (Fax)
msbdc@portland.maine.edu
www.usm.maine.edu/~sbdc
Portland (04103) - John Entwistle,
    Subcenter Director
University of Southern Maine
15 Surrenden Street
96 Falmouth Street
P.O. Box 9300 (04104-9300)
(207) 780-4949/780-4810 (Fax)
msbdc@portland.maine.edu
Rockland (04841)
Wednesdays - Contact Wiscasset Office
Key Bank of Maine
331 Main Street
(207) 882-4340/882-4456 (Fax)
Rumford (04276)
By appointment - Contact Auburn Office
Hotel Harris Building
23 Hartford Street
(207) 783-9186/783-5211 (Fax)
Saco (04072) - Frederick Aiello,
    Counselor, Fridays
Chamber of Commerce and Industry
110 Main Street
(207) 282-1567/282-3149 (Fax)
Sanford (04073) - Joseph Vitko,
    Subcenter Director
255 Main Street
P.O. Box Q
(207) 324-0316/324-2958 (Fax)
Skowhegan (04976)
By appointment - Contact Augusta Office
Norridgewock Avenue
(207) 621-0245/622-9739 (Fax)

---

* Lead Small Business Development Center
† Specialized Center
‡ Historical Black College/University

South Paris (04281)
By appointment - Contact Auburn Office
166 Main Street
(207) 783-9186/783-5211 (Fax)
Waterville (04901)
Tuesday and Friday - by appointment -
   Contact Augusta Office
Thomas College
Administration Building, Library
180 West River Road
(207) 621-2045/622-9739 (Fax)
Wiscasset (04578) - James Burbank II,
   Subcenter Director
Water Street
P.O. Box 268
(207) 882-4340/882-4456 (Fax)
York (03909)
First Wednesday of the month - Contact
   Sanford Office
York Chamber of Commerce
449 Route One
(207) 363-4422/324-2958 (Fax)

MARYLAND
Baltimore (21201) - Sonia Stockton,
   Executive Director
The Maxima Corporation
3 West Baltimore Street
(410) 659-1930/659-1939 (Fax)
College Park (20740) - James
   N. Graham, State Director
7100 Baltimore Avenue, Suite 401
(301) 403-8300/403-8303 (Fax)
jgraham@umd.edu
Cumberland (21502) - Sam LaManna,
   Executive Director
Three Commerce Drive
(800) 457-SBDC/(301) 724-6716/777-
   7504 (Fax)
LaPlata (20646-0910) - Betsy Cooksey,
   Executive Director
Charles County Community College
P.O. Box 910
Mitchell Road
(800) 762-SBDC/(301) 934-7583/
   934-7681 (Fax)

www.eaglenet.com/tree1/SBDC
Largo (20774) - Avon Evans, Acting
   Executive Director
Prince George's County Minority
   Business Opportunities Commission
1400 McCormick Drive, Suite 282
(301) 883-6491/883-6479 (Fax)
Salisbury (21801) - Marty Green,
   Executive Director
Salisbury State University
Power Professional Building, Suite 170
(800) 999-SBDC/(410) 546-4325/
   548-5389 (Fax)

MASSACHUSETTS
Amherst (01003) - John Ciccarelli,
   State Director
University of Massachusetts*
205 School of Management
(413) 545-6301/545-1273 (Fax)
Boston (02210) - Paula Murphy,
   Director
Massachusetts Export Center[†]
World Trade Center, Suite 315
(800) 478-4133/(617) 478-4135 (Fax)
Boston (02125-3393) - Hank Turner,
   Director
Minority Business Assistance Center[†]
University of Massachusetts-Boston
College of Management, Fifth Floor
(617) 287-7750/287-7725 (Fax)
Chestnut Hill (02167) - Dr. Jack
   McKiernan, Regional Director
Boston College
96 College Road, Rahner House
(617) 552-4091/552-2730 (Fax)
Chestnut Hill (02167) - Don Rielly,
   Director
Capital Formation Service[†]
Boston College
96 College Road, Rahner House
(617) 552-4091/552-2730 (Fax)

---

* Lead Small Business Development Center
[†] Specialized Center
[‡] Historical Black College/University

**Fall River (02722) - Clyde L. Mitchell,
Regional Director**
University of Massachusetts/Dartmouth
200 Pocasset Street
P.O. Box 2785
(508) 673-9783/674-1929 (Fax)
**Salem (01970) - Frederick Young,
Director**
Salem State College
197 Essex Street
(508) 741-6343/741-6345 (Fax)
**Springfield (01103) - Dianne Fuller
Doherty, Director**
University of Massachusetts
101 State Street, Suite 424
(413) 737-6712/737-2312 (Fax)
**Worcester (01610) - Laurence Marsh,
Director**
Clark University
950 Main Street, Dana Commons
(617) 793-7615/793-8890 (Fax)

MICHIGAN
**Adrian (49221) - Sally Pinchock,
Director**
202 North Main Street, Suite A
(517) 266-1488/263-6065 (Fax)
spin@orchard.washtenaw.cc.mi.us
Albion (49224)
941 Austin Avenue
P.O. Box 725
(517) 629-3926/629-3929 (Fax)
Allegan (49010) - Chuck Birr, Director
2891 116th Avenue, M-222 East
P.O. Box 2777
(616) 673-8442/650-8042 (Fax)
aceda@accn.org
**Allendale (49401-0539) - Ken Rizzio,
Director**
6676 Lake Michigan Drive
P.O. Box 539
(616) 892-4120/895-6670 (Fax)
krizzio@altelco.net

**Alma (48801-0516) - Sherri O. Graham,
Director**
110 West Superior Street
P.O. Box 516
(517) 463-5525/463-6588
**Alpena (49707) - Carl Bourdelais,
Regional Director**
Alpena Community College
666 Johnson Street
(517) 356-9021 ext. 296/354-7507 (Fax)
bourdelc@alpena.cc.mi.us
**Ann Arbor (48104-6831) - Edward
Wollmann, Director**
2568 Packard Road
(313) 971-0277/971-0826 (Fax)
edwoll@provide.net
**Ann Arbor (48106-1485) - William
Loomis, Director**
2901 Hubbard Road
P.O. Box 1485
(313) 769-4110/769-4064 (Fax)
wrl@iti.org
**Bad Axe (48413) - Carl Osentoski,
Director**
Huron County Building, Room 303
250 East Huron Avenue
(517) 269-6431/269-7221 (Fax)
cjo@avci.net
**Battle Creek (49017) - Kevin R. Wells,
Director**
4 Riverwalk Center
34 West Jackson, Suite A, Lower Level
(616) 962-8996/962-3692 (Fax)
bizstore@net-link.net
**Bay City (48708) - Shirley Roberts,
Director**
901 Saginaw
(517) 893-4567/893-7016 (Fax)
**Benton Harbor (49022-1899) - Milt
Richter, Director**
Lake Michigan College
2755 East Napier
(616) 927-8179/927-8103 (Fax)
richter@raptor.lmc.cc.mi.us

---

* Lead Small Business Development Center
† Specialized Center
‡ Historical Black College/University

Boyne City (49712-0008) - Thomas Johnson, Director
1048 East Main Street
P.O. Box 8
(616) 582-6482/582-3213 (Fax)
johnsoth@msue.msu.edu

Brighton (48116) - Dennis Whitney, Director
131 South Hyne Street
(810) 227-3556/227-3080 (Fax)
livibusi@bizserve.com

Buchanan (49107) - Joni Tumbleson, Director
119 Main Street
(616) 695-3291/695-4250 (Fax)

Caro (48723) - James McLoskey, Director
194 North State Street, Suite 200
(517) 673-2849/673-2517 (Fax)

Coldwater (49036) - Colleen Knight, Interim Director
20 Division Street
(517) 278-4146/278-8369 (Fax)
bcega@orion.branch-co.lib.mi.us

Detroit (48201) - B. Kevin Lauderdale, Regional Director
2727 Second Avenue, Suite 121
(313) 577-4850/577-8933 (Fax)
lauderk@bizserve.com

Detroit (48219-0900) - Dr. Ram Kesavan, Director
University of Detroit-Mercy
Commerce & Finance Building, Room 105
4001 West McNichols
P.O. Box 19900
(313) 993-1115/993-1052 (Fax)
kesavar@udmercy.edu

Detroit (48201) - Ronald R. Hall, State Director
Wayne State University*
2727 Second Avenue, Suite 107
Mailing address: 2727 Second Avenue
Detroit (48201)
(313) 964-1798/964-3648/(Fax)/
    964-4164 (Fax)
ron@misbdc.wayne.edu
bizserve.com/sbdc

Dowagiac (49047)
Southwestern Michigan College
58900 Cherry Grove Road
(616) 782-1277/782-1382 (Fax)

Escanaba (49829) - David Gillis, Regional Director
2415 Fourteenth Avenue, South
(906) 786-9234/786-4442 (Fax)
cuppad@up.net

Flint (48503) - Kim D. Yarber, Regional Director
711 North Saginaw, Suite 123
Walter Reuther Center
(810) 239-5847/239-5575 (Fax)

Fraser (48026) - Dr. Donald Amboyer, Director
Macomb Community College
32101 Caroline
(810) 296-3516/293-0427 (Fax)
amboOld@macomb.cc.mi.us

Grand Haven (49417) - Karen K. Benson, Director
One South Harbor Avenue
P.O. Box 509
(616) 846-3153/842-0379 (Fax)
acisbdc@hotmail.com

Grand Rapids (49503-1423) - Raymond De Winkle, Director
820 Monroe Avenue Northwest, Suite 350
(616) 771-0571/458-3768 (Fax)
dewinkler@rightplace.org

Grand Rapids (49504) - Carol Lopucki, Regional Director
Grand Valley State University
301 West Fulton, Room 718S
Eberhard Center
(616) 771-6693/458-3872 (Fax)
lopuckic@gvsu.edu

Hart (49420-0168) - Charles Persenaire, Director
100 State Street
P.O. Box 168
(616) 873-7141/873-5914 (Fax)

Hastings (49058) - Joe Rahn, Director
1035 East State Street
(616) 948-2305/948-2947 (Fax)
edohast.im4u.net

---

* Lead Small Business Development Center
† Specialized Center
‡ Historical Black College/University

Ithaca (48847) - Don Schurr, Director
136 South Main
(517) 875-2083/875-2990 (Fax)
don.schurr@gratiot.com

**Jackson (49201) - Duane K. Miller,
Director**
414 North Jackson Street
(517) 787-0442/787-3960 (Fax)
jbdc@jacksonmi.com

**Kalamazoo (49006-3200) - Carl
R. Shook, Regional Director**
Kalamazoo College
Stryker Center for Management Studies
1327 Academy Street
(616) 337-7350/337-7415 (Fax)
sbdc@kzoo.edu

**Lansing (48901-7210) - Deleski (Dee)
Smith, Regional Director**
Lansing Community College
Continental Building
333 North Washington Square
P.O. Box 40010
(517) 483-1921/483-9803 (Fax)
ds1921@lois.lansing.cc.mi.us

**Lapeer (48446) - Patricia Lucas
Crawford, Director**
449 McCormick Drive
(810) 667-0080/667-3541 (Fax)
ldc@tir.com

**Midland (48640) - Christine Greve,
Director**
300 Rodd Street
(517) 839-9901/835-3701 (Fax)
chamber@macc.org

**Monroe (48161) - Dani Topolski,
Director**
111 Conant Avenue
(313) 243-5947/242-0009 (Fax)
mcidc@ic.net

**Mt. Clemens (48043) - Donald
Morandini, Director**
115 South Groesbeck Highway
(810) 469-5118/469-6787 (Fax)
bacmac@bizserve.com

**Mt. Pleasant (48859) - Charles
Fitzpatrick, Regional Director**
Central Michigan University
256 Applied Business Studies Complex
(517) 774-3270/774-2372 (Fax)
34ntjen@cmuvm.csv.cmich.edu

**Muskegon (49443-1087) - Mert
Johnson, Director**
230 Terrace Plaza
P.O. Box 1087
(616) 722-3751/728-7251 (Fax)

**New Buffalo (49117) - Peggy Klute,
Office Manager**
530 South Whittaker Street, #5
(616) 469-5409/469-2257 (Fax)
hccc@hc.cns.net

Niles (49120) - Sharon Witt, Director
1105 North Front Street
(616) 683-1833/683-7515 (Fax)

**Oscoda (48750) - Dave Wentworth,
Director**
Alpena Community College
Huron Shores Campus
5800 Skeel Avenue
(517) 739-1445/739-1161 (Fax)

Petoskey (49770) - Tom Nathe, Director
North Central Michigan College
1515 Howard Street
(616) 348-6600/348-6630 (Fax)
tnath@sunny.ncmc.cc.mi.us

**Pontiac (48341) - Wayne Nierman,
Director**
Executive Office Building
1200 North Telegraph Road,
Department 416
(810) 858-0880/858-1477 (Fax)
niermanw@msue.msu.edu

**Port Huron (48060-5015) - Todd Brian,
Director**
800 Military Street, Suite 320
(810) 982-9511/982-9531 (Fax)

**Roscommon (48653) - John Loiacano,
Director**
Kirtland Community College
10775 North Street Helen Road
(517) 275-5121 ext. 297/275-8745 (Fax)
loiacanj@k2.kirtland.cc.mi.us

* Lead Small Business Development Center
† Specialized Center
‡ Historical Black College/University

Saginaw (48601) - James Bockelman, Director
901 South Washington Avenue
(517) 752-7161/752-9055 (Fax)
jroe@voyager.net

Saginaw (48607) - Matthew F. Hufnagel, Director
301 East Genesee, 3rd Floor
(517) 754-8222/754-1715 (Fax)
matthuf@bizserve.com

St. Joseph (49058) - Suzanne Thursby, Director
508 Pleasant Street
(616) 983-4453/983-4564 (Fax)

Saline (48176) - Baldomero Garcia, Regional Director
740 Woodland Drive
(313) 944-1016/944-0165 (Fax)
dstotz@orchard.washtenaw.cc.mi.us

Scottville (49454-0277) - Mark Bergstrom, Director
West Shore Community College
Business & Industrial Dev. Institute
3000 North Stiles Road
P.O. Box 277
(616) 845-6211/845-0207 (Fax)
bergstr@westshore.cc.mi.us

Southfield (48075-1058) - Daniel Belknap, Regional Director
Lawrence Technological University
21000 West Ten Mile Road
(248) 204-4056/204-4016 (Fax)
belknap@bizserve.com

Southgate (48195) - Paula Boase, Director
15100 Northline Road
(313) 281-0700 ext. 190/281-3418 (Fax)
pboase@bizserve.com

South Haven (49090) - Larry King, Director
300 Broadway
(616) 637-5171/639-1570 (Fax)
cofc@southhavenmi.com

Standish (48658) - Ken Kernstock, Director
County Building
P.O. Box 745
(517) 846-4111
arenac@msue.msu.edu

Sterling Heights (48313) - Lillian Adams, Director
12900 Hall Road, Suite 110
(810) 731-5400/731-3521 (Fax)
suscc.com

Traverse City (49685-0506) - Richard Beldin, Director
2200 Dendrinos Drive
P.O. Box 506
(616) 929-5000/929-5017 (Fax)
dbeldin@nwm.cog.mi.us

Traverse City (49685-0387) - Charles Blankenship, Regional Director
202 East Grandview Parkway
P.O. Box 387
(616) 946-1596/946-2565 (Fax)
chamber@gtii.com

Traverse City (49684) - Matthew Meadors, Director and Vice-President
202 East Grandview Parkway
P.O. Box 387
(616) 947-5075/946-2565 (Fax)
chamber@gtii.com

Traverse City (49686) - Cheryl Throop, Director
Northwestern Michigan College
1701 East Front Street
(616) 922-1717/922-1722 (Fax)
cthroop@nmc.edu

University Center (48710) - Charles B. Curtiss, Jr., Interim Regional Director
Saginaw Valley State University
7400 Bay Road, Wickes 387
(517) 791-7746/249-1955 (Fax)

Warren (48093) - Jan Masi, Director
30500 Van Dyke, Suite 118
(810) 751-3939/751-3995 (Fax)
janetmorris@chambercom.com

---

* Lead Small Business Development Center
† Specialized Center
‡ Historical Black College/University

MINNESOTA
Bemidji (56601) - Susan Kozojed,
Director
Northwest Technical College
905 Grant Avenue, Southeast
(218) 755-4286/755-4289 (Fax)
Bloomington (55431) - Scott Harding,
Director
Normandale Community College
9700 France Avenue South
(612) 832-6398/832-6352 (Fax)
Brainerd (56401) - Pamela Thomsen,
Director
Central Lakes College
501 West College Drive
(218) 825-2028/825-2053 (Fax)
Duluth (55812-2496) - Lee Jensen,
Director
University of Minnesota at Duluth
150 School of Business & Economics
10 University Drive
(218) 726-8758/726-6338 (Fax)
ljensen@d.umn.edu
Ely (55731) - Allen Jackson, Director
Vermillion Community College
1900 East Camp Street, Room NS110
(218) 365-7295
Grand Rapids (55744) - Kirk Bustrom,
Director
19 Northeast Third Street
(218) 327-2241/327-2242 (Fax)
idsbdc@uslink.net
Hibbing (55746) - Jim Antilla, Director
Hibbing Community College
1515 East 25th Street
(218) 262-6703/262-6717 (Fax)
j.antilla@hi.cc.mn.us
International Falls (56649) - Tom West,
Director
Rainy River Community College
1501 Highway 71
(218) 285-2255/285-2239 (Fax)

Mankato (56002-3367) - Jill Miller,
Director
410 Jackson Street
P.O. Box 3367
(507) 389-8863/387-7105 (Fax)
jillm@rndc.mankato.mn.us
Marshall (56258) - Jack Hawk,
Director
Southwest State University
Science & Technology Resource Center
1501 State Street, Suite 105
(507) 537-7386/537-6094 (Fax)
hawk@ssu.southwest.msus.edu
Minneapolis (55403) - Michael
J. Lyons, SBDC Project Officer
610-C Butler Square
100 North Sixth Street
(612) 370-2343/370-2303 (Fax)
michael.lyons@sba.gov
Minneapolis (55401) - Pat Dillon,
Director
Minnesota Project Innovation[†]
111 Third Avenue South, Suite 100
(612) 347-6751/338-3483 (Fax)
pdillon@mpi.org
Minneapolis (55403) - Gregg Schneider,
Director
University of St. Thomas
1000 La Salle Avenue
Suite MPL 100
(612) 962-4505/962-4410 (Fax)
gwschneider@stthomas.edu
Moorhead (56563) - Len Sliwoski,
Director
Moorhead State University
MSU Box 303
1104 Seventh Avenue South
(218) 236-2289/236-2280 (Fax)
Owatonna (55060) - Ken Henrickson,
Director
Owatonna Incubator, Inc.
560 Dunnell Drive, Suite 203
P.O. Box 505
(507) 451-0517/455-2788 (Fax)

* Lead Small Business Development Center
† Specialized Center
‡ Historical Black College/University

Pine City (55063) - John Sparling, Director
Pine Technical College
1100 Fourth Street
(320) 629-7340/629-7603 (Fax)
Rochester (55904) - Michelle Pyfferoen, Director
Rochester Community & Technical
   College
Riverland Hall
851 30th Avenue, Southeast
(507) 285-7425/285-7110 (Fax)
mpyffero@ucrpo.roch.edu
Rosemount (55068) - Tom Trutna, Director
Dakota County Technical College
1300 145th Street East
(612) 423-8262/423-8761 (Fax)
ttrut@dak.tec.mn.us
Rushford (55971) - Terry Erickson, Director
111 West Jessie Street
P.O. Box 684
(507) 864-7557/864-2091 (Fax)
St. Cloud (56301) - Dawn Jensen-Regnier, Director
St. Cloud State University
720 4th Avenue South
(320) 255-4842/255-4957 (Fax)
St. Paul (55101-2146) - Mary Kruger, State Director
Minnesota Department of Trade and
   Economic Development*
500 Metro Square
121 Seventh Place East
(612) 297-5773/296-1290 (Fax)
mary.kruger@state.mn.us
Two Harbors (55616) - Allen Jackson, Director
5 Fairgrounds Road
P.O. Box 248
(218) 834-3494/834-5074 (Fax)
ajackso2@d.umn.edu

Virginia (55792)
Minnesota Technology, Inc.
Olcott Plaza Building
820 North 9th Street
(218) 741-4241/741-4249 (Fax)
cchristl@d.umn.edu
White Bear Lake (55110-1894)
Century College
3300 Century Avenue, North, Suite 230-H
(612) 773-1794/779-5802 (Fax)

MISSOURI
Cape Girardeau (63701) - Frank "Buz" Sutherland, Director
Southeast Missouri State University
222 North Pacific
(573) 290-5965/651-5005 (Fax, Call First)
Chillicothe (64601) - Brian Olson, Director
715 Washington
(816) 646-6920/646-6811 (Fax)
Columbia (65211) - Dr. Tom Henderson, Director
Business and Industrial Specialists
821 Clark Hall
(573) 882-4142/882-2595 (Fax)
Columbia (65211) - Max E. Summers, State Director
University of Missouri*
300 University Place
(573) 882-0344/884-4297 (Fax)
Columbia (65211) - Frank Siebert, Director
University of Missouri at Columbia
1800 University Place
(573) 882-9931/882-6156 (Fax)
Flat River (63601) - Eugene Cherry, Director
Mineral Area College
P.O. Box 1000
(573) 431-4593 ext. 283/431-6807 (Fax)

---

* Lead Small Business Development Center
† Specialized Center
‡ Historical Black College/University

Joplin (64801-1595) - Jim Krudwig, Director
Missouri Southern State College
#107 Matthews Hall
3950 Newman Road
(417) 625-9313/625-9782 (Fax)
Kansas City (64110-2599) - Rhonda Gerke, Director
Rockhurst College
1100 Rockhurst Road
(816) 501-4572/501-4646 (Fax)
Kirksville (63501) - Glen Giboney, Director
Truman State University
207 East Patterson
(816) 785-4307/785-4181 (Fax)
Maryville (64468) - Brad Anderson, Director
Northwest Missouri State University
423 North Market Street
(816) 562-1701/582-3071 (Fax)
Rolla (65401-0249) - Fred Goss, Director
Center for Technology Transfer and Economic Development[†]
University of Missouri at Rolla
Room 104, Building 1, Nagogami Terrace
(573) 341-4559/341-4922 (Fax)
Rolla (65401-0249) - Robert Laney, Director
University of Missouri at Rolla
223 Engineering Management Building
(314) 341-4561/341-2071 (Fax)
St. Louis (63108) - Virginia Campbell, Director
St. Louis University
3750 Lindell Boulevard
(314) 977-7232/977-7241 (Fax)
Springfield (65804-0089) - Jane Peterson, Director
Southwest Missouri State University
Center for Business Research
901 South National, Box 88
(417) 836-5685/836-6337 (Fax)

Warrensburg (64093-5037)
Central Missouri State University
Grinstead #75
(816) 543-4402/747-1653 (Fax)
Warrensburg (64093-5037) - Wes Savage, Assistant Director
Technology Development Center[†]
Central Missouri State University
Grinstead #9
(816) 543-4402/543-8159 (Fax)

MISSISSIPPI
Biloxi (39532) - Richard Speights, Executive Director
Mississippi Contract Procurement Center
1636 Popps Ferry Road, Suite 229
(601) 396-1288/396-2520 (Fax)
mprogoff@aol.com
Booneville (38829) - Kenny Holt, Director
Northeast Mississippi Community College
Cunningham Boulevard
Holliday Hall, Second Floor
(601) 720-7448/720-7464 (Fax)
kholt@necc.cc.ms.us
Cleveland (38733) - David Holman, Director
Delta State University
P.O. Box 3235 DSU
Whitfield Gymnasium Building, Suite 105
(601) 846-4236/846-4235 (Fax)
sbdc@dsu.deltast.edu
Decatur (39327) - Ronald Westbrook, Director
East Central Community College
275 Broad Street
P.O. Box 129
(601) 635-2111 ext. 297/635-4031 (Fax)
Ellisville (39437) - Gary Suddith, Director
Jones Junior College
900 Court Street
(601) 477-4165/477-4166 (Fax)
crc@jcjc.cc.ms.us

---

* Lead Small Business Development Center
[†] Specialized Center
[‡] Historical Black College/University

Gautier (39553) - Dean Brown, Director
Mississippi Gulf Coast Community
   College
Jackson County Campus
P.O. Box 100
(601) 497-7723/497-7788 (Fax)
KUMACHAN
Greenville (38704-5607) Chuck Herring, Director
Mississippi Delta Community College
1656 East Union
P.O. Box 5607
(601) 378-8183/378-5349 (Fax)
mdccsbdc@tecinfo.com
Hattiesburg (39401) - Heidi McDuffie, Director
Pearl River Community College
5448 U.S. Highway 49 South
(601) 554-9133/554-9149 (Fax)
Itta Bena (38941) - Dr. Jim Breyley, Director
Mississippi Valley State University
(601) 254-3601/254-3600 (Fax)
Jackson (39204) - Henry Thomas, Director
Jackson State University[‡]
Jackson Enterprise Center, Suite 2A-1
931 Highway 80 West, Unit 43
(601) 968-2795/968-2796 (Fax)
hthomas@ccaix.jsums.edu
Long Beach (39560) - Lucy Betcher, Director
University of Southern Mississippi
136 Beach Park Place
(601) 865-4578/865-4581 (Fax)
lbetcher@medea.gp.usm.edu
Lorman (39096-9402) - Sharon Witty, Director
Alcorn State University[‡]
1000 ASU Drive
P.O. Box 90
(601) 877-6684/877-6256 (Fax)

Meridian (39307) - W. Mac Hodges, Director
Meridian Community College
910 Highway 19 North
(601) 482-7445/482-5803 (Fax)
mhodges@mcc.cc.ms.us
Mississippi State (39762) - Sonny Fisher, Director
Mississippi State University
#1 Research Boulevard, Suite 201
P.O. Drawer 5288
(601) 325-8684/325-4016 (Fax)
sfisher@cobilan.msstate.edu
Natchez (39120) - Bob D. Russ, Director
Co-Lin Community College
11 Co-Lin Circle
(601) 445-5254/446-1221 (Fax)
RobertR@natl.colin.cc.ms.ns
Raymond (39154) - Marguerite Wall, Director
International Trade Center[†]
Hinds Community College
1500 Raymond Lake Road, 2nd Floor
P.O. Box 1170
(601) 857-3536/857-3474 (Fax)
hccrcu2@teclink.net
Ridgeland (39157) - John Deddens, Director
Homes Community College
413 West Ridgeland Avenue
(601) 853-0827/853-0844 (Fax)
Southaven (38671) - Jody Dunning, Director
Northwest Mississippi Community
   College
DeSoto Center
5197 West E. Ross Parkway, Room 208
(601) 342-7648/342-7648 (Fax)
smbusdev@nwcc.cc.ms.us
Summit (39666) - Kathryn "Sissy" Whittington, Director
Southwest Mississippi Community
   College
College Drive
(601) 276-3890/276-3883 (Fax)

---

[*] Lead Small Business Development Center
[†] Specialized Center
[‡] Historical Black College/University

Tupelo (38801) - Rex Hollingsworth, Director
Itawamba Community College
2176 South Eason Boulevard
(601) 680-8515/680-8547 (Fax)
iccsbdc@ebicom.net
University (38677) - Michael Vanderlip, Director
University of Mississippi
Room 1082, N.C.P.A.
(601) 234-2120/232-1220 (Fax)
sbdc@olemiss.edu
University (38677) - Raleigh Byars, State Director
University of Mississippi*
Old Chemistry Building, Suite 216
(601) 232-5001/232-5650 (Fax)
rbyars@olemiss.edu

NEBRASKA
Chadron (69337) - Cliff Hanson, Director
Chadron State College
Administration Building
(308) 432-6282/432-6430 (Fax)
chanson@cscl.csc.edu
Kearney (68849-3035) - Kay Payne, Director
University of Nebraska at Kearney
Welch Hall, 19th and College Drive
(308) 865-8344/865-8153 (Fax)
Lincoln (68508) - Irene Cherhoniak, Director
University of Nebraska at Lincoln
1135 M Street, Suite 200
(402) 472-3358/472-0328 (Fax)
North Platte (69101) - Dean Kurth, Director
Mid-Plains Community College
416 North Jeffers, Room 26
(308) 635-7513
Omaha (68110) - Tom McCabe, Director
Omaha Business & Technology Center†
2505 North 24th Street, Suite 101
(402) 595-3511/595-3524 (Fax)

Omaha (68182-0248) - Robert Bernier, State Director
University of Nebraska at Omaha*
60th & Dodge Streets
CBA Room 407
(402) 554-2521/554-3747 (Fax)
Omaha (68182-0248) - Jeanne Eibes, Director
University of Nebraska at Omaha
Peter Kiewit Conference Center
1313 Farnam-on-the-Mall, Suite 132
(402) 595-2381/595-2385 (Fax)
Peru (68421) - David Ruenholl, Director
Peru State College
T.J. Majors Hall, Room 248
(402) 872-2274/872-2422 (Fax)
Scottsbluff (69361) - Ingrid Battershell, Director
Nebraska Public Power Building
1721 Broadway, Room 400
(308) 635-7513/635-6596 (Fax)
Wayne (68787) - Loren Kucera, Director
Wayne State College
Gardner Hall
1111 Main Street
(402) 375-7575/375-7574 (Fax)

NEVADA
Carson City (89701) - Larry Osborne, Director
Carson City Chamber of Commerce
1900 South Carson Street, #100
(702) 882-1565/882-4179 (Fax)
Elko (89801) - John Pryor, Director
Northern Nevada Community College
901 Elm Street
(702) 753-2245/753-2242 (Fax)
Incline Village (89451) - Sheri Woods, Executive Director
969 Tahoe Boulevard
(702) 831-4440/832-1605 (Fax)

---

* Lead Small Business Development Center
† Specialized Center
‡ Historical Black College/University

Las Vegas (89119) - Robert Holland, Bus. Dev. Specialist
Foreign Trade Zone Office
1111 Grier Drive
(702) 896-4496/896-8351 (Fax)
Las Vegas (89154-6011) - Sharolyn Craft, Director
University of Nevada at Las Vegas
P.O. Box 456011
(702) 895-0852/895-4095 (Fax)
North Las Vegas (89030) - Janis Stevenson, Management Consultant
19 West Brooks Avenue
(702) 399-6300/399-6301 (Fax)
Reno (89557-0100) - Sam Males, State Director
University of Nevada Reno*
College of Business Administration
Room 411032
(702) 784-1717/784-4337 (Fax)
Winnemucca (89446) - Teri Williams, Director
Tri-County Development Authority
50 West Fourth Street
P.O. Box 820
(702) 623-5777/623-5999 (Fax)

NEW HAMPSHIRE
Durham (03824-3593) - Mary Collins, State Director
University of New Hampshire*
108 McConnell Hall
(603) 862-2200/862-4876 (Fax)
Keene (03431) - Gary Cloutier, Regional Manager
Blake House
Keene State College
(603) 358-2602/358-2612 (Fax)
Littleton (03561) - Elizabeth Ward, Regional Manager
120 Main Street
(603) 444-1053/444-5463 (Fax)
Manchester (03101) - Bob Ebberson, Regional Manager
1000 Elm Street, 12th Floor
(603) 624-2000/647-4410 (Fax)

Manchester (03101) - Amy Jennings, Director
Office of Economic Initiatives
1000 Elm Street, 12th Floor
(603) 624-2000/647-4410 (Fax)
Nashua (03060) - Judy Orfao, Acting Regional Manager
Center for Economic Development
One Indiana Head Plaza, Suite 510
(603) 886-1233/598-1164 (Fax)
Plymouth (03264) - Janice Kitchen, Regional Manager
Outreach Center, MSC#24A
Plymouth State College
(603) 535-2523/535-2850 (Fax)
Rochester (03867) - Jeanine DiMario, Regional Manager
Chamber of Commerce, Suite 3A
18 South Main Street
(603) 330-1929/330-1948 (Fax)

NEW JERSEY
Atlantic City (08401) - William R. McGinley, Director
Greater Atlantic City Chamber of Commerce
1125 Atlantic Avenue
(609) 345-5600/345-1666 (Fax)
Camden (08102) - Patricia Peacock, Ed.D., Director
Rutgers University/Camden
Schools of Business
227 Penn Street, 3rd Floor, Room 334
(609) 225-6221/225-6621 (Fax)
ppeacock@camden.rutgers.edu
Lincroft (07738) - Bill Nunnally, Co-Director; Larry Novick, Co-Director
Brookdale Community College
Newman Springs Road
(908) 842-8685/842-0203 (Fax)

* Lead Small Business Development Center
† Specialized Center
‡ Historical Black College/University

**Newark (07102) - Brenda B. Hopper,
    State Director**
Rutgers University*
Ackerson Hall, 3rd Floor
49 Bleeker Street
(973) 353-5950/353-1110 (Fax)
bhopper@andromeda.rutgers.edu
**Newark (07102) - Leroy A. Johnson,
    Director**
Rutgers University
Ackerson Hall, 3rd Floor
180 University Avenue
(201) 648-5950/648-1175 (Fax)
leroyj@andromeda.rutgers.edu
**Paramus (07652) - Melody Irvin,
    Director**
Bergen County Community College
400 Paramus Road, Room A328
(201) 447-7841/447-9405 (Fax)
mirvin@pilot.njin.net
**Paterson (07505) - Joseph M. Bair,
    Director**
131 Ellison Street
(201) 754-8695
jbair@andromeda.rutgers.edu
**Trenton (08690) - Herbert Spiegel,
    Director**
Mercer County Community College
West Windsor Campus
1200 Old Trenton Road
P.O. Box B
(609) 586-4800 ext. 469/890-6338 (Fax)
hss@mccc.edu
Union (07083) - Mira Kostak, Director
Kean College
East Campus, Room 242
(908) 527-2946/527-2960 (Fax
**Washington (07882-9605) - James
    H. Smith, Director**
Warren County Community College
475 Route 57 West
(908) 689-9620/689-2247 (Fax)
smith@mail.warren.cc.nj.us

NEW MEXICO
**Alamogordo (88310) - Dwight Harp,
    Director**
New Mexico State University/Alamogordo
2230 Lawrence
(505) 434-5272/434-1432 (Fax, Call First)
**Albuquerque (87102) - Steven Becerra,
    Director**
700 4th Street, Southwest, Suite A
(505) 248-0132/248-0127 (Fax)
**Albuquerque (87106) - Ray Garcia,
    Director**
Albuquerque Technical Vocational
    Institute
801 University Southeast, Suite 300
Mailing Address: 525 Buena Vista,
    Southeast
(505) 272-7980/224-4251 (Fax)
**Carlsbad (88220) - Larry Coalson,
    Director**
New Mexico State University/Carlsbad
301 South Canal
P.O. Box 1090
(505) 887-6562/885-0818 (Fax)
**Clovis (88101) - Sandra Taylor-Smith,
    Director**
Clovis Community College
417 Schepps Boulevard
(505) 769-4136/769-4190 (Fax)
**Espanola (87532) - Darien Cabral,
    Director**
Northern New Mexico Community
    College
1002 North Onate Street
(505) 747-2236/747-2180 (Fax)
**Farmington (87402) - Calvin A. Tingey,
    Director**
San Juan College
4601 College Boulevard
(505) 599-0528/325-3964 (Fax)
Gallup (87301) - Elsie Sanchez, Director
University of New Mexico/Gallup
103 West Highway 66
P.O. Box 1395
(505) 722-2220/863-6006 (Fax)

---

* Lead Small Business Development Center
† Specialized Center
‡ Historical Black College/University

Grants (87020) - Clemente Sanchez, Director
New Mexico State University/Grants
709 East Roosevelt Avenue
(505) 287-8221/287-2125 (Fax)
Hobbs (88240) - Don Leach, Director
New Mexico Junior College
5317 Lovington Highway
(505) 392-4510/392-2526 (Fax)
Las Cruces (88033-0001) - Terry Sullivan, Director
Dona Ana Branch Community College
3400 South Espina Street
P.O. Box 30001, Department 3DA
(505) 527-7540/527-7515 (Fax)
Las Vegas (87701) - Don Bustos, Director
Luna Vocational Technical Institute
Luna Campus, P.O. Box 1510
(505) 454-2595/454-2518 (Fax)
Los Alamos (87544) - Jay Weschler, Acting Director
University of New Mexico/Los Alamos
901 18th Street, #11800
P.O. Box 715
(505) 662-0001/662-0099 (Fax)
Los Lunas (87031) - David Ashley, Director
University of New Mexico/Valencia
280 La Entrada
(505) 925-8980/925-8981 (Fax)
dashley@unm.edu
www.unm.edu/~vcsbdc/
Roswell (88201-6000) - Eugene D. Simmons, Director
Eastern New Mexico University
57 University Avenue
P.O. Box 6000
(505) 624-7133/624-7132 (Fax)
Santa Fe (87505) - J. Roy Miller, State Director
Santa Fe Community College*
6401 Richards Avenue
(800) 281-SBDC/(505) 438-1362/
     471-9469 (Fax)

Santa Fe (87505) - Monica Montoya, Director
Santa Fe Community College
6401 Richards Avenue
(505) 438-1343/471-9469 (Fax)
Silver City (88062) - Linda Kay Jones, Director
Western New Mexico University
P.O. Box 2672
(505) 538-6320/538-6341 (Fax)
Tucumcari (88401) - Richard Spooner, Director
Mesa Technical College
911 South 10th
P.O. Box 1143
(505) 461-4413/461-1901 (Fax)

NEW YORK
Albany (12222) - Peter George III, Director
State University of New York at Albany
Draper Hall, Room 107
135 Western Avenue
(518) 442-5577/442-5582 (Fax)
Albany (12246) - James L. King, State Director
State University of New York (SUNY)*
SUNY Plaza, S-523
(800) 732-SBDC/(518) 443-5398/465-
     4992 (Fax)
kingjl@cc.sunycentral.edu
Binghamton (13902-6000) - Joanne Bauman, Director
Binghamton University
P.O. Box 6000
(607) 777-4024/777-4029 (Fax)
sbdcbu@spectra.net
Brockport (14420) - Wilfred Bordeau, Director
State University of New York
74 North Main Street
(716) 637-6660/637-2102 (Fax)

---

* Lead Small Business Development Center
† Specialized Center
‡ Historical Black College/University

Bronx (10453) - Eugene Williams, Director
Bronx Community College
McCracken Hall, Room 14
West 181st Street & University Avenue
(718) 563-3570/563-3472 (Fax)
Bronx (10451)
Contact Bronx Community College
Con Edison
560 Cortlandt Avenue
(718) 563-9204
Brooklyn (11235) - Edward O'Brien, Director
Kingsborough Community College
2001 Oriental Boulevard
Building T4, Room 4204
(718) 368-4619/368-4629 (Fax)
Brooklyn (11201)
Contact Kingsborough Community
College
395 Flatbush Avenue, Extension Room 413
(718) 260-9783/260-9797 (Fax)
Buffalo (14222) - Susan McCartney, Director
State University College at Buffalo
Bacon Hall 117
1300 Elmwood Avenue
(716) 878-4030/878-4067 (Fax)
Canton (12617)
Contact Jefferson Community College
SUNY Canton
(315) 386-7312/386-7945 (Fax)
Cobleskill (12043)
Cobleskill Outreach Center
Contact SUNY at Albany
SUNY Cobleskill
Warner Hall, Room 218
(518) 234-5528/234-5272 (Fax)
Corning (14830) - Bonnie Gestwicki, Director
Corning Community College
24 Denison Parkway West
(607) 962-9461/936-6642 (Fax)

Dobbs Ferry (10522-1189) - Tom Milton, Coordinator
Mercy College Outreach Center
555 Broadway
(914) 674-7485/693-4996 (Fax)
Farmingdale (11735) - Joseph Schwartz, Director
State University College of Technology at
Farmingdale
Campus Commons
(516) 420-2765/293-5343 (Fax)
Fishkill (12524-2001)
Marist College Outreach Center
Contact Kingston SBDC
2600 Route 9, Unit 90
(914) 897-2607/897-4653 (Fax)
Geneseo (14454-1485) - Charles VanArsdale, Director
Geneseo Outreach Center
Contact Niagara Community College
SUNY Geneseo
One College Circle
South Hall #111
(716) 245-5429/245-5430 (Fax)
Geneva (14456) - Sandy Bordeau, Administrative Director
Geneva Outreach Center
122 North Genesee Street
(315) 781-1253
Hempstead (11550)
Hempstead Outreach Center
Contact State University College of
Technology
269 Fulton Avenue
(516) 564-1895/564-8672/481-4938 (Fax)
Jamaica (11451) - James A. Heyliger
York College/The City University of
New York
Science Building, Room 107
94-50 159th Street
(718) 262-2880/262-2881 (Fax)

---

* Lead Small Business Development Center
† Specialized Center
‡ Historical Black College/University

Jamestown (14702-0020) - Irene Dobies,
    Director
Jamestown Community College
P.O. Box 20
(800) 522-7232/(716) 665-5754/
    665-6733 (Fax)
Kingston (12401) - Patricia LaSusa,
    Director
One Development Court
(914) 339-0025/339-1631 (Fax)
New York (10010) - Cheryl Fenton,
    Director
Baruch College
360 Park Avenue South, Room 1101
(212) 802-6620/802-6613 (Fax)
New York (10010) - Barrie Phillip,
    Coordinator
Baruch College Mid-Town Outreach
    Center
360 Park Avenue South, Room 1101
(212) 802-6620/802-6613 (Fax)
New York (10027) - Anthony Sanchez,
    Coordinator
Central Harlem Outreach Center
163 West 125th Street, Room 1307
(212) 346-1900/534-4576 (Fax)
New York (10029) - Anthony Sanchez,
    Coordinator
East Harlem Outreach Center
145 East 116th Street, Third Floor
(212) 346-1900/534-4576 (Fax)
New York (10038) - Ira Davidson,
    Director
Pace University
One Pace Plaza, Room W483
(212) 346-1900/346-1613 (Fax)
Niagara Falls (14303-1117)
Contact Niagara Community College
Carborundum Center
345 Third Street
(716) 285-4793/285-4797 (Fax)

Oswego (13126)
State University of New York at Oswego
Contact Onondaga Community College
Oswego Outreach Center
Operation Oswego County
44 West Bridge Street
(315) 343-1545/343-1546 (Fax)
Plattsburgh (12901) - Merry Gwynn,
    Coordinator
Clinton Community College
Lake Shore Road, Route 9 South
136 Clinton Point Drive
(518) 562-4260/563-9759 (Fax)
Riverhead (11901)
Sulfolk County Community College
Contact SUNY at Stony Brook
Rochester Outreach Center
(516) 369-1409/369-1507/369-3255 (Fax)
Rochester (14604)
State University of Brockport
Contact SUNY at Brockport
Temple Building
14 Franklin Street, Suite 200
(716) 232-7310/637-2182 (Fax)
Sanborn (14132) - Richard Gorko,
    Director
Niagara Community College at Sanborn
3111 Saunders Settlement Road
(716) 693-1910/731-3595 (Fax)
Southampton (11968)
Long Island University at Southampton
Contact SUNY at Stony Brook
Southampton Outreach Center
Abney Peak, Montauk Highway
(516) 287-0059/287-0071/287-8287 (Fax)
Staten Island (10314-9806) - Dr. Ronald
    Sheppard, Acting Director
College of Staten Island
2800 Victory Boulevard
Building 1A, Room 211
(718) 982-2560/982-2323 (Fax)

---

* Lead Small Business Development Center
† Specialized Center
‡ Historical Black College/University

Stony Brook (11794-3775) - Judith McEvoy, Director
SUNY at Stony Brook
Harriman Hall, Room 109
(516) 632-9070/632-7176 (Fax)
Suffern (10901-3620) - Thomas J. Morley, Director
Rockland Community College
145 College Road
(914) 356-0370/356-0381 (Fax)
Syracuse (13215-1944) - Robert Varney, Director
Onondaga Community College
Excell Building, Room 108
4969 Onondaga Road
(315) 498-6070/492-3704 (Fax)
Troy (12180-7602) - Bill Brigham, Acting Director
Manufacturing Field Office[†]
Rensselaer Technology Park
385 Jordan Road
(518) 286-1014/286-1006 (Fax)
Utica (13504-3050) - David Mallen, Director
State University Institute of Technology at Utica/Rome
P.O. Box 3050
(315) 792-7546/792-7554 (Fax)
Watertown (13601) - John F. Tanner, Director
Jefferson Community College
Coffeen Street
(315) 782-9262/782-0901 (Fax)
White Plains (10605-1500) - Maria Circosta, Coordinator
222 Bloomingdale Road, Third Floor
(914) 644-4116/644-2184 (Fax)

NORTH CAROLINA
Boone (28608) - Bill Parrish, Regional Director
Appalachian State University Northwestern Region
Walker College of Business
2123 Raley Hall
(704) 262-2492/262-2027 (Fax)

Chapel Hill (27514) - Dan Parks, Director
University of North Carolina at Chapel Hill
608 Airport Road, Suite B
(919) 962-0389/962-3291 (Fax)
Charlotte (28262) - George McAllister, Director
University of North Carolina at Charlotte
The Ben Craig Center
8701 Mallard Creek Road
(704) 548-1090/548-9050 (Fax)
Cullowhee (28723) - Allan Steinberg, Director
Western Carolina University Western Region
Center for Improving Mountain Living
Bird Building
(704) 227-7494/227-7422 (Fax)
Elizabeth City (27909) - Wauna Dooms, Director
Elizabeth City State University[‡]
1704 Weeksville Road
P.O. Box 874
(919) 335-3247/335-3648 (Fax)
Fayetteville (28302) - Dr. Sid Gautam, Director
Fayetteville State University[‡]
Continuing Education Center
P.O. Box 1334
Fed Ex Delivery: Fayetteville State University
1200 Murchison Road
(910) 486-1727/486-1949 (Fax)
Greensboro (27411) - Cynthia Clemons, Director
North Carolina A&T State University[‡]
CH Moore Agricultural Research Center
1601 East Market Street
P.O. Box D-22
(910) 334-7005/334-7073 (Fax)

* Lead Small Business Development Center
[†] Specialized Center
[‡] Historical Black College/University

Greenville (27858-4353) - Walter Fitts, Director
East Carolina University Eastern Region
300 East First Street, Willis Building
(919) 328-6157/328-6992 (Fax)
Hickory (28601-4738) - Blair Abee, Director
514 Highway 321 Northwest, Suite A
(704) 345-1110/326-9117 (Fax)
Pembroke (28372) - Joanne Zakowski, Director
Pembroke State University
P.O. Box 1510
(910) 521-6198/521-6164 (Fax)
Raleigh (27601) - Mike Seibert, Director
North Carolina State University Capital
   Region
MCI Small Business Resource Center
800½ South Salisbury Street
(919) 715-0520/715-0518 (Fax)
Raleigh (27601-1742) - Scott R. Daugherty, Executive Director
University of North Carolina*
333 Fayetteville Street Mall, #1150
(800) 2580-UNC/(919) 715-7272/
   715-7777 (Fax)
Rocky Mount (27804) - Michael Twiddy
North Carolina Wesleyan College
400 North Wesleyan Boulevard
(919) 985-5130/977-3701 (Fax)
Wilmington (28403) - Dr. Warren Gulko, Director
University of North Carolina at
   Wilmington
601 South College Road
(910) 395-3744/962-3014 (Fax)
Winston-Salem (27110) - Bill Dowe, Director
Winston-Salem State University‡
P.O. Box 13025
Fed Ex Delivery: Winston-Salem State
   University
Albert Anderson Center, Room 118
MLK & Reynolds Park Road
(910) 750-2030/750-2031 (Fax)

OHIO
Akron (44308-1192) - Charles Smith, Director
One Cascade Plaza, 8th Floor
(216) 379-3170/379-3164 (Fax)
Athens (45701) - Karen Patton, Director
Enterprise Development Corporation
900 East State Street
(614) 592-1188/593-8283 (Fax)
Athens (45701) - Debra McBride, Director
Ohio University
Enterprise and Technology Building
20 East Circle Drive, Suite 190
(614) 593-1797/593-1795 (Fax)
Canton (44720) - Amy DeGeorge, Coordinator
Kent State University/Stark Campus
6000 Frank Avenue Northwest
(216) 499-9600/494-6121 (Fax)
Celina (45882) - Tom Knapke, Director
Wright State University/Lake Campus
West Central Office
7600 State Route 703
(800) 237-1477/(419) 586-0355/
   586-0358 (Fax)
Cincinnati (45212-3597) - Danielle K. Remmy, Director
1776 Mentor Avenue
(513) 632-8292/351-0610 (Fax)
HCDCSBDC@aol.com
Cincinnati (45245) - Dennis Begue, Director
Clermont County Chamber of Commerce
4440 Glen Este-Withamsville Road
(513) 753-7141/753-7146 (Fax)
Cincinnati (45216-2265) - Bill Fioretti, Director
University of Cincinnati
IAMS Research Park
1111 Edison Avenue
(513) 948-2082/948-2007 (Fax)

---

* Lead Small Business Development Center
† Specialized Center
‡ Historical Black College/University

Cleveland (44103-4314) - Robert
Schauer, Manager
Prospect Park Building
4600 Prospect Avenue
(216) 432-5364/361-2900 (Fax)
Cleveland (44113-2291) - Ann Hach,
Director
200 Tower City Center/50 Public Square
(216) 621-3300/621-4617 (Fax)
Columbus (43215-6108) - Holly
I. Schick, State Director
Department of Development*
77 South High Street, 28th Floor
(614) 466-2711/466-0829 (Fax)
Dayton (45402-2400) - Harry
Bumgarner, Director
Dayton Area Chamber of Commerce
Chamber Plaza, 5th and Main Streets
(513) 226-8239/226-8254 (Fax)
Dayton (45433) - Marsha Adams,
Director
Wright State University/Dayton Satellite
College of Business, 120 Rike Hall
(513) 873-3503/873-3545 (Fax)
Defiance (43512) - Don Wright,
Director
1935 East Second Street, Suite D
(419) 784-3777/782-4649 (Fax)
Fremont (43420) - Joe Wilson, Director
Terra Community College
2830 Napoleon Road
(800) 825-2431/(419) 334-8400 ext.
255/334-9414 (Fax)
Hillsboro (45133) - Bill Grunkemeyer,
Interim Director
129 East Main Street
(513) 393-9599/393-8159 (Fax)
Jefferson (44047) - Sarah Bogardus,
Director
36 West Walnut Street
(216) 576-9134/576-5003 (Fax)
Kent (44242) - Linda Yost, Director
Kent State University Partnership
College of Business Administration
Room 300A
(216) 672-2772 ext. 254/672-2448 (Fax)

Kettering (45420) - Harry Bumgarner,
Director
3155 Research Park, Suite 206
(513) 258-6180/258-6189 (Fax)
Kirkland (44094) - Catherine
C. Haworth, Director
Lakeland Community College
7750 Clocktower Drive
(216) 951-1290/951-7336 (Fax)
Lima (45801-4717) - Gerald
J. Biedenharn, Director
Lima Technical College
West Central Office
545 West Market Street, Suite 305
(419) 229-5320/229-5424 (Fax)
Lorain (44053) - Dennis Jones, Director
Lorain County Chamber of Commerce
6100 South Broadway
(216) 233-6500/246-4050 (Fax)
Mansfield (44901) - Barbara Harmony,
Director
246 East Fourth Street
P.O. Box 1208
(800) 366-7232/(419) 522-6811 (Fax)
Marietta (45750) - Emerson Shimp,
Director
Marietta College
213 Fourth Street, 2nd Floor
(614) 376-4832/376-4901 (Fax)
Marion (43302) - Lynn Lovell, Director
Heart of Ohio Marion Area Chamber of
Commerce
206 South Prospect Street
(614) 387-0188/387-7722 (Fax)
New Philadelphia (44663-9447) - Tom
Farbizo, Director
Kent State University
300 University Drive, Northeast
(216) 339-3391 ext. 279/339-2637 (Fax)
Piqua (45356) - Jon Heffner, Acting
Director
Upper Valley Joint Vocational School
8811 Career Drive, North County Road
25A
(800) 589-6963/(513) 778-8419/778-9237
(Fax)

* Lead Small Business Development Center
† Specialized Center
‡ Historical Black College/University

**Portsmouth (45662-4344) - Patrick
Dengel, Director**
Shawnee State University
940 Second Street, Room 008, Massie Hall
(614) 355-2274/355-2598 (Fax)
**Salem (44460) - Deanne Taylor,
Director**
Kent State University/Salem Campus
2491 State Route 45 South
(216) 332-0361/332-9256 (Fax)
**South Point (45680) - Lou-Ann Walden,
Director**
Lawrence County Chamber of Commerce
U.S. Route 52 & Solida Road
P.O. Box 488
(614) 894-3838/894-3836 (Fax)
**Springfield (45505) - Rafeal
Underwood, Executive Director**
300 East Auburn Avenue
(513) 322-7821/322-7874 (Fax)
**Toledo (43604-1575) - Linda
Fayerweather, Director**
300 Madison Avenue
Enterprise Suite 200
(419) 243-8191/241-8302 (Fax)
**Youngstown (44503) - Patricia Veisz,
Manager**
Youngstown State University
Cushwa Center for Business Development
241 Federal Plaza
(216) 746-3350/746-3324 (Fax)
**Zanesville (43701) - Bonnie J. Winnett,
Director**
Zanesville Area Chamber of Commerce
217 North Fifth Street
(614) 452-4868/454-2963 (Fax)

OKLAHOMA
Ada (74820) - Frank Vater, Director
East Central University
1036 East Tenth
(405) 436-3190/436-3190 (Fax)
osbdcecu@chickasaw.com

**Alva (73717) - Clance Doelling,
Director**
Northwestern Oklahoma State University
709 Oklahoma Boulevard
(405) 327-8608/327-0560 (Fax)
clance@okla.net
**Durant (74701) - Dr. Grady
Pennington, State Director**
Southeastern Oklahoma State University*
517 University
Station A, Box 2584
(800) 522-6154/(405) 924-0277/
920-7471 (Fax)
gpennington@sosu.edu
**Durant (74701) - Claire Livingston,
Bus. Dev. Specialist**
Southeastern Oklahoma State University
517 University
(405) 924-0277/920-7471 (Fax)
clivingston@sosu.edu
**Enid (73701) - Bill Gregory,
Coordinator**
Phillips University
100 South University Avenue
(405) 242-7989/237-1607 (Fax)
b9finger@enid.com
**Langston (73050) - Robert Allen,
Director**
Langston University Minority Assistance
Center†
Highway 33 East
(405) 466-3256/466-2909 (Fax)
**Lawton (73501) - James C. Elliott,
Business Dev. Specialist**
American National Bank Building
601 Southwest D, Suite 209
(405) 248-4946/248-4946 (Fax)
**Miami (74354) - Hugh Simon, Bus. Dev.
Specialist**
Northeast Oklahoma A&M
215 I Street, Northeast
(918) 540-0575/540-0575 (Fax)
hsimon@neoam.cc.ok.us

---

* Lead Small Business Development Center
† Specialized Center
‡ Historical Black College/University

Midwest City (73110) - Judy Robbins, Director
Rose State College Procurement
  Speciality Center[†]
6420 Southeast 15th Street
(405) 733-7348/733-7495 (Fax)
jrobbins@ms.rose.cc.ok.us
Oklahoma City (73101-1439) - Susan Urbach, Director
University of Central Oklahoma
115 Park Avenue
P.O. Box 1439
(405) 232-1968/232-1967 (Fax)
surbach@aixl.ucok.edu
Poteau (74953) - Dean Qualls, Director
Carl Albert College
1507 South McKenna
(918) 647-4019/647-1218 (Fax)
Tahlequah (74464) - Danielle Coursey, Bus. Dev. Specialist
Northeastern Oklahoma State University
(918) 458-0802/458-2105 (Fax)
Tulsa (74119) - Jeff Horvath, Director
Tulsa State Office Building
616 South Boston
(918) 583-2600/599-6173 (Fax)
Weatherford (73096) - Chuck Felz, Director
Southwestern Oklahoma State University
100 Campus Drive
(405) 774-1040/774-7091 (Fax)
sbdcswsu@brightok.net

OREGON
Albany (97321) - Dennis Sargent, Director
Linn-Benton Community College
6500 Southwest Pacific Boulevard
(541) 917-4923/917-4445 (Fax)
Sargend@Peak.org
sargend@gw.lbcc.cc.or.us
Bend (97701) - Bob Newhart, Director
Central Oregon Community College
2600 Northwest College Way
(541) 383-7290/383-3445 (Fax)
BDC@cocc.edu

Coos Bay (97420) - Jon Richards, Director
Southwestern Oregon Community College
2110 Newmark Avenue
(541) 888-7100/888-7113 (Fax)
jrichards@ortel.org
The Dalles (97058) - Bob Cole, Director
Columbia Gorge Community College
400 East Scenic Drive, Suite 257
(541) 298-3118/(503) 298-3119 (Fax)
Eugene (97401) - Jane Scheidecker, Director
Lane Community College
1059 Williamette Street
(541) 726-2255/686-0096 (Fax)
scheideckerj@lanecc.edu
Eugene (97401-3021) - Dr. Sandy Cutler, State Director
Lane Community College*
44 West Broadway, Suite 501
(541) 726-2250/345-6006 (Fax)
cutlers@lanecc.edu
Grants Pass (97526) - Lee Merritt, Director
Rogue Community College
214 Southwest Fourth Street
(514) 471-3515/471-3589 (Fax)
sbdclee@MAGICK.NET
Gresham (97030) - Billi Jo Schmuck, Acting Director
Mount Hood Community College
323 Northeast Roberts Street
(503) 667-7658/666-1140 (Fax)
Klamath Falls (97601) - Jamie Albert, Director
Oregon Institute of Technology
3201 Campus Drive, South 314
(541) 885-1760/885-1855 (Fax)
ALBERTJ@oit.osshe.edu
LeGrande (97850) - John Prosnik, Jr., Director
Eastern Oregon State College
1410 L Avenue
(541) 962-3391/962-3668 (Fax)
prosnij@eosc.osshe.edu

* Lead Small Business Development Center
[†] Specialized Center
[‡] Historical Black College/University

**Lincoln City (97367) - Guy Faust,
Director**
Oregon Coast Community College
4157 Northwest Highway 101, Suite 123
P.O. Box 419
(541) 765-2515/994-4166/996-4958 (Fax)
Newport Office: (541) 265-2283 ext. 122/
   265-3520 (Fax)
Medford (97501) - Liz Shelby, Director
Southern Oregon State College/Medford
Regional Services Institute
332 West Sixth Street
(541) 772-3478/734-4813 (Fax)
Shelby@wpo.sosc.osshe.edu
**Milwaukee (97222) - Jan Stennick,
Director**
Clackamas Community College
7616 Southeast Harmony Road
(503) 656-4447/652-0389 (Fax)
jans@clackamas.cc.or.us
Ontario (97914) - Kathy Simko, Director
Treasure Valley Community College
88 Southwest Third Avenue
(541) 889-2617/889-8331 (Fax)
simko@Mailman.tvcc.cc.or.us
**Pendleton (97801) - Gerald Wood,
Director**
Blue Mountain Community College
37 Southeast Dorion
(541) 276-6233/276-6819 (Fax)
jerry_wood@ortel.org
**Portland (97204) - Tom Niland,
Director**
International Trade Program[†]
Portland Community College
121 Southwest Salmon Street, Suite 210
(503) 274-7482/228-6350 (Fax)
tniland@pcc.edu
tniland@ortel.com
**Portland (97210) - Robert Keyser,
Director**
Portland Community College
Montgomery Park, Suite 499
2701 Northwest Vaughn Street
(503) 978-5080/222-2570 (Fax)

**Roseburg (97470) - Terry Swagerty,
Director**
Umpqua Community College
744 Southeast Rose
(541) 672-2535/672-3679 (Fax)
swagert@rosenet.net
Salem (97301) - Tom Nelson, Director
Chemeketa Community College
365 Ferry Street Southeast
(503) 399-5088/581-6017 (Fax)
nelt@chemek.cc.or.us
**Seaside (97138) - Paul Mallonee,
Interim Director**
Clatstop Community College
1761 North Holladay Drive
(503) 738-3347/738-7843 (Fax)
**Tillamook (97141) - Kathy Wilkes,
Director**
Tillamook Bay Community College
401 B Main Street
(503) 842-2551/842-2555 (Fax)

PENNSYLVANIA
**Bethlehem (18015) - Dr. John Bonge,
Director**
Lehigh University
Rauch Business Center #37
(610) 758-3980/758-5205 (Fax)
**Clarion (16214) - Dr. Woodrow Yeaney,
Director**
Clarion University of Pennsylvania
Dana Still Building
(814) 226-2060/226-2636 (Fax)
Erie (16541) - Ernie Post, Director
Gannon University
Carlisle Building, Third Floor
(814) 871-7714/871-7383 (Fax)
**Harrisburg (17110) - Katherine Wilson,
Director**
Kutztown University
2986 North Second Street
(717) 720-4230/720-4262 (Fax)
Latrobe (15650) - Jack Fabean, Director
St. Vincent College
Alfred Hall, Fourth Floor
(412) 537-4572/537-0919 (Fax)

---

* Lead Small Business Development Center
† Specialized Center
‡ Historical Black College/University

Lewisburg (17837) - Dr. Charles Coder, Director
Bucknell University
Dana Engineering Building, First Floor
(717) 524-1249/524-1768 (Fax)
Loretto (15940) - John A. Palko, Director
St. Francis College
Business Resource Center
(814) 472-3200/472-3202 (Fax)
Philadelphia (19122) - Sandra Sowell-Scott, Acting Director
Temple University
Room Six, Speakman Hall - 006-00
(215) 204-7282/204-4554 (Fax)
Philadelphia (19104-6374) - Gregory L. Higgins, State Director
University of Pennsylvania*
The Wharton School
423 Vance Hall
3733 Spruce Street
(215) 898-1219/573-2135 (Fax)
Philadelphia (19104) - Clark Callahan, Director
University of Pennsylvania
The Wharton School
409 Vance Hall
(215) 898-4861/898-1063 (Fax)
Pittsburgh (15282) - Dr. Mary T. McKinney, Director
Duquesne University
Rockwell Hall, Room 10 Concourse
600 Forbes Avenue
(412) 396-6233/396-5884 (Fax)
Pittsburgh (15213) - Ann Dugan, Director
University of Pittsburgh
208 Bellefield Hall
315 South Bellefield Avenue
(412) 648-1544/648-1636 (Fax)
Scranton (18510) - Elaine M. Tweedy, Director
University of Scranton
St. Thomas Hall, Room 588
(717) 941-7588/941-4053 (Fax)

Wilkes-Barre (18766-0001) - Kostas Mallios, Director
Wilkes University
192 South Franklin Street
(717) 831-4340/824-2245 (Fax)

RHODE ISLAND
Lincoln (02865-1105) - Sheila Hoogeboom, Case Manager
Northern Rhode Island Chamber of Commerce
6 Blackstone Valley Place, Suite 105
(401) 334-1000 ext. 113/334-1009 (Fax)
Middletown (02842-6377) - Sam Carr, Case Manager
Newport County Chamber of Commerce
45 Valley Road
(401) 849-6900/849-5848 (Fax)
North Kingstown (02852-7556) - Liz Kroll, Case Manager
South County RISBDC, QP/D Industrial Park
35 Belver Avenue #212
(401) 294-1227/294-6897 (Fax)
Providence (02905-1445) - Jaime Aguayo/Ann-Marie Marshall
550 Broad Street
(401) 272-1083/272-1186 (Fax)
Providence (02903-1793) - Erwin Robinson, Program Manager
Greater Providence Chamber of Commerce
Bryant College RISBDC
30 Exchange Terrace, 4th Floor
(401) 831-1330/274-5410 (Fax)
Providence (02903-1111) - O. J. Silas, Program Manager
Rhode Island Department of Transportation
2 Capitol Hill, Room 106
(401) 277-4576/277-6168 (Fax)
Smithfield (02917-1284) - Douglas H. Jobling, State Director
Bryant College*
1150 Douglas Pike
(401) 232-6111/232-6933 (Fax)

---

* Lead Small Business Development Center
† Specialized Center
‡ Historical Black College/University

Smithfield (02917-1284) - Raymond Fogarty, Director
Bryant College EAC
1150 Douglas Pike
(401) 232-6407/232-6416 (Fax)
Smithfield (02917-1284) - Cheryl Faria, Assistant Director; Dennis McCarthy, Program Manager
Entrepreneurship Training Program
Bryant College
1150 Douglas Pike
(401) 232-6115/232-6933 (Fax)
Smithfield (02917-1284) - Kate Dolan, Managing Director
NYNEX Telecommunications Center
Bryant College Koffler Technology Center
1150 Douglas Pike
(401) 232-0220/232-0242 (Fax)
Warren (02885-0250) - Sam Carr, Case Manager
Bristol County Chamber of Commerce
P.O. Box 250
(401) 245-0750/245-0110 (Fax)
Warwick (02886-7151) - Thomas J. Moakley, Case Manager
Central Rhode Island Chamber of Commerce
3288 Post Road
(401) 732-1100/732-1107 (Fax)

SOUTH CAROLINA
Aiken (29801) - Jackie Moore, Area Manager
171 University Parkway, Suite 100
(803) 641-3646/641-3647 (Fax)
Beaufort (29902) - Martin Goodman, Area Manager
University of South Carolina/Beaufort
801 Carteret Street
(803) 521-4143/521-4142 (Fax)
Clemson (29634-1392) - Rebecca Hobart, Regional Director; Jill Burroughs, Area Manager
Clemson University
425 Sirrine Hall, College of Commerce
(803) 656-3227/656-4869 (Fax)

Columbia (29208) - John Lenti, State Director
University of South Carolina*
College of Business Administration
Hipp Building
1710 College Street
(803) 777-4907/777-4403 (Fax)
lenti@darla.badm.scarolina.edu
Columbia (29208-9980) - Jim Brazell, Regional Director; Shawn Mewborn, Area Manager
University of South Carolina
College of Business Administration
(803) 777-5118/777-4403 (Fax)
brazell@univscvm.csd.scarolina.edu
Conway (29528-6054) - Tim Lowery, Area Manager
Costal Carolina University
Wall School of Business Administration
P.O. Box 261994
(803) 349-2170/349-2455 (Fax)
Florence (29501-0548) - David Raines, Area Manager
Florence Darlington Technical College
P.O. Box 100548
(803) 661-8256/661-8041 (Fax)
Greenville (29606) - Susan Dunlap, Area Manager
Greenville Chamber of Commerce
24 Cleveland Street
(864) 271-4259/282-8506 (Fax)
Greenville (29607)
University Center
216 South Pleasantburg Drive, Room 140
(864) 250-8894/250-8897 (Fax)
Greenwood (29648) - George Long, Area Manager
Upper Savannah Council of Government
P.O. Box 1366
(803) 941-8071/941-8090 (Fax)
Hilton Head (29928) - Jim DeMartin, Consultant
University of South Carolina/Hilton Head
1 College Center Drive
(803) 785-3995/777-0333 (Fax)

---

* Lead Small Business Development Center
† Specialized Center
‡ Historical Black College/University

Kingstree (29556)
128 Mill Street
P.O. Box 428
(803) 354-9070
**North Charleston (29406) - Merry
  Boone, Area Manager**
5900 Core Drive, Suite 104
(803) 740-6160/740-1607 (Fax)
**Orangeburg (29117) - John W. Gadson,
  Regional Director; Francis Heape,
  Area Manager**
South Carolina State University‡
114/116 Belcher Hall
300 College Avenue
(803) 536-8445/536-8066 (Fax)
**Rock Hill (29733) - Nate Barber,
  Regional Director; Diane Hockett,
  Area Manager**
Winthrop University
School of Business Administration
119 Thurmond Building
(803) 323-2283/323-4281 (Fax)
Sumter (29150-2498)
University of South Carolina/Sumter
200 Miller Road
(803) 775-6341

SOUTH DAKOTA
**Aberdeen (57401) - Belinda
  G. Engelhart, Regional Director**
620 15th Avenue Southeast
(605) 626-2565/626-2667 (Fax)
**Rapid City (57701) - Valerie
  S. Simpson, Regional Director**
444 North Mt. Rushmore, Suite 208
(605) 394-5311/394-6140 (Fax)
**Sioux Falls (57104) - Wade D. Druin,
  Regional Director**
405 South Third Avenue, Suite 101
(605) 367-5757/367-5755 (Fax)
**Sioux Falls (57104) - Matthew
  D. Johnson, Assistant State Director**
405 South Third Avenue, Suite 101
(605) 367-5757/367-5755 (Fax)
mdjohnso@sundance.usd.edu

**Vermillion (57069-2390) - Robert
  E. Ashley, Jr., State Director**
University of South Dakota*
School of Business
414 East Clark Street
(605) 677-5498/677-5272 (Fax)
rashley@iw.net

TENNESSEE
**Chattanooga (37405-0757) - Sherri
  E. Bishop, Business Specialist**
25 Cherokee Boulevard
P.O. Box 4757
(423) 266-5781/267-7705 (Fax)
**Chattanooga (37405-3878) - Donna
  Marsh, Small Business Specialist**
Chattanooga State Technical Community
  College
100 Cherokee Boulevard, Suite 202
(423) 752-1774/752-1925 (Fax)
**Clarksville (37044-0001) - John Volker,
  Director**
Austin Peay State University
College of Business
(615) 648-7764/648-6316 (Fax)
**Cleveland (37320-3570) - Don Geren,
  Director**
Cleveland State Community College
Adkisson Drive
P.O. Box 3570
(423) 478-6247/478-6251 (Fax)
**Columbia (38402) - Eugene Osekowsky,
  Business Specialist**
P.O. Box 8069
(615) 898-2745/893-7089 (Fax)
**Dyersburg (38024-2450) - Bob Wylie,
  Senior Business Specialist**
Dyersburg State Community College
Office of Extension Services
1510 Lake Road
(901) 286-3201/286-3271 (Fax)
**Hartsville (37074-0063) - Dorothy
  Vaden, Small Business Specialist**
P.O. Box 63
(615) 374-9521/374-4608 (Fax)

* Lead Small Business Development Center
† Specialized Center
‡ Historical Black College/University

Jackson (38305-3797) - David
    L. Brown, Business Counselor
Jackson State Community College
2046 North Parkway Street
(901) 424-5389/425-2647 (Fax)
Johnson City (37614-0698) - Bob
    Justice, Director
East Tennessee State University
College of Business
P.O. Box 70698
(423) 439-5630/439-7080 (Fax)
Kingsport (37660-8488) - Rob Lytle,
    Business Counselor
East Tennessee State University
Kingsport University Center
1501 University Boulevard
(423) 392-8017/392-8017 (Fax)
Knoxville (37915-2572) - Richard
    Vogler, IT Specialist
International Trade Center[†]
301 East Church Avenue
(423) 637-4283/523-2071 (Fax)
Knoxville (37915-2572) - Teri Brahams,
    Director
Pellissippi State Technical Community
    College
Chamber of Commerce
301 East Church Avenue
(423) 525-0277/971-4439 (Fax)
Memphis (38152-0001) - Philip
    Johnson, Director
International Trade Center[†]
University of Memphis
(901) 678-4174/678-4072 (Fax)
Memphis (38104-3206) - Earnest Lacey,
    Director
University of Memphis
320 South Dudley Street
(901) 527-1041/527-1047 (Fax)
Memphis (38152-0001) - Dr. Kenneth
    J. Burns, State Director
University of Memphis*
South Campus (Getwell Road), Building 1
(901) 678-2500/678-4072 (Fax)

Memphis (38152-0001) - Dr. Paul
    Jennings, Director
University of Memphis
Technology and Energy Services
(901) 678-4057/678-4072 (Fax)
Morristown (37813-6889) - Jack
    Tucker, Director
Walters State Community College
500 South Davy Crockett Parkway
(423) 585-2675/585-2679 (Fax)
Murfreesboro (37129-0001) - Patrick
    Geho, Director
Middle Tennessee State University
Rutherford County Chamber of
    Commerce Building
501 Memorial Boulevard
(615) 898-2745/893-7089 (Fax)
Nashville (37203-3401) - Billy E. Lowe,
    Director
Tennessee State University*
College of Business
330 Tenth Avenue North
(615) 963-7179/963-7160 (Fax)
Oak Ridge (37830-8026) - Dan Collier,
    Business Specialist
Technology 2020 Office
1020 Commerce Park Drive
(423) 483-2668/220-2030 (Fax)

TEXAS
Abilene (79601) - Judy Wilhelm,
    Director
Abilene Christian University
College of Business Administration
648 East Highway 80
(915) 670-0300/670-0311 (Fax)
Alpine (79832) - Michael Levine,
    Director
Sul Ross State University
P.O. Box C-47, Room 319
(915) 837-8694/837-8104 (Fax)
Amarillo (79102) - Don Taylor, Director
West Texas A&M University
T. Boone Pickens School of Business
1800 South Washington, Suite 209
(806) 372-5151/372-5261 (Fax)

---

* Lead Small Business Development Center
[†] Specialized Center
[‡] Historical Black College/University

Athens (75751) - Judy Loden, Director
Trinity Valley Community College
500 South Prairieville
(800) 335-7232/(903) 675-7403/
    675-5199 (Fax)
Austin (78767) - Larry Lucero, Director
Lower Colorado River Authority
3700 Lake Austin Boulevard
Jack Miller Building Mail Stop M104
(512) 473-3510/473-3285 (Fax)
**Baytown (77522-0818) - Tommy
    Hathaway, Director**
Lee College
200 Lee Drive
Rundell Hall
P.O. Box 818
(281) 425-6309/425-6307 (Fax)
**Beaumont (77705) - Gene Arnold,
    Director**
Lamar University
855 Florida Avenue
(409) 880-2367/880-2201 (Fax)
**Bonham (75418) - Darroll Martin,
    Coordinator**
Sam Rayburn Library
1201 East 9th Street, Building 2
(903) 583-7565/583-6706 (Fax)
**Brenham (77833) - Phillis Nelson,
    Director**
Blinn College
902 College Avenue
(409) 830-4137/830-4135 (Fax)
Bryan (77805) - Sam Harwell, Director
Bryan College Station
4001 East 29th Street, Suite 175
P.O. Box 3695
(409) 260-5222/260-5229 (Fax)
www.bvsbdc.org
**Corpus Christi (78403) - Oscar
    Martinez, Director**
Greater Corpus Christi Business Alliance
1201 North Shoreline
(512) 881-1847/882-4256 (Fax)

**Corsicana (75110) - Leon Allard,
    Director**
120 North 12th Street
(800) 320-7232/(903) 874-0658/
    874-4187 (Fax)
**Dallas (75215) - Gerald Chandler,
    Director**
Center for Government Contracting/
    Technology Assistance Center
1402 Corinth Street
(800) 348-7232/(214) 860-5841/
    860-5881 (Fax)
**Dallas (75215) - Liz Klimback,
    Regional Director**
Dallas County Community College*
1402 Corinth Street
(800) 350-7232/(214) 860-5835/
    860-5813 (Fax)
**Dallas (75215) - Earnest Castillo,
    Director**
Dallas County Community College
1402 Corinth Street
(214) 860-5850/860-5881 (Fax)
**Dallas (75258) - Beth Huddleston,
    Director**
International Assistance Center[†]
World Trade Center, Suite 150
2050 Stemmons Freeway
P.O. Box 58299
(800) 337-7232/(214) 747-1300/
    748-5774 (Fax)
**Denison (75020) - Karen Stidham,
    Director**
Grayson County College
6101 Grayson Drive
(800) 316-7232/(903) 463-8787/
    463-5437 (Fax)
**Denton (76201) - Carolyn Birkhead,
    Coordinator**
P.O. Drawer P
(254) 380-1849/382-0040 (Fax)

* Lead Small Business Development Center
† Specialized Center
‡ Historical Black College/University

Duncanville (75116) - Neil Small, Director
214 South Main, Suite 102A
(800) 317-7232/(972) 709-5878/
  709-6089 (Fax)
Edinburg (78539-2999) - Juan Garcia, Director
University of Texas/Pan American
1201 West University
(210) 316-2610/316-2612 (Fax)
El Paso (79902-3929) - Roque R. Segura, Director
El Paso Community College
103 Montana Avenue, Suite 202
(915) 534-3410/534-4625 (Fax)
Ft. Worth (76118) - Jo-An Weddle, Director
7300 Jack Newell Boulevard, South
(817) 272-5930/272-5952 (Fax)
Ft. Worth (76102) - David Edmonds, Director
Tarrant County Junior College
7917 Highway 80 West
Mailing address: 1500 Houston Street,
  Room 163
(817) 871-6028/871-0031 (Fax)
Gainesville (76240) - Cathy Keeler, Director
North Central Texas College
1525 West California
(800) 351-7232/(254) 668-4220/
  668-6049 (Fax)
Galveston (77550) - Georgette Peterson, Director
Galveston College
5001 Avenue U
Mailing address: 4015 Avenue Q
(409) 740-7380/740-7381 (Fax)
Houston (77060) - Kay Hamilton, Director
250 North Sam Houston Parkway East
(281) 933-7932/591-9374 (Fax)
Houston (77099) - Joe Harper, Director
Houston Community College System
10405 Stancliff, Suite 100
(281) 933-7932/568-3690 (Fax)

Houston (77002) - Dr. Elizabeth Gatewood, Executive Director
University of Houston*
1100 Louisiana, Suite 500
(713) 752-8444/756-1500 (Fax)
Houston (77002) - Carlos Lopez, Director
UH International Trade Center†
University of Houston
1100 Louisiana, Suite 500
(713) 752-8404/756-1515 (Fax)
Houston (77002) - Jacqueline Taylor, Director
UH Texas Information Procurement
  Service†
University of Houston
1100 Louisiana, Suite 500
(800) 252-7232/(713) 752-8477
  /756-1515 (Fax)
Huntsville (77341) - Bob Barragan, Director
Sam Houston State University
843 South Sam Houston Avenue
Mailing address: P.O. Box 2058
(409) 294-3737/294-3738 (Fax)
Kingsville (78363) - Elizabeth Soliz, Director
Kingsville Chamber of Commerce
635 East King
(512) 595-5088/592-0866 (Fax)
Lake Jackson (77566) - Patricia Leyendecker, Director
500 College Drive
(409) 266-3380/266-3482 (Fax)
Laredo (78041) - David Puig, Director
Laredo Development Foundation
616 Leal Street
(210) 722-0563/722-6247 (Fax)
Longview (75601) - Brad Bunt, Director
Kilgore College
Triple Creek Shopping Plaza
110 Triple Creek Drive, Suite 70
(800) 338-7232/(903) 757-5857/
  753-7920 (Fax)

---

* Lead Small Business Development Center
† Specialized Center
‡ Historical Black College/University

Lubbock (79423) - Craig Bean,
  Regional Director
Texas Tech University*
Spectrum Plaza
2579 South Loop 289, Suite 114
(806) 745-3973/745-6207 (Fax)
odbea@ttacs.ttu.edu

Lubbock (79423) - Steve Anderson,
  Director
Texas Tech University
Spectrum Plaza
2579 South Loop 289, Suite 210
(806) 745-1637/745-6717 (Fax)

Lufkin (75902) - Brian McClain,
  Director
Angelina Community College
P.O. Box 1768
(409) 639-1887/639-3863 (Fax)

Mt. Pleasant (75455) - Bob Wall,
  Director
P.O. Box 1307
(800) 357-7232/(903) 572-1991/
  572-0598 (Fax)
www.bizcoach.org

Odessa (79762) - Karl Painter, Director
University of Texas/Permian Basin
4901 East University
(915) 552-2455/552-2433 (Fax)

Paris (75460) - Pat Bell, Director
Paris Junior College
2400 Clarksville Street
(903) 784-1802/784-1801 (Fax)

Plano (75093) - Chris Jones, Director
Courtyard Center for Professional and
  Economic Development
4800 Preston Park Boulevard,
  Suite A126
P.O. Box 15
(972) 985-3770/985-3775 (Fax)

San Angelo (76909) - Patti Warrington,
  Director
Angelo State University
2610 West Avenue N
Campus Box 10910
(915) 942-2098/942-2096 (Fax)

San Antonio (78212) - Sara Jackson,
  Director
International Trade Center†
University of Texas at San Antonio
1222 North Main, Suite 450
(210) 458-2470/458-2464 (Fax)

San Antonio (78212) - Judith Ingalls,
  Director
Technology Center†
University of Texas at San Antonio
1222 North Main, Suite 450
(210) 458-2458/458-2464 (Fax)

San Antonio (78212) - Morrison Woods,
  Director
University of Texas at San Antonio
  Downtown
1222 North Main, Suite 450
(210) 458-2460/458-2464 (Fax)

San Antonio (78212) - Robert
  McKinley, Regional Director
University of Texas at San Antonio
  Downtown*
USTA Downtown
1222 North Main, Suite 450
(210) 458-2450/458-2464 (Fax)
rmckinley@utsa.edu

Stephenville (76402) - Rusty Freed,
  Director
Tarleton State University
College of Business Administration
Box T-0650
(817) 689-4373/689-4374 (Fax)

Texas City (77591) - Elizabeth
  Boudreau, Director
College of the Mainland
1200 Amburn Road
(409) 938-1211 ext. 494/(281) 280-3991
  ext. 494/(409) 938-7578 (Fax)

Tyler (75701) - Frank Viso, Director
Tyler Junior College
1530 South Southwest Loop 323, Suite 100
(903) 510-2975/510-2978 (Fax)

Uvalde (78801) - Mario Riojas,
  Director
Middle Rio Grande Development Council
209 North Getty Street
(210) 278-2527/278-2929 (Fax)

---

* Lead Small Business Development Center
† Specialized Center
‡ Historical Black College/University

Uvalde (78801) - Patrick Gibbons, Director
Middle Rio Grande Development Council
209 North Getty Street
(210) 278-2527/278-2929 (Fax)
Victoria (79901) - Carole Parks, Director
University of Houston/Victoria
700 Main Center, Suite 102
(512) 575-8944/575-8852 (Fax)
parks@jade.vic.uh.edu
Waco (76701) - Lu Billings, Director
McLennan Community College
401 Franklin
(800) 349-7232/(254) 714-0077/
    714-1668 (Fax)
Wharton (77488) - Lynn Polson, Director
Lower Colorado River Authority Coastal
    Plains
301 West Milam
P.O. Box 148
(409) 532-1007/532-0056 (Fax)
Wharton (77488-0080) - Lynn Polson, Director
Wharton County Junior College
Administration Building, Room 102
911 Boling Highway
(409) 532-0604/532-2410 (Fax)
Wichita Falls (76308) - Tim Thomas, Director
Midwestern State University
3410 Taft Boulevard
(817) 689-4373/689-4374 (Fax)

UTAH
Cedar City (84720) - Greg Powell, Director
Southern Utah University
351 West Center
(801) 586-5400/586-5493 (Fax)
Ephraim (84627) - Russell Johnson, Director
Snow College
345 West 100 North
(801) 283-4021/283-6913 (Fax)

Logan (84322-8330) - Franklin C. Prante, Director
Utah State University
East Campus Building, Room 24
(801) 797-2277/797-3317 (Fax)
Moab (84532)
Utah State University Extension Office
125 West 200 South
Ogden (84720) - Bruce Davis, Director
Weber State University
College of Business and Economics
(801) 626-6070/626-7423 (Fax)
Orem (84058) - Michael Finnerty, Director
Utah Valley State University
800 West 1200 South
(801) 222-8230/225-1229 (Fax)
Price (84501) - Patrick Glenn, Director
Price Center
South Eastern Utah AOG
451 East 400 North
(801) 637-1995/637-4102 (Fax)
Roosevelt (84066) - Matt Redd, Director
Uintah Basin Applied Technology Center
987 Lagoon Street
(801) 722-2294/722-5804 (Fax)
St. George (84770) - Jill Ellis, Director
Dixie College
225 South 700 East
(801) 652-7751/652-7870 (Fax)
Salt Lake City (84115) - Pamela Hunt, Director
Salt Lake Community College
1623 State Street
(801) 957-3480/957-3489 (Fax)
Sandy (84070) - Barry Bartlett, Director
Salt Lake Community College
8811 South 700 East
(801) 255-5878/255-6393 (Fax)

* Lead Small Business Development Center
† Specialized Center
‡ Historical Black College/University

VERMONT

Brattleboro (05301-1177) - William McGrath, Executive Vice President
Brattleboro Development Credit
Corporation
72 Cotton Mill Hill
(802) 257-7731/257-0294 (Fax)
bdcc@sover.net

Burlington (05402-0786) - Thomas D. Schroeder, SBDC Specialist; Norbert Lavigne, President
Greater Burlington Industrial Corporation
Northwest Vermont Small Business
Development Center[†]
P.O. Box 786
(802) 658-9228/860-1899 (Fax)
gbic@vermont.org

Middlebury (05753) - James B. Stewart, Executive Director
Addison County Economic Development
Corp.
RD #4, Box 1309A
(802) 388-7953/388-0119 (Fax)
acedc@sover.net

Montpelier (05601-1439) - Richard Angney, Executive Director
Central Vermont Economic Development
Corporation
P.O. Box 1439
(802) 223-4654/223-4655 (Fax)
cvedc@plainfield.bypass.com

Morrisville (05661-0455) - John Sullivan, Executive Director
Lamoille Economic Development
Corporation
P.O. Box 455
(802) 888-5640/888-7612 (Fax)
ledc@together.net

North Bennington (05257-0357) - Lance Matteson, Executive Director
Bennington County Industrial
Corporation
P.O. Box 357
(802) 442-8975/447-1101 (Fax)
lance@bcic.org

North Hero (05474-0213) - Barbara Mooney, Executive Director
Lake Champlain Islands Chamber of
Commerce
P.O. Box 213
(802) 372-5683/372-3205 (Fax)
ilandfun@together.net

Randolph Center (05060-0422) - Donald L. Kelpinski, State Director
Vermont Technical College*
P.O. Box 422
(800) 464-SBDC/(802) 728-9101/
728-3026 (Fax)
dkelpins@vtc.vsc.edu

Rutland (05701) - Wendy Wilton, SBDC Specialist; David O'Brien, Executive Director
Rutland Economic Development
Corporation
Southwestern Vermont Small Business
Development Center[†]
256 North Main Street
(802) 773-9147/773-2772 (Fax)
wwilton@vtc.vsc.edu

St. Albans (05478-1099) - Timothy J. Soule, Executive Director
Franklin County Industrial Development
Corporation
P.O. Box 1099
(802) 524-2194/524-6793 (Fax)
fcidc@together.net

St. Johnsbury (05819-0630) - Joseph P. Wynne, SBDC Specialist; Charles E. Carter, Executive Director
Northeastern Vermont Development
Association
Northeastern Vermont Small Business
Development Center[†]
P.O. Box 630
(802) 748-1014/748-1223 (Fax)
nvda@plainfield.bypass.com

---

* Lead Small Business Development Center
† Specialized Center
‡ Historical Black College/University

Springfield (05156-0058) - Steve Casabona, SBDC Specialist; Pat Moulton-Powden, Executive Director
Springfield Regional Development Corporation
Southeastern Vermont Small Business Development Center[†]
P.O. Box 58
(802) 885-2071/885-3027 (Fax)
srdc@sover.net

White River Junction (05001-0246) - Jim Saudade, Executive Director; Lenae Quillen-Blume, SBDC Specialist
Green Mount Economic Development Corporation
Central Vermont Small Business Development Center[†]
P.O. Box 246
(802) 295-3710/295-3779 (Fax)
gmedc@aol.com

VIRGINIA

Abingdon (24212) - Jim Tilley, Director
P.O. Box 828, Route 372 off Route 140
(540) 676-5615/628-7576 (Fax)
vhtillj%vccscent.bitnet@vtbit.cc.vt.edu

Alexandria (22306) - Gwendolyn Reape
6911 Richmond Highway, Suite 290
(703) 768-1440/768-0547 (Fax)

Alexandria (22314) - Bill Reagan, Director
Alexandria Graduate Education Center
1775-B Duke Street
(703) 299-9146/299-0295 (Fax)
bill@agec.dup.gwu.edu

Arlington (22001) - Paul Hall, Director
GMU Arlington Campus
4001 North Fairfax Drive, Suite 400
(703) 993-8129/993-8130 (Fax)
phall@gmu.edu

Belle Haven (23306) - Susan Tyler, Business Analyst
P.O. Box 395
(757) 442-7179/442-7181 (Fax)

Big Stone Gap (24219) - Tim Blankenbecler, Director
Mountain Empire Community College
Drawer 700, Route 23 South
(540) 523-6529/523-8139 (Fax)
meblant@me.cc.va.us

Charlottesville (22903) - Robert A. Hamilton, Jr., Director
918 Emmet Street North, Suite 200
(804) 295-8198/295-7066 (Fax)
Hamilton@sbdc.acs.virginia.edu

Fairfax (22030-3409) - Julie Janoski, Director
4031 University Drive, Suite 200
(703) 277-7700/277-7722 (Fax)
jjanoski@gmu.edu

Farmville (23909) - Gerald L. Hughes, Jr., Director
Longwood College
515 Main Street
(804) 395-2086/395-2359 (Fax)
jhughes@longwood.lwc.edu

Fredericksburg (22401) - Jeff Sneddon, Director
1301 College Avenue
Seacobeck Hall
(540) 654-1060/654-1070 (Fax)
jsneddon@mwcgw.mwc.edu

Hampton (23666) - William J. Holloran, Jr., Executive Director
525 Butler Farm Road, Suite 102
(757) 825-2957/825-2960 (Fax)
bhollora@chespo.hrccva.com

Harrisonburg (22807) - Karen Wigginton, Director
James Madison University
JMU College of Business
Zane Showker Hall, Room 527
(540) 568-3227/568-3106 (Fax)
vancesn@jmu.edu

Lynchburg (24502) - Barry Lyons, Director
147 Mill Ridge Road
(800) 876-7232/(804) 582-6170/ 582-6169 (Fax)
lrsbdc@aol.com

---

* Lead Small Business Development Center
[†] Specialized Center
[‡] Historical Black College/University

Manassas (22109-2962) - Linda Decker, Director
10311 Sudley Manor Drive
(703) 335-2500/335-1700 (Fax)
florysbdc@aol.com

Martinsville (24114) - Ken Copeland, Director
115 Broad Street
P.O. Box 709
(540) 632-4462/632-5059 (Fax)

Middletown (22645) - Robert Crosen, Director
Lord Fairfax Community College
P.O. Box 47, 173 Skirmisher Lane
(540) 869-6649/868-7002 (Fax)
lfcrosr@lf.cc.va.us

Petersburg (23804) - Kathryn Culbertson, Director
325 Washington Street
(804) 643-7232
kgbus@sprynet.com

Radford (24141) - David O. Shanks, Director
Radford University
600-H Norwood Street
(540) 831-6056/831-6057 (Fax)
dshanks@runet.edu

Richlands (24641) - Jim Boyd, Director
Southwest Virginia Community College
P.O. Box SVCC, Route 19
(540) 964-7345/964-5788 (Fax)
jim_boyd@sw.cc.va.us

Richmond (23219) - Taylor Cousins, Executive Director
1 North Fifth Street, Suite 510
(800) 646-SBDC/(804) 648-7838/
    648-7849 (Fax)
pwinter@richmond.infi.net

Richmond (23219) - Robert D. Wilburn, State Director
Commonwealth of Virginia
Department of Economic Development*
901 East Byrd Street, Suite 1400
(804) 371-8253/225-3384 (Fax)
rwilburn@dba.state.va.us

Roanoke (24011) - Doug Murray, Director
212 South Jefferson Street, Mez. level
(540) 983-0717/983-0723 (Fax)
djmr@roanoke.infi.net

South Boston (24592) - Vincent Decker, Director
515 Broad Street
P.O. Box 1116
(804) 575-0044/572-1762 (Fax)

Sterling (20164) - Ted London, Director
207 East Holly Avenue, Suite 214
(703) 430-7222/430-7258 (Fax)
tedlondon@aol.com

Warsaw (22572) - John Clickener, Director
5559 West Richmond Road
P.O. Box 490
(800) 524-8915/(804) 333-0286/
    333-0187 (Fax)
sbdcwarsaw@sylvaninfo.net

Wytheville (24382) - Rob Edwards, Director
Wytheville Community College
1000 East Main Street
(800) 468-1195 ext. 4798/
(540) 223-4798/223-4778 (Fax)
redwards@naxs.com

WASHINGTON
Aberdeen (98520)
Aberdeen/Grays Harbor College
1620 Edward P. Smith Drive
(360) 538-4021

Bellevue (98007-6484) - Bill Huenefeld, BDS
Bellevue Community College
300 Landerholm Circle Southeast
(206) 643-2888/649-3113 (Fax)

Bellingham (98225-9073) - Lynn Trzynka, BDS
Bellingham Western Washington
    University
College of Business and Economics
300 Parks Hall
(360) 650-3899/650-4844 (Fax)

---

* Lead Small Business Development Center
† Specialized Center
‡ Historical Black College/University

Bellingham (98226)
Whatcom Community College
237 West Kellogg Road
(360) 676-2170
Centralia (98036) - Don Hays, BDS
Centralia College
600 West Locust Street
(360) 736-9391/753-3404 (Fax)
Lynwood (98036) - Jack Wicks, BDS
Edmonds Community College
6600 196th Street, Southwest
(206) 640-1435/640-1532 (Fax)
Mt. Vernon (98273) - Peter Stroosma,
    BDS
Mt. Vernon Skagit Valley College
2405 College Way
(360) 428-1282/336-6116 (Fax)
Olympia (98501) - Douglas Hammel,
    BDS
South Puget Sound Community College
721 Columbia Street, Southwest
(360) 753-5616/586-5493 (Fax)
Port Angeles (98362)
102 East Front Street
P.O. Box 1085
(360) 457-7793
Pullman (99164-4851) - Carol
    Reisenberg, Acting State Director
Washington State University*
College of Business and Economics
501 Johnson Tower
(509) 335-1576/335-0949 (Fax)
Seattle (98109) - Bill Jacobs, BDS
180 Nickerson, Suite 207
(206) 464-5450/464-6357 (Fax)
Seattle (98121) - Ann Tamura, IT
    Specialist
North Seattle Community College
U.S. Export Assistance Center
2001 Sixth Avenue, Suite 650
(206) 553-5615

Seattle (98108-3405) - Ruth Ann
    Halford, BDS
South Seattle Community College
Duwamish Industrial Educational Center
6770 East Marginal Way South
(206) 764-5375/764-5838 (Fax)
Tacoma (98401-1933) - Neil Delisanti,
    BDS
950 Pacific Avenue, Suite 300
P.O. Box 1933
(206) 272-7232/597-7305 (Fax)

WEST VIRGINIA
Beckley (25802) - Tom Hardiman,
    Program Manager
College of West Virginia
306 South Kanawha Street
P.O. Box AG
(800) 766-4556/(304) 255-4022/
    252-9584 (Fax)
SBDC@CWV.edu
Charleston (25301) - Joseph Ciccarello,
    Program Manager
950 Kanawha Boulevard East, 2nd Floor
(304) 558-2960/558-0127 (Fax)
jcicca@mail.wvnet.edu
Charleston (25301) - Dr. Hazel
    Kroesser Palmer, State Director
Governor's Office of Community and
    Industrial Development*
950 Kanawha Boulevard East, 2nd Floor
(304) 558-2960/558-0127 (Fax)
Elkins (26241) - James Martin,
    Business Analyst
10 11th Street, Suite One
(304) 637-7205/637-4902 (Fax)
jrjm@access.mountain.net
Fairmont (26554) - Jack Kirby,
    Program Manager
Fairmont State College
1000 Technology Drive
(304) 367-2712/367-2717 (Fax)
sbdc@fscvax.fairmont.wvnet.edu

---

* Lead Small Business Development Center
† Specialized Center
‡ Historical Black College/University

Huntington (25755-2126) - Edna McClain, Program Manager
Marshall University
1050 Fourth Avenue
(304) 696-6789/696-6277 (Fax)
emcclain@rcbins.redc.marshall.edu

Morgantown (26506) - Sharon Stratton, Business Development Specialist
West Virginia University
439 B&E Building
P.O. Box 6025
(304) 293-5839/293-7061 (Fax)
Stratton@wvubel.be.wvu.edu

Oak Hill (25901) - James Epling, Program Manager
West Virginia Institute of Technology
912 East Main Street
(304) 465-1434/465-8680 (Fax)

Parkersburg (26101) - Greg Hill, Program Manager
West Virginia University at Parkersburg
Route 5, Box 167-A
(304) 424-8277/424-8320 (Fax)
ghill@alpha.wvup.wvnet.edu

Shepherdstown (25443) - Fred Baer, Program Manager
Shepherd College
Gardiner Hall
(304) 876-5261/876-3101 (Fax)
fbaer@shepherd.wvnet.edu

Wheeling (26003) - Ron Trevellini, Program Manager
West Virginia Northern Community
College
College Square
(304) 233-5900 ext. 206/232-0965 (Fax)

WISCONSIN
Eau Claire (54702-4004) - Fred Waedt, Director
University of Wisconsin at Eau Claire
P.O. Box 4004
(715) 836-5811/836-5263 (Fax)

Green Bay (54301) - Jan Thornton, Director
University of Wisconsin at Green Bay
Wood Hall, Suite 460
(920) 465-2089/465-2660 (Fax)

Kenosha (53141) - Patricia Duetsch, Director
University of Wisconsin at Parkside
284 Tallent Hall
(414) 595-2189/595-2513 (Fax)

La Crosse (54601) - Jan Gallagher, Director
University of Wisconsin at La Crosse
120 North Hall
(608) 785-8782/785-6919 (Fax)

Madison (53706) - Erica McIntire, State Director
University of Wisconsin
432 North Lake Street, Room 423
(608) 263-7794/262-3878 (Fax)

Madison (53706) - Neil Lerner, Director
University of Wisconsin at Madison
975 University Avenue
(608) 263-2221/263-0818 (Fax)

Milwaukee (53204)
University of Wisconsin at Milwaukee
161 West Wisconsin Avenue, Suite 6000
(414) 227-3240/227-3142 (Fax)

Oshkosh (54901) - John Mozingo, Director
University of Wisconsin at Oshkosh
157 Clow Faculty Building
(920) 424-1453/424-7413 (Fax)

Platteville (53818)
University of Wisconsin at Platteville
133 Warner Hall
1 University Plaza
(608) 342-1038/342-1454 (Fax)

Stevens Point (54481) - Vicki Lobermeier
University of Wisconsin at Stevens Point
Main Building, Lower Lever
(715) 346-3838/346-4045 (Fax)

* Lead Small Business Development Center
† Specialized Center
‡ Historical Black College/University

Superior (54880) - Loren Erickson, Director
University of Wisconsin at Superior
29 Sundquist Hall
(715) 394-8351/394-8454 (Fax)
Whitewater (53190) - Carla Lenk, Director
University of Wisconsin at Whitewater
2000 Carlson Building
(414) 472-3217/472-4863 (Fax)
Whitewater (53190) - Debra Malewicki, Director
Wisconsin Innovation Service
    Center/Technology[†]
University of Wisconsin at Whitewater
402 McCutchen Hall
(414) 472-3217/472-1600 (Fax)

WYOMING
Casper (82601) - Leonard Holler, Director
111 West Second Street, Suite 502
(800) 348-5207/(307) 234-6683/
    577-7014 (Fax)
Cheyenne (82007-3298) - Arlene Soto, Regional Director
1400 East College Drive
(800) 348-5208/(307) 632-6141/632-6061
    (Fax)
Laramie (82071-3622) - Diane Wolverton, State Director; Matt Edwards, Assistant to the Director
University of Wyoming*
P.O. Box 3622
(800) 348-5194/(307) 766-3505/
    766-3406 (Fax)
Powell (82435) - Dwane Heintz, Director
146 South Bent Street
(800) 383-0371/(307) 754-2139/
    754-0368 (Fax)
Rock Springs (82902) - Bill Ellis, Director
P.O. Box 1168
(800) 348-5205/(307) 352-6894
    352-6876 (Fax)

GUAM
UOG Station, Mangilao (96923) - Dr. Stephen L. Marder, Executive Director
University of Guam*
P.O. Box 5061
(671) 735-2590/734-2002 (Fax)

PUERTO RICO
Arecibo (00614) - Wanda Vega Rosado, Regional Director
Inter American University Arecibo
    Campus
P.O. Box 4050
(787) 878-5475 ext. 2236/880-1624 (Fax)
wanvega@ns.inter.edu
Fajardo (00738) - Joy C. Vilardi de Camacho, Regional Director
Inter American University Fajardo
    Campus
P.O. Box 70003
(787) 863-2390 ext. 2219/860-3470 (Fax)
jvilardi@ns.inter.edu
Hato Rey (00918) - Carmen Marti, Executive Director
Edificio Union Plaza, Suite 701
416 Ponce De Leon Avenue
(787) 763-6811/763-4629 (Fax)
cmarti@ns.inter.edu
Hato Rey (00918) - Dr. Mario Sverdlik, Regional Director
Union Plaza Building, Suite 701
416 Ponce de Leon Avenue
(787) 763-5108/763-4529 (Fax)
msverdik@ns.inter.edu
Mercedita (00715) - Carlos Maldonado, Regional Director
Inter American University Ponce Campus
Carr. #1, Km. 123.2
(787) 284-1912 ext. 2023/841-0103 (Fax)
carmaldo@ns.inter.edu

---

* Lead Small Business Development Center
† Specialized Center
‡ Historical Black College/University

**San German (00683) - Luis
E. Valderrama, Regional Director**
Inter American University San German
  Campus
P.O. Box 5100
(787) 264-1912 ext. 7715/892-6350 (Fax)
lvalderr@ns.inter.edu

VIRGIN ISLANDS
**St. Croix (00820-4487) - Ian Hodge,
Director**
University of the Virgin Islands
United Shopping Plaza
Suite 5, Sion Farm
(809) 778-8270/778-7629 (Fax)
**St. Thomas (00802-5804) - Chester
Williams, Director**
University of the Virgin Islands*‡
8000 Nisky Center, Suite 202
Charlotte Amalie
(809) 776-3206/775-3756 (Fax)

Small Business Exporters Association
4603 John Tyler Court, Suite 203
Annandale, VA 22003
(703) 642-2490
FAX: (703) 750-9655
www.sbea.org/sbea/index.html
Contact: E. Martin Duggan,
  President

Small Business Foundation of America
1155 15th Street
Washington, DC 20005
(202) 223-1103
FAX: (202) 628-8392
web.miep.org/sbfa

Small Business Resource Centers
Contact your local Chamber of
Commerce

Society of Competitive Intelligence Professionals
1700 Diagonal Road, Suite 520
Alexandria, VA 22314
(703) 739-0696
FAX: (703) 739-2524
www.scip.org/homepage.html

STATE INFORMATION CENTERS

Environmental Protection Agency
regional offices handle pollution
and environmental issues, and can
also suggest local sources:

ALABAMA
State Information Office
(334) 242-2591

ALASKA
State Information Office
(907) 465-2111

ARIZONA
State Information Office
(602) 542-4900

ARKANSAS
State Information Center
(501) 682-3000

CALIFORNIA
State Information Office
(916) 322-9900

COLORADO
State Information Office
(303) 866-5000

CONNECTICUT
State Information Office
(860) 566-2211

DELAWARE
State Information Office
(302) 739-4000

---

* Lead Small Business Development Center
† Specialized Center
‡ Historical Black College/University

FLORIDA
State Information Office
(904) 488-1234

GEORGIA
State Information Office
(404) 656-2000

HAWAII
State Information Office
(808) 586-0222

IDAHO
State Information Office
(208) 334-2411

ILLINOIS
State Information Office
(217) 782-2000

INDIANA
State Information Office
(317) 232-1000

IOWA
State Information Office
(515) 281-5011

KANSAS
State Information Office
(913) 296-0111

KENTUCKY
State Information Office
(502) 564-3130

LOUISIANA
State Information Office
(504) 342-6600

MAINE
State Information Office
(207) 582-9500

MARYLAND
State Information Office
(410) 767-0100

MASSACHUSETTS
State Information Office
(617) 727-2121

MICHIGAN
State Information Office
(517) 373-1837

MINNESOTA
State Information Office
(612) 296-6013

MISSISSIPPI
State Information Office
(601) 359-1000

MISSOURI
State Information Office
(573) 751-2000

MONTANA
State Information Office
(406) 444-2511

NEBRASKA
State Information Office
(402) 471-2311

NEVADA
State Information Office
(702) 687-5000

NEW HAMPSHIRE
State Information Office
(603) 271-1110

NEW JERSEY
State Information Office
(609) 292-2121

NEW MEXICO
State Information Office
(505) 827-4011

NEW YORK
State Information Office
(518) 474-2121

NORTH CAROLINA
State Information Office
(919) 733-1110

NORTH DAKOTA
State Information Office
(701) 328-2000

OHIO
State Information Office
(614) 466-2000

OREGON
State Information Office
Not Available

PENNSYLVANIA
State Information Office
(717) 787-2121

RHODE ISLAND
State Information Office
(401) 277-2000

SOUTH CAROLINA
State Information Office
(803) 734-1000

SOUTH DAKOTA
State Information Office
Not Available

TENNESSEE
State Information Office
(615) 741-3011

TEXAS
State Information Office
(512) 463-4630

UTAH
State Information Office
(801) 538-3000

VERMONT
State Information Office
(802) 828-1110

VIRGINIA
State Information Office
(804) 786-0000

WASHINGTON
State Information Office
Not available

WEST VIRGINIA
State Information Office
(304) 558-3456

WISCONSIN
State Information Office
(608) 266-2211

WYOMING
State Information Office
(307) 777-7220

Storage Council
8720 Red Oak Boulevard, Suite 201
Charlotte, NC 28217
(705) 522-8644
FAX: (704) 522-7826

Support Services Alliance
P.O. Box 130
Schoharie, NY 12157-0130
(518) 295-7966
FAX: (518) 295-8556
www.ssainto.com
Contact: Gary Swan, Vice
President, Public Affairs

Trademark Research Corporation
300 Park Avenue South
New York, NY 10010
(212) 228-4084
FAX: (212) 228-5090
Contact: Charles Williams, Vice
President, Development

U.S. Department of Commerce
1615 H Street, NW
Washington, DC 20062

Bureau of the Census
(301) 457-2800

Bureau of Economic Analysis
(202) 606-9600

Bureau of Export Administration
(202) 482-1455

Economic Development Administration
(202) 482-5112

Economics and Statistics Administration
(202) 482-2235

**Export Assistance Centers -
Office of Domestic Operations**
(202) 482-4767

**International Trade
Administration**
(202) 482-3809

Minority Business Development
(202) 482-4547

**National Technical Information
Service**
(202) 487-4650

Office of Business Liaison
(202) 482-1360

**Office of Small and
Disadvantaged Business
Utilization**
(202) 482-3387

Patent and Trademark Office
(703) 308-4357

Technology Administration
(202) 482-1397

**Trade Adjustment Assistance
Program**
(202) 482-4031

**Trade Information Center
(Government and Private Web
Sites)**
800-USA-TRADE

**U.S. and Foreign Commercial
Service**
(202) 482-5777

ARIZONA
Phoenix (85012) - Pompeya Lambrecht
2901 North Central Avenue, Suite 970
(602) 640-2513/640-2518 (Fax)
PLambrech@doc.gov

ARKANSAS
Little Rock (72201) - Lon J. Hardin
425 West Capitol Avenue, Suite 700
(501) 324-5794/324-7380 (Fax)
LHardin@doc.gov

CALIFORNIA
**Newport Beach (92660) - Richard
 Swanson**
3300 Irvine Avenue, Suite 305
(714) 660-1688/660-8039 (Fax)
RSwanson@doc.gov
San Francisco (94104) - Moira Jacobs
250 Montgomery Street, 14th Floor
(415) 705-2300/705-2297 (Fax)
MJACOBS1@doc.gov
San Jose (95113) - Martha Murphy
101 Park Center Plaza, Suite 1001
(408) 271-7300/271-7307 (Fax)
MMurphy7@doc.gov
**Santa Clara (95054) - Sara Kent
 Deluca and Rick deLambert**
5201 Great American Parkway, #456
(408) 970-4610/970-4618 (Fax)
SKentDeluca@doc.gov
RdeLamb1@doc.gov

COLORADO
Denver (80202) - Mark O'Grady
1625 Broadway, Suite 680
(303) 844-6622/844-5651 (Fax)
MOGrady@doc.gov

CONNECTICUT
**Middletown (06457-3346) - Carl
 Jacobsen and Sharon McKendry**
213 Court Street, Suite 903
(860) 638-6950/638-6970 (Fax)
CJacobse@doc.gov
SMcKendr@doc.gov

FLORIDA
Miami (33159) - Karl Koslowski
P.O. Box 590570
5600 Northwest 36th Street, Suite 617
(305) 526-7425/526-7434 (Fax)
KKoslows@doc.gov

ILLINOIS
Chicago (60603) - Thelma Young
55 West Monroe Street, Suite 2440
(312) 353-8040/353-8098 (Fax)
TYoung@doc.gov
Wheaton (60187) - Roy Dube
c/o Illinois Institute of Technology
201 East Loop Road
(312) 353-4332/353-4336 (Fax)
RDube@doc.gov

INDIANA
Indianapolis (46032) - Dan Swart
11405 North Pennsylvania Street,
    Suite 106
(317) 582-2300/582-2301
DSwart@doc.gov

IOWA
Des Moines (50309) - Randall
J. LaBounty
210 Walnut Street, Room 817
(515) 284-4222/284-4021 (Fax)
RLaBount@doc.gov

MARYLAND
Baltimore (21202) - Arica Young
World Trade Center, Suite 2432
401 East Pratt Street
(410) 962-4539/962-4529 (Fax)
AYoung4@doc.gov

MASSACHUSETTS
Boston (02210) - Christina Ravekes,
Nancy Russell, and Keith
Yatsuhashi
164 Northern Avenue
World Trade Center, Suite 307
(617) 424-5990/424-5992 (Fax)
CRavekes@doc.gov
NRussell@doc.gov
KYatsuha@doc.gov
Marlborough (01752) - Kathleen Walsh
100 Granger Boulevard, Unit 102
(508) 624-6000/624-7145 (Fax)
KWalsh3@doc.gov

MICHIGAN
Ann Arbor (48104) - Paul Litton
425 South Main Street, Suite 103
(313) 741-2430/741-2432 (Fax)
PLitton@doc.gov

Pontiac (48341) - Tristina Toll-Kirsten
Oakland Pointe Office Building
250 Elizabeth Lake Road
(810) 975-9600/975-9606 (Fax)
TTollKir@doc.gov

NEBRASKA
Omaha (68137) - Meredith Bond
11135 O Street
(402) 221-3664/221-3668 (Fax)
MBond1@doc.gov

NEW JERSEY
Newark (07102) - Carmella Mammas
7-45 Raymond Plaza, West, 9th Floor
(201) 645-4682/645-4783 (Fax)
CMammas@doc.gov

NEW YORK
New York (10048) - Thomas Mottley
6 World Trade Center, Room 635
(212) 264-0635/264-1356 (Fax)
TMottle1@doc.gov

OHIO
Cleveland (44114) - Amy Shaughnessy
600 Superior Avenue, East, Suite 700
(216) 522-4750/522-2235 (Fax)
AShaugn@doc.gov

OKLAHOMA
Oklahoma City (73116) - Marcus
Verner
301 Northwest 63rd Street
(405) 231-5302/231-4211 (Fax)
MVerner@doc.gov

OREGON
Portland (97204) - Valerie Buss
One World Trade Center, Suite 242
121 Southwest Salmon Street
(503) 326-3001/326-6351 (Fax)
VBuss1@doc.gov

PENNSYLVANIA
Pittsburgh (15222) - Ted Arnn and
Andrea Scheibel
2002 Federal Boulevard
1000 Liberty Avenue
(412) 644-2850/644-4875 (Fax)
TArnn@doc.gov
AScheibe@doc.gov

TEXAS
Austin (78711) - Karen Parker
1700 Congress, 2nd Floor
P.O. Box 12728
(512) 916-5939/916-5940 (Fax)
KParker@doc.gov
Dallas (75207) - Donie Sasser
2050 North Stemmons Freeway, Suite 170
P.O. Box 420069
(214)767-0542/767-8240 (Fax)
DSasser@doc.gov

WASHINGTON
Seattle (98121) - Kelly Butler and Jay Field
2001 6th Avenue, Suite 650
(206) 553-5615
KButler2@doc.gov
JField2@doc.gov

WISCONSIN
Milwaukee (53202) - Patrick Hope
517 East Wisconsin Avenue, Room 596
(414) 297-3473/297-3470 (Fax)
PHope@doc.gov

U.S. DEPARTMENT OF COMMERCE COMMERCIAL SERVICE POSTS ABROAD

ALGERIA
Washington, DC (20521-6030) - American Embassy Algiers
U.S. Dept. of State (Algiers)
4 Chemin Cheich Bachir Brahimi
011-213-2-60-39-73/
    011-213-2-69-39-79 (Fax)

ARMENIA
Washington, DC (20521-7020) - American Embassy Yerevan
U.S. Dept. of State (Yerevan)
18 Gen Bagramian
011-3742-151-144/
    011-3742-151-138 (Fax)

ARGENTINA
APO AA 34034 - American Embassy Buenos Aires
Unit 4334
4300 Colombia 1425
011-54-1-777-4533 ext. 2226/
    011-54-1-777-0673 (Fax)

AUSTRALIA
APO AP (96554-0002) - American Consultate General Sydney
Unit 11024
Hyde Park Tower, 36th Floor, Park and Elizabeth Streets
011-612-9373-9200/
    011-612-9221-0573 (Fax)
OSydney@doc.gov
APO AP (96553-0002) - American Consulate Brisbane
Unit 11018
383 Wickham Terrace
011-61-7-831-3330/
    011-61-7-832-6247 (Fax)
APO AP (96551-0002) - American Consulate General Melbourne
Unit 11011
553 St. Kilda Road
011-613-9526-5925/
    011-613-9510-4660 (Fax)
OMelbour@doc.gov
APO AP (96553-0002) - American Consulate General Perth
Unit 11021
16 St. George's Terrace, 13th Floor
011-61-9-231-9410/
    011-61-9-231-9444 (Fax)

AUSTRIA
American Embassy Vienna
Boltzmanngasse 16, A-1091
011-431-313-39-2296/
    011-431-310-6917 (Fax)

AZERBAIJAN
Washington, DC (20521-7050) - American Embassy Baku
U.S. Dept. of State (Baku)
Azadliq Prospetati 83
011-9-9412-98-03-35/
    011-9-9412-96-04-69 (Fax)

BELARUS
Washington, DC (20521-7010) - American Embassy Minsk
U.S. Dept. of State (Minsk)
Starivilenskaya 346-220002
011-375-172-31-50-00/
    011-375-172-34-78-53 (Fax)

BELGIUM
APO AE (09724-1015) - American Embassy Brussels
PSC 82, Box 002
27 Boulevard du Regent
011-32-2-508-2425/
    011-32-2-512-6653 (Fax)
APO AE (09724) - U.S. Mission to the European Community (Brussels)
PSC 82, Box 002
40 Boulevard du Regent, B-1000
011-32-2-513-2746/
    011-32-2-513-1228 (Fax)

BOSNIA
Washington, DC (20521-7030) - American Embassy Sarajevo
U.S. Dept. of State (Sarajevo)
43 ul. Dure, Dakovica
011-387-71-445-700/
    011-387-71-659-722 (Fax)

BRAZIL
APO AA (34030-0002) - American Consulate General Sao Paulo
Rua Estados Unidos 1812
011-55-11-853-2811/
    011-55-11-853-2744 (Fax)
APO AA (34030) - American Consular Agency Belem
011-55-91-223-0800/
    011-55-91-223-0413 (Fax)
APO AA (34030-3505) - American Consular Agency Belo Horizonte
Minas Trade Center Rua Timbiras, 1200, 7th Floor
011-55-31-213-1571/
    011-55-31-213-1575 (Fax)
Unit 3500 APO AA (34030) - American Embassy Brasilia
Avenida das Nocoes, Lote 3
011-55-61-321-7272/
    011-55-61-225-3981 (Fax)
APO AA (34030) - American Consulate General Rio de Janeiro
Avenida Presidente Wilson, 147 Castelo
011-55-21-292-7117/
    011-55-21-240-9738 (Fax)

BULGARIA
Unit 1335 APO AE (09213-1335) - American Embassy Sofia
1 Saborna Street
011-359-2-980-5241/
    011-359-2-980-68-50 (Fax)

CANADA
Champlain, NY (12919-0847) - American Consulate General Montreal
P.O. Box 847
455 Rene Levesque Boulevard, 19th Floor
Montreal, Quebec H2Z-1Z2
(514) 398-9695/398-0711 (Fax)
Lewiston, NY (14092) - American Consulate General Toronto
P.O. Box 135
360 University Avenue, Suite 602
Toronto, Ontario, M5G-1S4
(416) 595-1700/595-0051 (Fax)
Ogdensburg, NY (13669-0430) - American Embassy Ottawa
P.O. Box 5000
World Exchange Plaza, 45 O'Connor, Suite 1140
K1P-1A4
1-613-238-5335/1-613-238-5999 (Fax)
Ogdensburg, NY (13669) - American Consulate General Calgary
c/o AmEmbassy Ottawa
P.O. Box 5000
615 MacLeod Trail Southeast, Room 1050
(403) 266-8962/266-6630 (Fax)
Ogdensburg, NY (13669) - American Consulate General Halifax
c/o AmEmbassy Ottawa
P.O. Box 5000
Suite 910, Cogswell Tower
Scotia Square
Halifax, Nova Scotia B3J 3K1
(902) 429-2480/429-7690 (Fax)
Point Roberts, Washington (98281-5002) - American Consulate General Vancouver
P.O. Box 5002
1095 West Pender Street, 20th Floor
Vancouver, British Columbia V6E-2M6
(604) 685-4311/687-6095 (Fax)

CHILE
APO AA (34033) - American Embassy
Santiago
Unit 4111
Andres Bello 2800, Los Condes
011-56-2-330-3310/
011-56-2-330-3172 (Fax)

CHINA
FPO AP (96521-0002) - American
Embassy Beijing
PSC 461Box 50
Xiu Shui Bei Jie 3
011-86-10-6532-6924/
011-86-10-6532-3297 (Fax)
OBeijing@doc.gov
FPO AP (96521-0002) - American
Consulate General Chengdu
PSC 461 Box 100
No. 1 South Shamian St. Shamian Island
011-86-28-558-9642/
011-86-28-558-9221 (Fax)
uscscd@public.cd.sc.cn
FPO AP (96521-0002) - American
Consulate General Guangzhou
PSC 461 Box 100
China Hotel 14/F Liu Hua Road
011-86-20-8667-4011/
011-86-20-8666-6409 (Fax)
OGuangzh@doc.gov
FPO AP (96521-0002) - American
Consulate General Shanghai
PSC 461 Box 200
1469 Huai Hai Middle Road
011-86-21-6279-7630/
011-86-21-6279-7639 (Fax)
OShangha@doc.gov
U.S. Commercial Center Shanghai
Shanghai Centre Suite 631,
East Tower 1376
Nanjing Xi Lu
011-86-21-6279-7640/
011-86-21-6279-7639 (Fax)
AChang1@doc.gov
FPO AP (96521-0002) - American
Consulate General Shenyang
PSC 461 Box 45
40 Lane 4, Section 5 Sanjing Street,
Heping District
011-86-21-6279-7640/
011-86-21-6279-7649 (Fax)

COLOMBIA
APO AA (34038) - American Embassy
Bogota
Unit 5120
Calle 22 D bis No. 47-51 Santa Fe de
Bogota
011-57-1-315-2126 ext. 2684/
011-57-1-315-2171 (Fax)

COSTA RICA
APO AA (34020) - American Embassy
San Jose
Embajada de los Estados Unidos, Frentel
al Centro,
Commercial del Oeste, Unit 2508, Pavas,
San Jose, Costa Rica
011-506-220-2454 ext.3939/
011-506-231-4783 (Fax)

COTE D'IVOIRE
Washington, DC (20521-2010) -
American Embassy Abidjan
U.S. Dept. of State (Abidjan)
O I.B.P. 1712
011-225-21-4616/
011-225-22-2437 (Fax)

CROATIA
APO AE (09213-1345) - American
Embassy Zagreb
Unit 345
Andrije Hebranga 2
011-359-2-980-5241/
011-359-2-981-8977 (Fax)

CZECH REPUBLIC
Washington, DC (20521-5630) -
American Embassy Prague
U.S. Dept. of State (Prague)
Hybernska 7a 117 16 Praha 1
011-422-2421-9844/
011-422-2421-9965 (Fax)

DENMARK
APO AE (09176) - American Embassy
Copenhagen
Dag Hammarskjolds Alle 24
011-45-3142-3144/
011-45-3142-0175 (Fax)

DOMINICAN REPUBLIC
APO AA (34041-0008) - American
 Embassy Santo Domingo
Unit 5515
Corner of Calle Cesar Nicolas Penson &
 Calle Leopoldo Navarro
(809) 221-2171/688-4838 (Fax)

ECUADOR
APO AA (34039-3420) - American
 Embassy Quito
Unit 5334
Avenida 12 de Octubre y Avenida Patria
011-593-2-561-404/
 011-593-2-504-550 (Fax)
APO AA (34039) - American Consulate
 General Guayaquil
9 de Octubre y Garcia Moreno
011-593-4-323-570/
 011-593-4-325-286 (Fax)

EGYPT
APO AE (09839-4900) - American
 Embassy Cairo
Unit 64900 Box 11
3 Lazougi Street, Garden City, Cairo
 (Sunday-Thursday)
011-20-2-357-2340/
 011-20-2-355-8368 (Fax)
FPO AE (09839-4900) - American
 Consulate General Alexandria
Unit 64900, Box 24
3 El Faranna Street
011-20-3-482-5607/
 011-20-3-482-9199 (Fax)

FINLAND
APO AE (09723) - American Embassy
 Helsinki
Itainen Puistotie 14ASF
011-358-9-171-931/
 011-358-9-635-332 (Fax)

FRANCE
APO AE (09777) - American Embassy
 Paris
2 Avenue Gabriel
011-33-1-4312-2370/
 011-33-1-4312-2172 (Fax)

APO AE (09777) - U.S. Mission to the
 OECD (Paris)
19 Rue de Franqueville 75016 Paris
011-33-1-4524-7437/
 011-33-1-4524-7410 (Fax)
APO AE (09777) - American Consulate
 General Bordeaux
c/o American Embassy Paris
22 Cours du Marechal Foch
011-33-56-526595/011-33-56-51-60-42
 (Fax)
APO AE (09777) - American Consulate
 General Lyon
c/o American Embassy Paris
7 Quai General Sarrail
011-33-472-407-220/
 011-33-478-391-409 (Fax)
APO AE (09777) - American Consulate
 General Marseille
c/o American Embassy Paris
12 Boulevard Paul Peytral
011-33-491-549-200/
 011-33-491-550-947 (Fax)
APO AE (09777) - U.S. Commercial
 Office Nice
c/o American Embassy Paris
31 Rue du Marechal Joffre
011-33-93-88-89-55/
 011-33-93-87-07-38 (Fax)
APO AE (09777) - American Consulate
 General Strasbourg
Unit 21551
c/o American Embassy Paris
15 Avenue d'Alsace
011-33-88-35-31-04/
 011-33-88-24-06-95 (Fax)

GEORGIA
Washington, DC (20521-7060) -
 American Embassy Tbilisi
U.S. Dept. of State (Tbilisi)
25 Atoneli
011-995-32-989-967/
 011-995-32-933-759 (Fax)

GERMANY
APO AE (09080) PSC 117 - American
 Embassy Bonn
Unit 21701, Box 53170, Bonn
Deichmanns Avenue 29
011-49-228-339-2895/
 011-49-228-334-649 (Fax)

APO AE (09235-5500) - American Embassy Office Berlin
Unit 10117
Neustaedtische Kirchstrasse 4-5 10117
  Berlin
011-49-30-238-5174/
  011-49-30-238-6290 (Fax)

APO AE (09080) - U.S. Commercial Office Dusseldorf
Unit 21701, Box 30
Emmanual Lutz Str. 1B
011-49-211-431-744/
  011-49-211-431-431 (Fax)

APO AE (09213-0115) - American Consulate General Frankfurt
PSC 115
Platenstrasse 1 60320 Frankfurt/Main
011-49-69-956-79-013/
  011-49-69-561-114 (Fax)

Washington, DC (20521-5180) - American Consulate General Hamburg
U.S. Dept. of State (Hamburg)
Alsterufer 27/28, 20354
011-49-40-4117-1304/
  011-49-40-410-6598 (Fax)

APO AE (09265) - American Consulate General Leipzig
PSC 120, Box 1000
Wilhelm-Seyfferth-Strasse 4 04107
  Leipzig
011-49-341-213-8421/
  011-49-341-213-8441 (Fax)

APO AE (09178) - American Consulate General Munich
Koeniginstrasse 5
011-49-89-2888-748/
  011-49-89-285-261 (Fax)

GREECE
APO AE (09482) - American Embassy Athens
PSC 108
91 Vasilissia Sophias Boulevard
011-30-1-729-4302/
  011-30-1-721-8660 (Fax)

GUATEMALA
APO AA (34024) - American Embassy Guatemala
Unit 3306
7-01 Avenida de la Reforma, Zona 10
011-502-3-31-1541 ext. 259/
  011-502-3-31-7373 (Fax)

HONDURAS
APO AA (34022) - American Embassy Tegucigalpa
Avenido La Paz
011-504-36-9230/38-5114/
  011-504-38-2888 (Fax)

HONG KONG
FPO AP (96522-0002) - American Consulate General Hong Kong
PSC 464, Box 30
26 Garden Road, 17th Floor
011-85-22-521-1467/
  011-85-22-845-9800 (Fax)
OHongKon@doc.gov

HUNGARY
Washington, DC (20521-5270) - American Embassy Budapest
U.S. Dept. of State (Budapest)
V. Szabadsag Ter 7
011-36-1-302-6100/
  011-36-1-302-0089 or 0091 (Fax)

INDIA
Washington, DC (20521-9000) - American Embassy New Delhi
U.S. Dept. of State (New Delhi)
Shanti Path, Chanakyapuri 110021
011-91-11-611-3033/
  011-91-11-419-0025 (Fax)

Bangalore (560042) - Commercial Office, US&FCS Bangalore
W-202, 2nd Floor, West Wing, Sunrise
  Chambers
22 Ulsoor Road
011-91-80-558-1452/
  011-91-80-558-3630 (Fax)
Cable to AmConGen, who will pass to
  Bangalore

Washington, DC (20521-6250) - American Consulate General Calcutta
U.S. Dept. of State (Calcutta)
5/1 Ho Chi Minh Sarani, Calcutta 700071
011-91-33-242-1074/
  011-91-33-242-2335 (Fax)

Washington, DC (20521-6260) - American Consulate General Chennai
U.S. Dept. of State (Chennai)
220 Mount Road, Chennai 600006
011-91-44-827-7542/
  011-91-44-827-0240 (Fax)

Washington, DC (20521-6240) - American Consulate General Mumbai (Formerly Bombay)
U.S. Dept. of State (Bombay)
4, New Marine Lines, Mumbai 400020
011-91-22-265-2511/
  011-91-22-262-3851/3850 (Fax)

INDONESIA
APO AP (96520) - American Embassy Jakarta
Box 1
Medan Merdeka Selatan 5
011-62-21-344-2211/
  011-62-21-385-1632 (Fax)
OJakarta@doc.gov

Jakarta (12920) - U.S. Commercial Center Jakarta
World Trade Center Wisma Metropolital II, 3rd Floor
Jalan Jenral Sudiman 29-31
011-62-21-526-2850/
  011-62-21-526-2855 (Fax)
OJakart1@doc.gov

APO AP (96520) - American Consulate General Surabaya
Jalan Raya Dr. Sutomo 33, Box 18131
011-62-31-561923/5676880/
  011-62-31-5677748/5674492 (Fax)
OSurabay@doc.gov

IRAQ
Washington, DC (20521-6060) - American Embassy Baghdad
U.S. Dept. of State (Baghdad)
Opp. For. Ministry Club (Masbah Quarter) (Sunday-Thursday)
011-964-1-719-6138/
  011-964-1-718-9297 (Fax)

IRELAND
Washington, DC (20521-5290) - American Embassy Dublin
U.S. Dept. of State (Dublin)
42 Elgin Road, Ballsbridge
011-353-1-667-4755/
  011-353-1-667-4754 (Fax)

ISRAEL
APO AE (09830) - American Embassy Tel Aviv
PSC 98, Box 100
71 Rehov, Tel Aviv 63432
011-972-3-519-7327/
  011-972-3-510-7215 (Fax)

ITALY
APO AE (09624) - American Embassy Rome
PSC 59
Via Veneto 119/A
011-39-6-46741/011-4674-2113 (Fax)

APO AE (09624) - American Consulate General Florence
Lungarno Amerigo Vespucci 38
011-39-55-211-676/
  011-39-55-283-780 (Fax)

APO AE (09624) - American Consulate General Genoa
PSC 59, Box G
Banca d'Americae d'Italia Building Piazza Portello
011-39-10-247-1412/
  011-39-10-290-027 (Fax)

APO AE (09624) - American Consulate General Milan
PSC 59, Box M
Via Principe Amerdeo 2/10, 20121 Miliano
011-39-2-6592-260/
  011-39-2-6592-561 (Fax)

FPO AE (09619-0002) - American
Consulate General Naples
PSC 810, Box 18
Piazza della Repubblica
011-39-81-761-1592/
    011-39-81-761-1869 (Fax)

JAMAICA
Washington, DC (20521-3210) -
American Embassy Kingston
U.S. Dept. of State (Kingston)
Jamaica Mutual Life Center, 2 Oxford
    Road, 3rd Floor, Kingston 5
(876) 926-8115/(809) 920-2580 (Fax)

JAPAN
APO AP (96337-5004) - American
Embassy Tokyo
Unit 45004, Box 204
1-10-5 Akasaka 1-chome Minato-ku (107)
011-81-3-3224-5060/
    011-81-3-3589-4235 (Fax)
OTokyo@doc.gov
APO AP (96337-0001) - U.S. Trade
Center Tokyo
Unit 45004, Box 258
7th Floor, World Import Mart, 1-3
    Higoshi Ikebukuro
3-chome Toshima-ku, Tokyo 170
011-81-3-3987-2441/
    011-81-3-3987-2447 (Fax)
OTokyo1@doc.gov
FPO AP (98766) - American Consulate
Fukuoka
Box 10
5-26 Ohori 2-chome Chuo-ku Fukuoka-810
011-81-92-751-9331/
    011-81-92-713-9222 (Fax)
APO AP (96337-0001) - American
Consulate Nagoya
c/o AmEmbassy Tokyo, Unit 45004,
    Box 280
10-33 Nishiki 3-chome Naka-ku, Nagoya
    460, Japan
011-81-52-203-4277/
    011-81-52-201-4612 (Fax)
ONagoya@doc.gov

APO AP (96337-0002) - American
Consulate General Osaka-Kobe
Unit 45004, Box 239
11-5, Nishitnma 2-Chrome Kita-Ku Osaka
    (530)
011-81-6-315-5957/
    011-81-6-315-5963 (Fax)
OOsakaKo@doc.gov
APO AP (96337-0003) - American
Consulate Sapporo
Kita 1-Jo Nishi 28-chome Chuoku
    Sapporo 064
011-81-11-641-1115/
    011-81-11-643-1283 (Fax)

KAZAKHSTAN
Washington, DC (20521-7030) -
American Embassy Almaty
U.S. Dept. of State (Almaty)
99/97 Furmanova Street Almaty, 480012
011-7-3275-81-15-77/
    011-7-3275-81-15-76 (Fax)

KENYA
APO AE (09831) - American Embassy
Nairobi
P.O. Box 30137, Unit 64100
Moi/Haile Selassie Avenue
011-254-2-212-354/
    011-254-2-216-648 (Fax)

KOREA
APO AP (96205-0001) - American
Embassy Seoul
Unit 15550
82 Sejong-Ro Chongro-Ku
011-82-2-397-4535/
    011-82-2-739-1628 (Fax)
OSeoul@doc.gov

KUWAIT
APO AE (09880-9000) - American
Embassy Kuwait
Unit 6900, Box 10
Al Masjeed Al Aqsa Street, Plot 14,
    Block 14, Bayan Plan 3602
(Saturday-Wednesday)
011-965-539-6362/5307/
    011-965-538-0281 (Fax)

MACEDONIA
**Washington, DC (20521-7120) -
American Embassy Skopje**
U.S. Dept. of State (Skopje)
Bul Linden BB, 9100 Skopje
011-389-91-116-180/
011-389-91-117-103 (Fax)

MALAYSIA
**APO AP (96535-5000) - American
Embassy Kuala Lumpur**
376 Jalan Tun Razak
011-603-457-2724/
011-603-242-1866 (Fax)

MEXICO
**Laredo, TX (78044-3087) - American
Embassy Mexico**
P.O. Box 3087
Paseo de la Reforma 305, Colonia
Cuauhtemoc, 06500 Mexico, D.F.
Mexico
011-52-5-209-9100/
011-52-5-207-8837 (Fax)
**Laredo, TX (78044-3087) - U.S. Trade
Center Mexico**
P.O. Box 3087
Liverpool 31, Co. Juarez, 06600 Mexico,
D.F. Mexico
011-52-5-591-0155/
011-52-5-566-1115 (Fax)
**Laredo, TX (78044-3098) - American
Consulate General Guadalajara**
P.O. Box 3088
Jal. Progreso 175
011-52-3-825-2700 ext. 371/
01152-3-827-0258/
011-52-3-826-3576 (Fax)
**Laredo, TX (78044-3098) - American
Consulate General Monterrey**
P.O. Box 3098
N.L. Avenida Constitucion 411 Poniente
011-52-83-45-2120/011-52-83-45-5172/
343-4440 (Fax)

MOROCCO
**APO AE (09718) - American Consulate
General Casablanca**
PSC 74, Box 24
8 Boulevard, Moulay Youssef
011-212-2-26-45-50/
011-212-2-22-02-59 (Fax)

**APO AE (09718) - American Embassy
Rabat**
PSC 74, Box 003
2 Ave de Marrakech
011-212-7-622-65/011-212-7-656-61 (Fax)

NETHERLANDS
**APO AE (09715) - American Embassy
The Hague**
PSC 71, Box 1000
Lange Voorhout 102
011-31-70-310-9417/
011-31-70-363-2985 (Fax)
**APO AE (09715) - American Consulate
General Amsterdam**
Box 1000
Museumplein 19
011-31-20-575-5351/
011-31-20-575-5350 (Fax)

NEW ZEALAND
**FPO AP (96531-1099) - American
Consulate General Auckland**
PSC 467, Box 99
4th Floor, Yorkshire General Building,
Shortland and O'Connell Streets
011-649-303-2038/
011-649-302-3156 (Fax)
OAucklan@doc.gov
**FPO AP (96531-1001) - American
Embassy Wellington**
PSC 467, Box 1
29 Fitzherbert Terr., Thorndon
011-644-472-2068/
011-644-471-2380 (Fax)

NIGERIA
**Washington, DC (20521-8300) -
American Embassy Lagos**
U.S. Dept. of State (Lagos)
2 Eleke Crescent, Victoria Island
011-234-1-261-0078 ext. 383/
011-234-1-261-9856 (Fax)

NORWAY
**APO AE (09707) - American Embassy
Oslo**
PSC 69, Box 1000
Drammensveien 18
011-47-22-44-8550/
011-47-22-55-8803 (Fax)

PAKISTAN
APO AE (09812-2200) - American
  Embassy Islamabad
Diplomatic Enclave, Ramna 5
P.O. Box 1048, Unit 6220
  (Sunday–Thursday)
011-92-51-826-161/
  011-92-51-823-981 (Fax)
APO AE (09812-2216) - American
  Consulate General Lahore
Unit 62216
50 Shahrah-E-Bin Badees
  (Sunday–Thursday)
011-92-42-636-5530/
  011-92-42-636-5177 (Fax)

PANAMA
APO AA (34002) - American Embassy
  Panama
Unit 0945
Avenida Balboa Y Calle 38 Apartado
  6959
011-507-227-1777/
  011-507-227-1713 (Fax)

PERU
APO AA (34031) - American Embassy
  Lima
Unit 3780
Avenida la Encalada Cuadro 17, Lima 33
011-51-1-434-3040/
  011-51-1-434-3041 (Fax)

PHILIPPINES
APO AP (96440) - American Embassy
  Manila
395 Senator Gil Puyat Avenue, Extension
  Makati
011-632-890-9362/
  011-632-895-3028 (Fax)
OManila@doc.gov

POLAND
APO AE (09213-1340) - American
  Embassy Warsaw
c/o AmConGen (WAW) Unit 1340
Aleje Ujazdowskle 29/31
011-48-2-628-3041/
  011-48-2-628-8298 (Fax)

U.S. Trade Center Warsaw
Aleje Jerozolimski 56C IKEA Building,
  2nd Floor, 00-803 Warsaw
011-48-2-621-4515/
  011-48-2-621-6327 (Fax)

PORTUGAL
APO AE (09726) - American Embassy
  Lisbon
PSC 83, Box FCS
Avenida das Forcas Armadas
011-351-1-727-5086/
  011-351-1-726-8914 (Fax)
APO AE (09726) - American Business
  Center Oporto
c/o AmEmbassy Lisbon
Apartado No. 88 Rua Julio Dinis 826 3rd
  Floor
011-351-2-606-3094/
  011-351-2-600-2737 (Fax)

ROMANIA
Washington, DC (20521-5260) -
  American Embassy Bucharest
The Commercial Service U.S. Embassy
  (Bucharest-5260)
c/o U.S. Department of State
Strada Tudor Arghezi 7-9
011-40-1-210-4042/
  011-40-1-210-0690 (Fax)

RUSSIA
APO AE (09721) - American Embassy
  Moscow
Novinsky Bulvar 19/23
011-7-502-224-1105/
  011-7-402-224-1106 (Fax)
APO AE (09723) - American Consulate
  General St. Petersburg
Box L
Furshatskaya 15
011-7-812-850-1902/
  011-7-812-850-1903 (Fax)
APO AE (09721) - American Consulate
  General Vladivostok
Ulitsa Mordovtseva 12
011-7-4232-268-458/
  011-7-4232-268-445 (Fax)

SAUDI ARABIA
APO AE (09803-1307) - American Embassy Riyadh
Unit 61307
Collector Road M, Diplomatic Quarter
   (Saturday–Wednesday)
011-966-1-488-3800/
   011-966-1-488-3237 (Fax)
APO AE (09858-6803) - American Consulate General Dhahran
Unit 66803
Between Aramco Headquarters and
   Dhahran International Airport
P.O. Box 81, Dhahran Airport, 31932
   (Saturday–Wednesday)
011-966-3-891-3200/
   011-966-3-891-8332 (Fax)
APO AE (09811-2112) - American Consulate General Jeddah
Unit 62112
Palestine Road Ruwais, P.O. Box 149
   (Saturday–Wednesday)
011-966-2-667-0040/
   011-966-2-665-8106 (Fax)

SINGAPORE
FPO AP (96534-0001) - American Embassy Singapore
1 Columbo Court, #05-16
011-65-476-9037/011-65-476-9080 (Fax)
OSingapo@doc.gov

SLOVAK REPUBLIC
Washington, DC (20521-5840) - American Embassy Bratislava
U.S. Dept. of State (Bratislava)
Hviezdoslavovo Namestie 4 81102
   Bratislava
011-421-7-533-0861/
   011-421-7-335-096 (Fax)
American Business Center Bratislava
Grosslingova 35 81109 Bratislava
011-421-7-361-079/
   011-421-7-361-085 (Fax)

SOUTH AFRICA
Washington, DC (20521-2500) - American Consulate General Johannesburg
U.S. Dept. of State (Johannesburg)
1 Commercial Service Office 15 Chaplin
   Road, Illovo 2196
P.O. Box 2155, Johannesburg 2000,
   South Africa
011-27-11-442-3571/
   011-27-11-442-3200
Washington, DC (20521-2480) - American Consulate General Cape Town
U.S. Dept. of State (Cape Town)
Broadway Industries Center
   Herrengracht, Foreshore
011-27-21-214-269/
   011-27-21-254-151 (Fax)

SPAIN
APO AE (09642) - American Embassy Madrid
PSC 61, Box 0021
Serrano 75
011-34-1-577-4000/
   011-34-1-577-2301 (Fax)
APO AE (09642) - American Consulate General Barcelona
PSC 61, Box 0005
Paseo Leina Elisenda, 23 08034
   Barcelona, Spain
011-34-3-280-2227/
   011-34-3-205-7705 (Fax)

SWEDEN
Washington, DC (20521-5750) - American Embassy Stockholm
U.S. Dept. of State (Stockholm)
Strandvagen 101
011-46-8-783-5346/
   011-46-8-660-9181 (Fax)

SWITZERLAND
Washington, DC (20521-5110) - American Embassy Bern
U.S. Dept. of State (Bern)
Jubilaeumstrasse 93
011-41-31-357-7270/
   011-41-31-357-7336 (Fax)

Washington, DC (20521-5130) - U.S. Mission to the GATT (Geneva)
U.S. Dept. of State (Geneva)
Botanic Building 1-3 Avenue de la Paix
011-41-22-749-5281/
   011-41-22-749-4885 (Fax)
Washington, DC (20521-5130) - American Consulate General Zurich
U.S. Dept. of State (Zurich)
Zolliikerstrasse 141
011-41-1-552-070/
   011-41-1-382-2655 (Fax)

THAILAND
APO AP (96546) - American Embassy Bangkok
Diethelm 93/1 Wireless Road, Towers
   Building
011-662-255-4365/
   011-662-255-2915 (Fax)
OBangkok@doc.gov

TURKEY
APO AE (09823) - American Embassy Ankara
PSC 93, Box 5000
110 Ataturk Boulevard
011-90-312-467-0949/
   011-90-312-467-1366 (Fax)
APO AE (09827-0002) - American Consulate General Istanbul
PSC 97, Box 0002
104-108 Mesrutiyet Caddesi, Tepebasi
011-90-1-251-1651/
   011-90-1-252-2417 (Fax)
APO AE (09821) - American Consulate General Izmir
PSC 88, Box 5000
92 Ataturk Caddesi (3rd Floor)
011-90-232-421-3643/
   011-90-232-463-5040 (Fax)

TURKMENISTAN
Washington, DC (20521-7070) - American Embassy Ashgabat
U.S. Dept. of State (Ashgabat)
9 Pushkin Street
011-9-7-3632-35-00-45/
   001-9-7-3632-51-13-05 (Fax)

UKRAINE
Washington, DC (20521-5850) - American Embassy Kiev
U.S. Dept. of State (Kiev)
10 Yuria Kotsyubinskono
011-380-44-417-2669/
   011-380-44-417-1419 (Fax)

UNITED ARAB EMIRATES
Washington, DC (20521-6020) - American Consulate General Dubai
U.S. Dept. of State (Dubai)
Dubai International Trade Center,
   21st Floor
   (Saturday–Wednesday)
011-971-4-313-584/
   011-971-4-313-121 (Fax)
Washington, DC (20521-6010) - American Embassy Abu Dhabi
U.S. Dept. of State (Abu Dhabi)
8th Floor, Blue Tower Building, Shaikh
   Khalifa Bin Zayed Street
   (Saturday–Wednesday)
011-971-2-273-666/
   011-971-2-271-377 (Fax)

UNITED KINGDOM
FPO AE (09498-4040) - American Embassy London
PSC 801, Box 40
24-31 Grosvenor Square
011-44-71-408-8019/
   011-44-71-408-8020 (Fax)

UZBEKISTAN
Washington, DC (20521-7110) - American Embassy Tashkent
U.S. Dept. of State (Tashkent)
82 Chelanzanskaya
011-7-3712-771-407/
   011-7-3712-776-953 (Fax)

VENEZUELA
APO AA (34037) - American Embassy Caracas
Unit 4958
Calle F con Calle Suapure Colinas de
   Valle Arriba
Codigo Postal 1060
011-58-2-977-2792/
   011-58-2-977-2177 (Fax)

VIETNAM
Commercial Service Hanoi
U.S. Commercial Center 31 Hai Ba Trung
   4th Floor, Hanoi
011-844-824-2422/
   011-844-824-2421 (Fax)
10313.3220@compuserve.com

TAIPEI
**Washington, DC (20521) - The
   American Institute in Taiwan**
U.S. Dept. of State (Taipei)
American Institute in Taiwan Commercial
   Unit
600 Min Chuan East Road, Taipei
011-886-2-720-1550/
   011-886-2-757-7162 (Fax)
**Washington, DC (20521) - American
   Institute in Taiwan**
U.S. Dept. of State (Kaohsiung)
3rd Floor, #2 Chung Cheng 3d Road,
   Kaohsiung
011-886-7-224-0154/
   011-886-7-223-8237 (Fax)
OKaohsiu@doc.gov

Trade Information Center
800-USA-TRADE
www.ita.doc.gov/tic

U.S. GOVERNMENT EXPORT
TRADE LEADS SITES

Business America Magazine
www.ita.doc.gov/bizam/
**Business Information Service for the
   Newly Independent States**
www.iep.doc.gov/bisnis/bisnis.html
**Central & Eastern Europe Business
   Information Center**
(800) USA-TRADE(E) selection 2
www.mac.doc.gov/eebic/ceebic.html
**Computerized Information Delivery
   Service**
(202) 720-5505/690-1131 (Fax)
**Environmental Technology Network for
   the Americas and Asia**
(800) 818-9911
www.info.usaid.gov/business/ctis/etna
   .html

Export Opportunity Hotline
(800) 243-7232
www.sba.gov/hotlist
Foreign Agriculture Service
www.fas.usda.gov
Infrastructure Division
www.ita.doc.gov/infrastructure/
Trade Opportunities Program
(800) 223-0243 ext. 7185
www.stat-usa.gov
U.S. Africa Technology Network
(202) 663-2672
U.S. Department of Commerce
(800) STAT-USA/USA-TRADE(E) for
   local federal depository library
www.stat-usa.gov

NON-U.S. GOVERNMENT SITES
PRIMARILY RELATED TO EXPORT
TRADE LEADS

American Shine Star Corp.
shinestar.com
Asian Sources On-Line
www.asiansources.com
Asia's Marketplace
www.asiatrade.com/Mkt.html
Bay Area World Trade Center
www.wtcsf.org
Chilnet
www.chilnet.cl/buscai.htm
Clearfreight
www.clearfreight.com
Export Hotline
www.exporthotline.com
Export-Leads
www.export-leads.com
Florida Trade Data Center
www.flatrade.org
Global Business Forum
www.pragmatix.com/gbf/
Global Marketplace
worldbusiness.net/english/marketplace
Hong Kong Development Council
www.tdc.org.hk/main/
Import-Export Bulletin Board
www.iebb.com/welcome.html

International Import Export Business
  Exchange
www.imex.com/imex/trade/opprt.html
Internet Directory for Exporters and
  Importers
www.interlink-cafe.com/eie
Japanese External Trading
  Organization
www.jetro.go.jp/
MSU-CIBER
ciber.bus.msu.edu/busres.htm
Net Source America/Asia
www.netsource-america.com/
www.netsource-asia.com/ (net site for
  Asia)
Owens Online
www.owens.com
Regent China BizInfo Network
china-inc.com
Rexco's International Trade
  Resources
www.rexco.com/index.html
Singapore Trade Development
  Board
www.tdb.gov.sg/
Swissinfo Net: Import-Export Bulletin
  Board
swissinfo.net.iebbs/index.shtml
Trade Broker
www.tradecompass.com/forum
  /trade_broker.html
Trade Express International
www.trade-express.com
Trade Leads.Com
www.tradeleads.com
Tradenet
tradenet.chipnet.cz/
Trade Net On-Line
www.TradeNet.com
Trade Point Program
www.unicc.org/untpdc/welcome.html
Trade Port
tradeport.org
Trade U.S.
www.tradeUS.com
Trading Floor
trading.wmw.com
World Trade Center Assoc.
www.wtca.org

NON-U.S. GOVERNMENT SITES THAT ALSO CONTAIN TRADE LEADS OR LINKS TO TRADE LEADS

Anew Net
www.anewnet.com
Asia Mart
www.anewnet.com/asiamart
Asia-Pacific International Trade
  Business Directory
www.cnctek.com/usa-import-export.html
Asiaville
www.asiaville.com
Business Strategies International
www.tradecompass.com/pages/bsi
Center for Global Development
www.cgtd.com/global/index.html
Center for International Trade &
  Commerce; Alabama
ns1.maf.mobile.al.us/~citcmob
Czech Information Center
www.muselik.com
EEurope Business Digest
www.tradeport.org/ts/
Exim Web Trade Leads
www.bigpage.net/eximweb/leads.html
The Exporter
www.exporter.com
Export Expert
www.cci2.com/cc.leads
Export Hotline
www.exporthotline.com
Export-Leads
www.export-leads.com
Export Today Magazine
www.exporttoday.com
Externa
www.externa.com.ar/
Free Trade Zone
www.tradehere.com
The Gateway
www.teknetsystems.co.uk
German American Trade Leads
www.gaccwest.org/greenpgx.html
Global Connexions
www.globalcon.com
Global Enterpreuners Network
www.entrepreneurs.net/

Global Recycling Network
grn.com.grn
Global Textile Network
www.g-t-n.com/
Hello Singapore
www.singapore.com/cgbin/var/online/
IGEME-Export Promotion Center of Turkey
www.igeme.org.tr
International Trade Database
www.netvisa.com/trade1
International Trade Net
www.intl-tradenet.com/tnetmain.htm
IntlTrade Zone
www.intltradezone.com
I-Trade
www.i-trade.com
Market net
www.us-market.com
on Trac
www.ontrac.yorku.ca
Pangaea.Net
www.pangaea.net
Russian Business & Trade Connection
www.publications-etc.com/russia
/business
Source Link International
www.africa.com/trade/slink
Taiwan Commerce
www.commerce.com.tw/
Taiwan Products
www.manufacture.com.tw/
Trade Leads Online
www.tradeline.com.at/
Trade Match
www.tradematch.co.uk/

Trade Matchmaker
www.trading.wmw.com
Traders Club
yotrinidad.com/traclub.htm
TradeScope
www.owens.com
Trade UK
www.tradeUK.wits.co.uk/
Trinity Business Solutions
www.trinitybusolution.com
Unibex web
www.unibex.com
Venture Web
www.venture-web.or.jp/
Wade World Trade
www.demon.co.uk/fernhart/wade/wade1
.html
World Business Source
www.wbs.com.au/
World Trade Data Base
www.wtdb.com
World Trade Center; Ft. Lauderdale
www.worldtradefl.com
World Trade Exchange
www.wte.net/
YO! Trinidad
www.yotrinidad.com

Warehousing Education and Research Council

1100 Jorie Boulevard, Suite 170
Oak Brook, IL 60521
(708) 990-0001
www.werc.org/

INDEX

profits/losses, reporting, 6, 80–86
  cost of goods sold, 82
  depreciation, 83–86
  expenses, 83, 86
  gross profit on sales, 82
  net sales, 81–82
promotion, 182–91
  advertising, 184–85
    agency selection, 187–89
  demographics, 190–91
  information sources, 185–87
  letterheads/stationery, 189–90
  public relations, 182–84
  recommended reading, 191
Property Management Association
    (PMA), 155
proprietorship (legal format), 24–25
  see also sole proprietorship
PRSA, *see* Public Relations Society of
    America (PRSA)
PTO, *see* United States Department of
    Commerce, Patent and Trademark
    Office (PTO)
public, accounting information needs,
    89
public relations, *see* promotion
Public Relations Society of America
    (PRSA), 186, 271
purchasing, 160–65
  researching purchases, 164
Purdue University, 240

Ramicitte, David F., 181
real estate investments, 75–76
real estate issues, 152–55
reading, recommended:
  accounting, 94
  business plan, 66–67
  capital, raising/using, 87
  compensation and benefits, 101
  consultants, 146–47
  ethics, 151
  human resource management, 129–30
  leasing office/storage space, 155

legal issues, 140
management, 114
manufacturing/processing, 168–69
marketing, 180–81
mergers/acquisitions/joint ventures,
    205
product testing/research, 159
public relations and advertising, 191
purchasing, 164
training and continuing education, 199
transportation and relocation, 226
record-keeping methods (in business
    plan), 6
recycling, 135
regulations/restrictions:
  accounting information needs, 89
  in business plan, 6
Rehabilitation Act, 123
relocation, *see* transportation and
    relocation
Reproduction Rights Organization (RRO),
    134
retail, 179, 180
retirement plans, 95–96, 98
Robb, Russel, 205
Rochester, University of, 241
Romania, 358
Rubin, Charles, 181
Russia, 358

Sachs, Randi Toler, 130
safety:
  Consumer Product Safety Commission
    (CPSC), 156
  National Highway Traffic Safety
    Administration, 224–25
  National Institute for Occupational
    Safety and Health (NIOSH),
    195–96
  National Safety Council, 196, 270
  National Safe Workplace Institute
    (NSWI), 196, 270
salary management, 95, 116
  see also compensation and benefits